# Tell us what you think about Shojo Beat Manga!

Our survey is now available online. Go to:

**shojobeat.com/mangasurvey**

Help us make our product offerings better!

Shojo Beat

THE REAL DRAMA BEGINS IN...

SAKURA HIME: SAKASHITA © 2001 by Arina Tanemura/SHUEISHA Inc.
Fushigi Yûgi: Genbu Kaiden © 2004 Yuu WATASE/Shogakukan Inc.
Ouran Koko Host Club © Bisco Hatori 2002/HAKUSENSHA, Inc.

# We Were There
## Vol. 9
Shojo Beat Edition

STORY & ART BY
YUUKI OBATA


Original Japanese edition "BOKURA GA ITA"
published by SHOGAKUKAN Inc.

Adaptation/Nancy Thistlethwaite
Translation/Tetsuichiro Miyaki
Touch-up Art & Lettering/Inori Fukuda Trant
Design/Courtney Utt
Editor/Nancy Thistlethwaite

VP, Production/Alvin Lu
VP, Sales & Product Marketing/Gonzalo Ferreyra
VP, Creative/Linda Espinosa
Publisher/Hyoe Narita



Printed in Canada

Published by VIZ Media, LLC
P.O. Box 77010
San Francisco, CA 94107

10 9 8 7 6 5 4 3 2 1
First printing, March 2010

www.viz.com

www.shojobeat.com

RATED T+ FOR OLDER TEEN

**PARENTAL ADVISORY**
WE WERE THERE is rated T+ for Older Teen and is recommended for ages 16 and up. This volume contains sexual themes.
ratings.viz.com

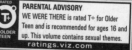

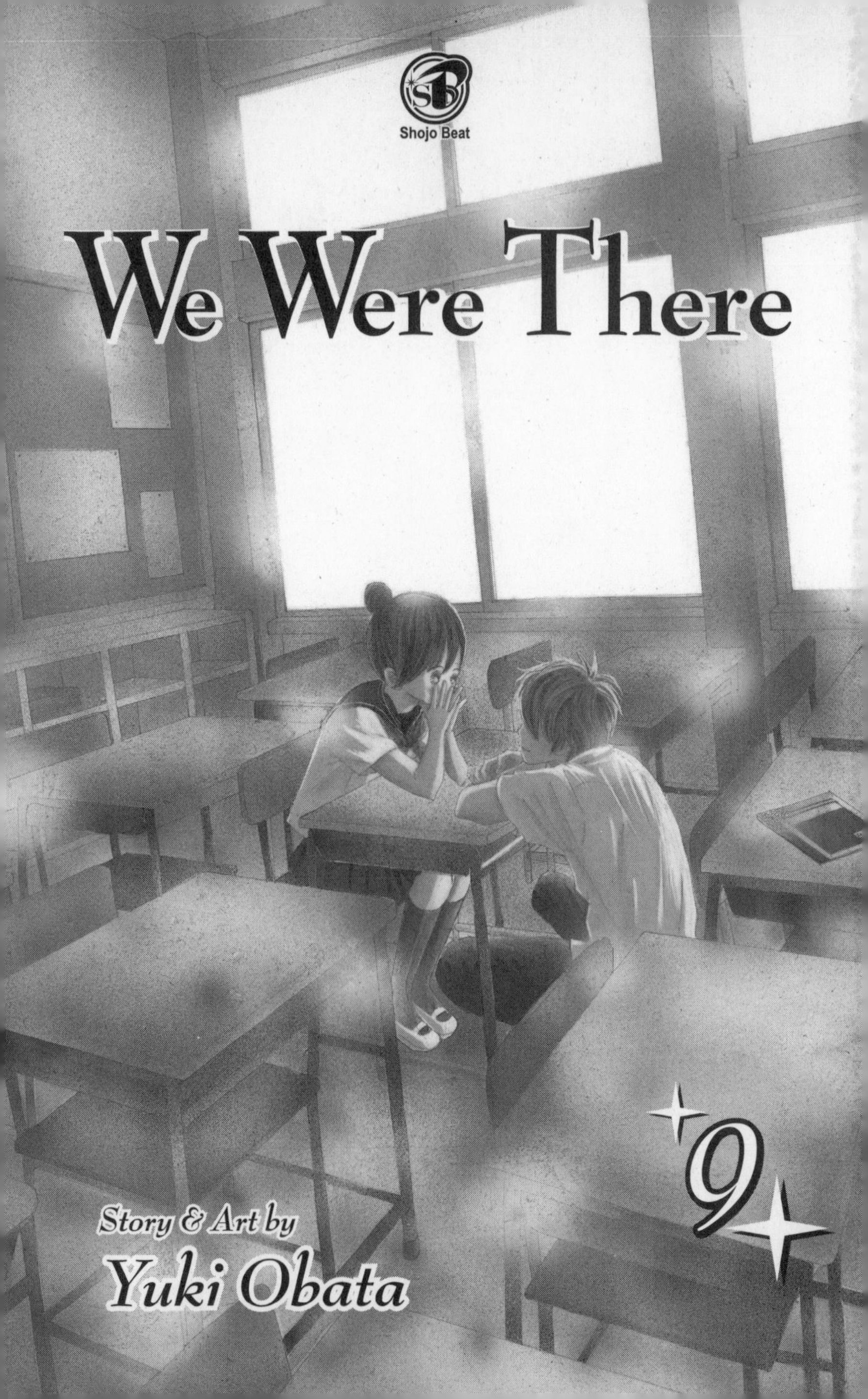
Shojo Beat
We Were There
9
Story & Art by
Yuki Obata

# Contents

# Characters

**Masafumi Takeuchi**
*Yano's childhood friend.
He's kinder and more
modest than Yano.*

**Nanami Takahashi**
*A 21-year-old college
student in Tokyo.
She's earnest but a bit
forgetful at times.*

**Motoharu Yano**
*Nanami's boyfriend. His
girlfriend Nana-san died.*

# Story

Yano has left for Tokyo because of his mother's divorce.
After promising to meet each other a year later, Nanami and
Yano begin their long-distance relationship. But the two
have not met since. It has been five years since Nanami saw
Yano off, and her graduation from college is drawing near.
Nanami is busy with her graduation thesis, job hunt, and...?!

# Chapter 32

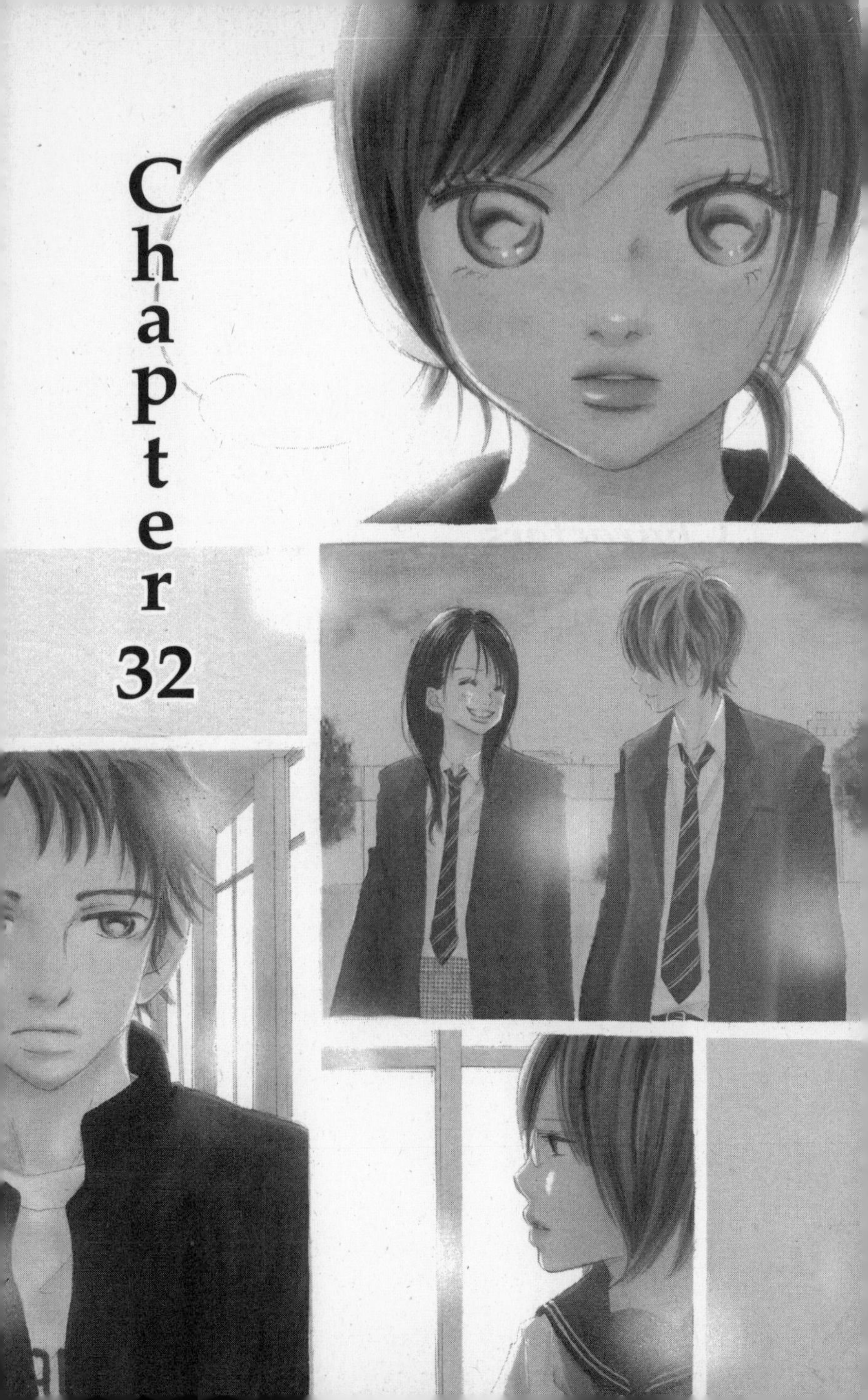

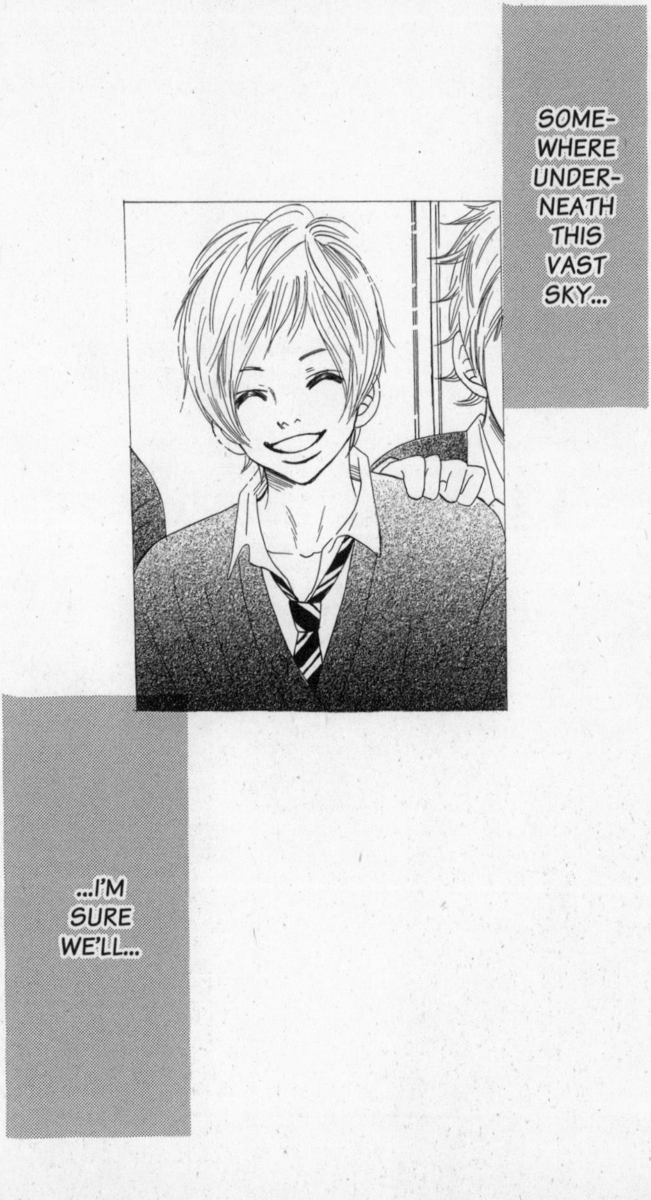
SOME-WHERE UNDER-NEATH THIS VAST SKY...
...I'M SURE WE'LL...

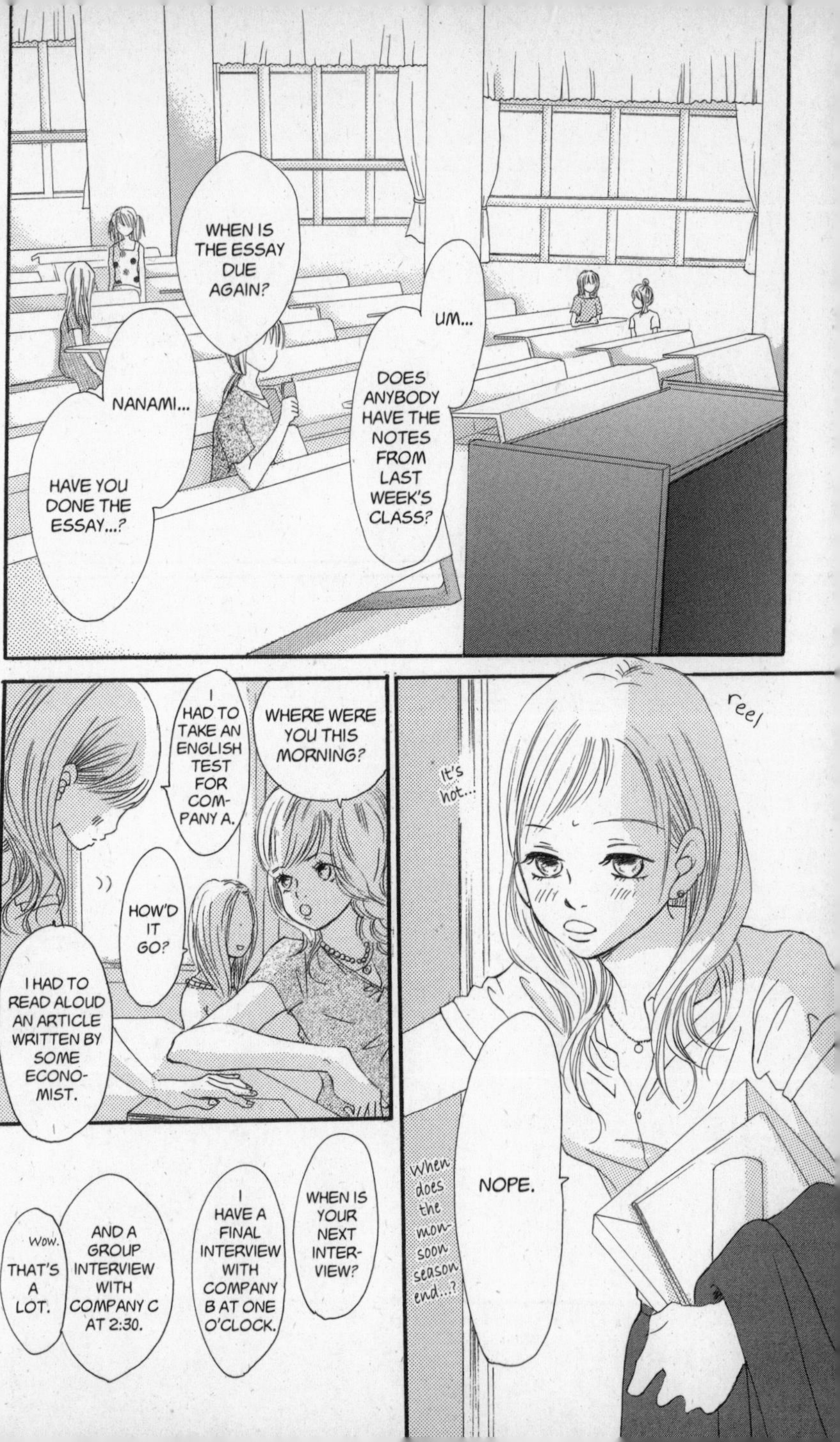
UM...
DOES ANYBODY HAVE THE NOTES FROM LAST WEEK'S CLASS?
WHEN IS THE ESSAY DUE AGAIN?
NANAMI...
HAVE YOU DONE THE ESSAY...?
reel
It's hot...
NOPE.
When does the mon-soon season end...?
WHERE WERE YOU THIS MORNING?
I HAD TO TAKE AN ENGLISH TEST FOR COM-PANY A.
HOW'D IT GO?
I HAD TO READ ALOUD AN ARTICLE WRITTEN BY SOME ECONO-MIST.
WHEN IS YOUR NEXT INTER-VIEW?
I HAVE A FINAL INTERVIEW WITH COMPANY B AT ONE O'CLOCK.
AND A GROUP INTERVIEW WITH COMPANY C AT 2:30.
Wow.
THAT'S A LOT.

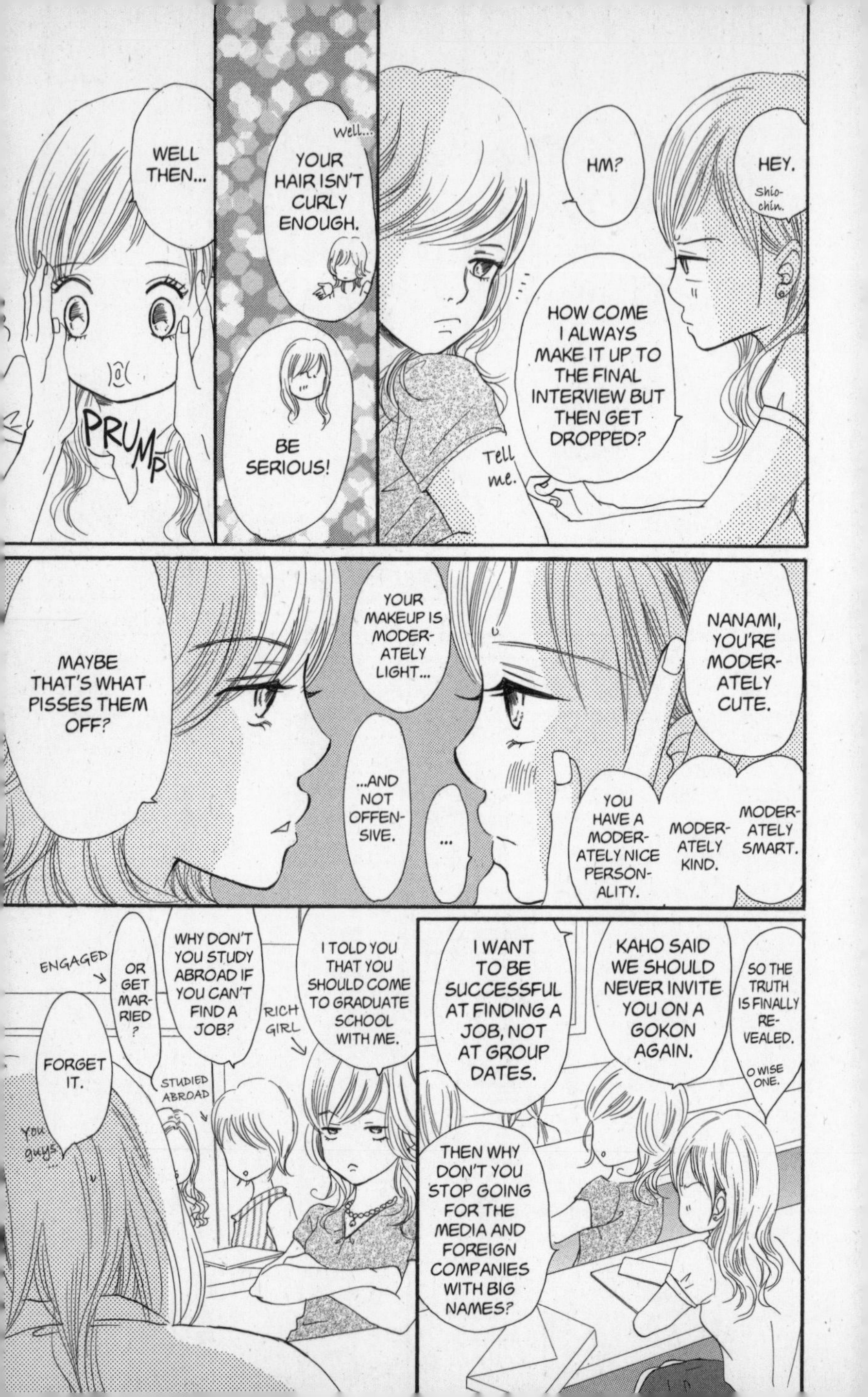
HEY.
Shio-chin.
HM?
HOW COME I ALWAYS MAKE IT UP TO THE FINAL INTERVIEW BUT THEN GET DROPPED?
Tell me.
Well...
YOUR HAIR ISN'T CURLY ENOUGH.
BE SERIOUS!
WELL THEN...
PRUMP
NANAMI, YOU'RE MODERATELY CUTE.
MODERATELY SMART.
MODERATELY KIND.
YOU HAVE A MODERATELY NICE PERSONALITY.
YOUR MAKEUP IS MODERATELY LIGHT...
...AND NOT OFFENSIVE.
...
MAYBE THAT'S WHAT PISSES THEM OFF?
SO THE TRUTH IS FINALLY REVEALED.
O WISE ONE.
KAHO SAID WE SHOULD NEVER INVITE YOU ON A GOKON AGAIN.
I WANT TO BE SUCCESSFUL AT FINDING A JOB, NOT AT GROUP DATES.
THEN WHY DON'T YOU STOP GOING FOR THE MEDIA AND FOREIGN COMPANIES WITH BIG NAMES?
I TOLD YOU THAT YOU SHOULD COME TO GRADUATE SCHOOL WITH ME.
RICH GIRL
WHY DON'T YOU STUDY ABROAD IF YOU CAN'T FIND A JOB?
STUDIED ABROAD
OR GET MARRIED?
ENGAGED
FORGET IT.
You guys.

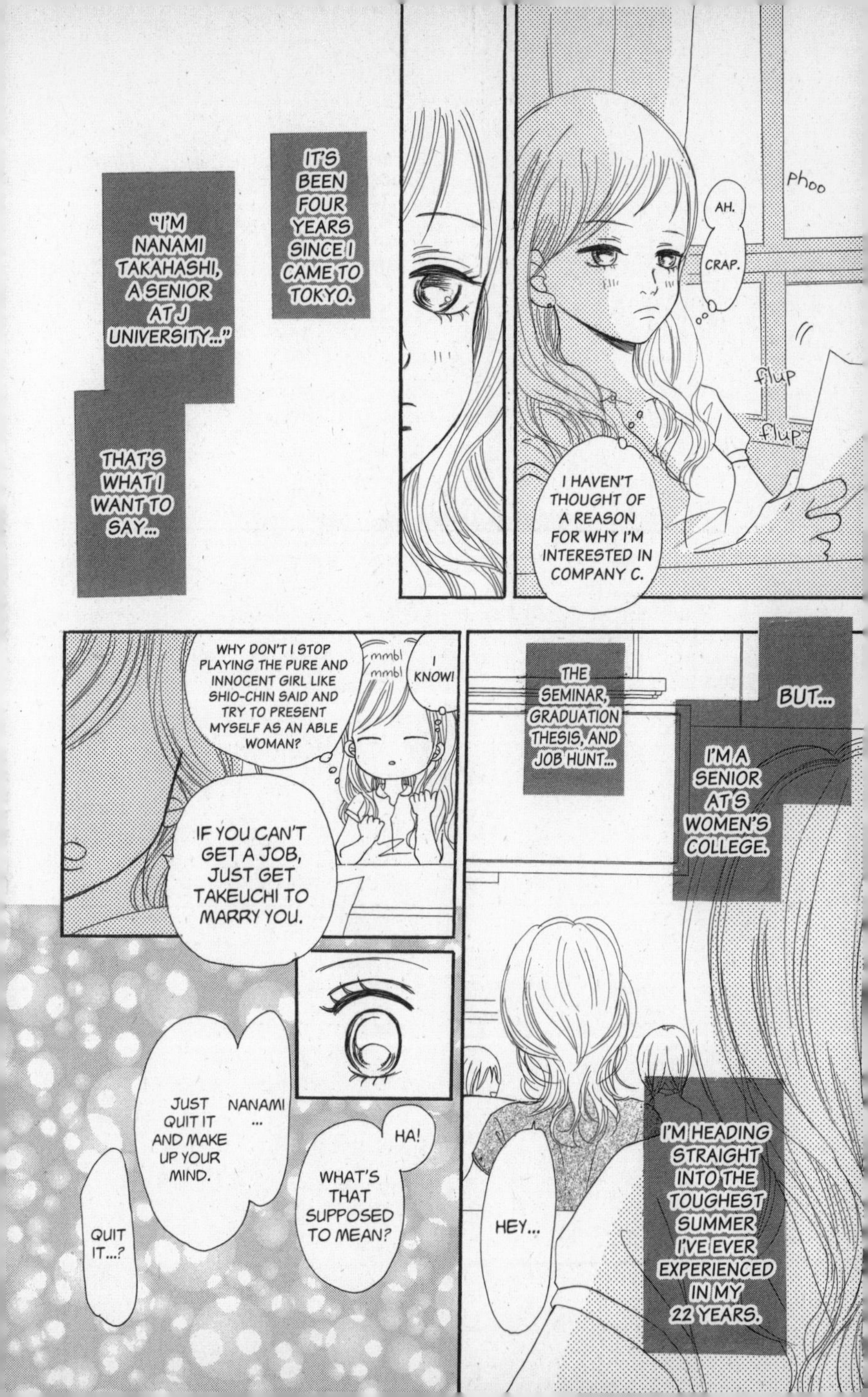
Phoo
AH.
CRAP.
flup
flup
I HAVEN'T THOUGHT OF A REASON FOR WHY I'M INTERESTED IN COMPANY C.
IT'S BEEN FOUR YEARS SINCE I CAME TO TOKYO.
"I'M NANAMI TAKAHASHI, A SENIOR AT J UNIVERSITY..."
THAT'S WHAT I WANT TO SAY...
BUT...
I'M A SENIOR AT S WOMEN'S COLLEGE.
THE SEMINAR, GRADUATION THESIS, AND JOB HUNT...
I'M HEADING STRAIGHT INTO THE TOUGHEST SUMMER I'VE EVER EXPERIENCED IN MY 22 YEARS.
HEY...
I KNOW!
mmbl mmbl
WHY DON'T I STOP PLAYING THE PURE AND INNOCENT GIRL LIKE SHIO-CHIN SAID AND TRY TO PRESENT MYSELF AS AN ABLE WOMAN?
IF YOU CAN'T GET A JOB, JUST GET TAKEUCHI TO MARRY YOU.
NANAMI ... JUST QUIT IT AND MAKE UP YOUR MIND.
HA!
WHAT'S THAT SUPPOSED TO MEAN?
QUIT IT...?

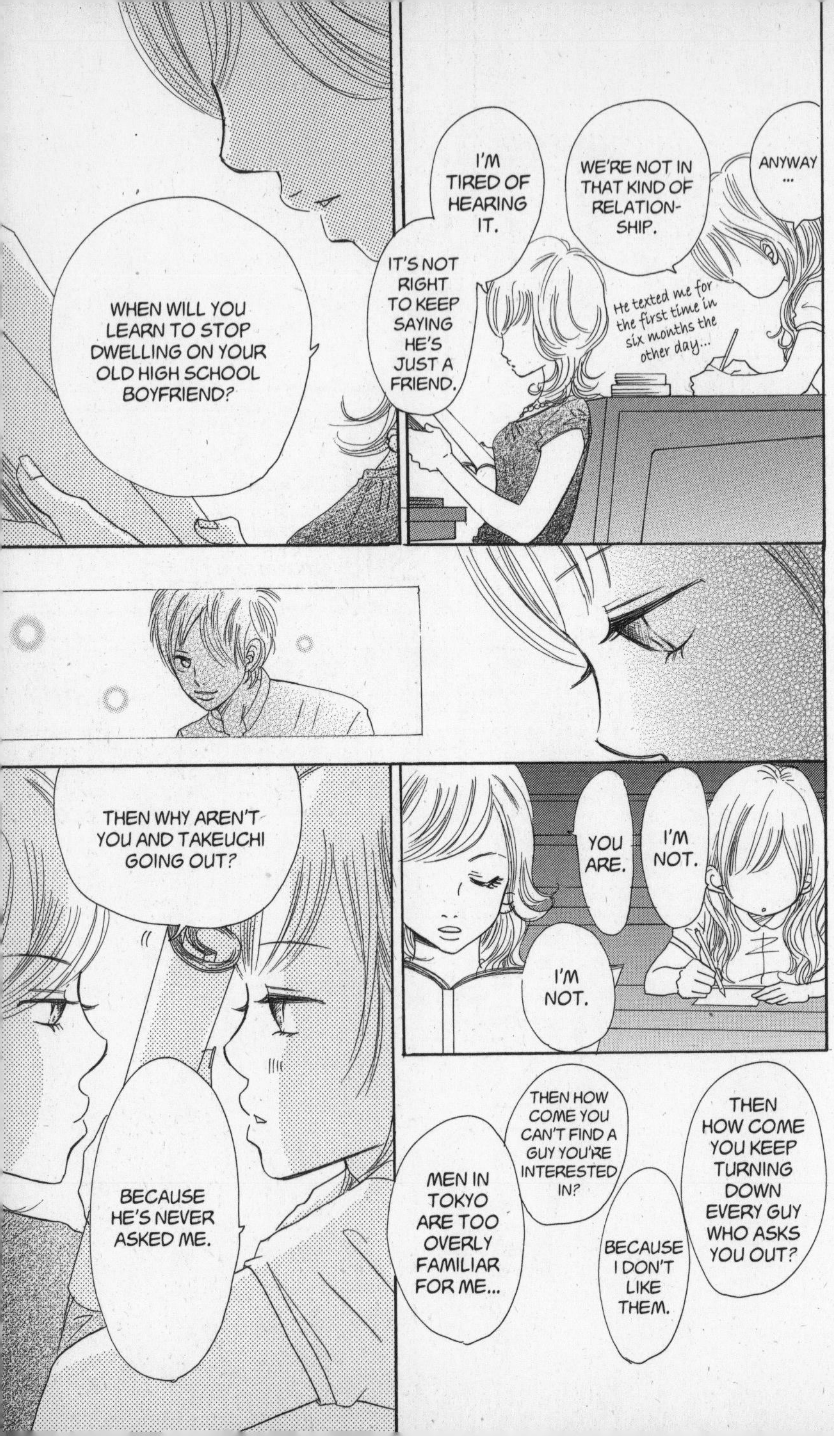
ANYWAY ...
WE'RE NOT IN THAT KIND OF RELATION-SHIP.
He texted me for the first time in six months the other day...
I'M TIRED OF HEARING IT.
IT'S NOT RIGHT TO KEEP SAYING HE'S JUST A FRIEND.
WHEN WILL YOU LEARN TO STOP DWELLING ON YOUR OLD HIGH SCHOOL BOYFRIEND?
I'M NOT.
YOU ARE.
I'M NOT.
THEN HOW COME YOU KEEP TURNING DOWN EVERY GUY WHO ASKS YOU OUT?
BECAUSE I DON'T LIKE THEM.
THEN HOW COME YOU CAN'T FIND A GUY YOU'RE INTERESTED IN?
MEN IN TOKYO ARE TOO OVERLY FAMILIAR FOR ME...
THEN WHY AREN'T YOU AND TAKEUCHI GOING OUT?
BECAUSE HE'S NEVER ASKED ME.

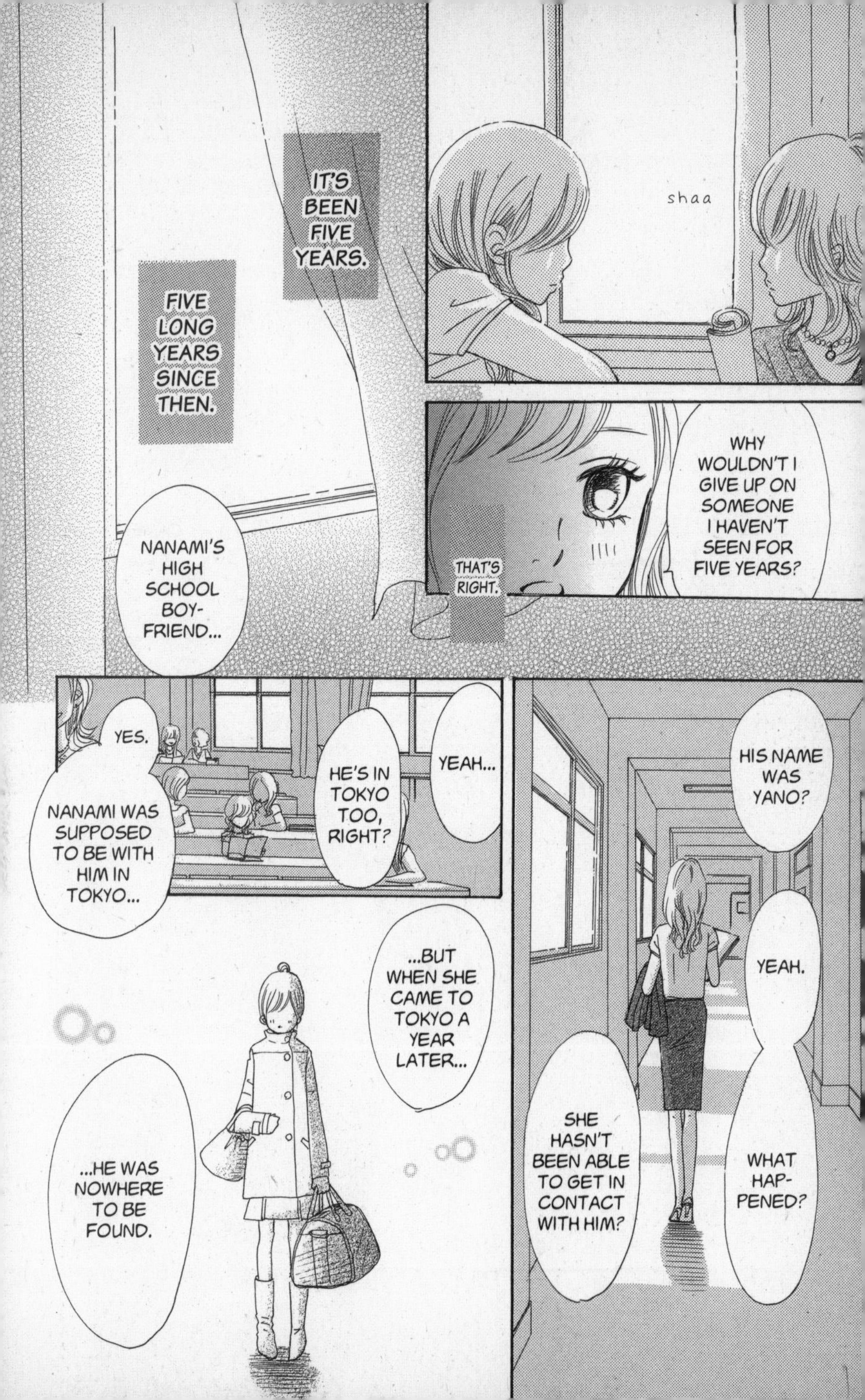
shaa
IT'S BEEN FIVE YEARS.
FIVE LONG YEARS SINCE THEN.
WHY WOULDN'T I GIVE UP ON SOMEONE I HAVEN'T SEEN FOR FIVE YEARS?
THAT'S RIGHT.
NANAMI'S HIGH SCHOOL BOY-FRIEND...
HIS NAME WAS YANO?
YEAH.
WHAT HAP-PENED?
SHE HASN'T BEEN ABLE TO GET IN CONTACT WITH HIM?
YEAH...
HE'S IN TOKYO TOO, RIGHT?
YES.
NANAMI WAS SUPPOSED TO BE WITH HIM IN TOKYO...
...BUT WHEN SHE CAME TO TOKYO A YEAR LATER...
...HE WAS NOWHERE TO BE FOUND.

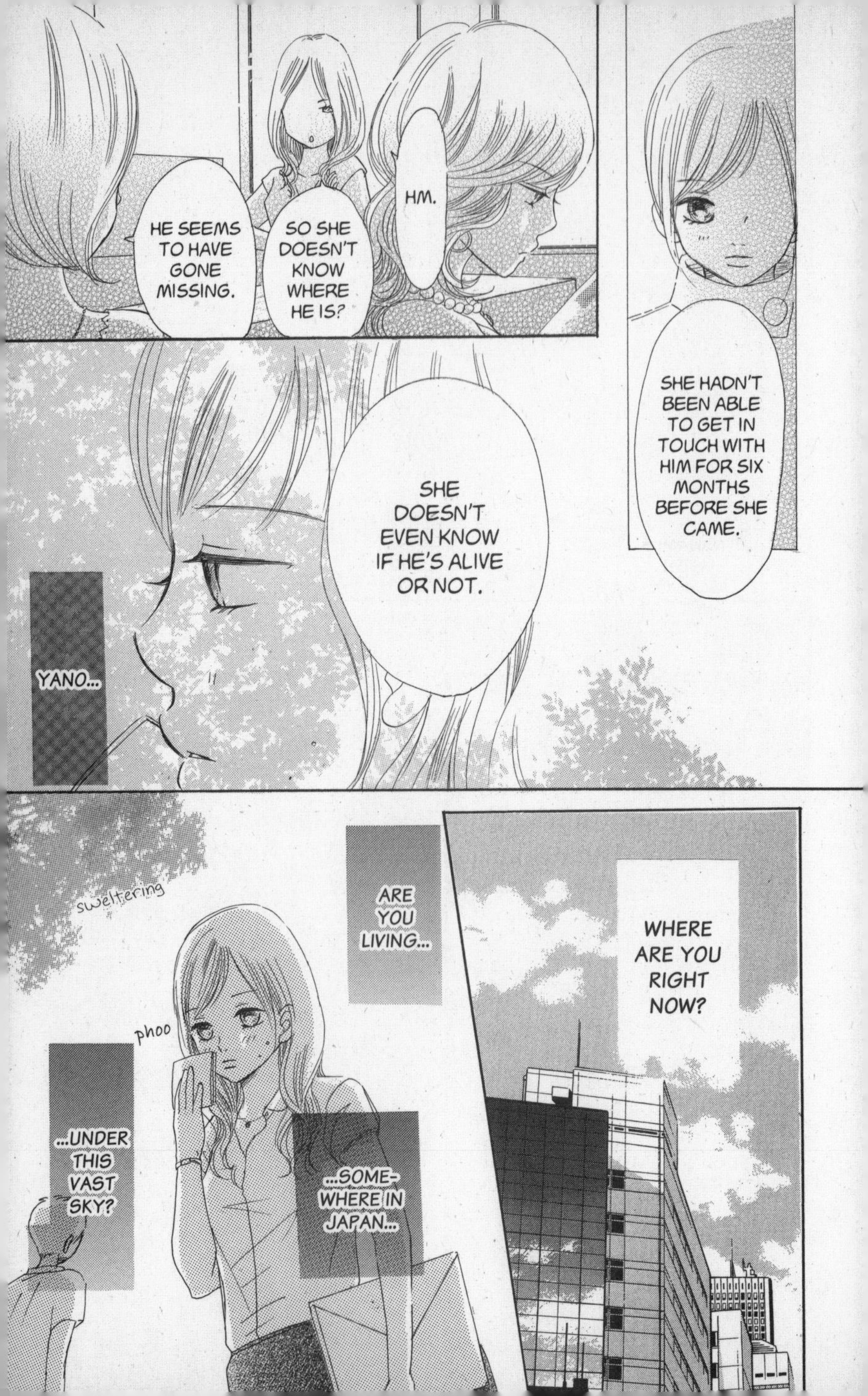
HE SEEMS TO HAVE GONE MISSING.
SO SHE DOESN'T KNOW WHERE HE IS?
HM.
SHE HADN'T BEEN ABLE TO GET IN TOUCH WITH HIM FOR SIX MONTHS BEFORE SHE CAME.
SHE DOESN'T EVEN KNOW IF HE'S ALIVE OR NOT.
YANO...
WHERE ARE YOU RIGHT NOW?
ARE YOU LIVING...
sweltering
phoo
...SOME-WHERE IN JAPAN...
...UNDER THIS VAST SKY?

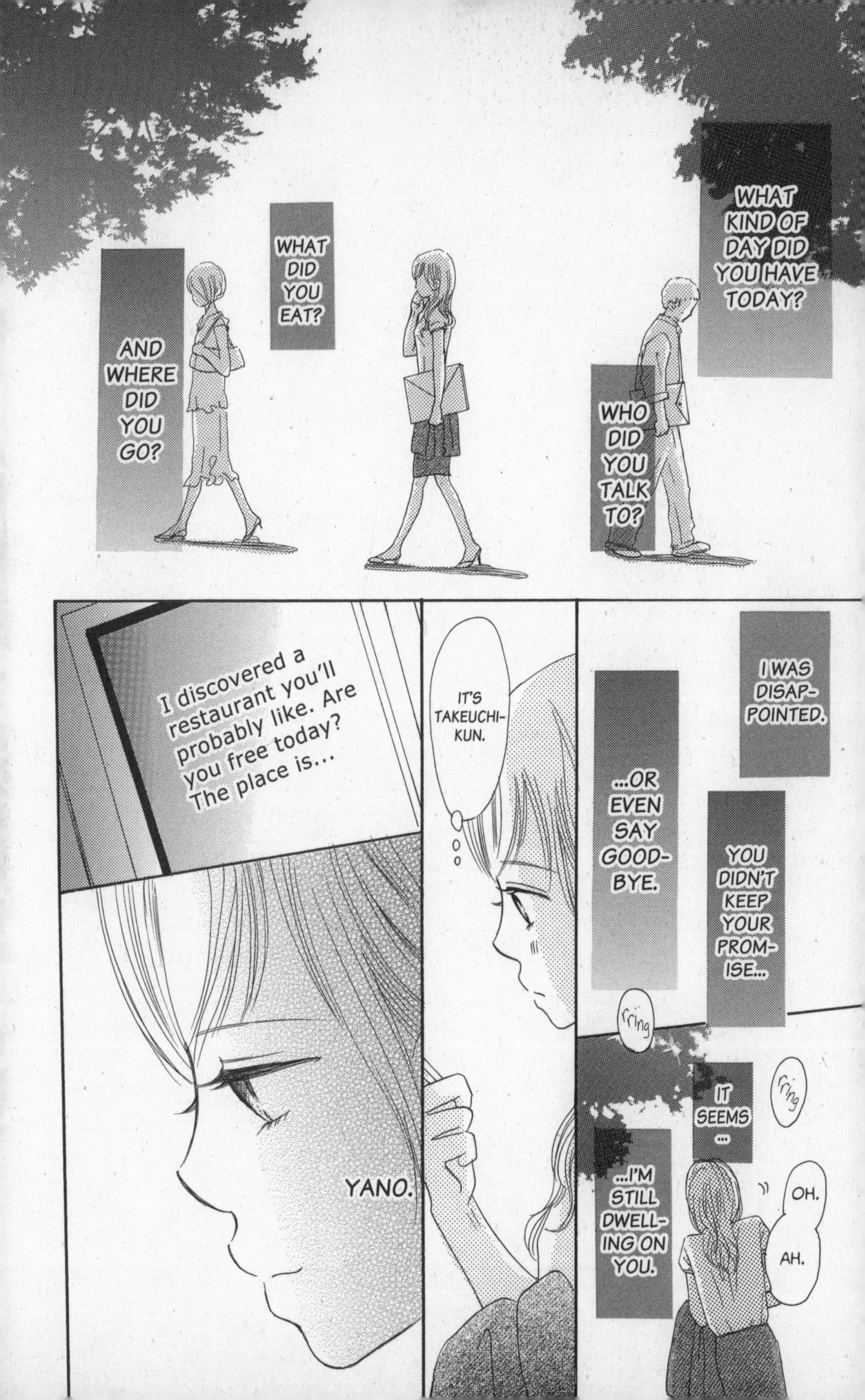
WHAT KIND OF DAY DID YOU HAVE TODAY?
WHO DID YOU TALK TO?
WHAT DID YOU EAT?
AND WHERE DID YOU GO?
I WAS DISAP-POINTED.
YOU DIDN'T KEEP YOUR PROM-ISE...
...OR EVEN SAY GOOD-BYE.
fring
IT SEEMS ...
...I'M STILL DWELL-ING ON YOU.
fring
OH.
AH.
IT'S TAKEUCHI-KUN.
I discovered a restaurant you'll probably like. Are you free today? The place is...
YANO.

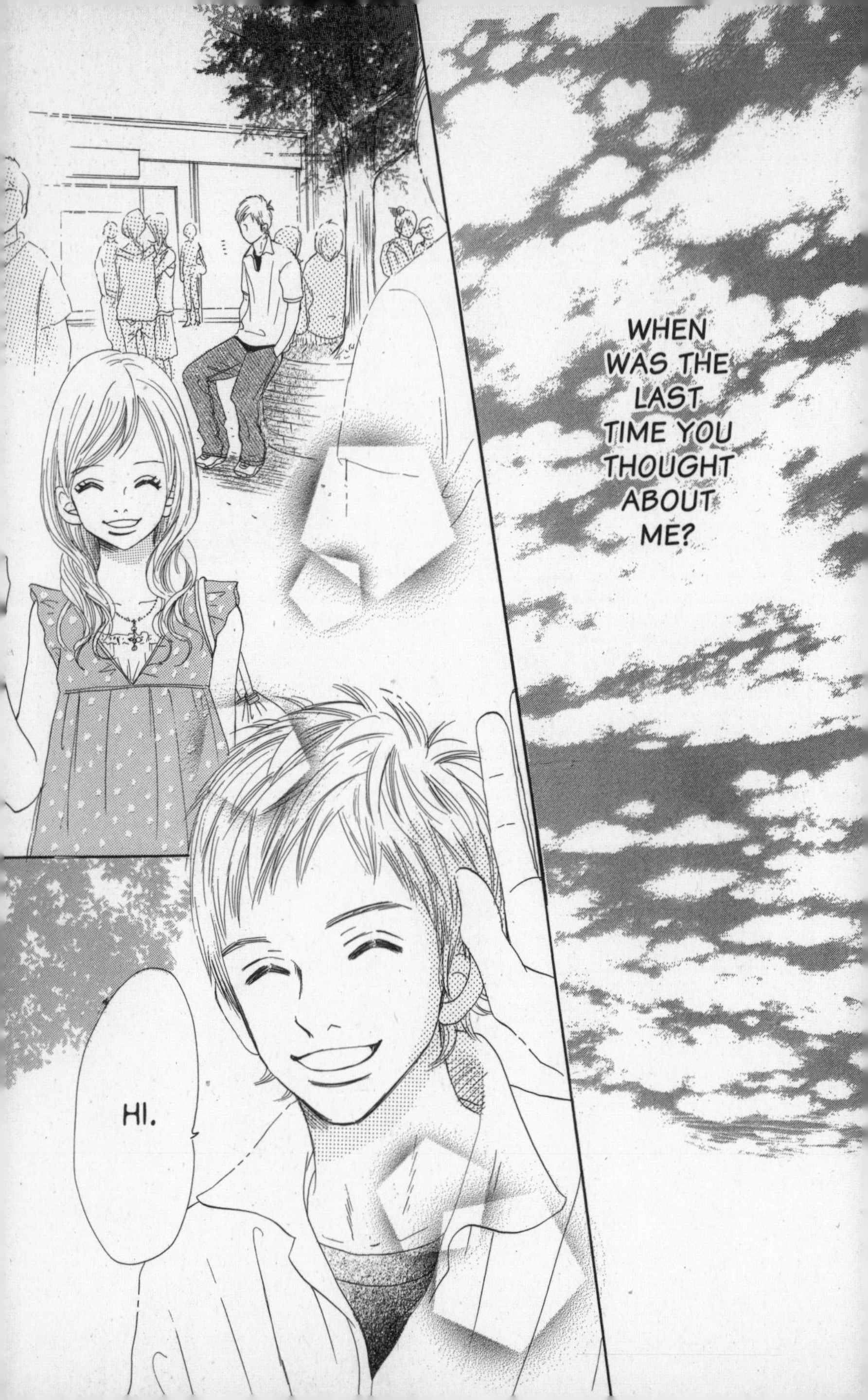
WHEN WAS THE LAST TIME YOU THOUGHT ABOUT ME?
HI.

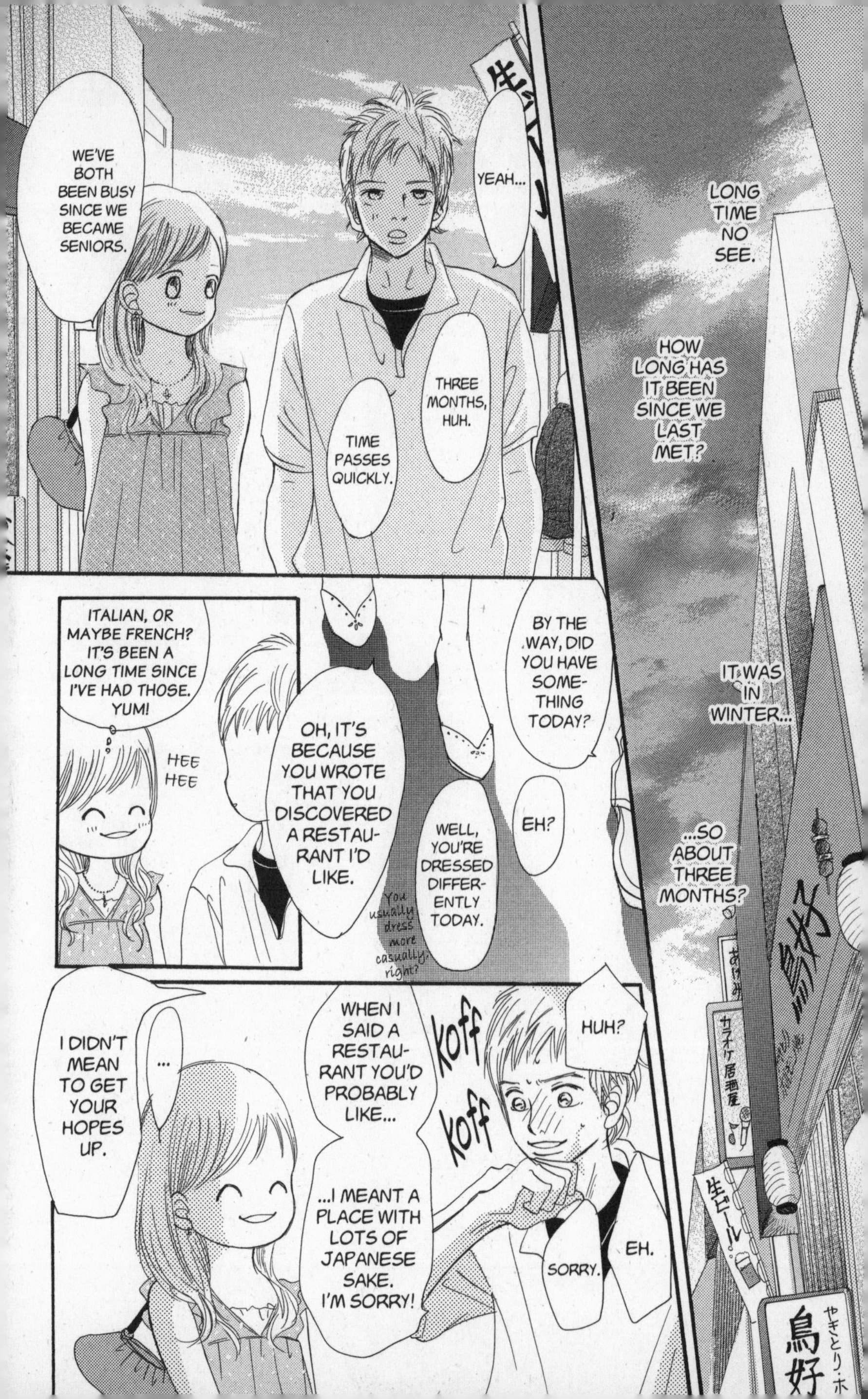
LONG TIME NO SEE.
HOW LONG HAS IT BEEN SINCE WE LAST MET?
IT WAS IN WINTER...
...SO ABOUT THREE MONTHS?
鳥好
やきとり・ホ
生ビール
カラオケ居酒屋
YEAH...
WE'VE BOTH BEEN BUSY SINCE WE BECAME SENIORS.
THREE MONTHS, HUH.
TIME PASSES QUICKLY.
BY THE WAY, DID YOU HAVE SOME-THING TODAY?
EH?
WELL, YOU'RE DRESSED DIFFER-ENTLY TODAY.
You usually dress more casually, right?
OH, IT'S BECAUSE YOU WROTE THAT YOU DISCOVERED A RESTAU-RANT I'D LIKE.
ITALIAN, OR MAYBE FRENCH? IT'S BEEN A LONG TIME SINCE I'VE HAD THOSE. YUM!
HEE HEE
HUH?
KOFF KOFF
WHEN I SAID A RESTAU-RANT YOU'D PROBABLY LIKE...
...I MEANT A PLACE WITH LOTS OF JAPANESE SAKE. I'M SORRY!
EH.
SORRY.
...
I DIDN'T MEAN TO GET YOUR HOPES UP.

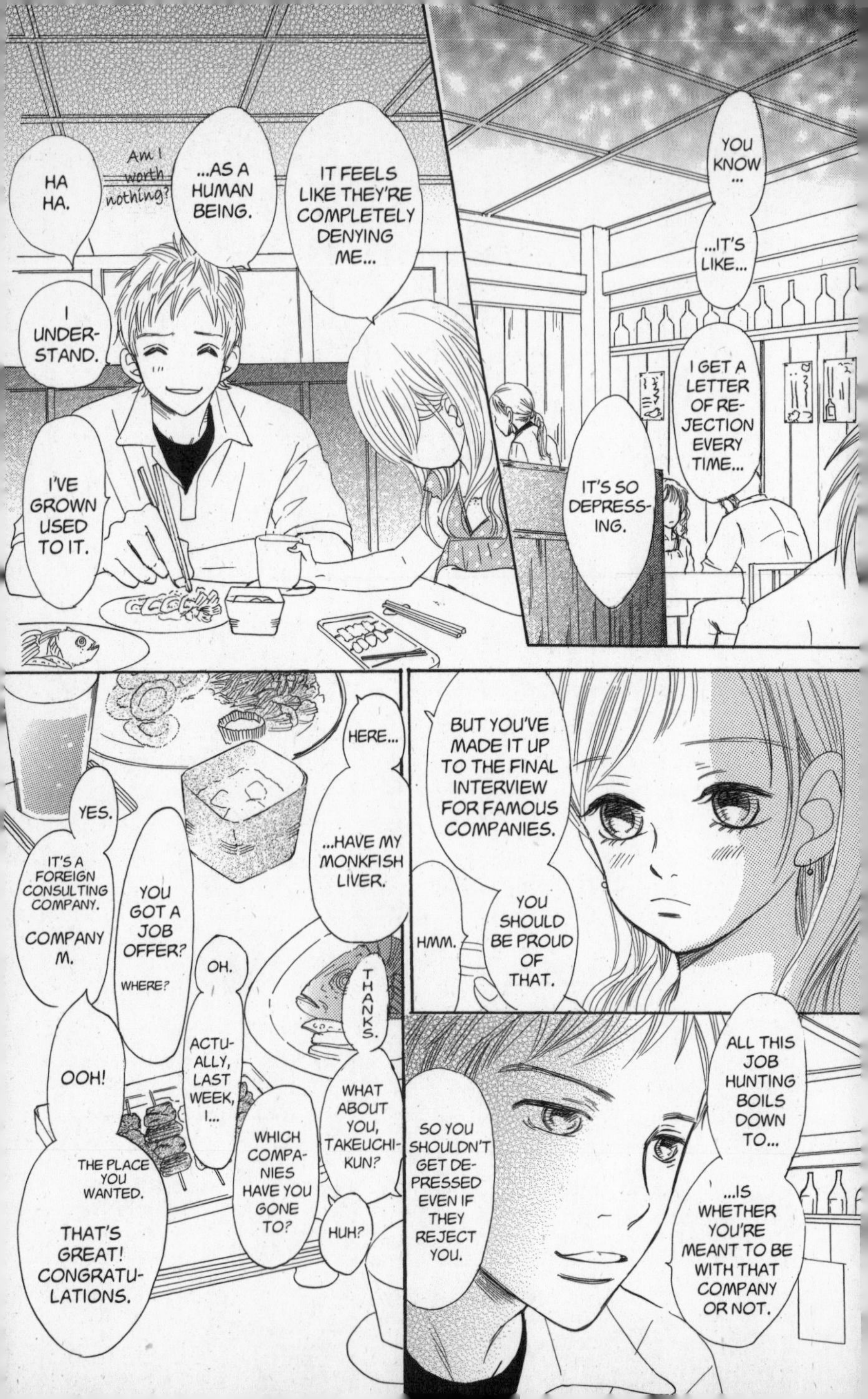
YOU KNOW ...
...IT'S LIKE...
I GET A LETTER OF RE-JECTION EVERY TIME...
IT'S SO DEPRESS-ING.
IT FEELS LIKE THEY'RE COMPLETELY DENYING ME...
...AS A HUMAN BEING.
Am I worth nothing?
HA HA.
I UNDER-STAND.
I'VE GROWN USED TO IT.
BUT YOU'VE MADE IT UP TO THE FINAL INTERVIEW FOR FAMOUS COMPANIES.
YOU SHOULD BE PROUD OF THAT.
HMM.
ALL THIS JOB HUNTING BOILS DOWN TO...
...IS WHETHER YOU'RE MEANT TO BE WITH THAT COMPANY OR NOT.
SO YOU SHOULDN'T GET DE-PRESSED EVEN IF THEY REJECT YOU.
HERE...
...HAVE MY MONKFISH LIVER.
THANKS.
WHAT ABOUT YOU, TAKEUCHI-KUN?
HUH?
WHICH COMPA-NIES HAVE YOU GONE TO?
OH.
ACTU-ALLY, LAST WEEK, I...
YOU GOT A JOB OFFER?
WHERE?
YES.
IT'S A FOREIGN CONSULTING COMPANY.
COMPANY M.
OOH!
THE PLACE YOU WANTED.
THAT'S GREAT! CONGRATU-LATIONS.

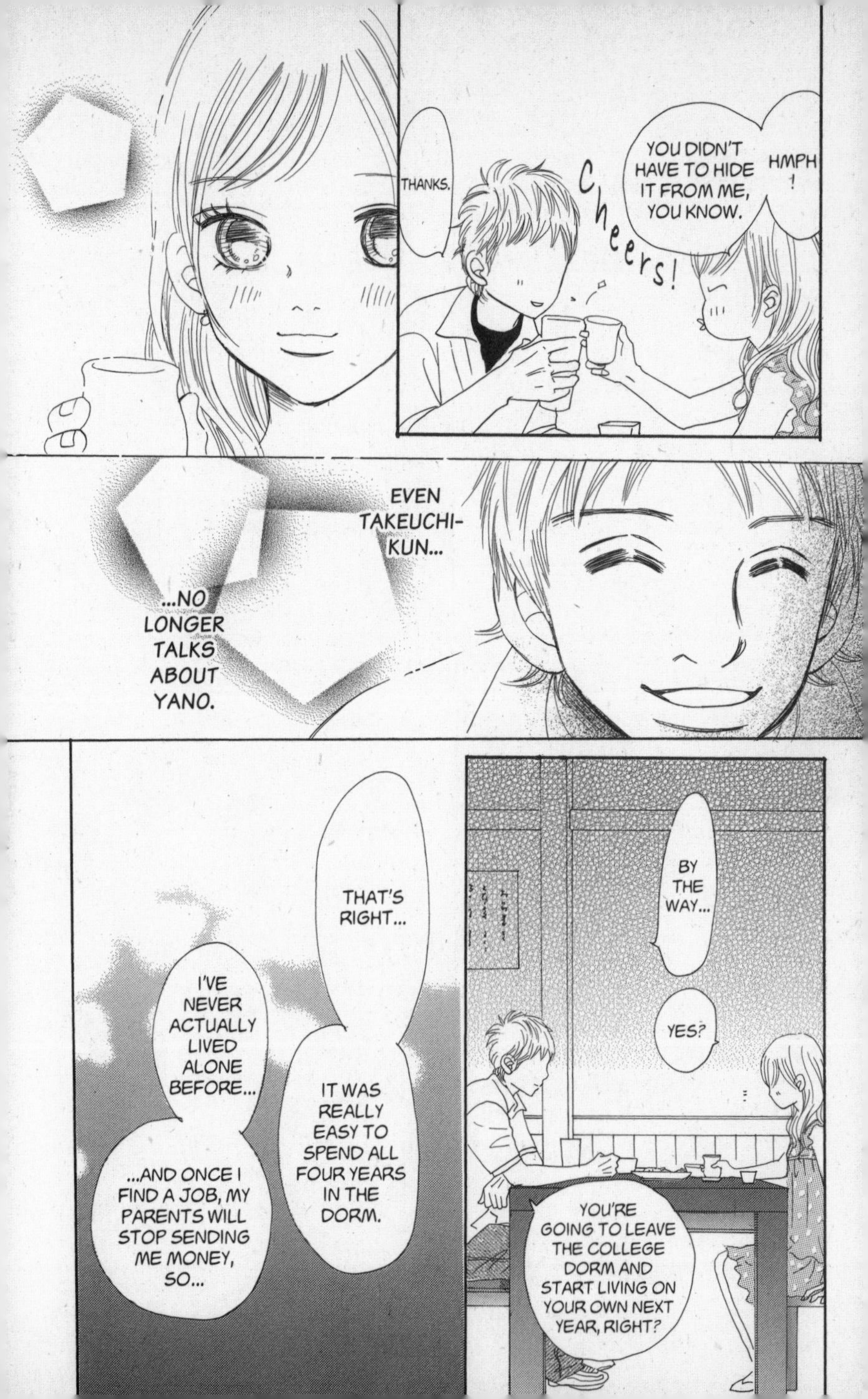
HMPH!
YOU DIDN'T HAVE TO HIDE IT FROM ME, YOU KNOW.
Cheers!
THANKS.
EVEN TAKEUCHI-KUN...
...NO LONGER TALKS ABOUT YANO.
BY THE WAY...
YES?
YOU'RE GOING TO LEAVE THE COLLEGE DORM AND START LIVING ON YOUR OWN NEXT YEAR, RIGHT?
THAT'S RIGHT...
IT WAS REALLY EASY TO SPEND ALL FOUR YEARS IN THE DORM.
I'VE NEVER ACTUALLY LIVED ALONE BEFORE...
...AND ONCE I FIND A JOB, MY PARENTS WILL STOP SENDING ME MONEY, SO...

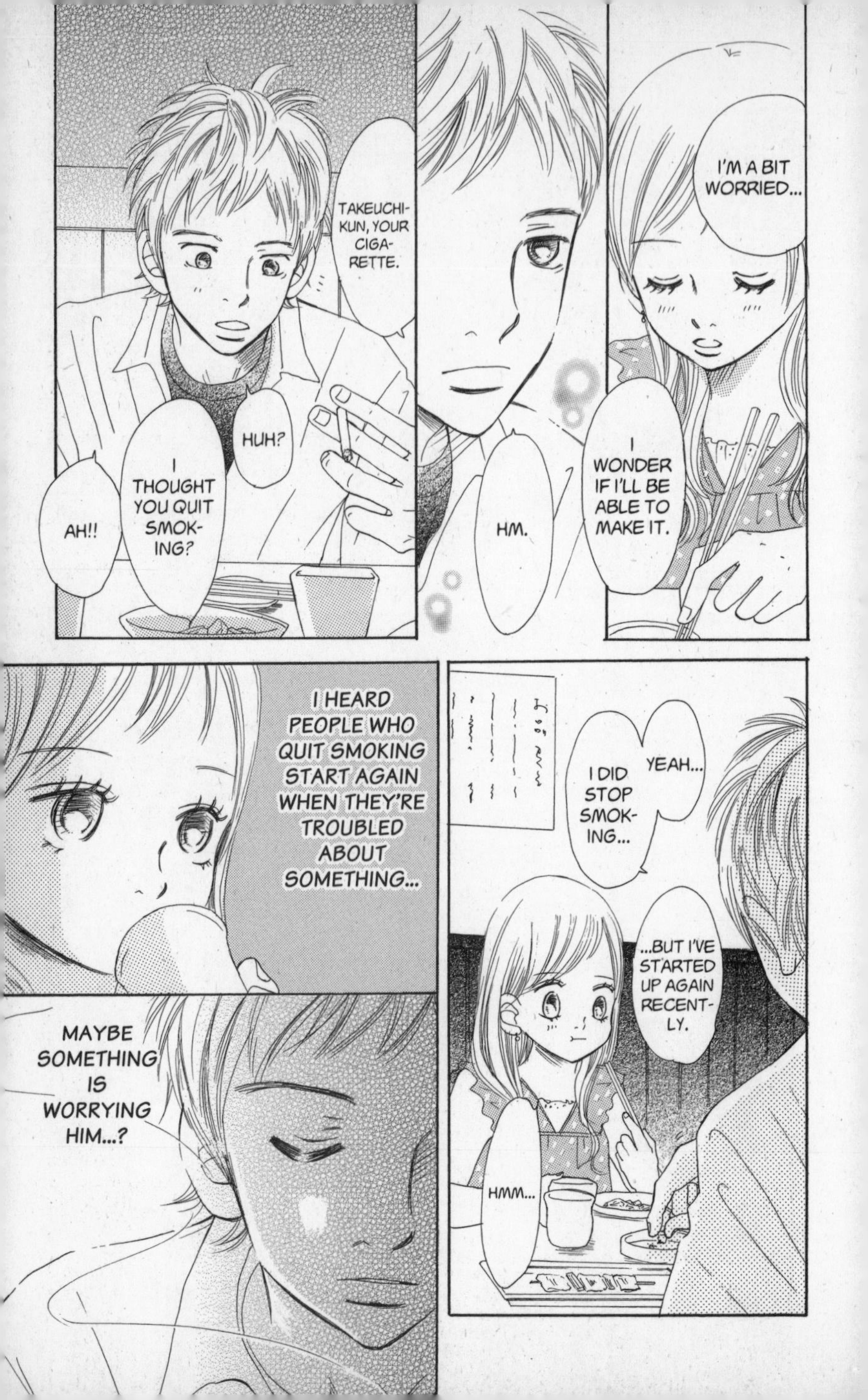
I'M A BIT WORRIED...
I WONDER IF I'LL BE ABLE TO MAKE IT.
HM.
TAKEUCHI-KUN, YOUR CIGA-RETTE.
HUH?
I THOUGHT YOU QUIT SMOK-ING?
AH!!
YEAH...
I DID STOP SMOK-ING...
...BUT I'VE STARTED UP AGAIN RECENT-LY.
HMM...
I HEARD PEOPLE WHO QUIT SMOKING START AGAIN WHEN THEY'RE TROUBLED ABOUT SOMETHING...
MAYBE SOMETHING IS WORRYING HIM...?

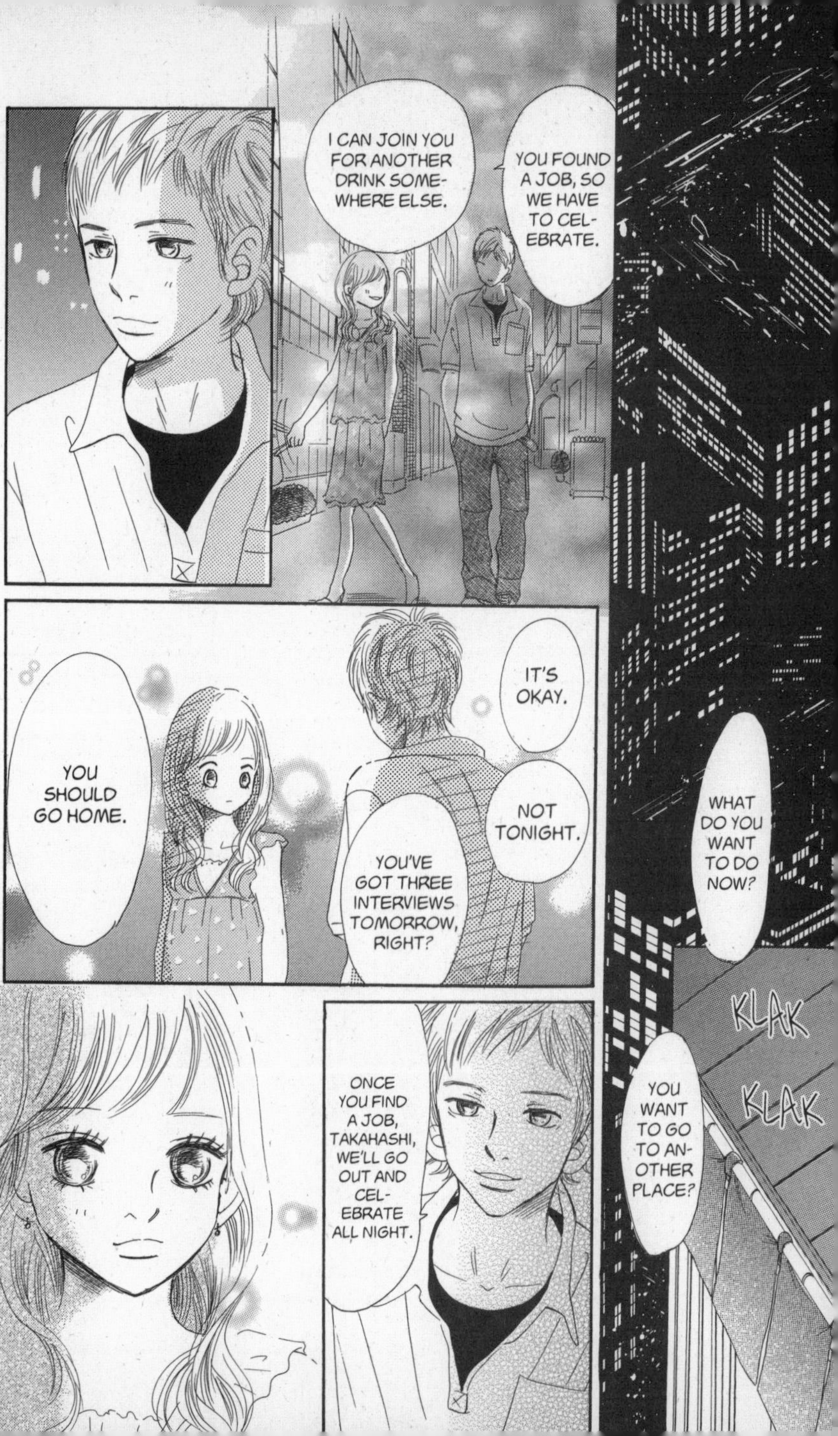
WHAT DO YOU WANT TO DO NOW?
KLAK KLAK
YOU WANT TO GO TO AN-OTHER PLACE?
YOU FOUND A JOB, SO WE HAVE TO CEL-EBRATE.
I CAN JOIN YOU FOR ANOTHER DRINK SOME-WHERE ELSE.
IT'S OKAY.
NOT TONIGHT.
YOU'VE GOT THREE INTERVIEWS TOMORROW, RIGHT?
YOU SHOULD GO HOME.
ONCE YOU FIND A JOB, TAKAHASHI, WE'LL GO OUT AND CEL-EBRATE ALL NIGHT.

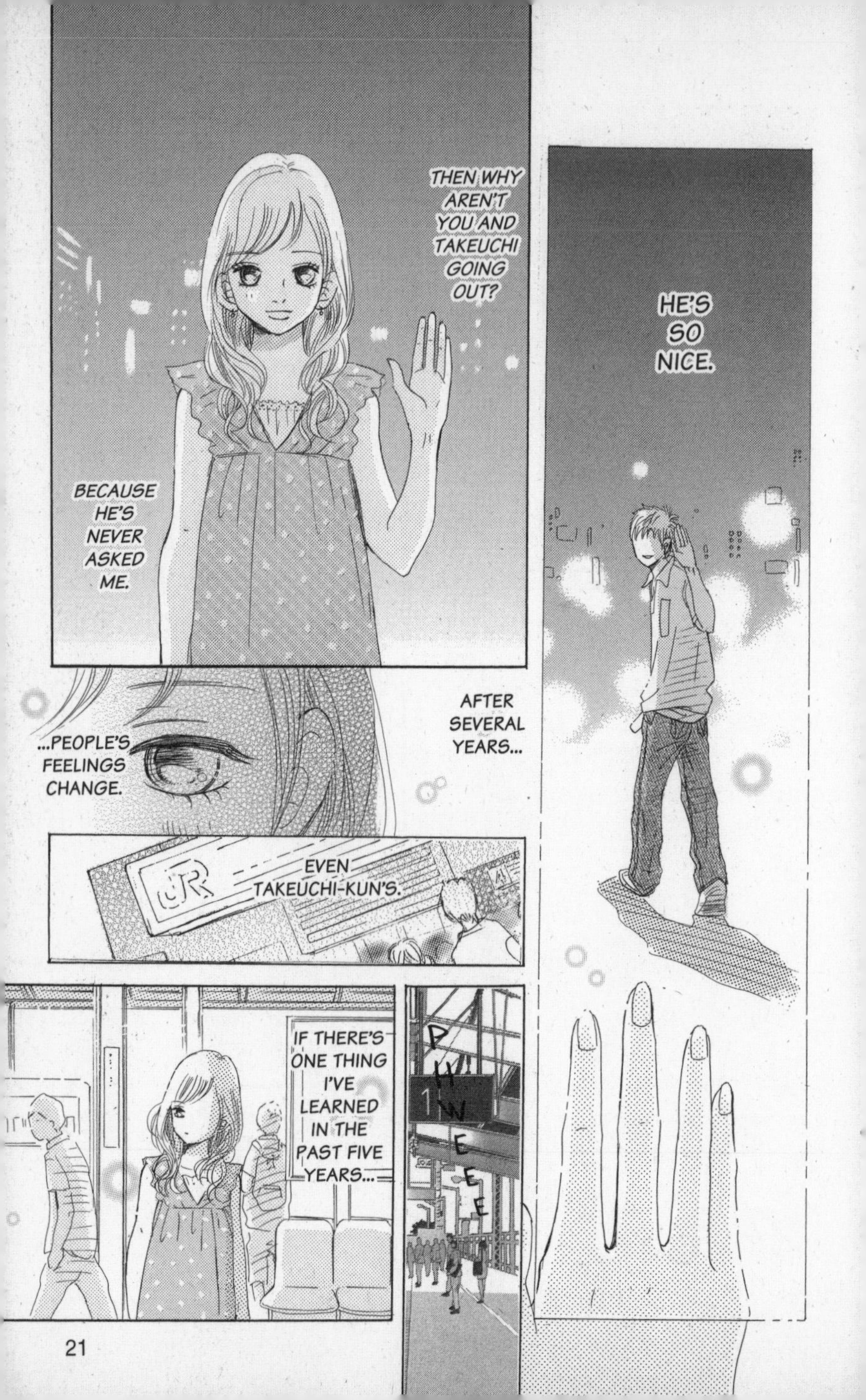
THEN WHY AREN'T YOU AND TAKEUCHI GOING OUT?
BECAUSE HE'S NEVER ASKED ME.
HE'S SO NICE.
AFTER SEVERAL YEARS...
...PEOPLE'S FEELINGS CHANGE.
EVEN TAKEUCHI-KUN'S.
PHWEEE
IF THERE'S ONE THING I'VE LEARNED IN THE PAST FIVE YEARS...

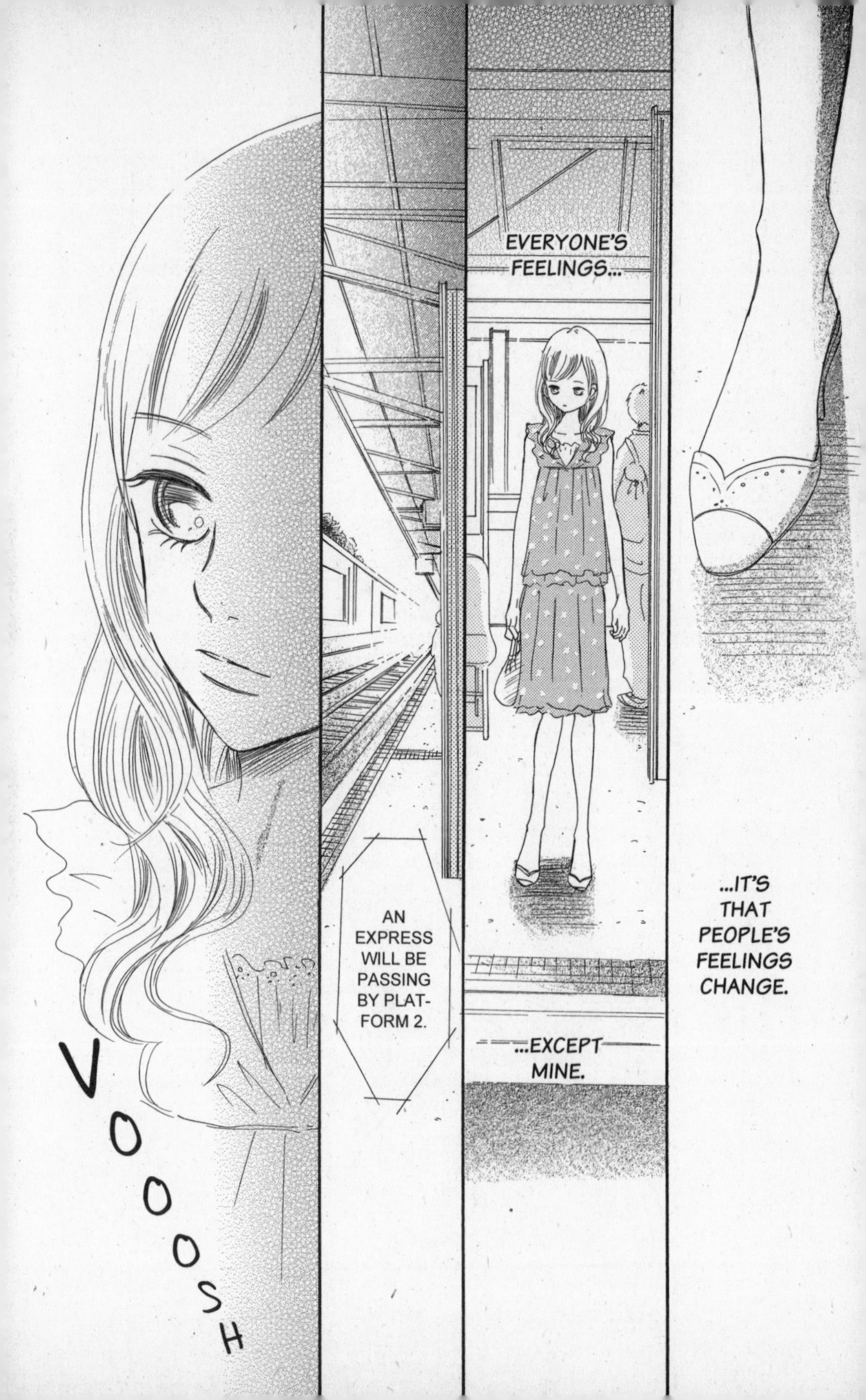
...IT'S THAT PEOPLE'S FEELINGS CHANGE.
EVERYONE'S FEELINGS...
...EXCEPT MINE.
AN EXPRESS WILL BE PASSING BY PLAT-FORM 2.
VOOOSH

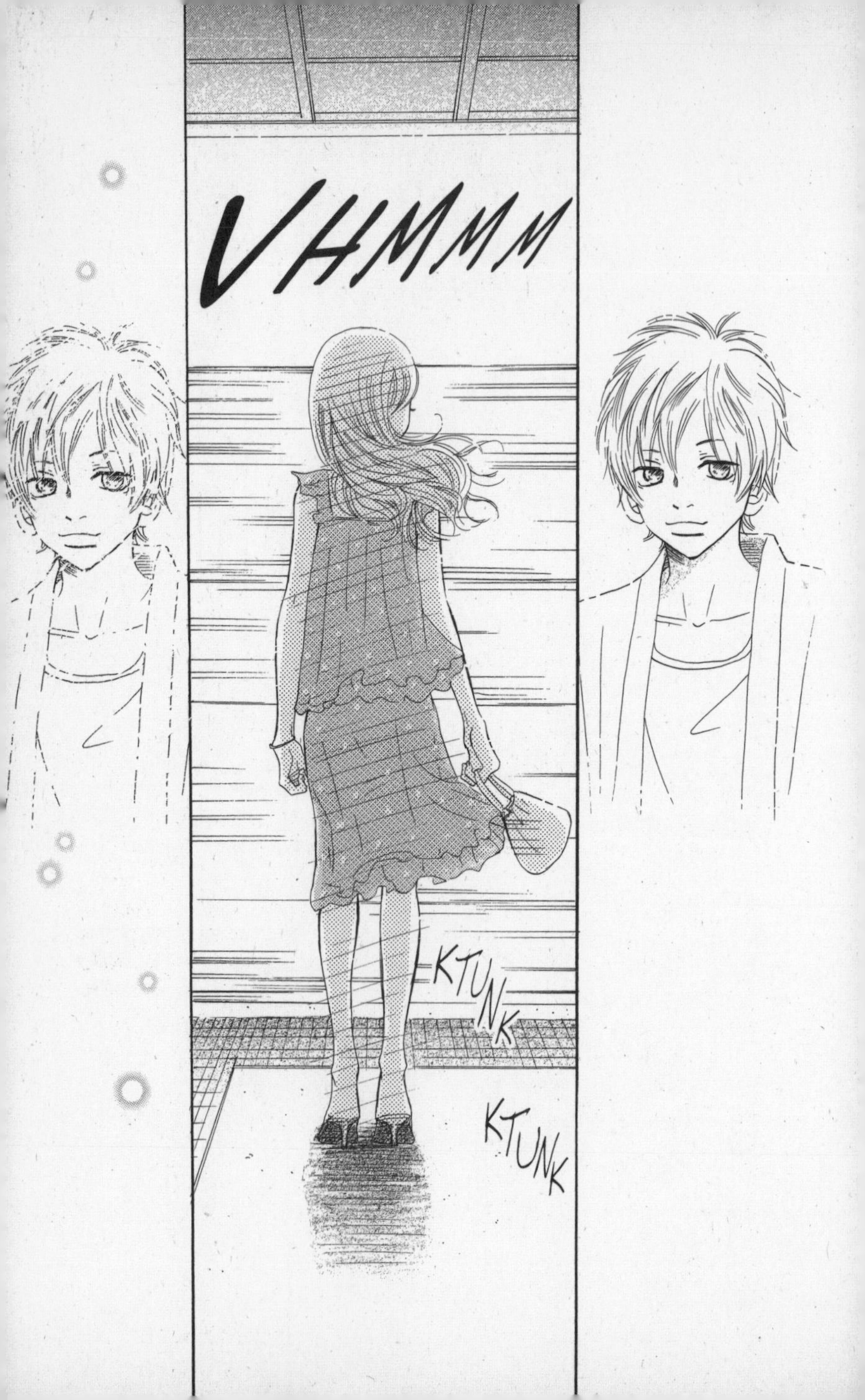
VHMMM
KTUNK
KTUNK

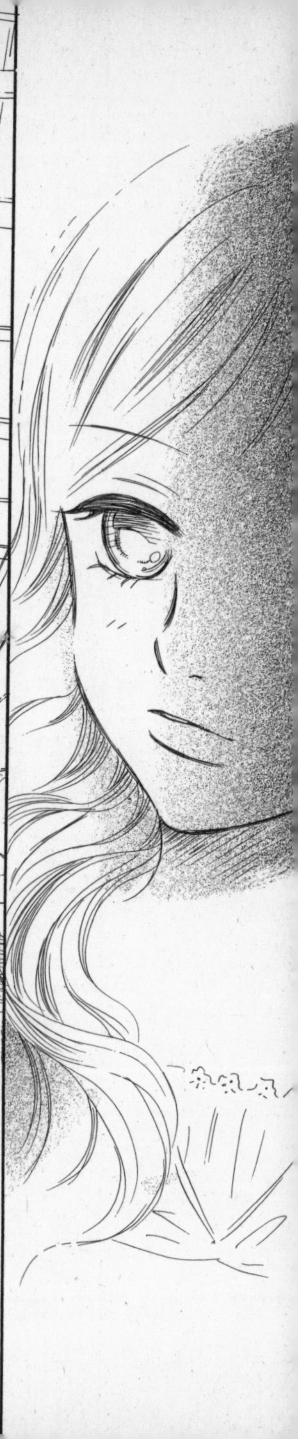

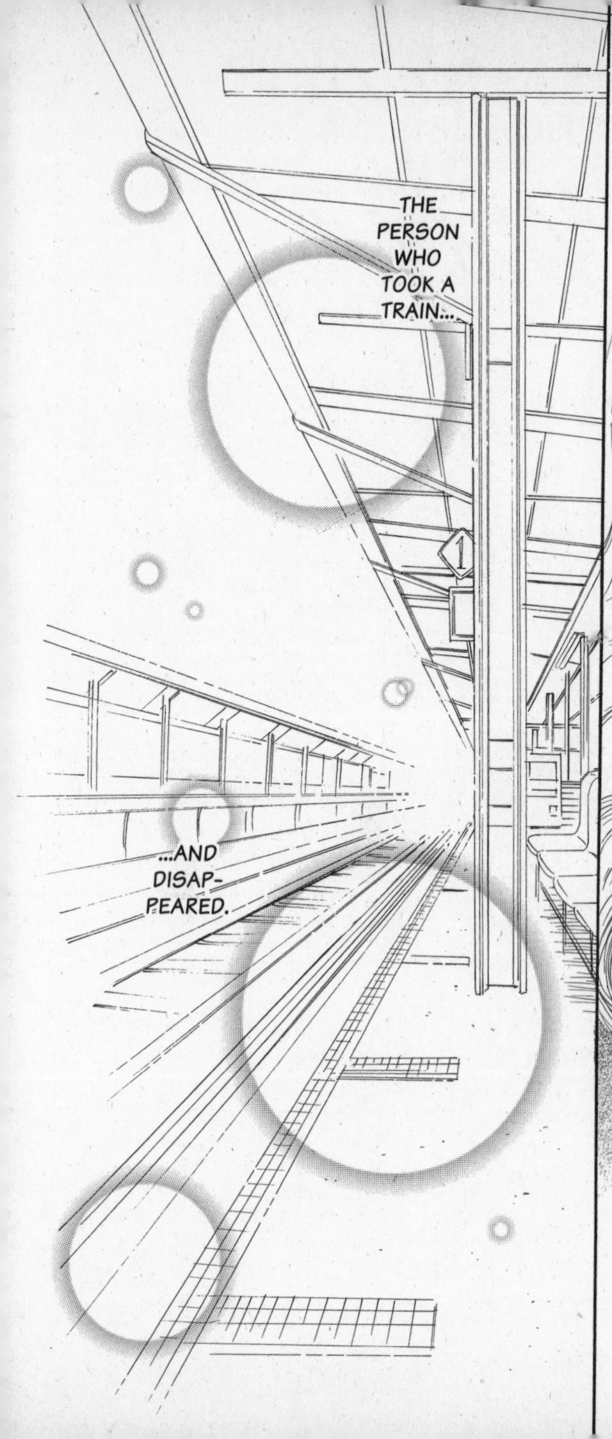
THE PERSON WHO TOOK A TRAIN...
...AND DISAP-PEARED.

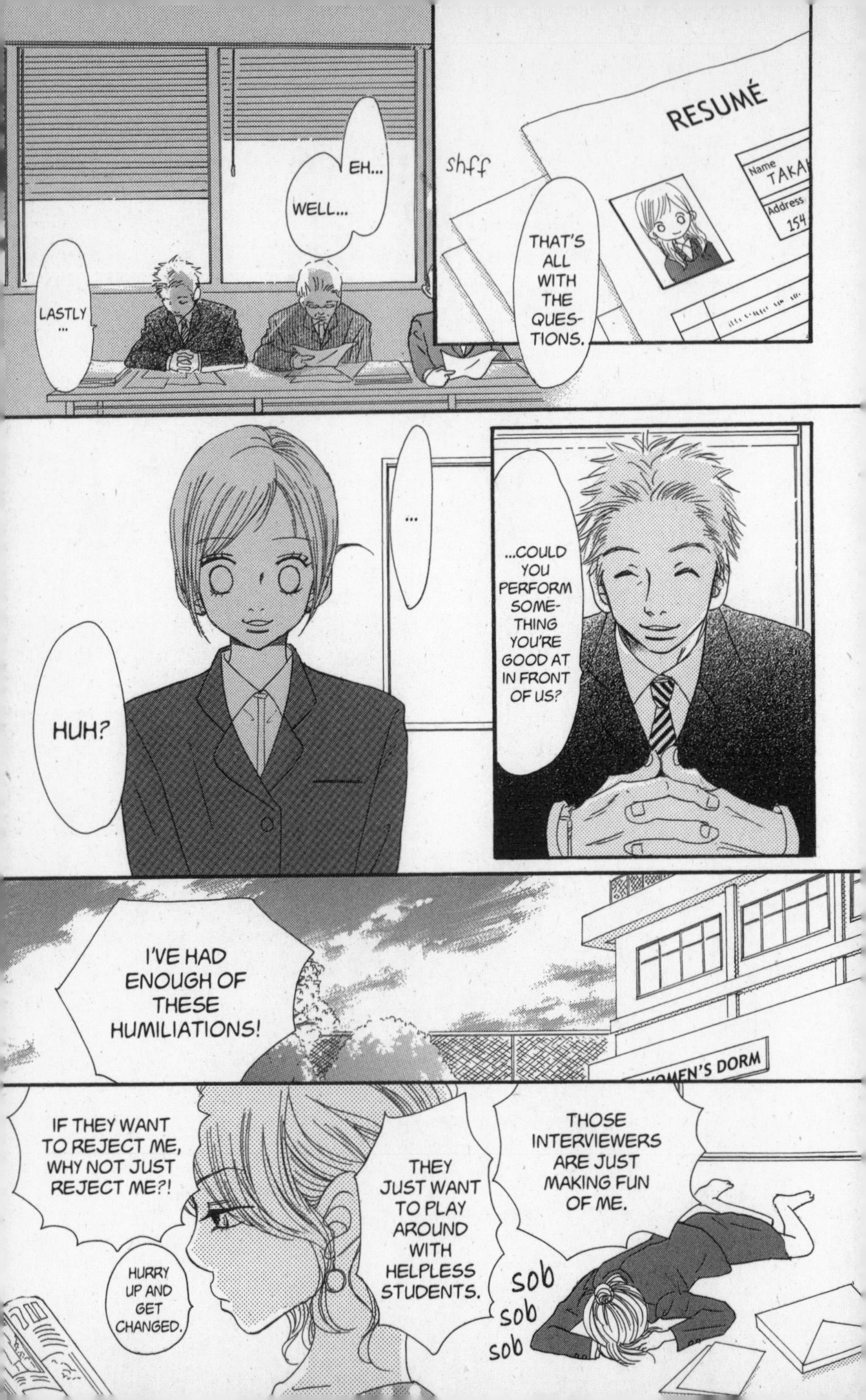
RESUMÉ
Name TAKA
Address 154
shff
THAT'S ALL WITH THE QUES-TIONS.
EH...
WELL...
LASTLY...
...COULD YOU PERFORM SOME-THING YOU'RE GOOD AT IN FRONT OF US?
...
HUH?
WOMEN'S DORM
I'VE HAD ENOUGH OF THESE HUMILIATIONS!
THOSE INTERVIEWERS ARE JUST MAKING FUN OF ME.
sob sob sob
THEY JUST WANT TO PLAY AROUND WITH HELPLESS STUDENTS.
IF THEY WANT TO REJECT ME, WHY NOT JUST REJECT ME?!
HURRY UP AND GET CHANGED.

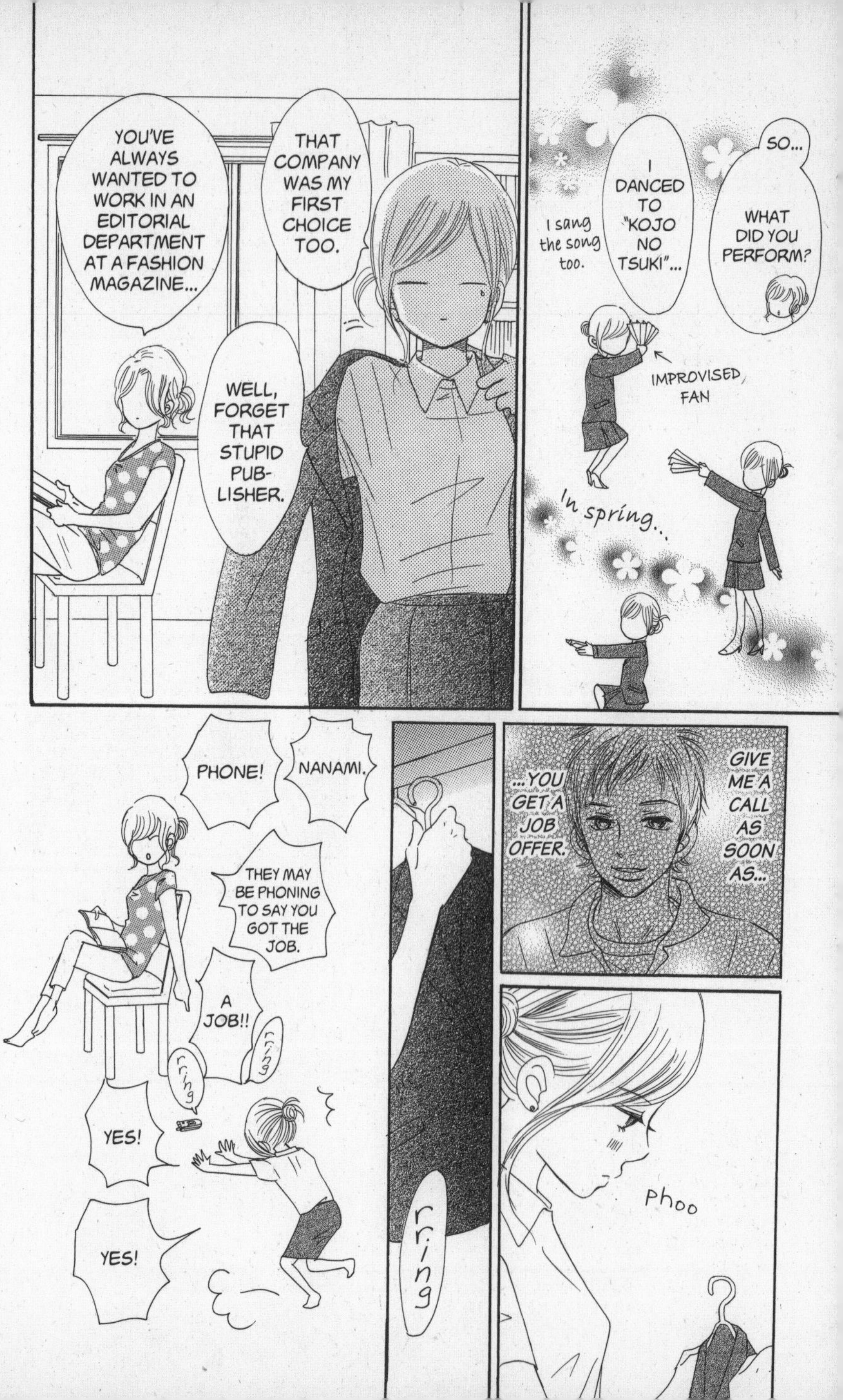
SO...
WHAT DID YOU PERFORM?
I DANCED TO "KOJO NO TSUKI"...
I sang the song too.
IMPROVISED FAN
In spring...
YOU'VE ALWAYS WANTED TO WORK IN AN EDITORIAL DEPARTMENT AT A FASHION MAGAZINE...
THAT COMPANY WAS MY FIRST CHOICE TOO.
WELL, FORGET THAT STUPID PUB-LISHER.
GIVE ME A CALL AS SOON AS...
...YOU GET A JOB OFFER.
Phoo
rring
NANAMI.
PHONE!
THEY MAY BE PHONING TO SAY YOU GOT THE JOB.
A JOB!!
rring
rring
YES!
YES!

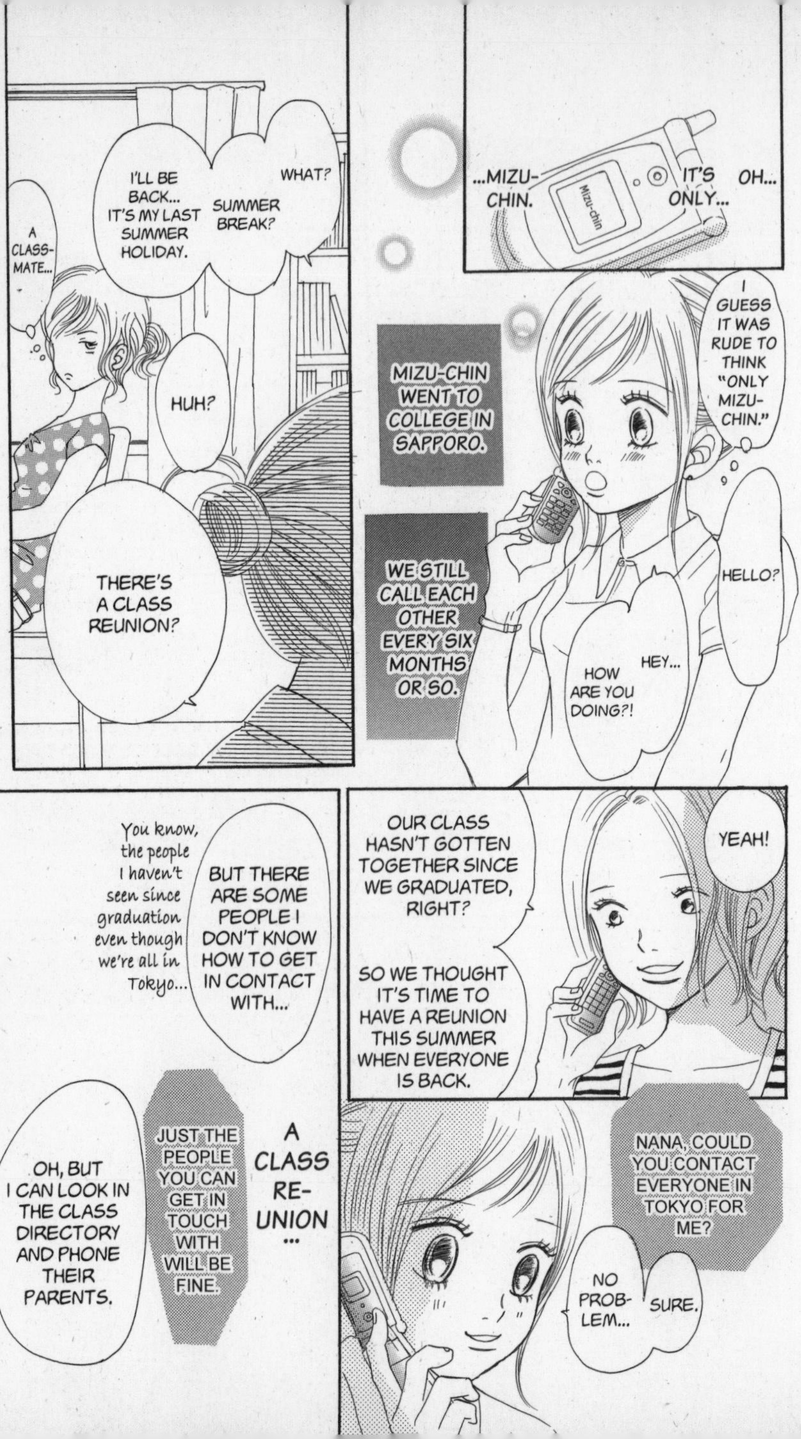
OH...
IT'S ONLY...
...MIZU-CHIN.
Mizu-chin
I GUESS IT WAS RUDE TO THINK "ONLY MIZU-CHIN."
MIZU-CHIN WENT TO COLLEGE IN SAPPORO.
HELLO?
HEY...
HOW ARE YOU DOING?!
WE STILL CALL EACH OTHER EVERY SIX MONTHS OR SO.
WHAT?
SUMMER BREAK?
I'LL BE BACK... IT'S MY LAST SUMMER HOLIDAY.
A CLASS-MATE...
HUH?
THERE'S A CLASS REUNION?
YEAH!
OUR CLASS HASN'T GOTTEN TOGETHER SINCE WE GRADUATED, RIGHT?
SO WE THOUGHT IT'S TIME TO HAVE A REUNION THIS SUMMER WHEN EVERYONE IS BACK.
NANA, COULD YOU CONTACT EVERYONE IN TOKYO FOR ME?
SURE.
NO PROB-LEM...
BUT THERE ARE SOME PEOPLE I DON'T KNOW HOW TO GET IN CONTACT WITH...
You know, the people I haven't seen since graduation even though we're all in Tokyo...
A CLASS RE-UNION...
JUST THE PEOPLE YOU CAN GET IN TOUCH WITH WILL BE FINE.
OH, BUT I CAN LOOK IN THE CLASS DIRECTORY AND PHONE THEIR PARENTS.

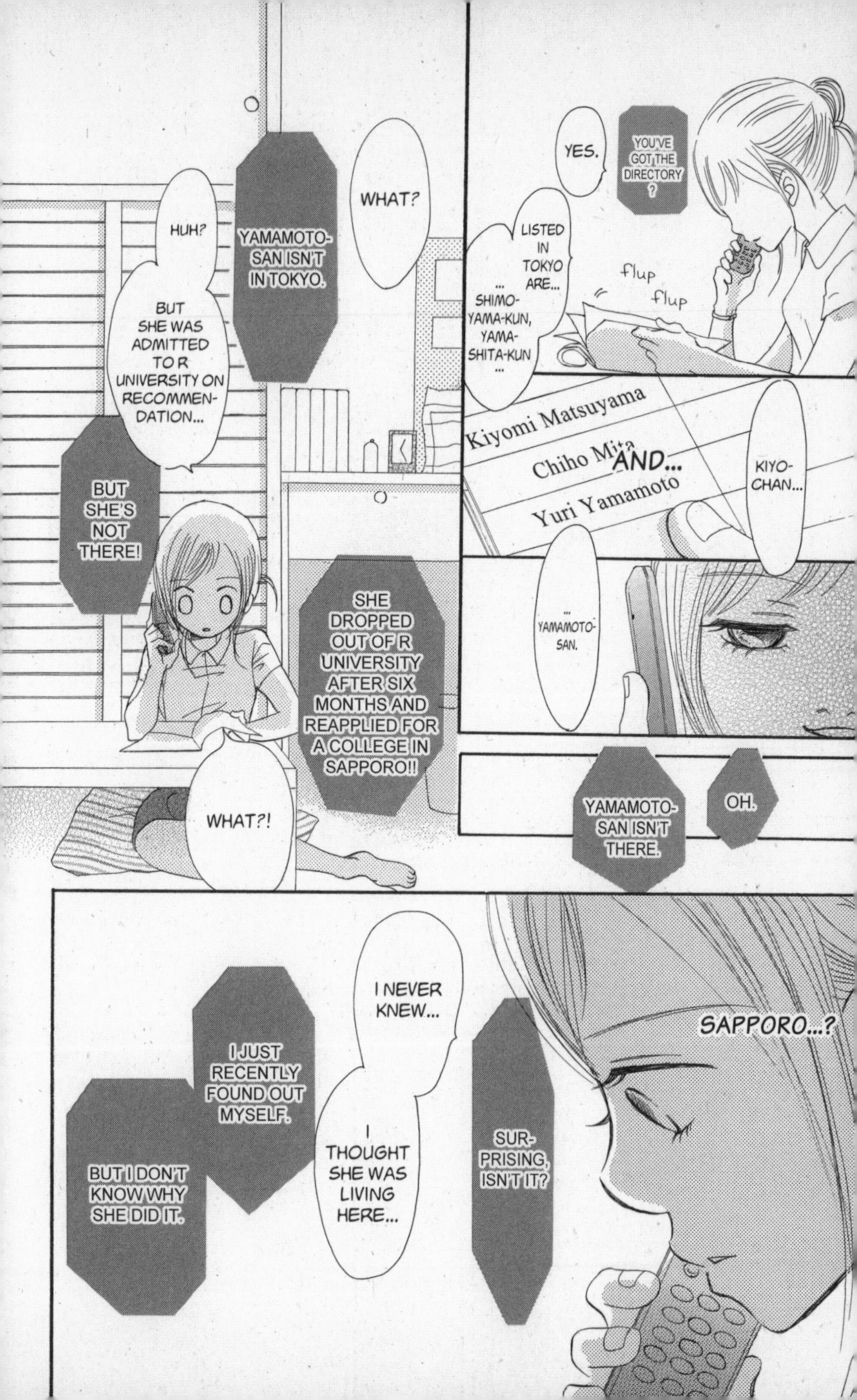
YOU'VE GOT THE DIRECTORY ?
YES.
LISTED IN TOKYO ARE... ... SHIMO-YAMA-KUN, YAMA-SHITA-KUN ...
flup
flup
Kiyomi Matsuyama
Chiho Mita
Yuri Yamamoto
AND...
KIYO-CHAN...
... YAMAMOTO-SAN.
OH.
YAMAMOTO-SAN ISN'T THERE.
WHAT?
YAMAMOTO-SAN ISN'T IN TOKYO.
HUH?
BUT SHE WAS ADMITTED TO R UNIVERSITY ON RECOMMEN-DATION...
BUT SHE'S NOT THERE!
SHE DROPPED OUT OF R UNIVERSITY AFTER SIX MONTHS AND REAPPLIED FOR A COLLEGE IN SAPPORO!!
WHAT?!
SAPPORO...?
SUR-PRISING, ISN'T IT?
I NEVER KNEW...
I THOUGHT SHE WAS LIVING HERE...
I JUST RECENTLY FOUND OUT MYSELF.
BUT I DON'T KNOW WHY SHE DID IT.

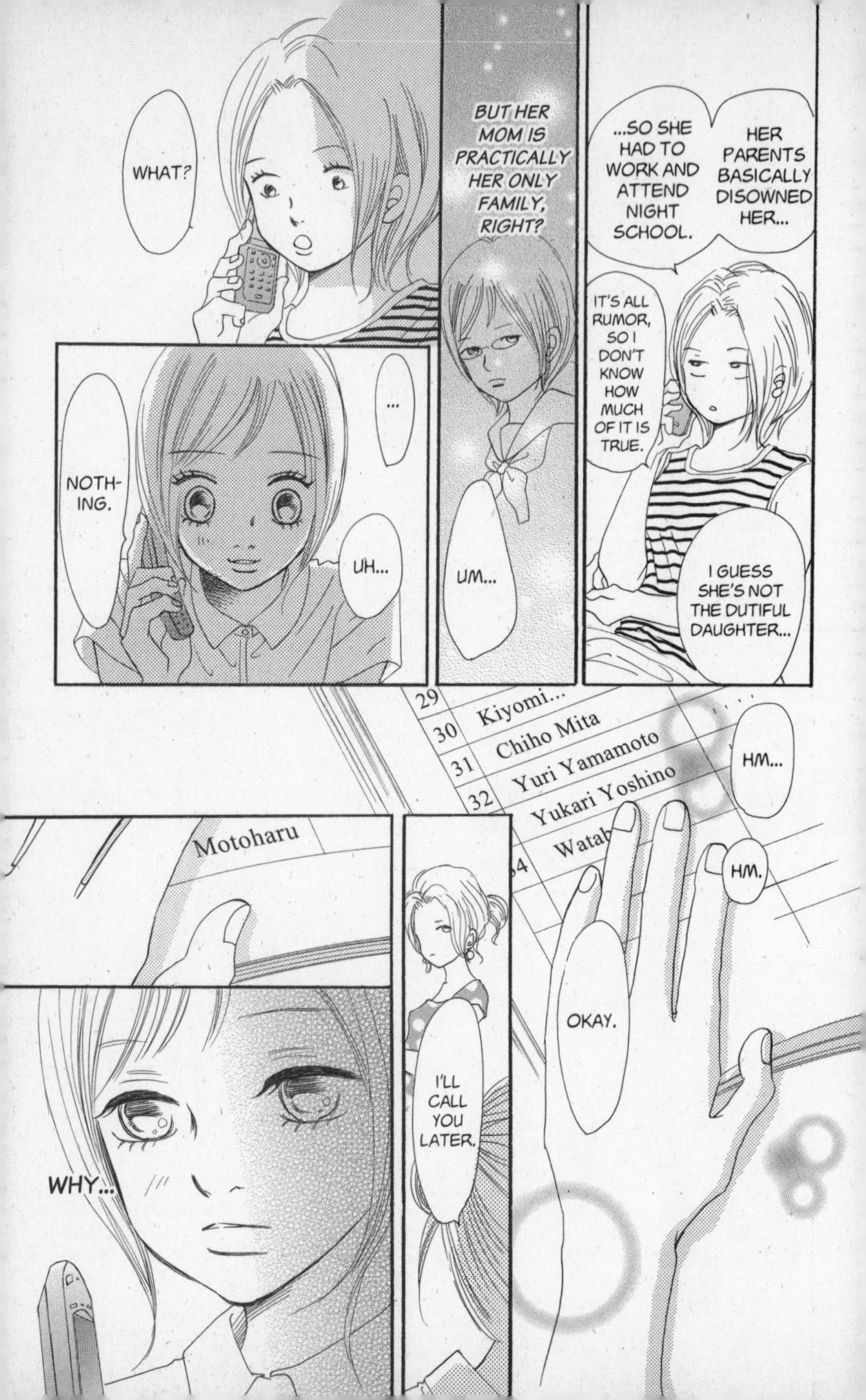
HER PARENTS BASICALLY DISOWNED HER...
...SO SHE HAD TO WORK AND ATTEND NIGHT SCHOOL.
IT'S ALL RUMOR, SO I DON'T KNOW HOW MUCH OF IT IS TRUE.
I GUESS SHE'S NOT THE DUTIFUL DAUGHTER...
BUT HER MOM IS PRACTICALLY HER ONLY FAMILY, RIGHT?
UM...
WHAT?
...
UH...
NOTH-ING.
29
30 Kiyomi...
31 Chiho Mita
32 Yuri Yamamoto
Yukari Yoshino
34 Watab
HM...
HM.
OKAY.
I'LL CALL YOU LATER.
Motoharu
WHY...

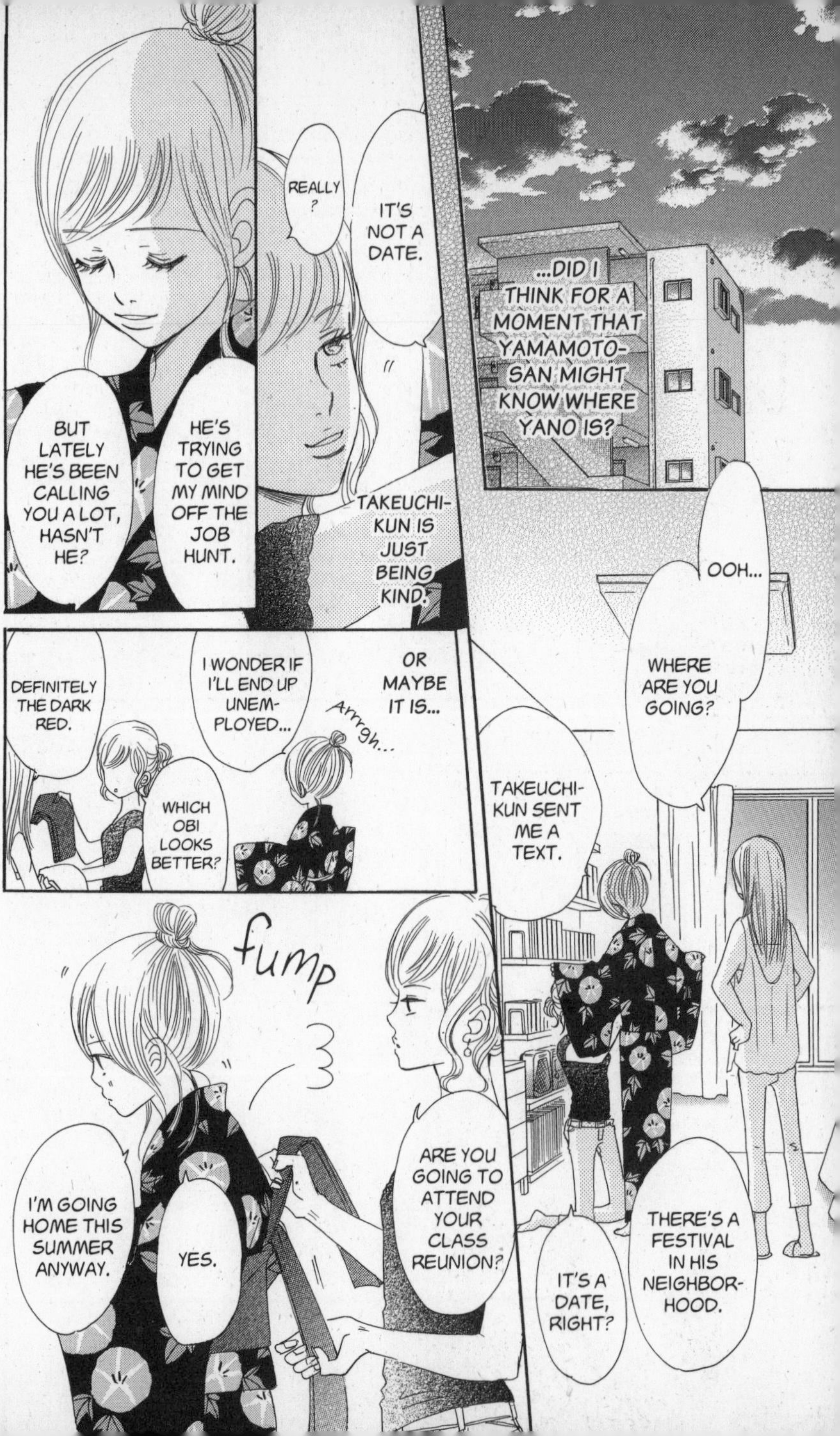
...DID I THINK FOR A MOMENT THAT YAMAMOTO-SAN MIGHT KNOW WHERE YANO IS?
OOH...
WHERE ARE YOU GOING?
TAKEUCHI-KUN SENT ME A TEXT.
THERE'S A FESTIVAL IN HIS NEIGHBOR-HOOD.
IT'S A DATE, RIGHT?
IT'S NOT A DATE.
REALLY?
TAKEUCHI-KUN IS JUST BEING KIND.
BUT LATELY HE'S BEEN CALLING YOU A LOT, HASN'T HE?
HE'S TRYING TO GET MY MIND OFF THE JOB HUNT.
OR MAYBE IT IS...
Arrrgh...
I WONDER IF I'LL END UP UNEM-PLOYED...
WHICH OBI LOOKS BETTER?
DEFINITELY THE DARK RED.
ARE YOU GOING TO ATTEND YOUR CLASS REUNION?
fump
I'M GOING HOME THIS SUMMER ANYWAY.
YES.

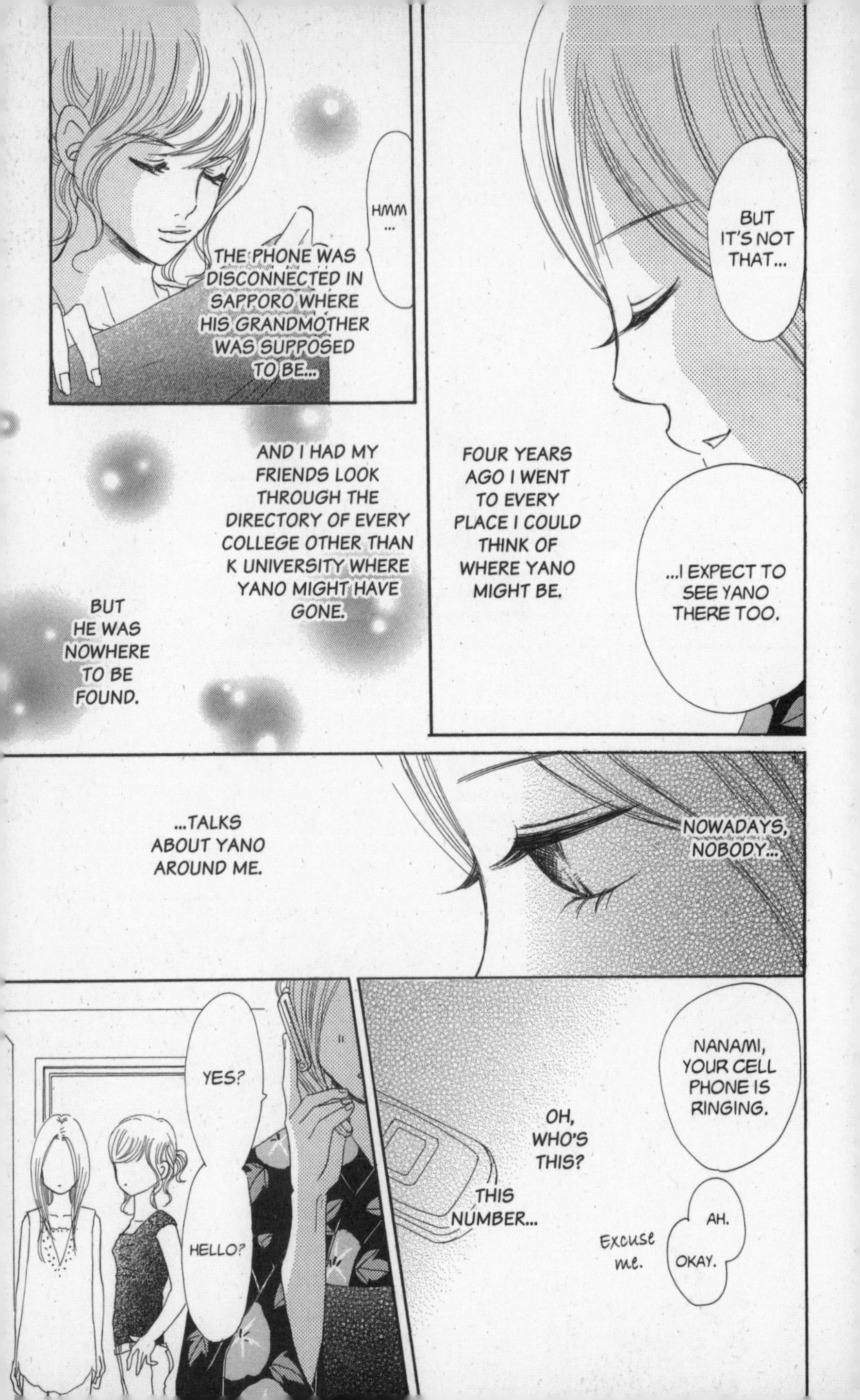
BUT IT'S NOT THAT...
...I EXPECT TO SEE YANO THERE TOO.
FOUR YEARS AGO I WENT TO EVERY PLACE I COULD THINK OF WHERE YANO MIGHT BE.
HMM...
THE PHONE WAS DISCONNECTED IN SAPPORO WHERE HIS GRANDMOTHER WAS SUPPOSED TO BE...
AND I HAD MY FRIENDS LOOK THROUGH THE DIRECTORY OF EVERY COLLEGE OTHER THAN K UNIVERSITY WHERE YANO MIGHT HAVE GONE.
BUT HE WAS NOWHERE TO BE FOUND.
NOWADAYS, NOBODY...
...TALKS ABOUT YANO AROUND ME.
NANAMI, YOUR CELL PHONE IS RINGING.
AH.
OKAY.
Excuse me.
OH, WHO'S THIS?
THIS NUMBER...
YES?
HELLO?

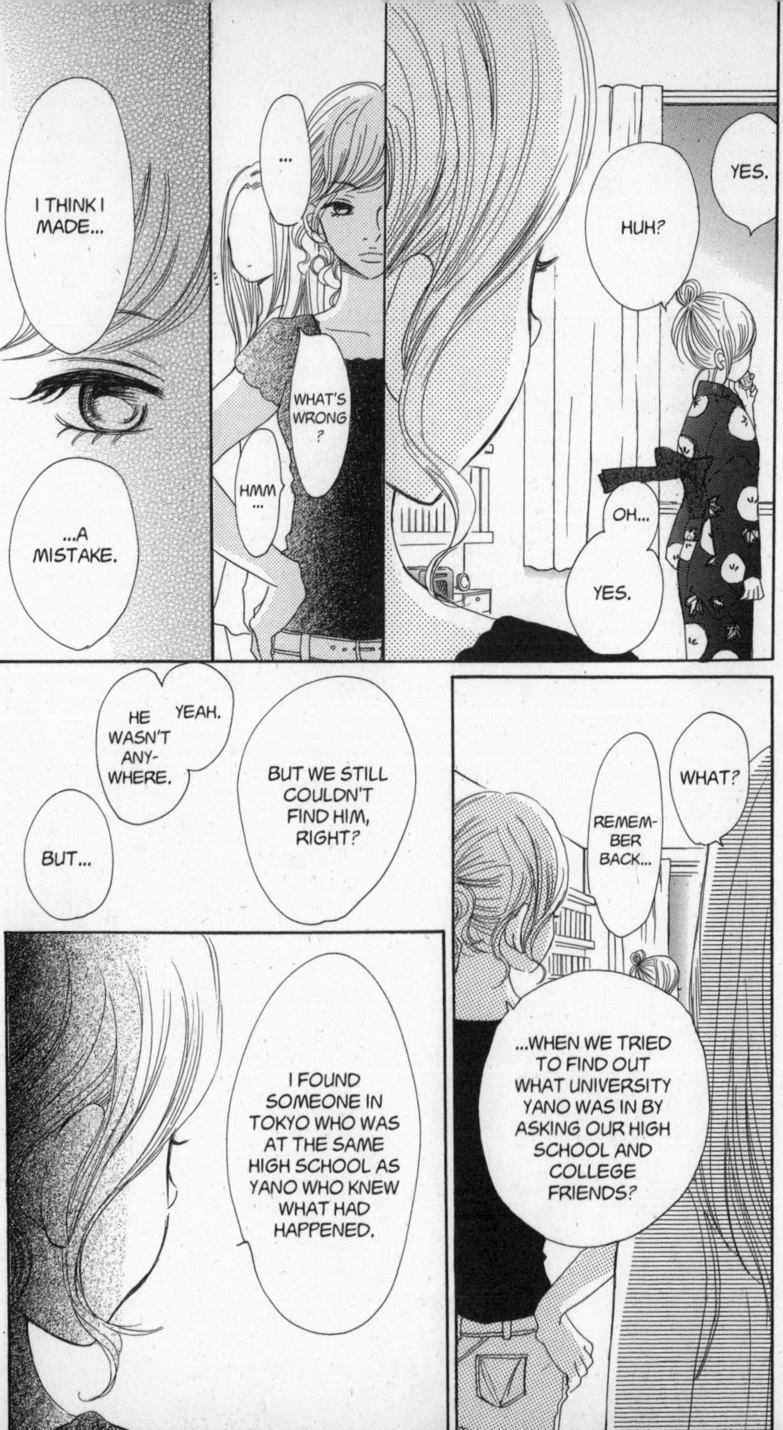
YES.
HUH?
OH...
YES.
...
WHAT'S WRONG?
HMM...
I THINK I MADE...
...A MISTAKE.
WHAT?
REMEMBER BACK...
...WHEN WE TRIED TO FIND OUT WHAT UNIVERSITY YANO WAS IN BY ASKING OUR HIGH SCHOOL AND COLLEGE FRIENDS?
BUT WE STILL COULDN'T FIND HIM, RIGHT?
YEAH.
HE WASN'T ANYWHERE.
BUT...
I FOUND SOMEONE IN TOKYO WHO WAS AT THE SAME HIGH SCHOOL AS YANO WHO KNEW WHAT HAD HAPPENED.

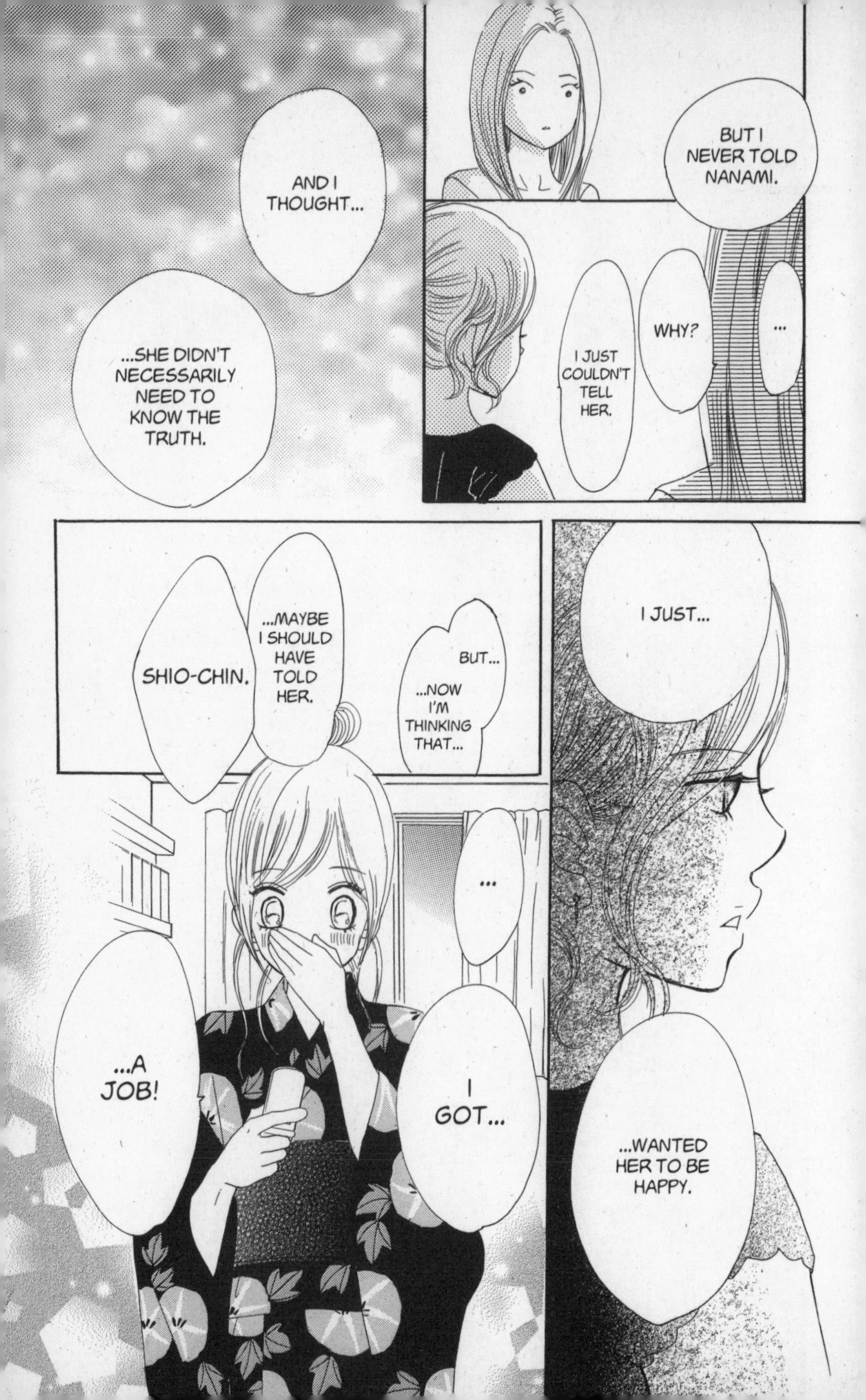
BUT I NEVER TOLD NANAMI.
...
WHY?
I JUST COULDN'T TELL HER.
AND I THOUGHT...
...SHE DIDN'T NECESSARILY NEED TO KNOW THE TRUTH.
I JUST...
...WANTED HER TO BE HAPPY.
BUT...
...NOW I'M THINKING THAT...
...MAYBE I SHOULD HAVE TOLD HER.
SHIO-CHIN.
...
I GOT...
...A JOB!

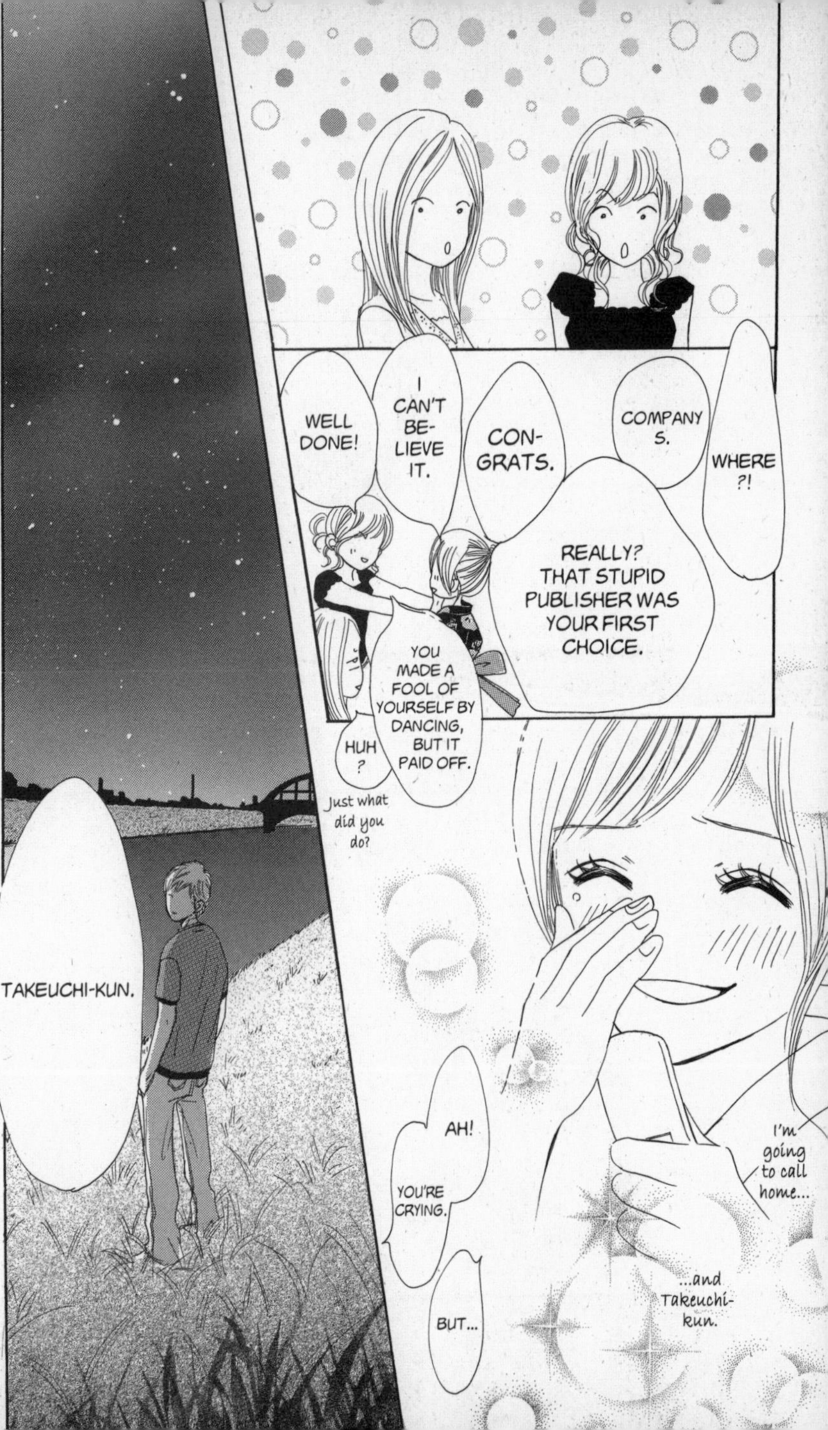
WHERE ?!
COMPANY S.
REALLY? THAT STUPID PUBLISHER WAS YOUR FIRST CHOICE.
CON-GRATS.
I CAN'T BE-LIEVE IT.
WELL DONE!
YOU MADE A FOOL OF YOURSELF BY DANCING, BUT IT PAID OFF.
HUH ?
Just what did you do?
I'm going to call home...
...and Takeuchi-kun.
AH!
YOU'RE CRYING.
BUT...
TAKEUCHI-KUN.

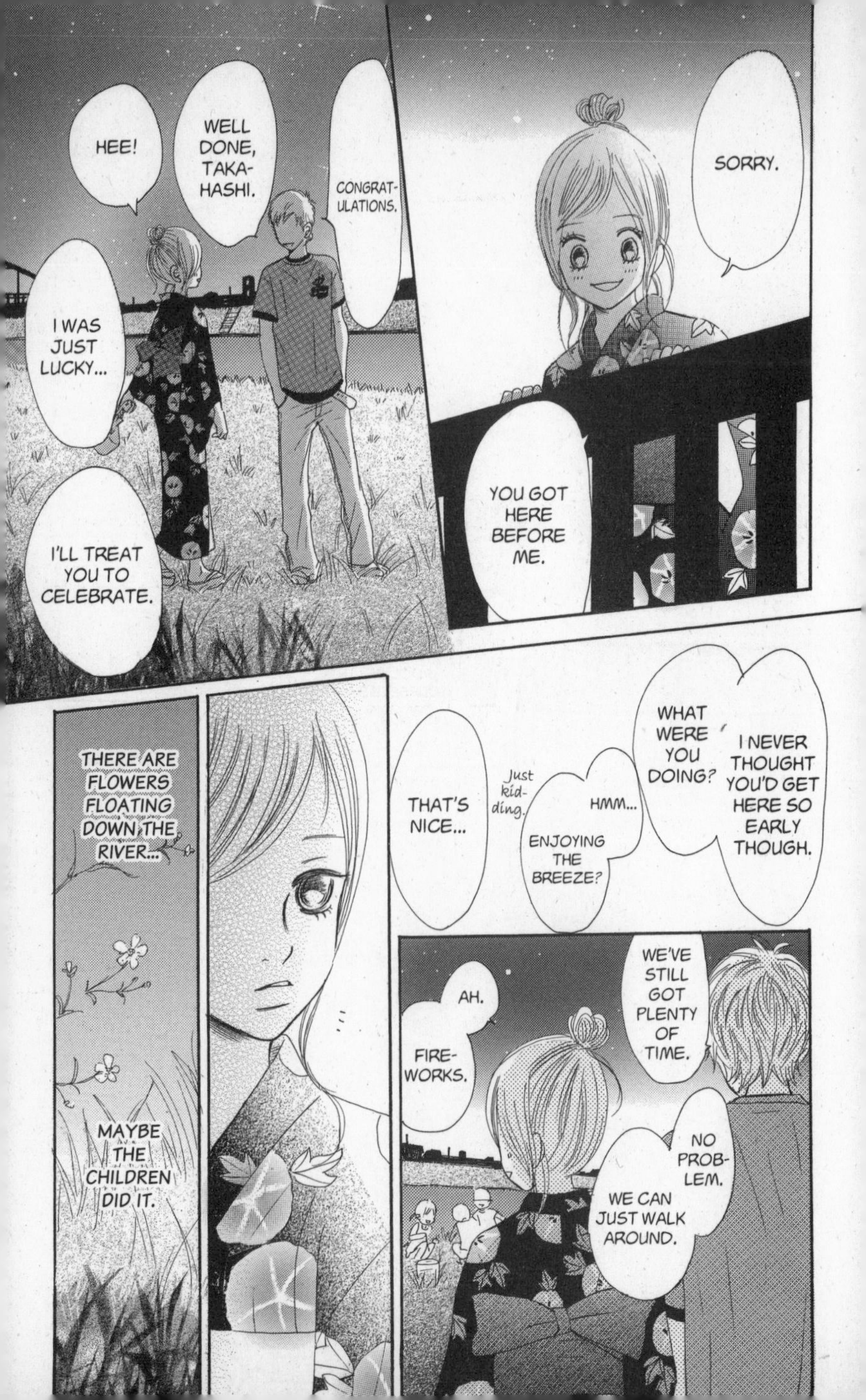
SORRY.
YOU GOT HERE BEFORE ME.
CONGRATULATIONS.
WELL DONE, TAKAHASHI.
HEE!
I WAS JUST LUCKY...
I'LL TREAT YOU TO CELEBRATE.
WHAT WERE YOU DOING? I NEVER THOUGHT YOU'D GET HERE SO EARLY THOUGH.
HMM... ENJOYING THE BREEZE?
Just kidding.
THAT'S NICE...
WE'VE STILL GOT PLENTY OF TIME.
AH. FIREWORKS.
NO PROBLEM. WE CAN JUST WALK AROUND.
THERE ARE FLOWERS FLOATING DOWN THE RIVER...
MAYBE THE CHILDREN DID IT.

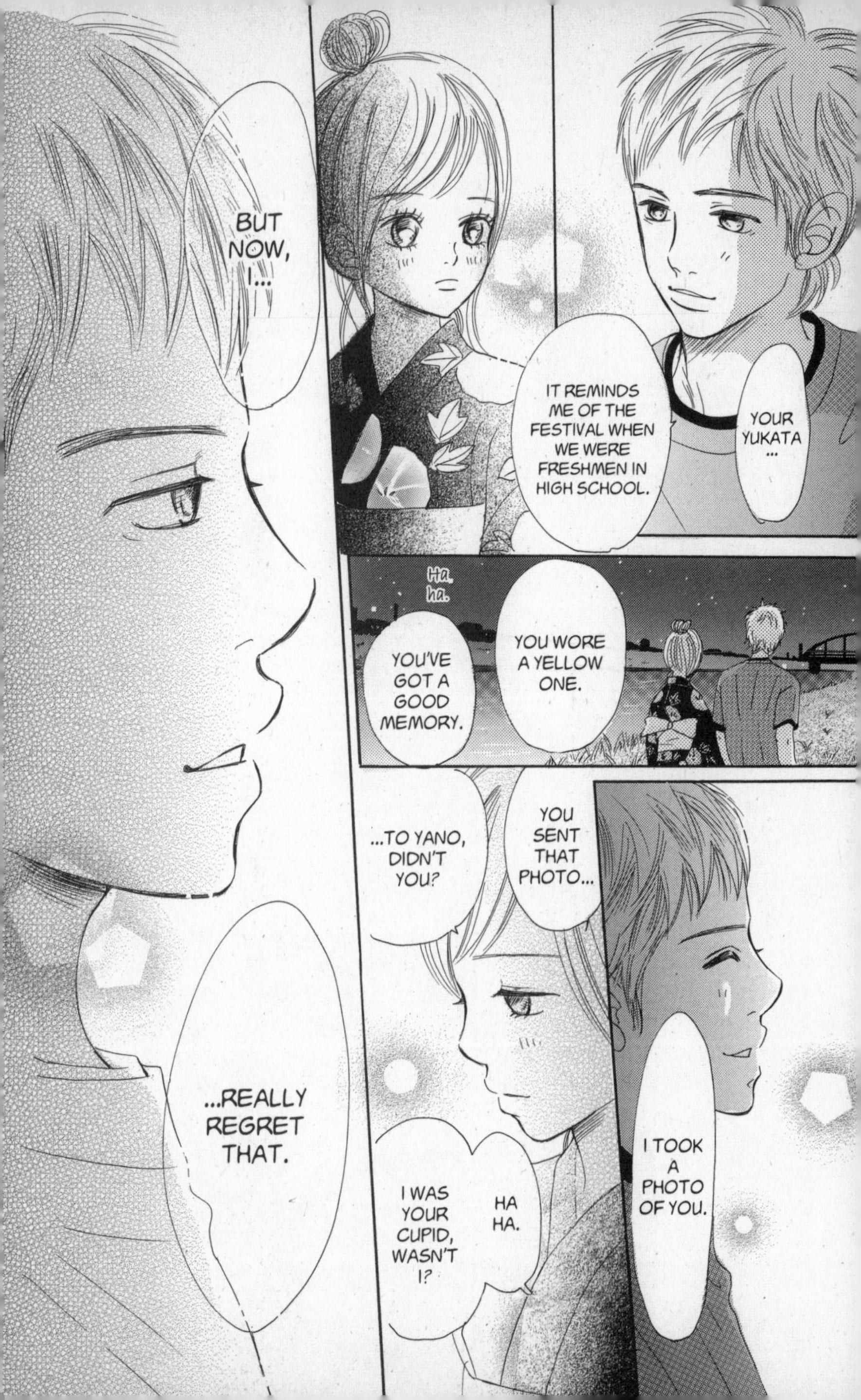
YOUR YUKATA...
IT REMINDS ME OF THE FESTIVAL WHEN WE WERE FRESHMEN IN HIGH SCHOOL.
YOU WORE A YELLOW ONE.
YOU'VE GOT A GOOD MEMORY.
Ha. ha.
I TOOK A PHOTO OF YOU.
YOU SENT THAT PHOTO...
...TO YANO, DIDN'T YOU?
HA HA.
I WAS YOUR CUPID, WASN'T I?
BUT NOW, I...
...REALLY REGRET THAT.

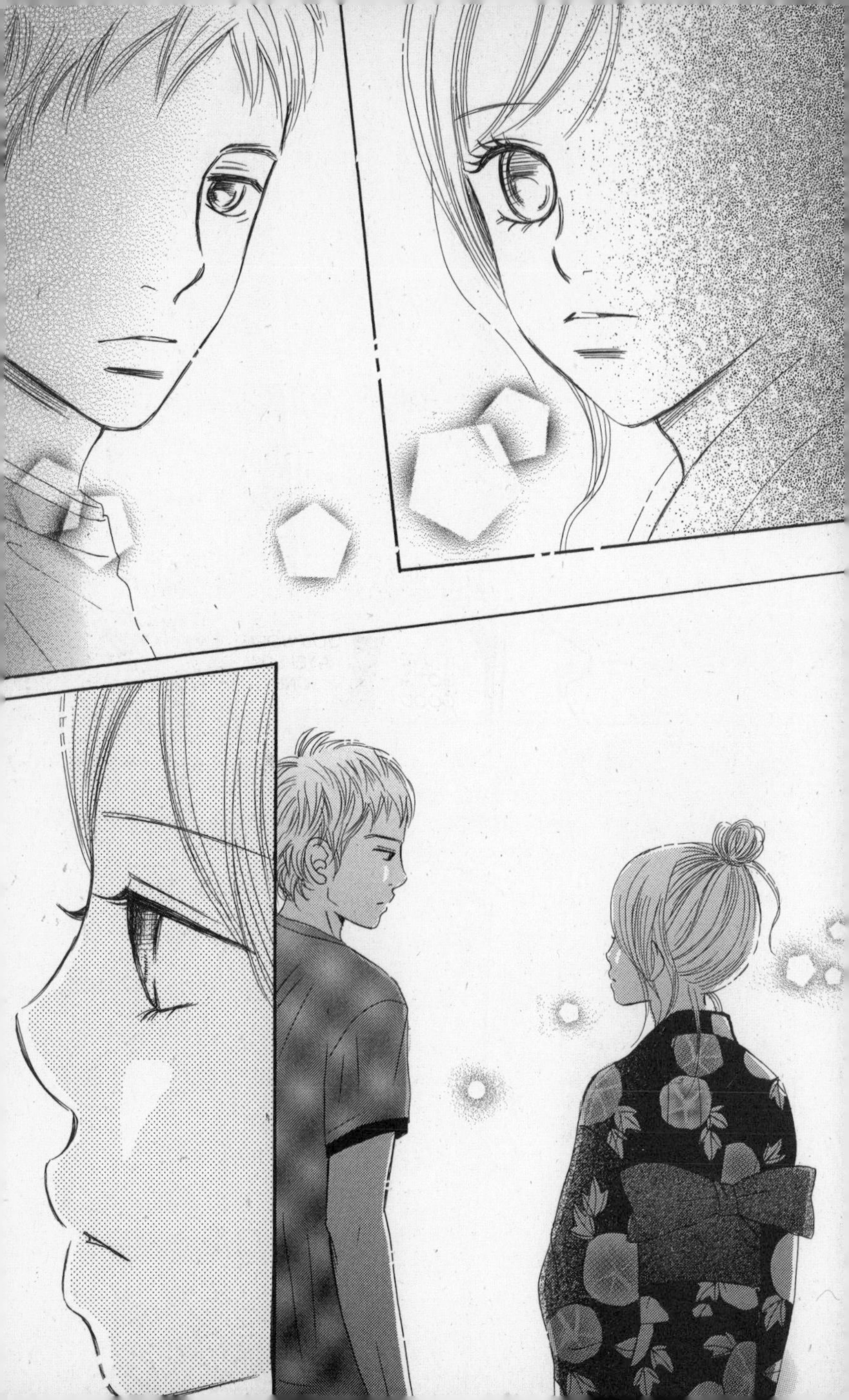

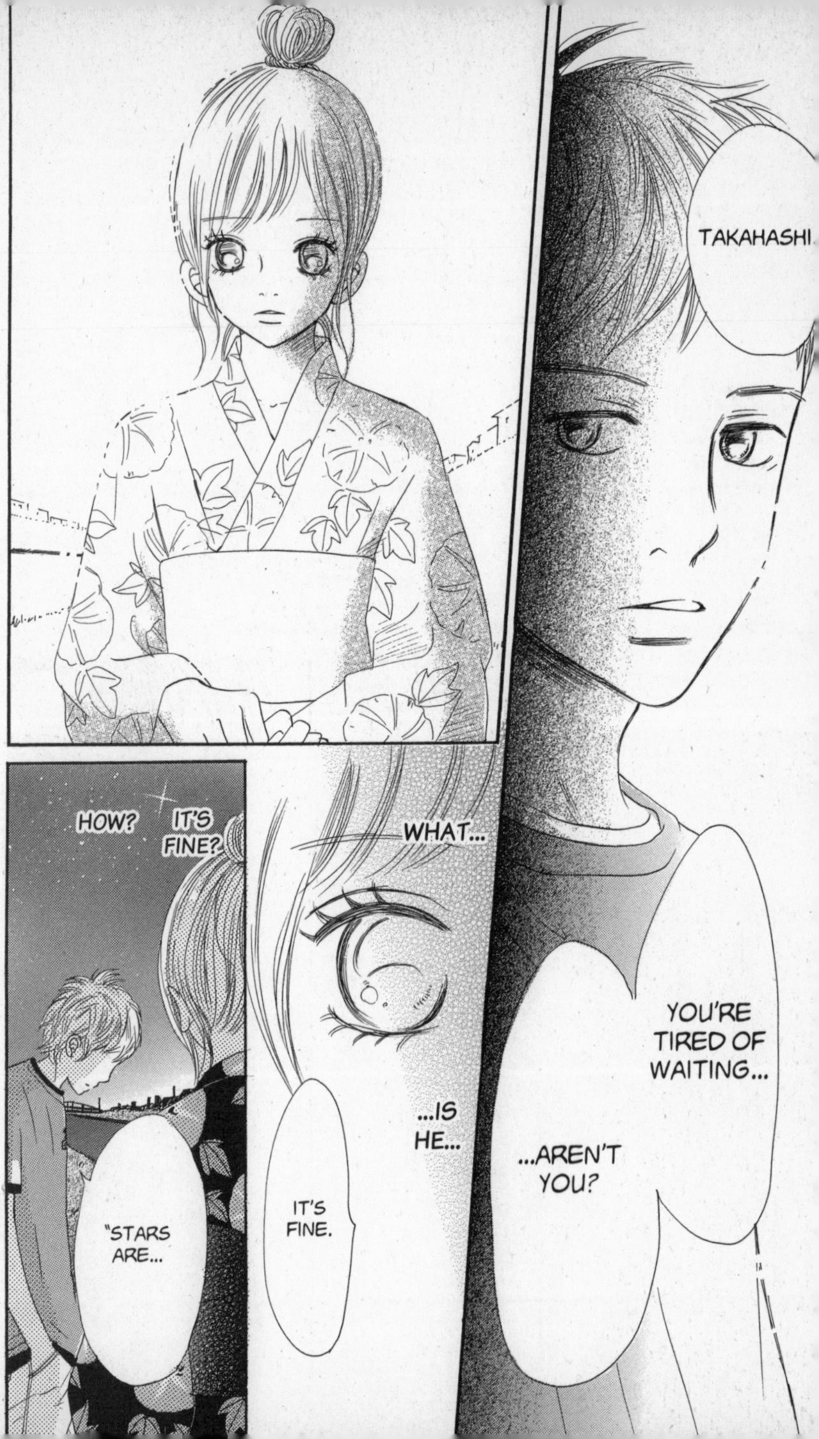
TAKAHASHI
YOU'RE TIRED OF WAITING...
...AREN'T YOU?
WHAT...
...IS HE...
IT'S FINE.
HOW? IT'S FINE?
"STARS ARE...

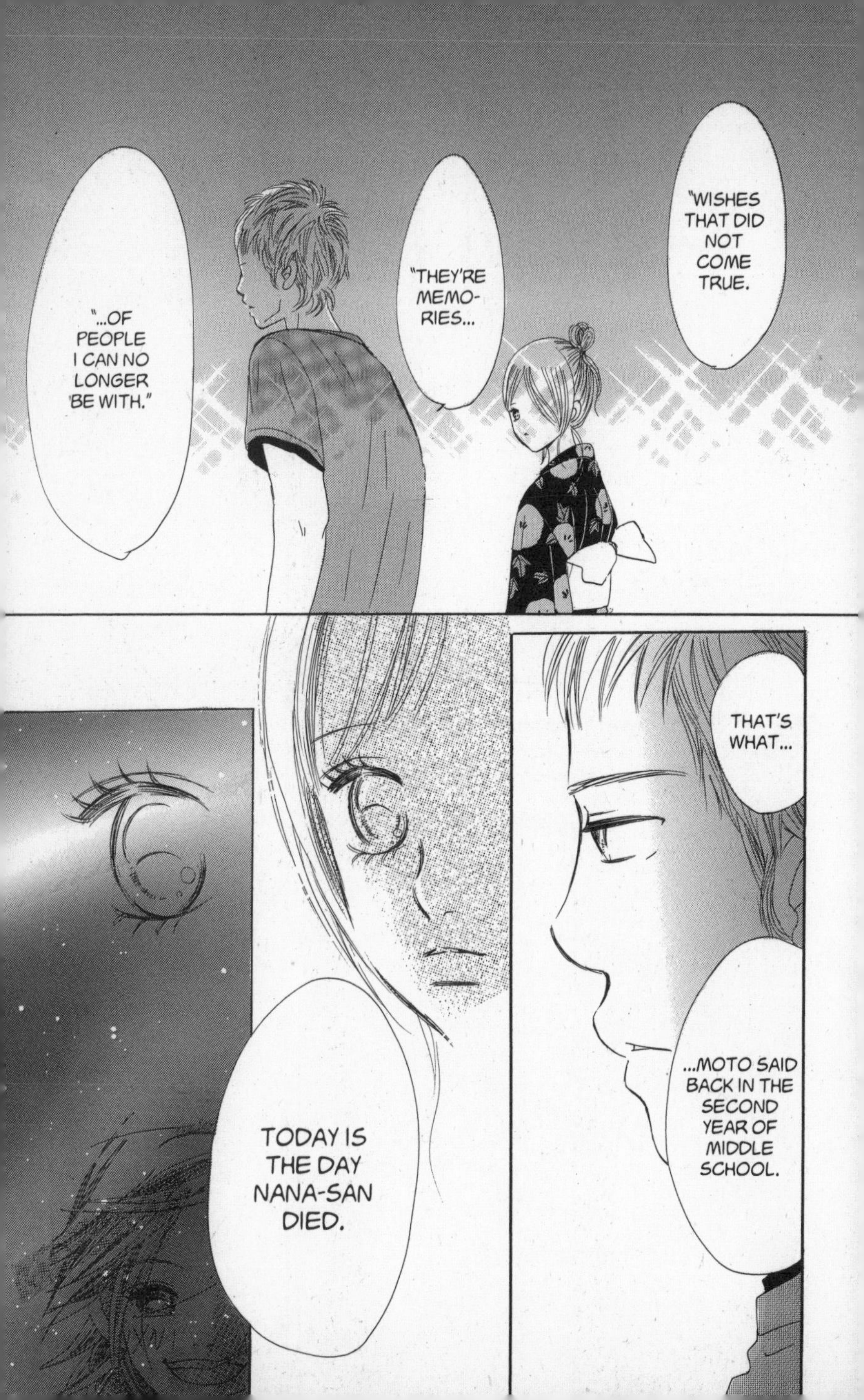
"WISHES THAT DID NOT COME TRUE.
"THEY'RE MEMO-RIES...
"...OF PEOPLE I CAN NO LONGER 'BE WITH."
THAT'S WHAT...
...MOTO SAID BACK IN THE SECOND YEAR OF MIDDLE SCHOOL.
TODAY IS THE DAY NANA-SAN DIED.

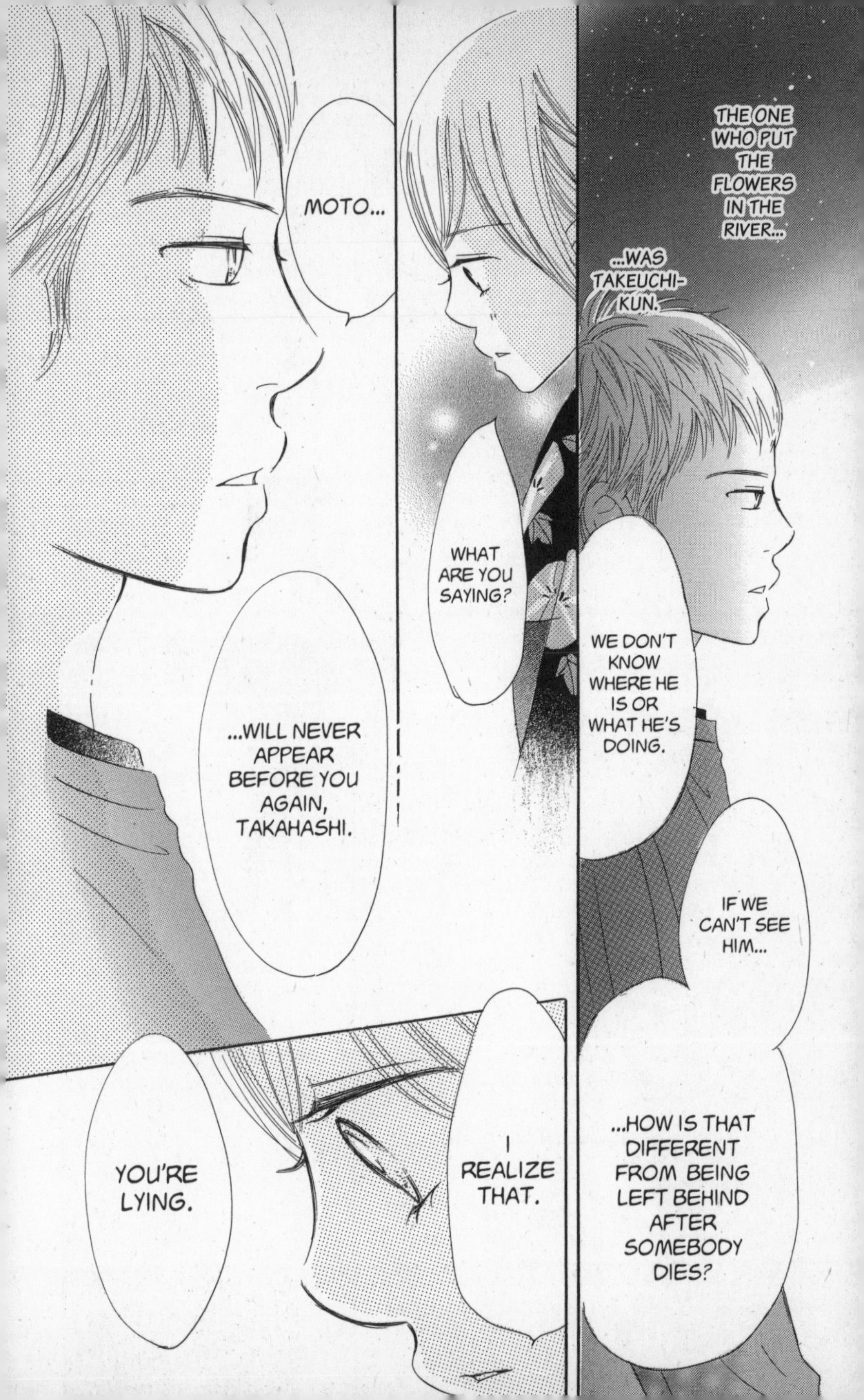
THE ONE WHO PUT THE FLOWERS IN THE RIVER...
...WAS TAKEUCHI-KUN.
WE DON'T KNOW WHERE HE IS OR WHAT HE'S DOING.
IF WE CAN'T SEE HIM...
...HOW IS THAT DIFFERENT FROM BEING LEFT BEHIND AFTER SOMEBODY DIES?
WHAT ARE YOU SAYING?
MOTO...
...WILL NEVER APPEAR BEFORE YOU AGAIN, TAKAHASHI.
I REALIZE THAT.
YOU'RE LYING.

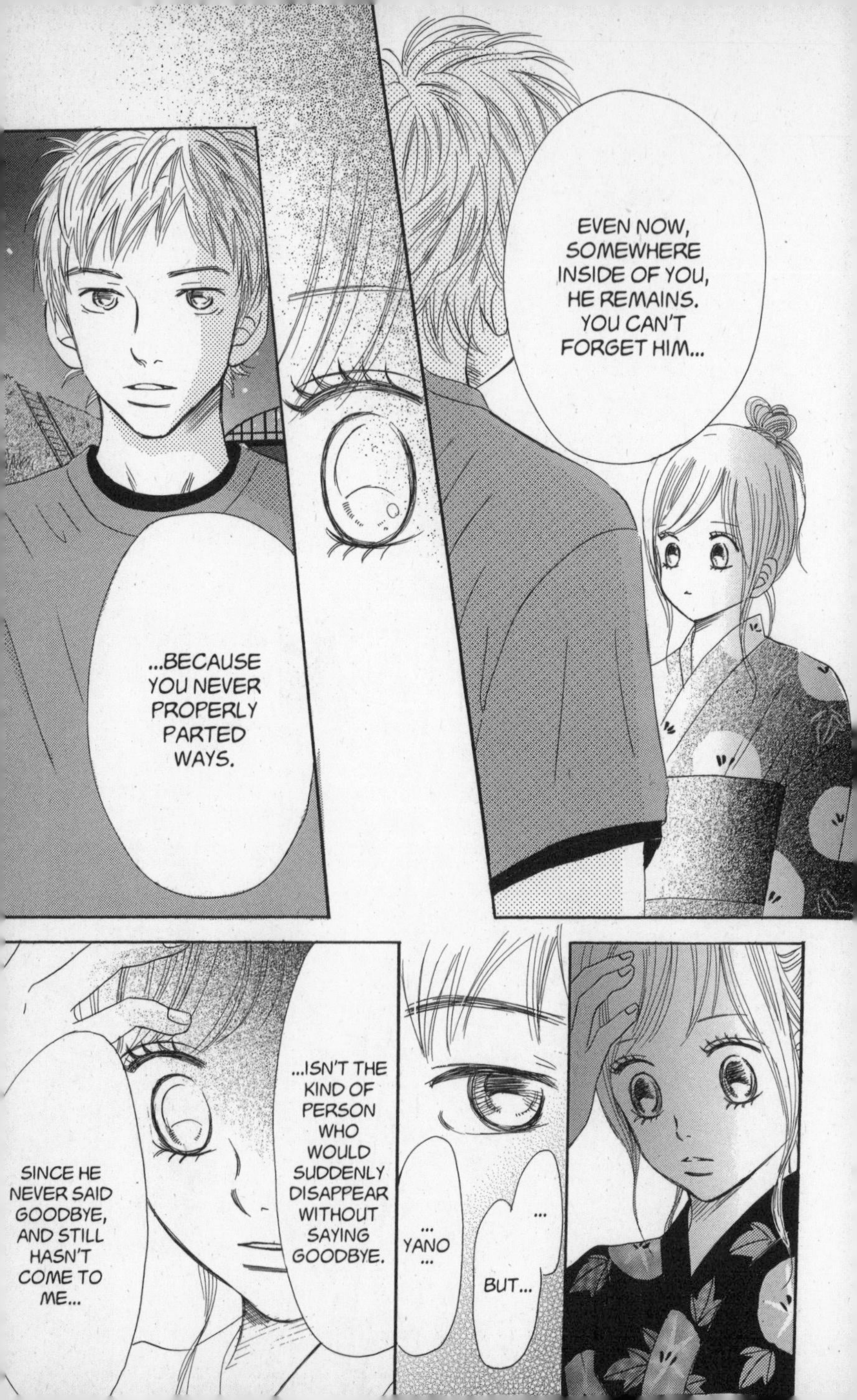
EVEN NOW, SOMEWHERE INSIDE OF YOU, HE REMAINS. YOU CAN'T FORGET HIM...
...BECAUSE YOU NEVER PROPERLY PARTED WAYS.
...
...YANO...
BUT...
...ISN'T THE KIND OF PERSON WHO WOULD SUDDENLY DISAPPEAR WITHOUT SAYING GOODBYE.
SINCE HE NEVER SAID GOODBYE, AND STILL HASN'T COME TO ME...

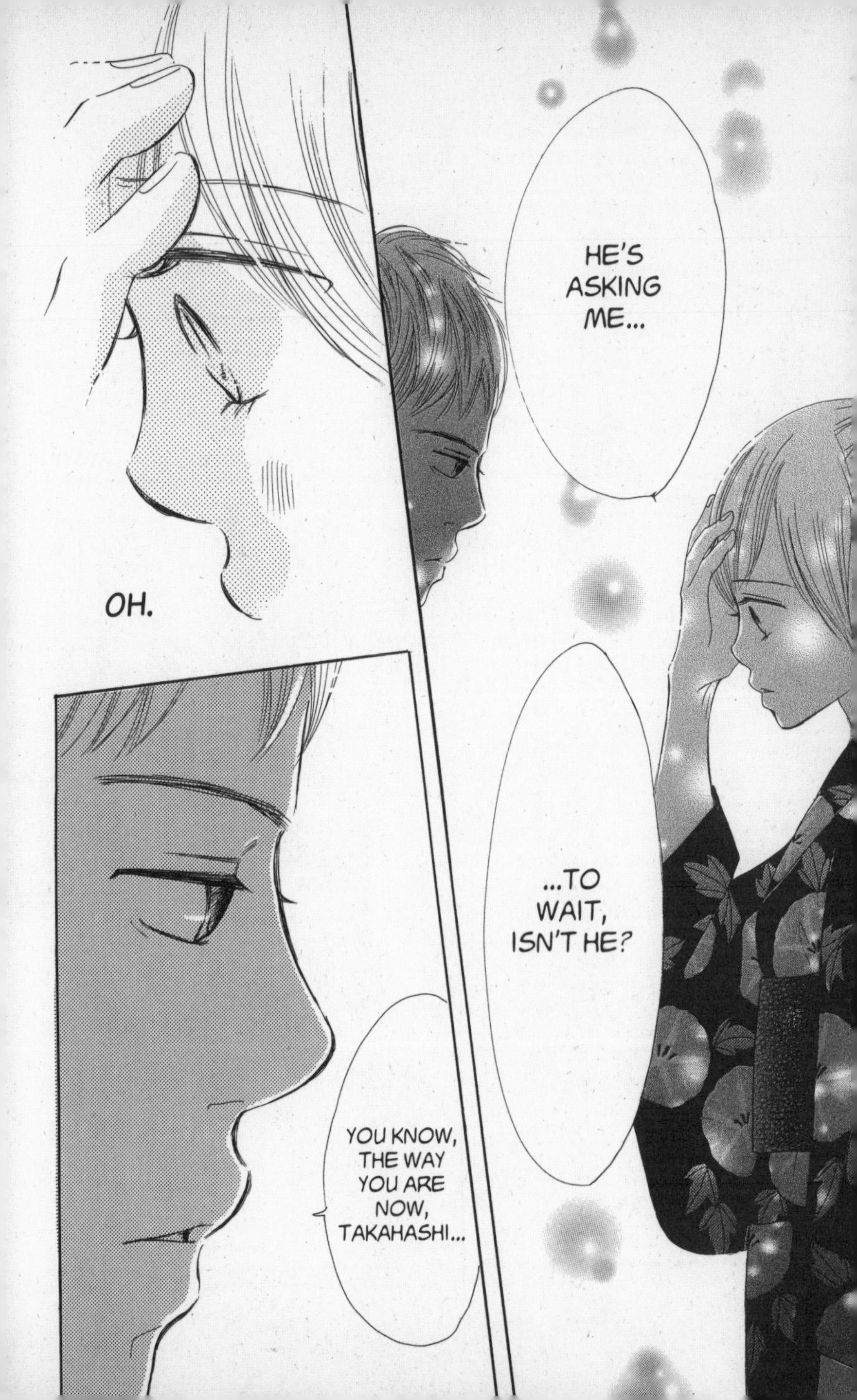
HE'S ASKING ME...
...TO WAIT, ISN'T HE?
OH.
YOU KNOW, THE WAY YOU ARE NOW, TAKAHASHI...

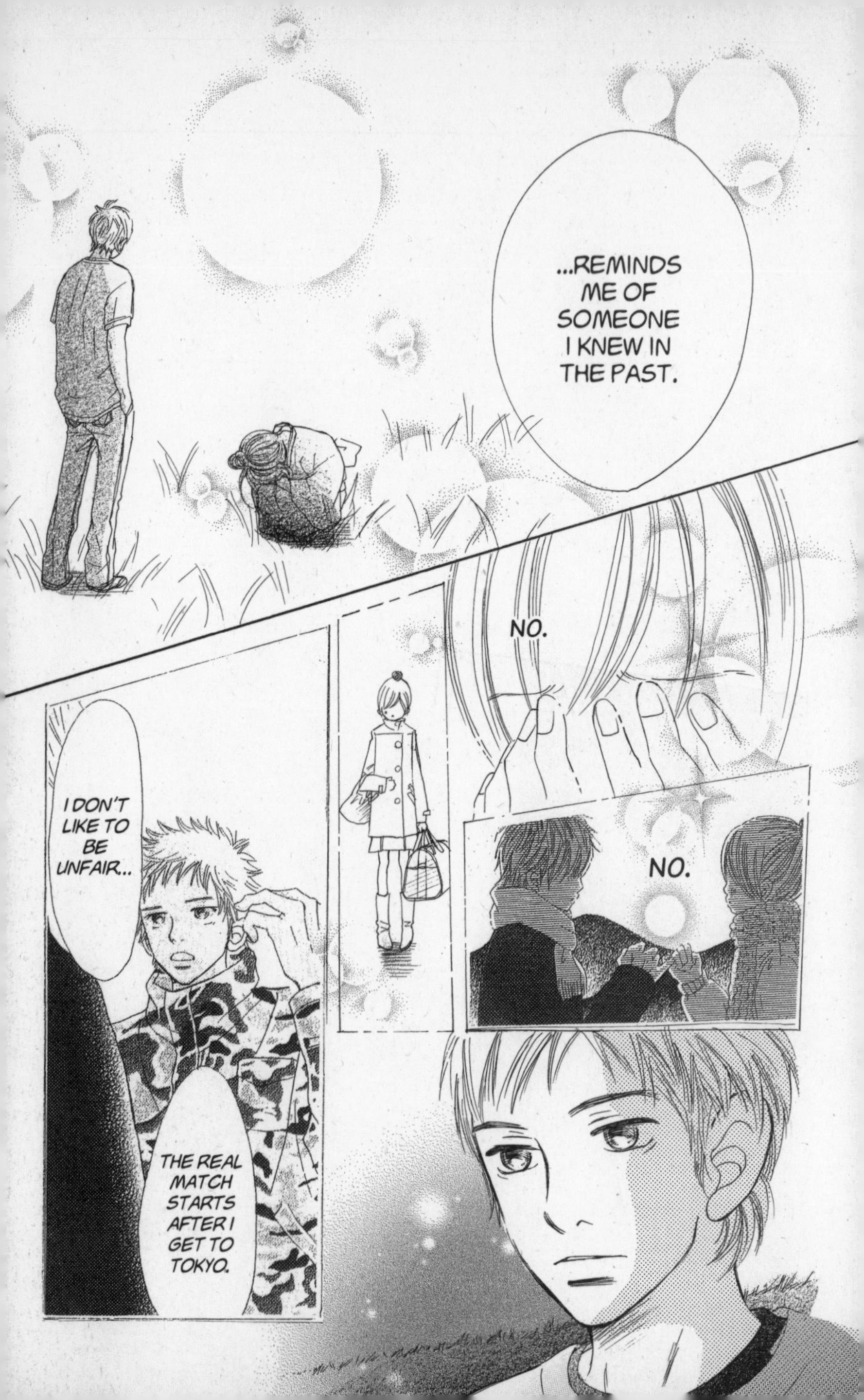
...REMINDS ME OF SOMEONE I KNEW IN THE PAST.
NO.
NO.
I DON'T LIKE TO BE UNFAIR...
THE REAL MATCH STARTS AFTER I GET TO TOKYO.

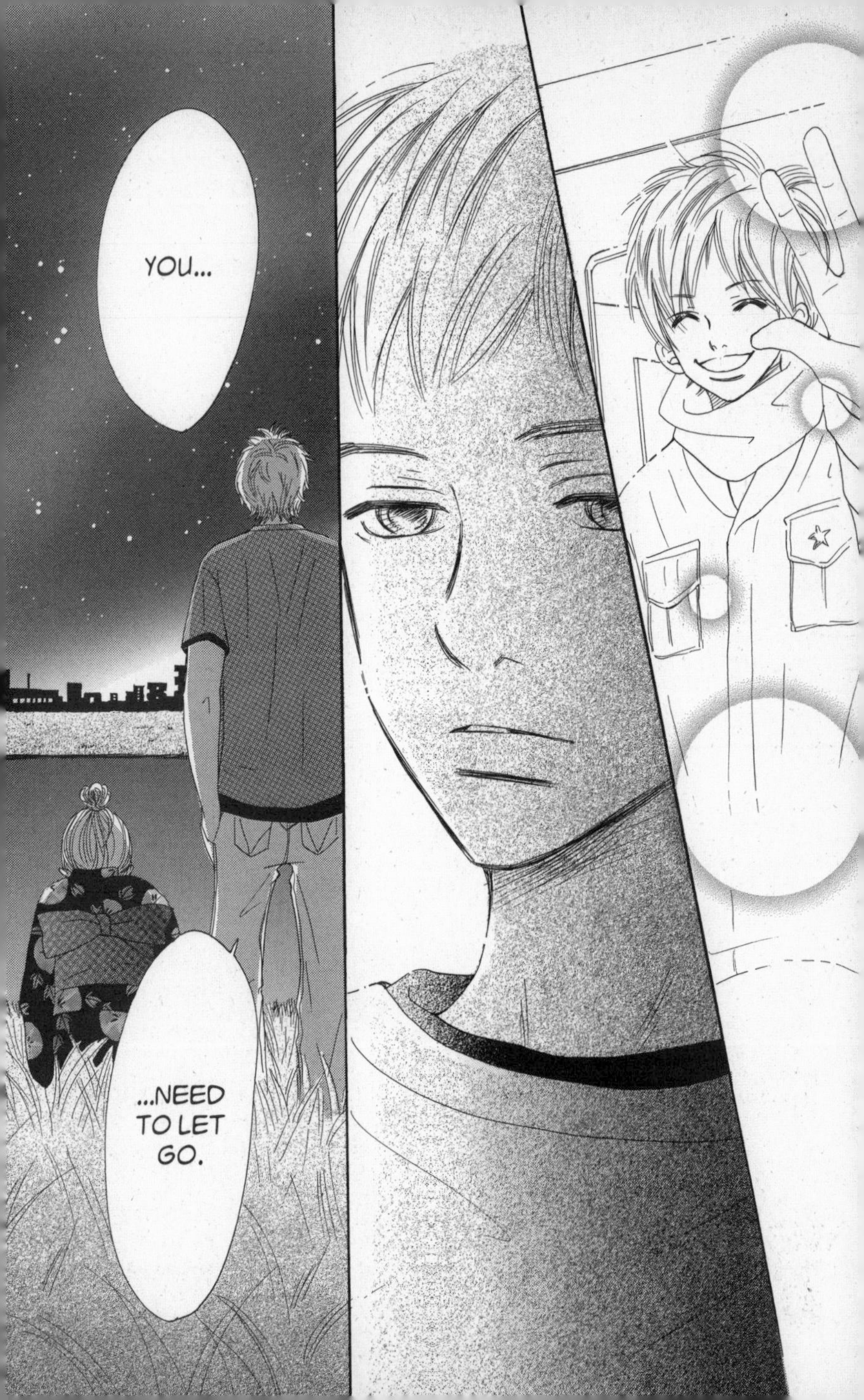
YOU...
...NEED TO LET GO.

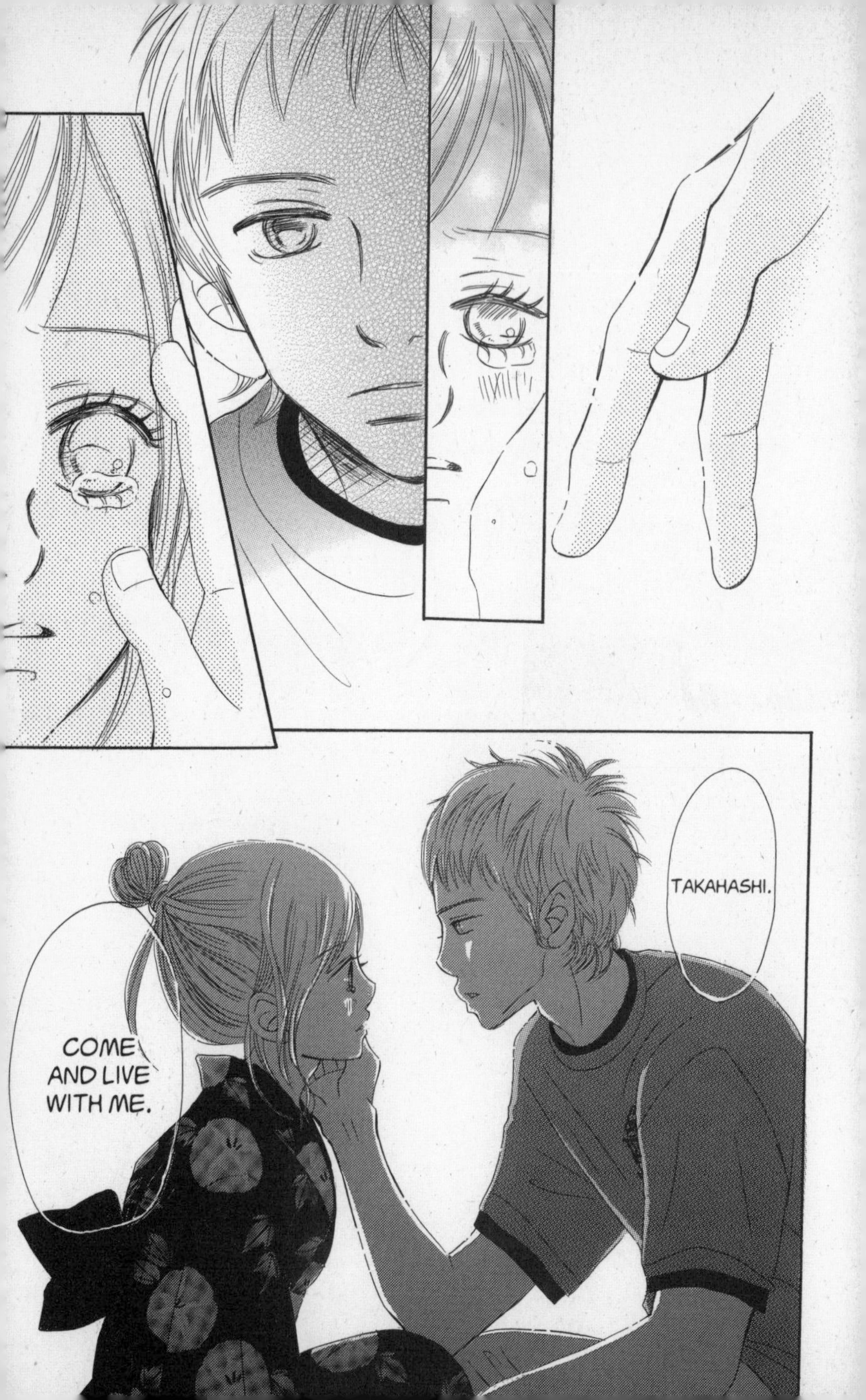
TAKAHASHI.
COME AND LIVE WITH ME.

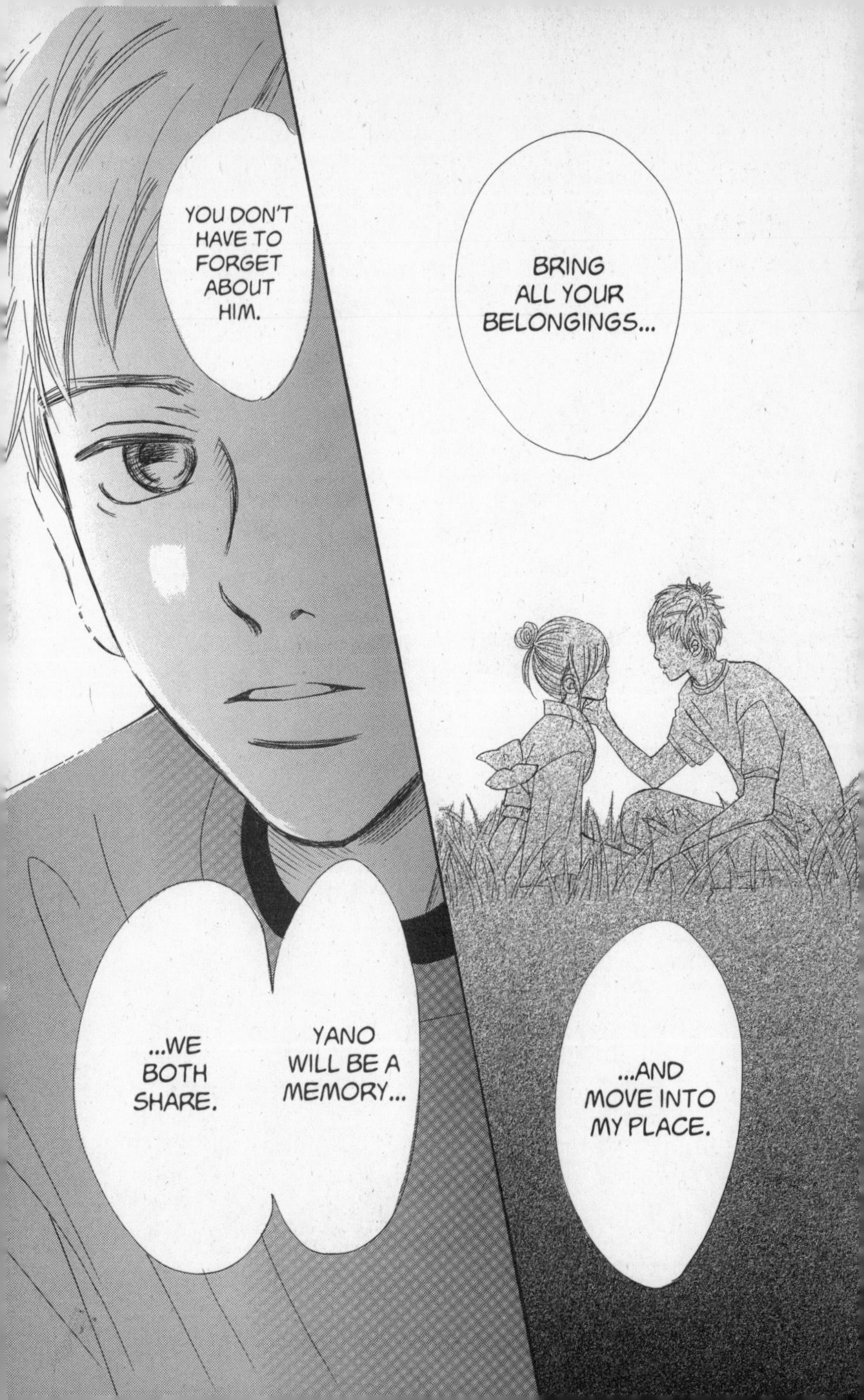
BRING ALL YOUR BELONGINGS...
...AND MOVE INTO MY PLACE.
YOU DON'T HAVE TO FORGET ABOUT HIM.
YANO WILL BE A MEMORY...
...WE BOTH SHARE.

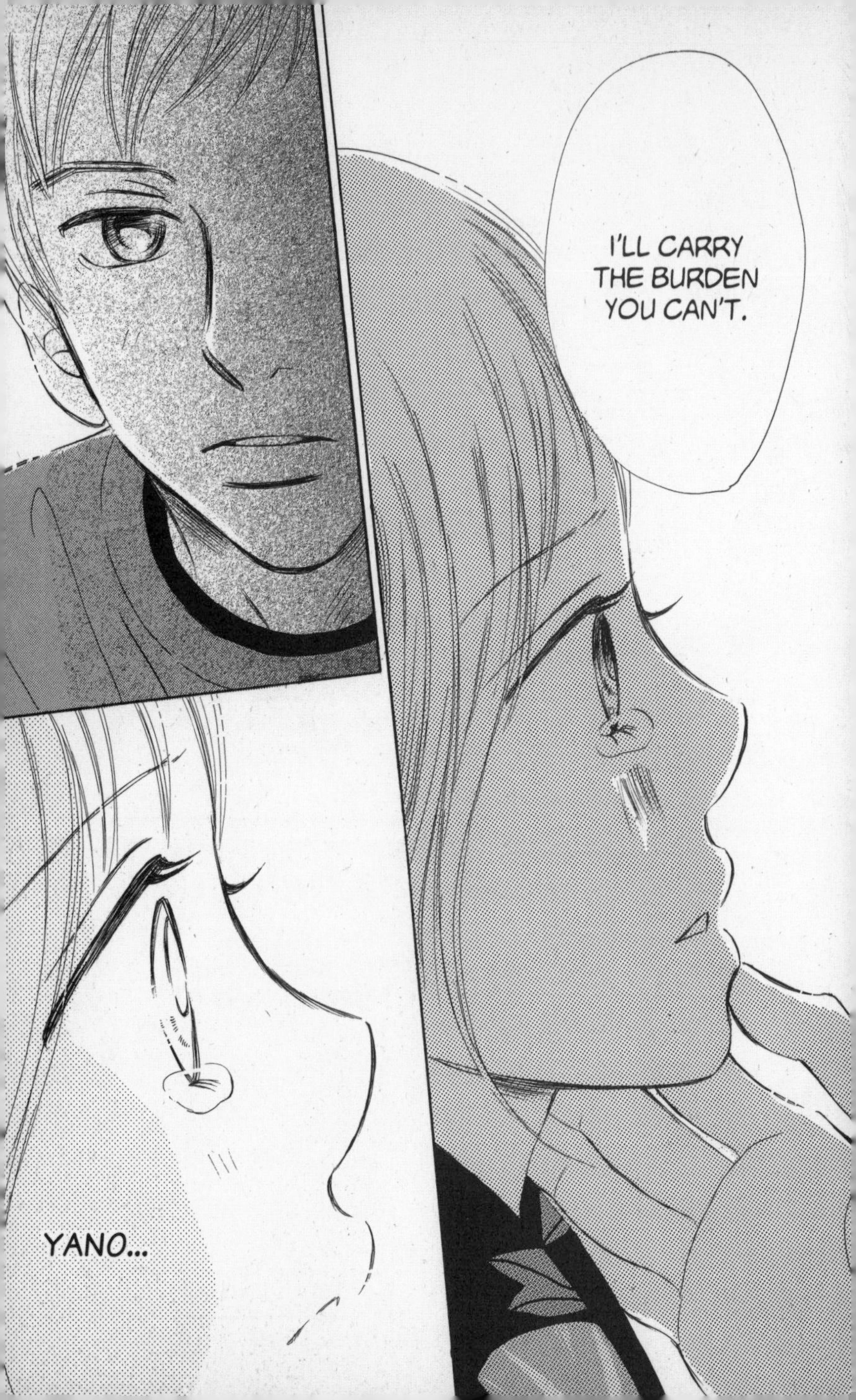
I'LL CARRY THE BURDEN YOU CAN'T.
YANO...

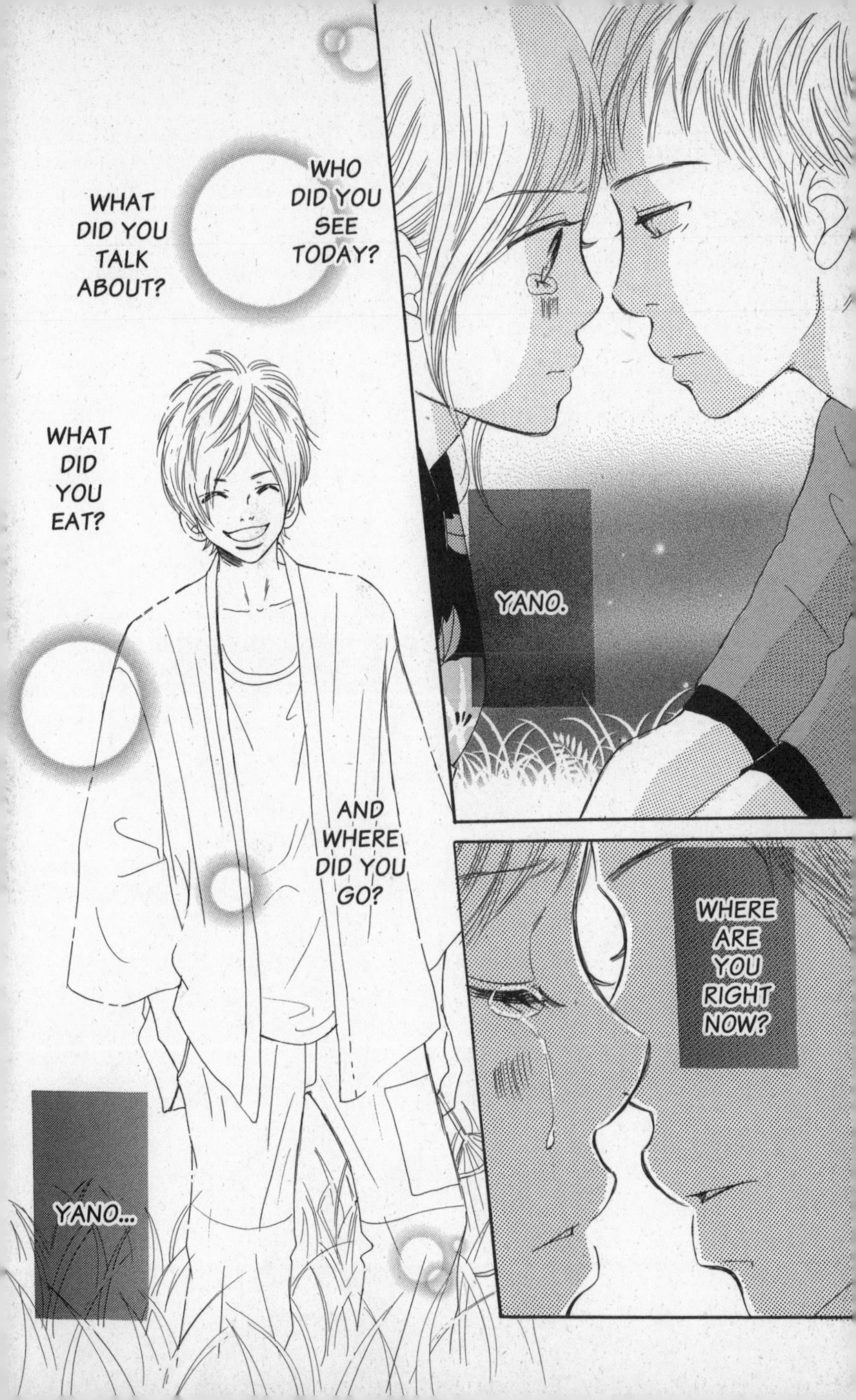
YANO.
WHERE ARE YOU RIGHT NOW?
WHO DID YOU SEE TODAY?
WHAT DID YOU TALK ABOUT?
WHAT DID YOU EAT?
AND WHERE DID YOU GO?
YANO...

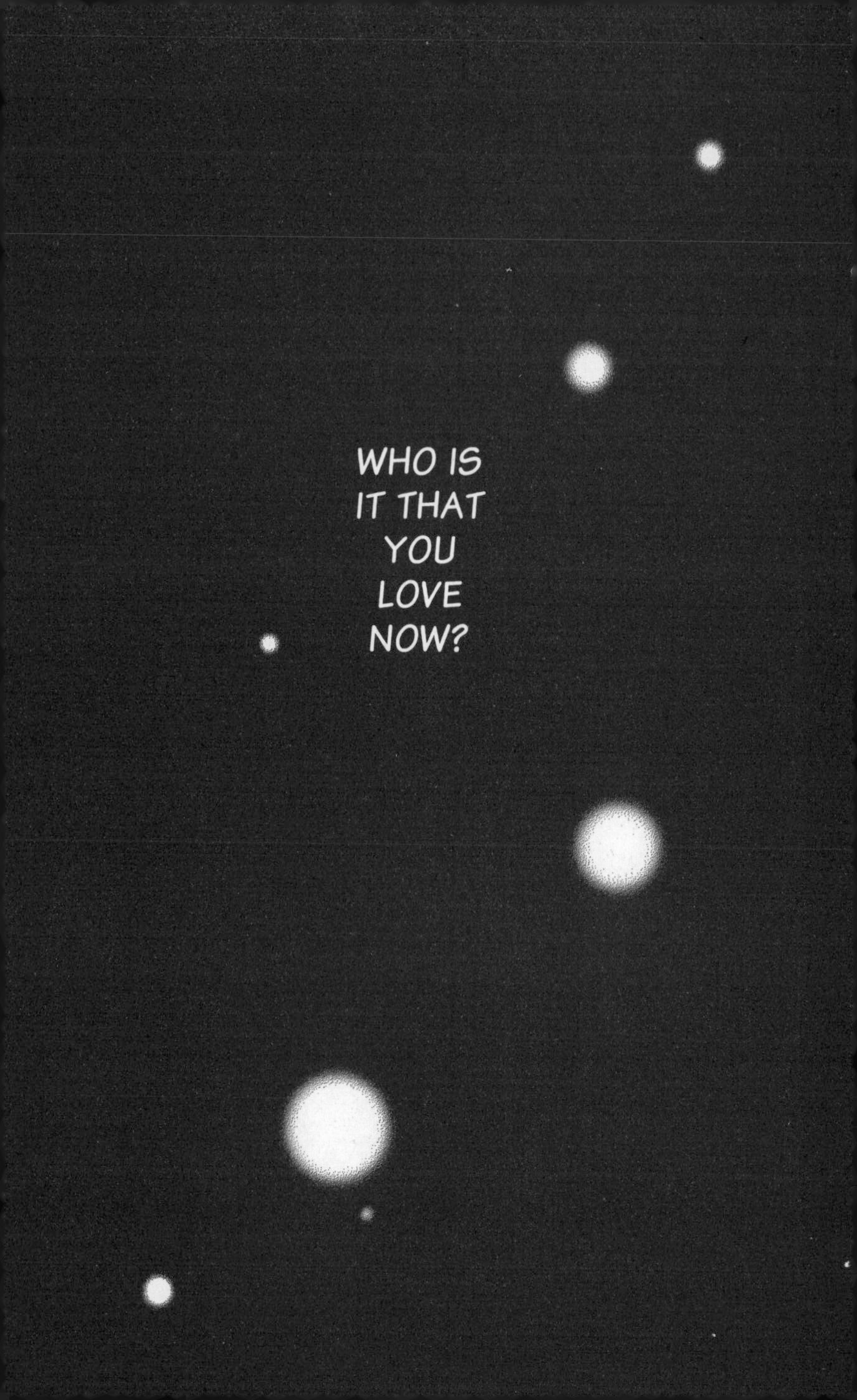
WHO IS IT THAT YOU LOVE NOW?

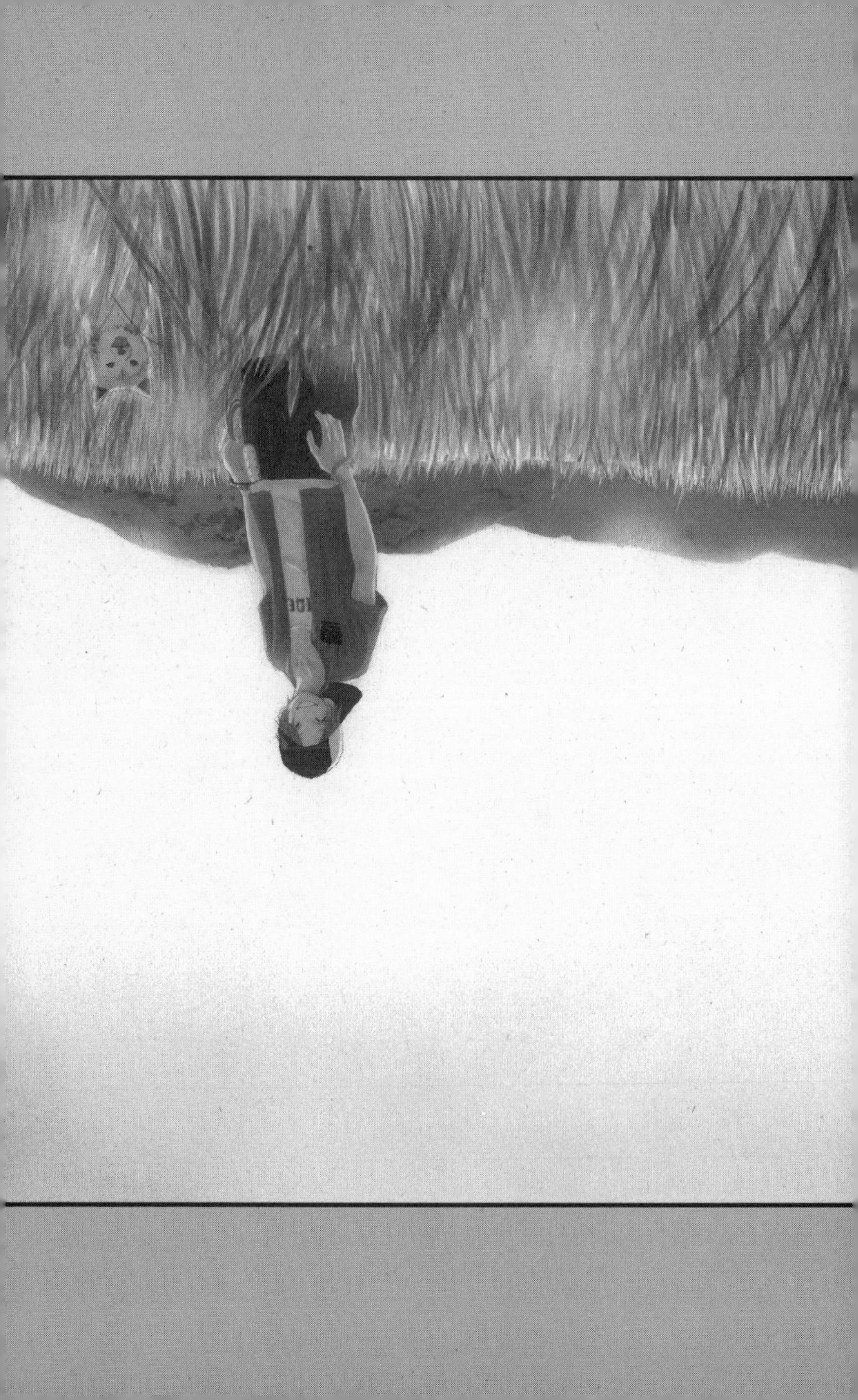

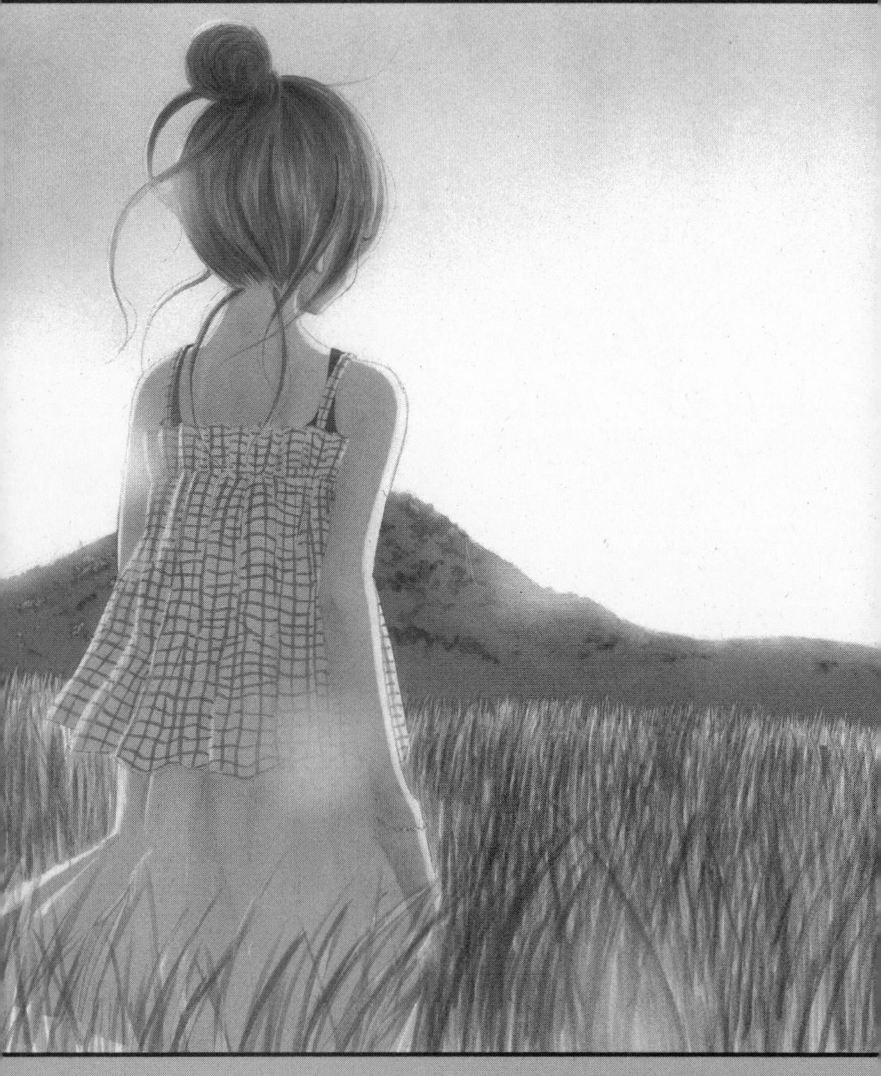

# Chapter 33

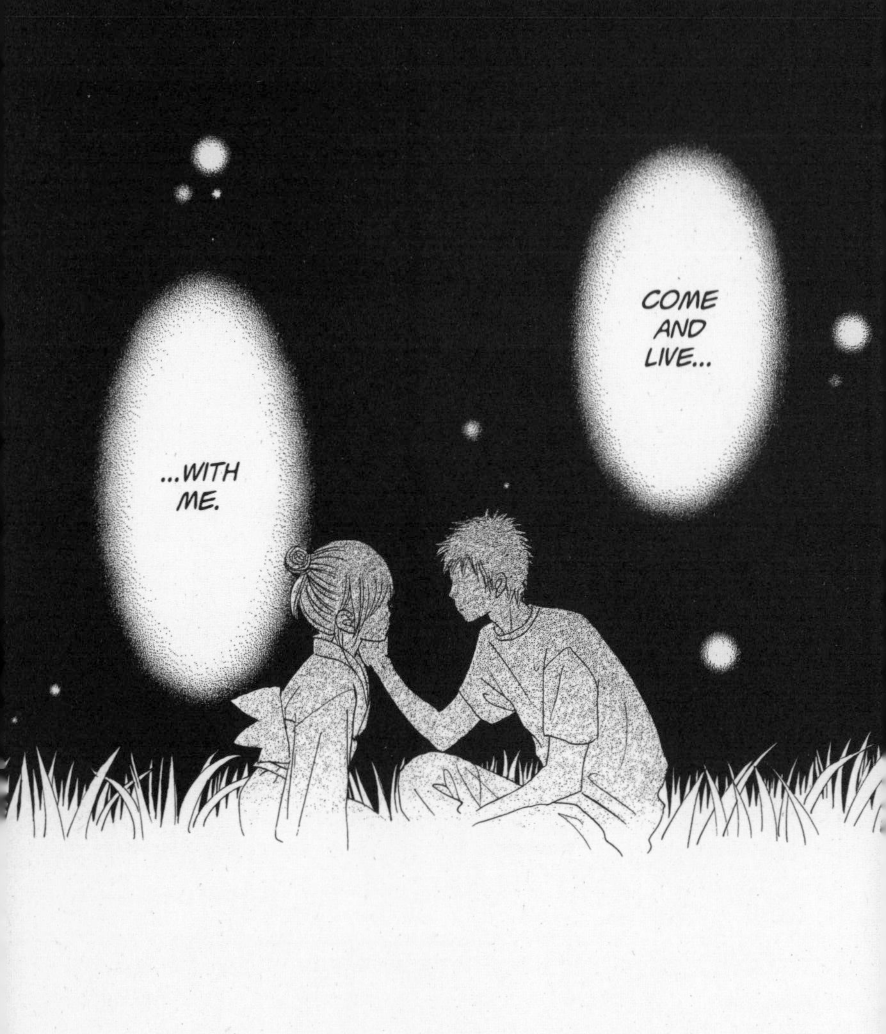
COME AND LIVE...
...WITH ME.

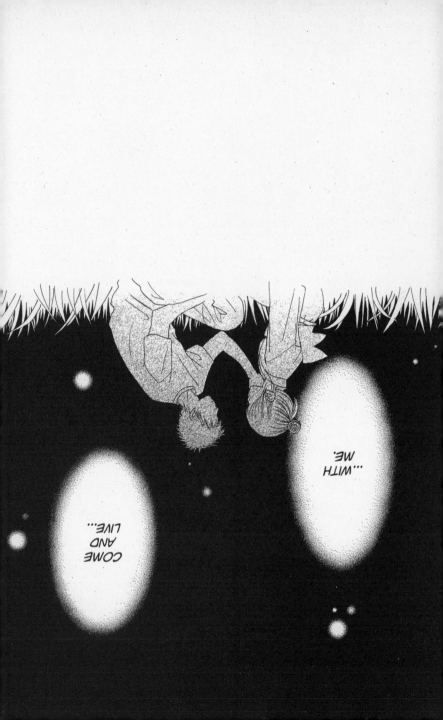

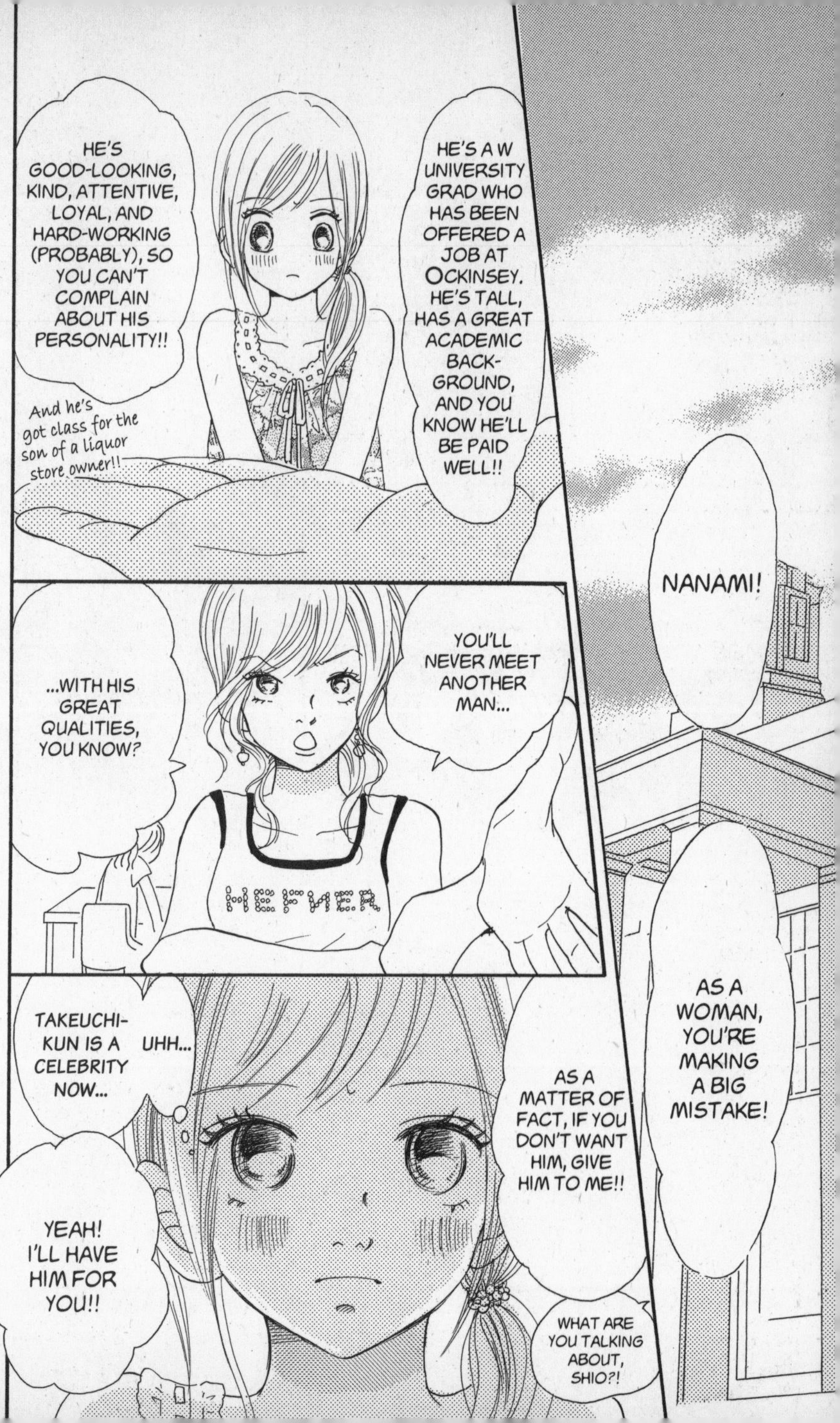
NANAMI!
AS A WOMAN, YOU'RE MAKING A BIG MISTAKE!
HE'S A W UNIVERSITY GRAD WHO HAS BEEN OFFERED A JOB AT OCKINSEY. HE'S TALL, HAS A GREAT ACADEMIC BACK-GROUND, AND YOU KNOW HE'LL BE PAID WELL!!
HE'S GOOD-LOOKING, KIND, ATTENTIVE, LOYAL, AND HARD-WORKING (PROBABLY), SO YOU CAN'T COMPLAIN ABOUT HIS PERSONALITY!!
And he's got class for the son of a liquor store owner!!
YOU'LL NEVER MEET ANOTHER MAN...
...WITH HIS GREAT QUALITIES, YOU KNOW?
TAKEUCHI-KUN IS A CELEBRITY NOW...
UHH...
AS A MATTER OF FACT, IF YOU DON'T WANT HIM, GIVE HIM TO ME!!
YEAH! I'LL HAVE HIM FOR YOU!!
WHAT ARE YOU TALKING ABOUT, SHIO?!

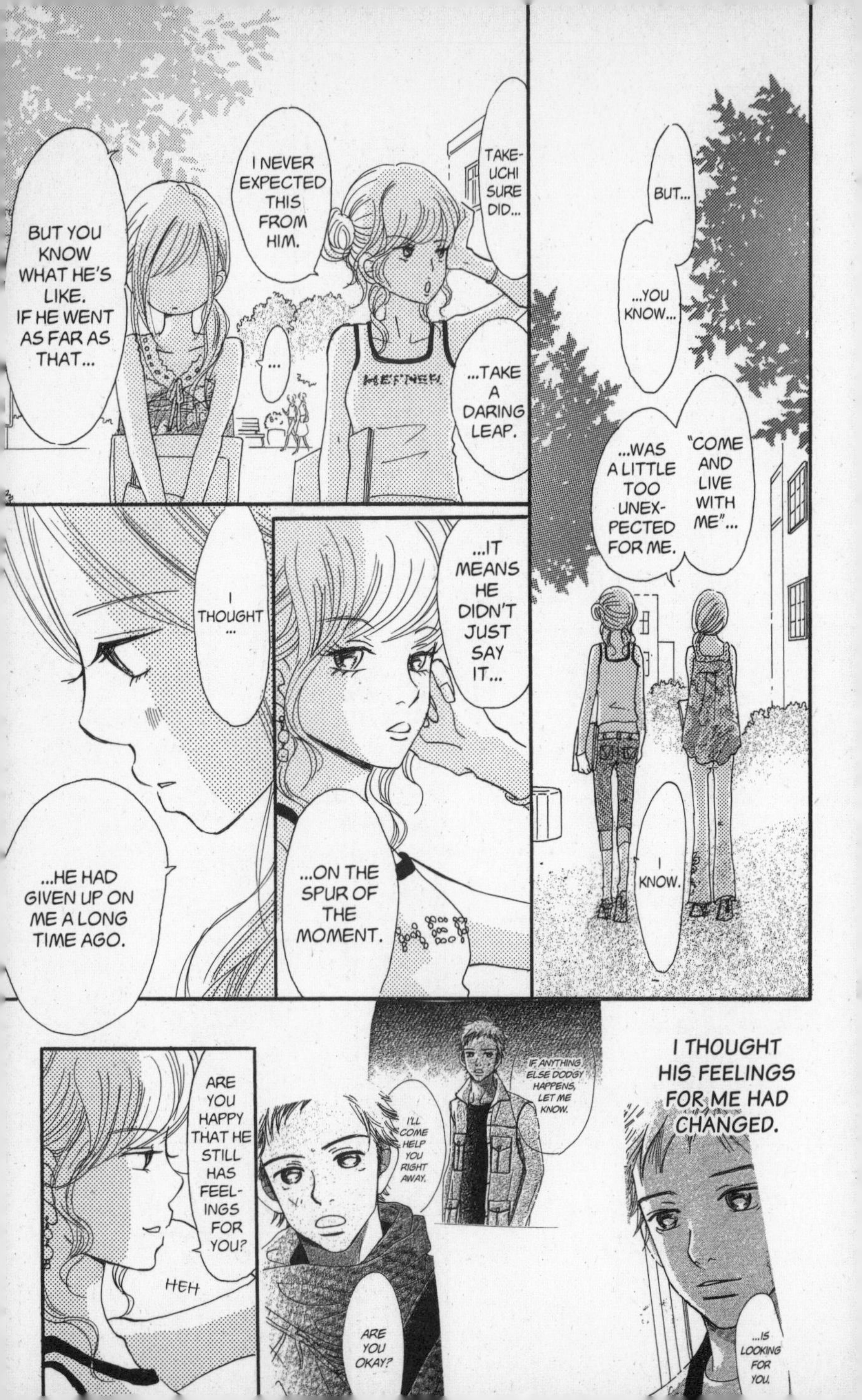
BUT...
...YOU KNOW...
"COME AND LIVE WITH ME"...
...WAS A LITTLE TOO UNEXPECTED FOR ME.
I KNOW.
TAKE-UCHI SURE DID...
I NEVER EXPECTED THIS FROM HIM.
...TAKE A DARING LEAP.
...
BUT YOU KNOW WHAT HE'S LIKE. IF HE WENT AS FAR AS THAT...
...IT MEANS HE DIDN'T JUST SAY IT...
...ON THE SPUR OF THE MOMENT.
I THOUGHT...
...HE HAD GIVEN UP ON ME A LONG TIME AGO.
I THOUGHT HIS FEELINGS FOR ME HAD CHANGED.
...IS LOOKING FOR YOU.
IF ANYTHING ELSE DODGY HAPPENS, LET ME KNOW.
I'LL COME HELP YOU RIGHT AWAY.
ARE YOU OKAY?
ARE YOU HAPPY THAT HE STILL HAS FEEL-INGS FOR YOU?
HEH

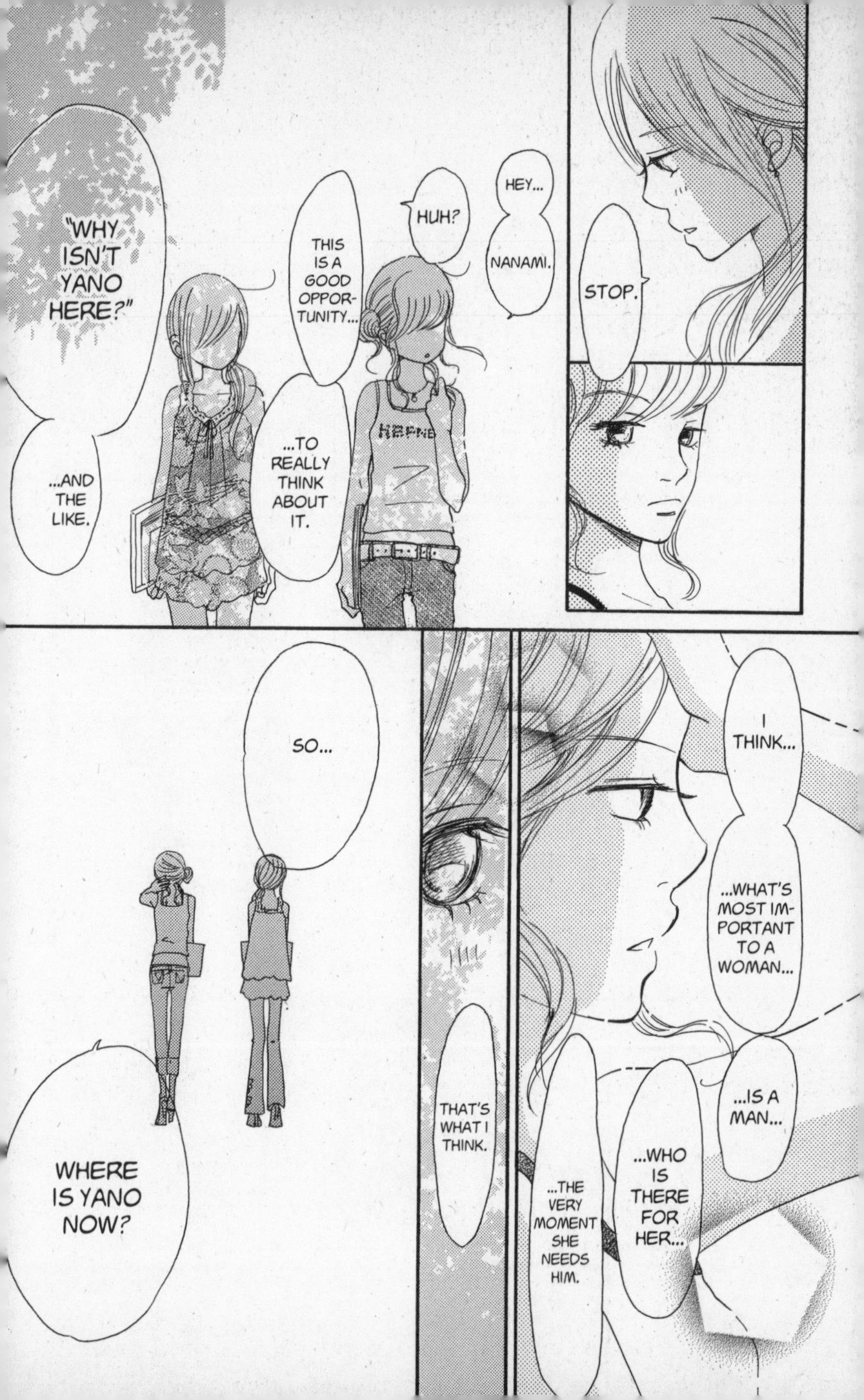
STOP.
HEY... NANAMI.
HUH?
THIS IS A GOOD OPPOR-TUNITY...
...TO REALLY THINK ABOUT IT.
"WHY ISN'T YANO HERE?"
...AND THE LIKE.
I THINK...
...WHAT'S MOST IM-PORTANT TO A WOMAN...
...IS A MAN...
...WHO IS THERE FOR HER...
...THE VERY MOMENT SHE NEEDS HIM.
THAT'S WHAT I THINK.
SO...
WHERE IS YANO NOW?

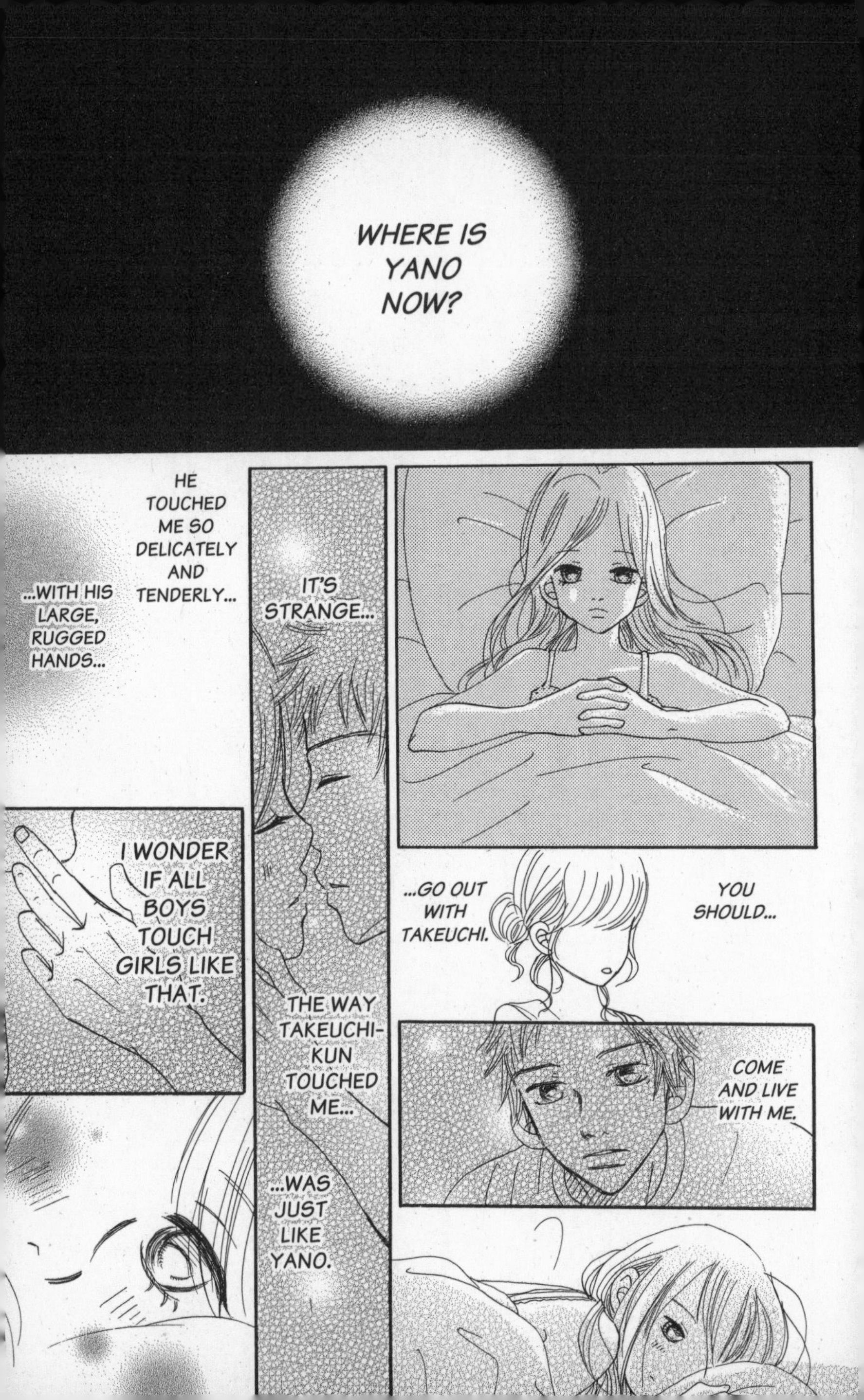
WHERE IS YANO NOW?
YOU SHOULD...
...GO OUT WITH TAKEUCHI.
COME AND LIVE WITH ME.
IT'S STRANGE...
THE WAY TAKEUCHI-KUN TOUCHED ME...
...WAS JUST LIKE YANO.
HE TOUCHED ME SO DELICATELY AND TENDERLY...
...WITH HIS LARGE, RUGGED HANDS...
I WONDER IF ALL BOYS TOUCH GIRLS LIKE THAT.

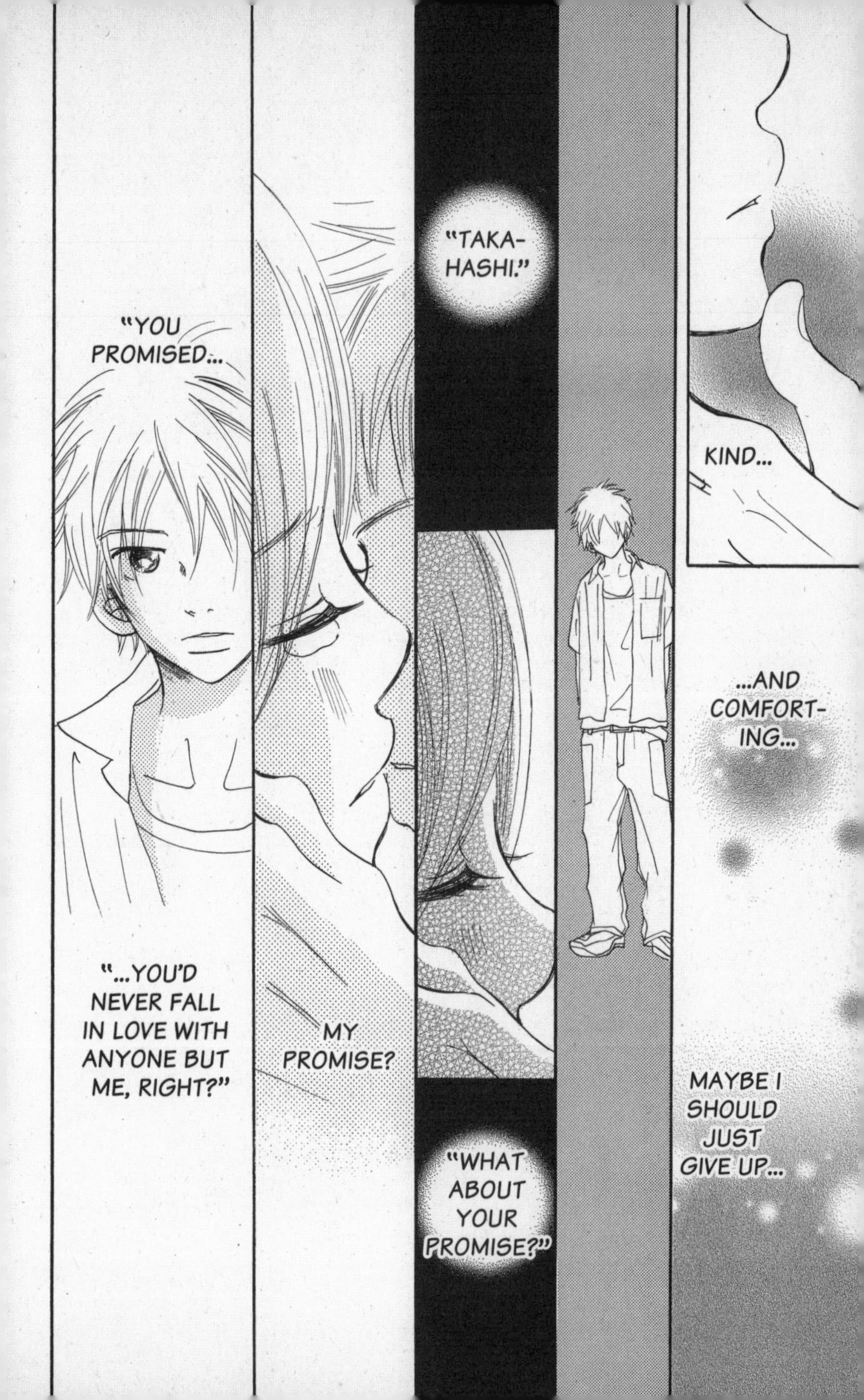
KIND...
...AND COMFORT-ING...
MAYBE I SHOULD JUST GIVE UP...
"TAKA-HASHI."
"WHAT ABOUT YOUR PROMISE?"
MY PROMISE?
"YOU PROMISED...
"...YOU'D NEVER FALL IN LOVE WITH ANYONE BUT ME, RIGHT?"

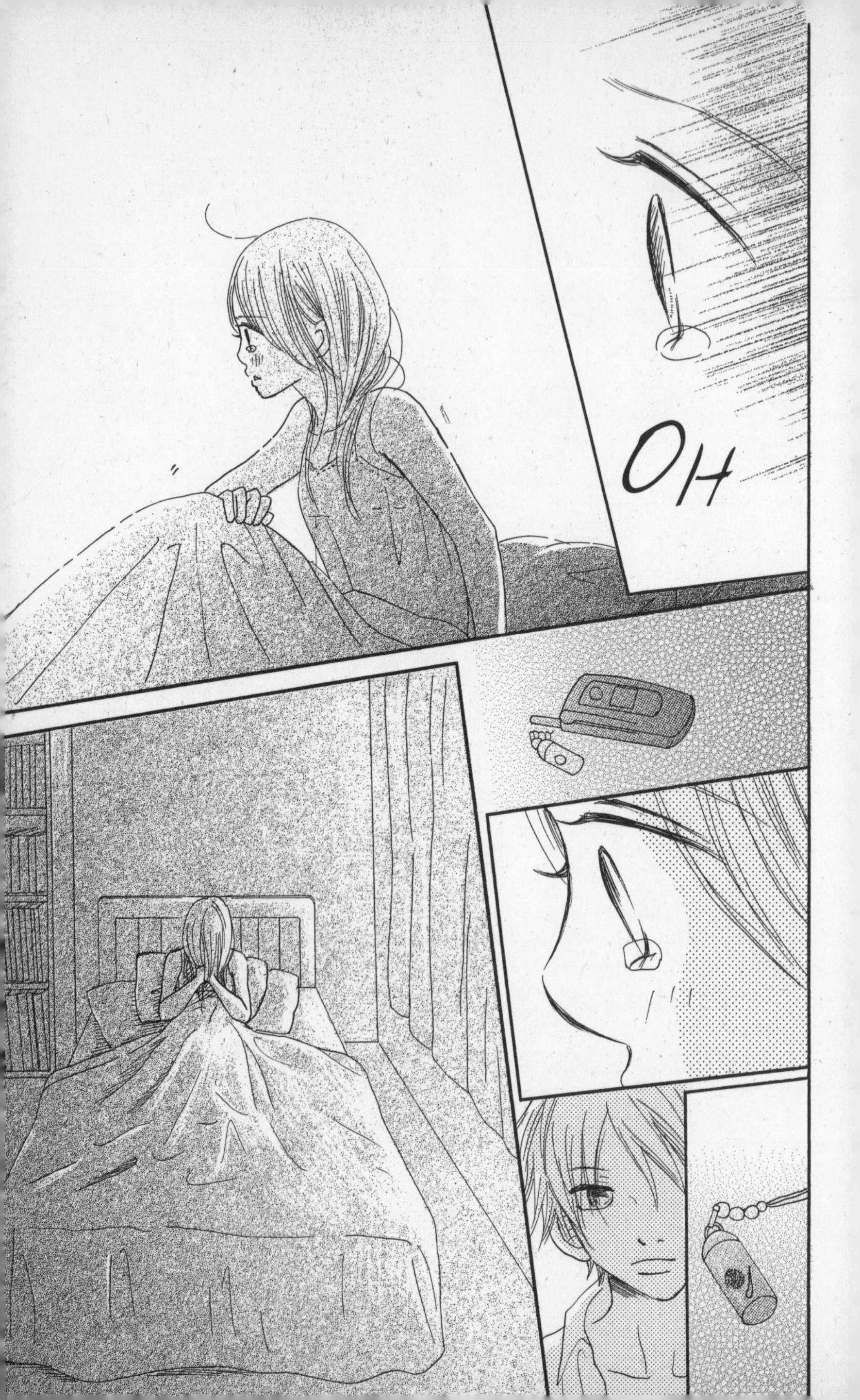
OH

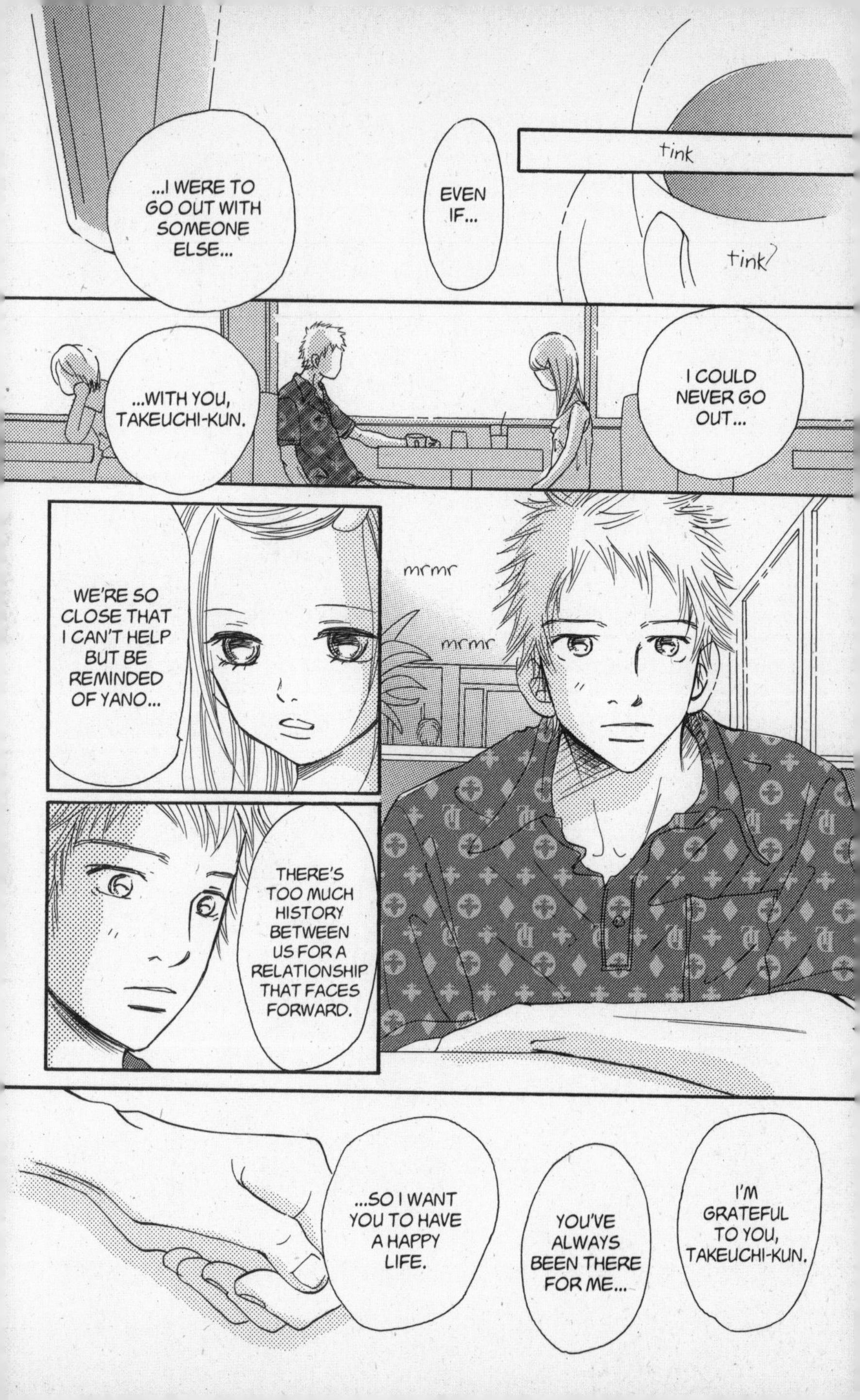
tink
tink
EVEN IF...
...I WERE TO GO OUT WITH SOMEONE ELSE...
I COULD NEVER GO OUT...
...WITH YOU, TAKEUCHI-KUN.
mrmr
mrmr
WE'RE SO CLOSE THAT I CAN'T HELP BUT BE REMINDED OF YANO...
THERE'S TOO MUCH HISTORY BETWEEN US FOR A RELATIONSHIP THAT FACES FORWARD.
I'M GRATEFUL TO YOU, TAKEUCHI-KUN.
YOU'VE ALWAYS BEEN THERE FOR ME...
...SO I WANT YOU TO HAVE A HAPPY LIFE.

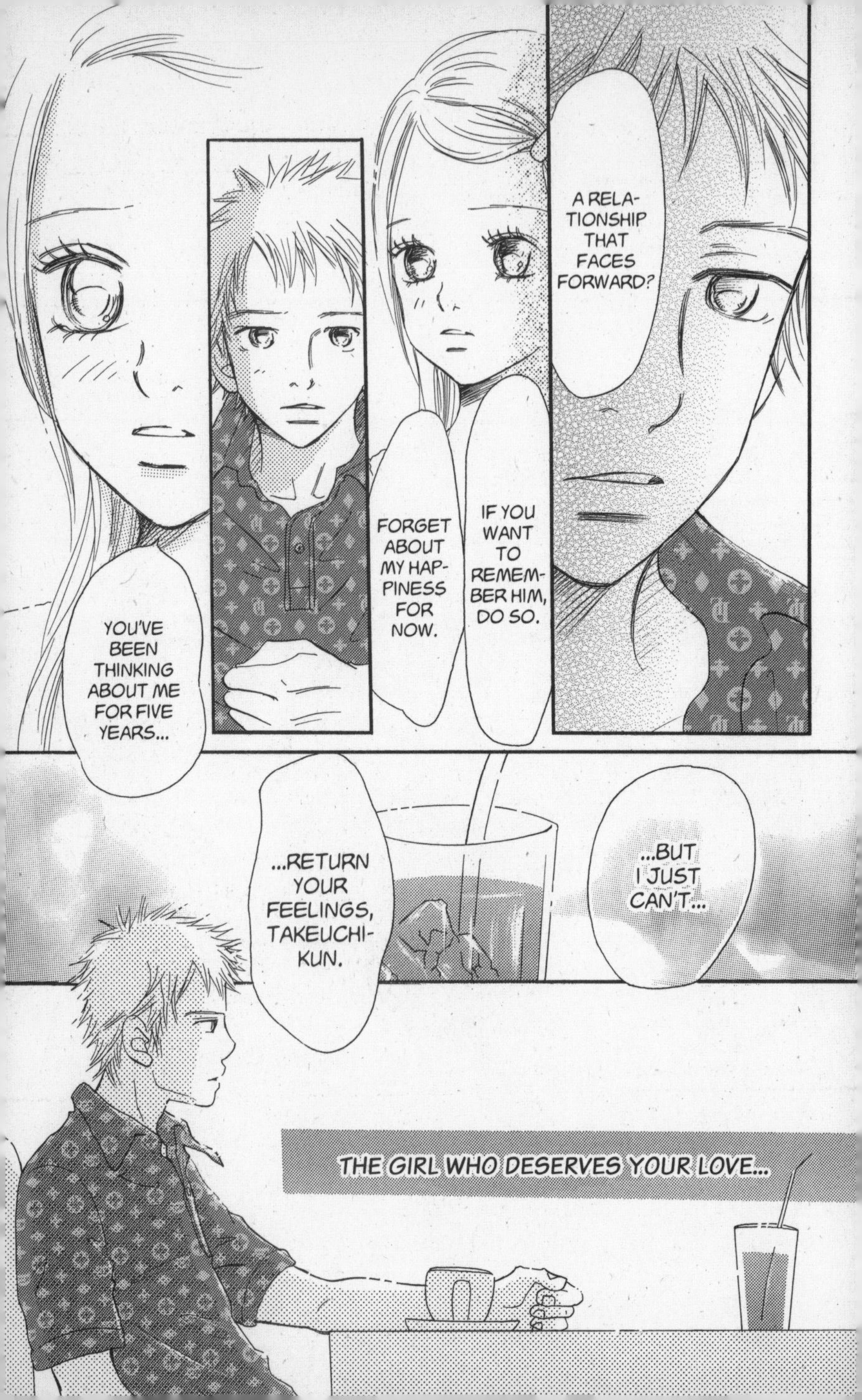
A RELA-
TIONSHIP
THAT
FACES
FORWARD?
IF YOU
WANT
TO
REMEM-
BER HIM,
DO SO.
FORGET
ABOUT
MY HAP-
PINESS
FOR
NOW.
YOU'VE
BEEN
THINKING
ABOUT ME
FOR FIVE
YEARS...
...BUT
I JUST
CAN'T...
...RETURN
YOUR
FEELINGS,
TAKEUCHI-
KUN.
THE GIRL WHO DESERVES YOUR LOVE...

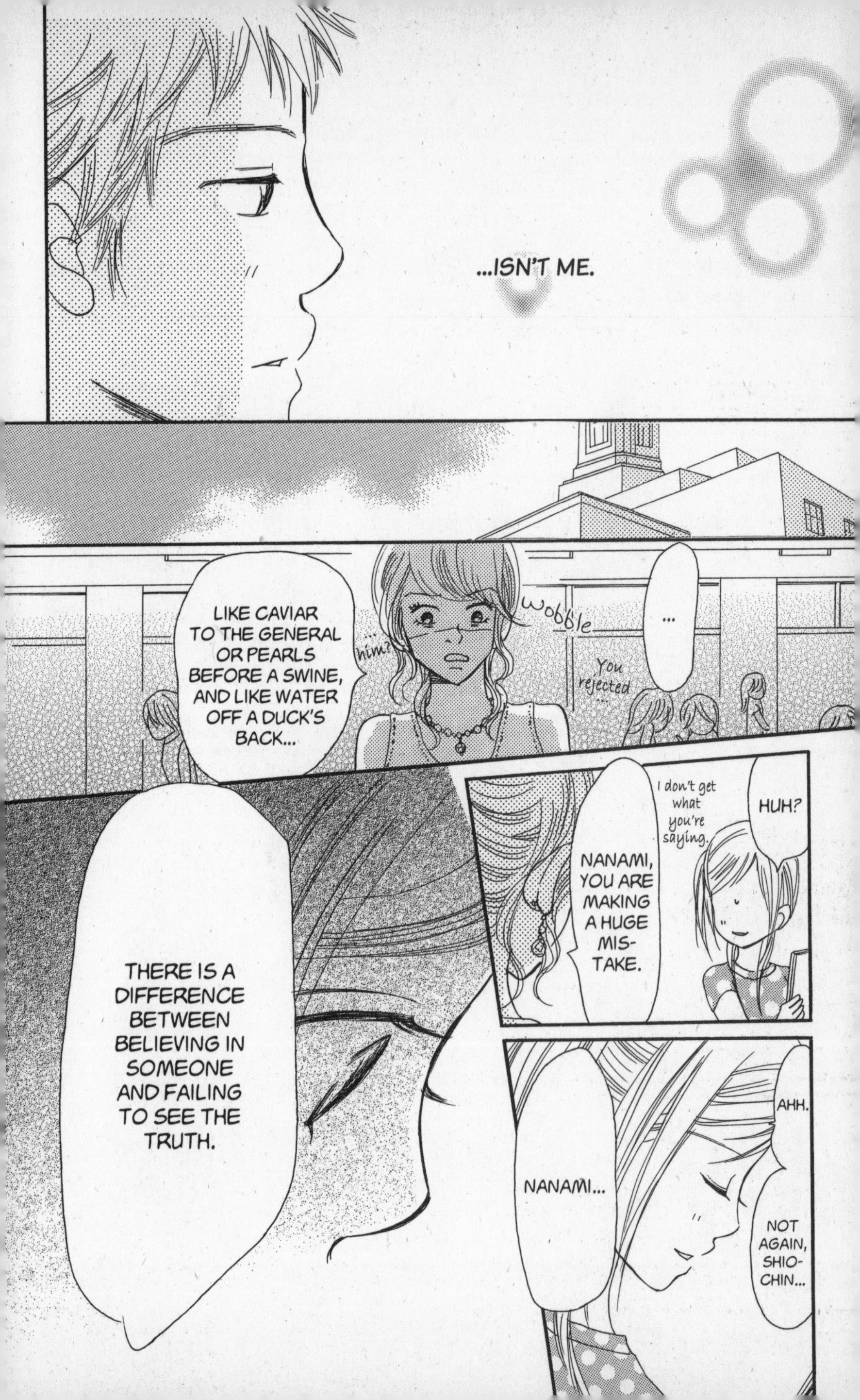
...ISN'T ME.
...
You rejected...
wobble
...him?
LIKE CAVIAR TO THE GENERAL OR PEARLS BEFORE A SWINE, AND LIKE WATER OFF A DUCK'S BACK...
HUH?
I don't get what you're saying.
NANAMI, YOU ARE MAKING A HUGE MIS-TAKE.
AHH.
NOT AGAIN, SHIO-CHIN...
NANAMI...
THERE IS A DIFFERENCE BETWEEN BELIEVING IN SOMEONE AND FAILING TO SEE THE TRUTH.

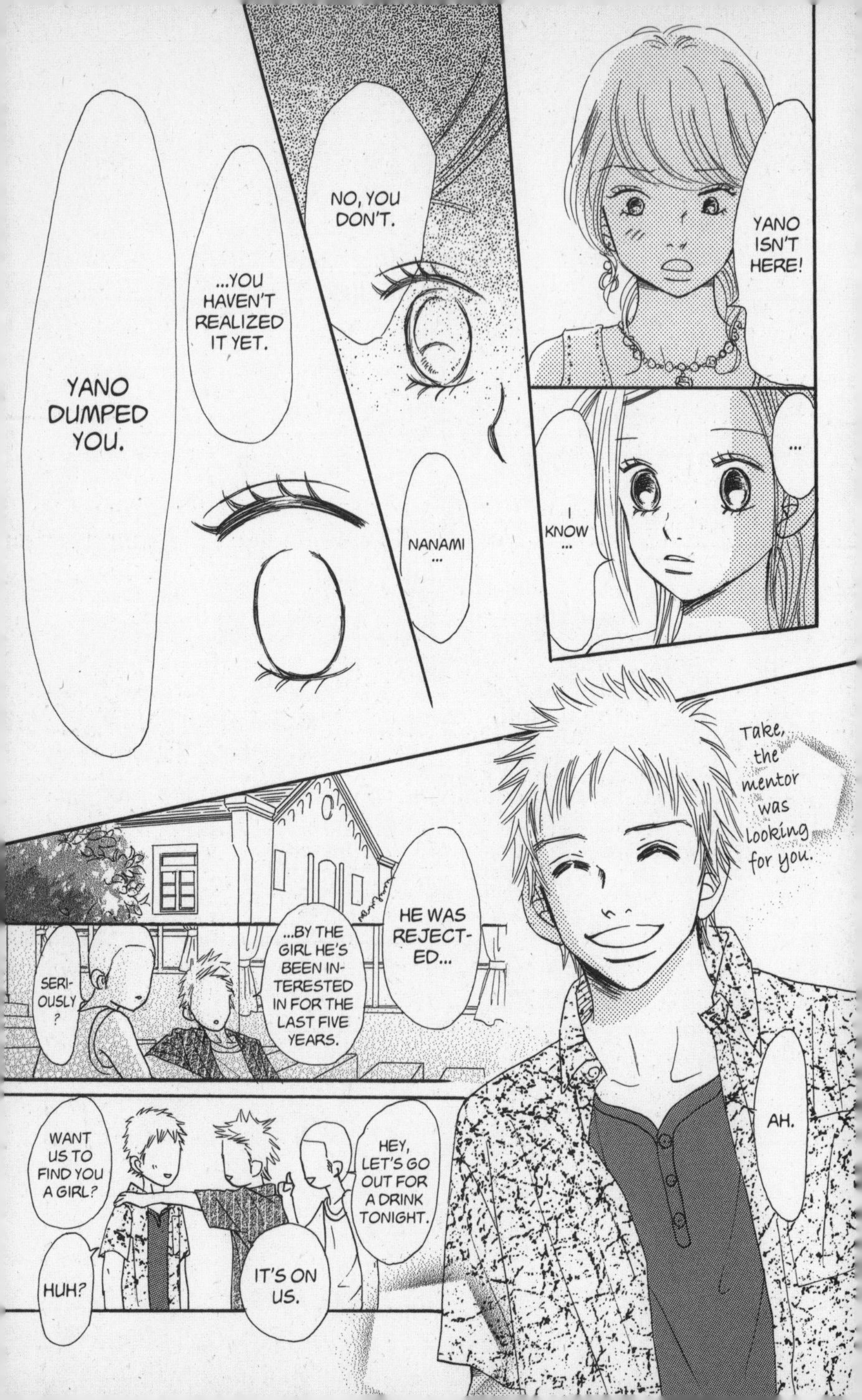
YANO ISN'T HERE!
...
I KNOW ...
NANAMI ...
NO, YOU DON'T.
...YOU HAVEN'T REALIZED IT YET.
YANO DUMPED YOU.
Take, the mentor was looking for you.
AH.
HE WAS REJECTED...
...BY THE GIRL HE'S BEEN INTERESTED IN FOR THE LAST FIVE YEARS.
SERIOUSLY?
HEY, LET'S GO OUT FOR A DRINK TONIGHT.
WANT US TO FIND YOU A GIRL?
IT'S ON US.
HUH?

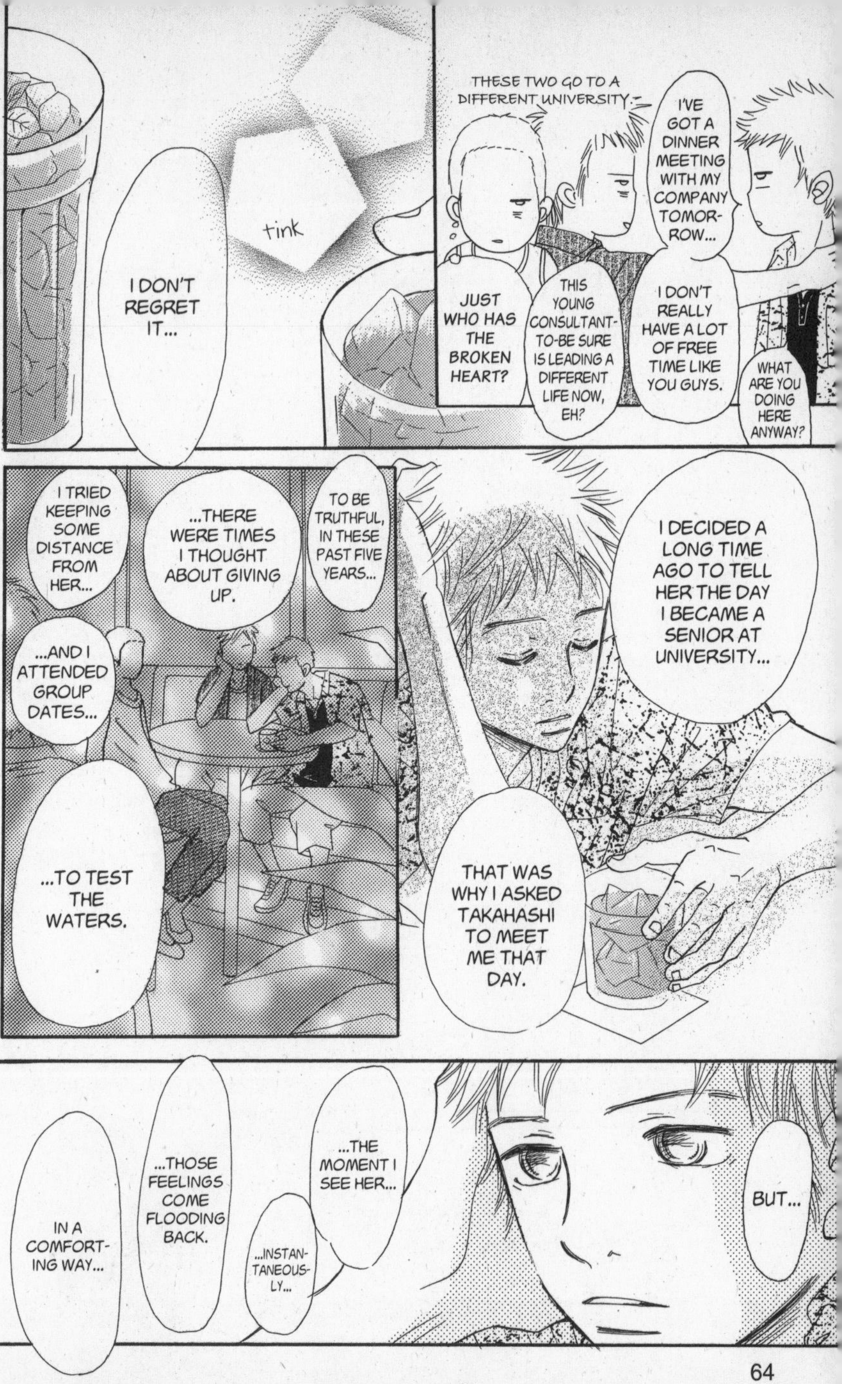
I'VE GOT A DINNER MEETING WITH MY COMPANY TOMORROW...
WHAT ARE YOU DOING HERE ANYWAY?
I DON'T REALLY HAVE A LOT OF FREE TIME LIKE YOU GUYS.
THESE TWO GO TO A DIFFERENT UNIVERSITY.
THIS YOUNG CONSULTANT-TO-BE SURE IS LEADING A DIFFERENT LIFE NOW, EH?
JUST WHO HAS THE BROKEN HEART?
tink
I DON'T REGRET IT...
I DECIDED A LONG TIME AGO TO TELL HER THE DAY I BECAME A SENIOR AT UNIVERSITY...
THAT WAS WHY I ASKED TAKAHASHI TO MEET ME THAT DAY.
TO BE TRUTHFUL, IN THESE PAST FIVE YEARS...
...THERE WERE TIMES I THOUGHT ABOUT GIVING UP.
I TRIED KEEPING SOME DISTANCE FROM HER...
...AND I ATTENDED GROUP DATES...
...TO TEST THE WATERS.
BUT...
...THE MOMENT I SEE HER...
...INSTANTANEOUSLY...
...THOSE FEELINGS COME FLOODING BACK.
IN A COMFORTING WAY...

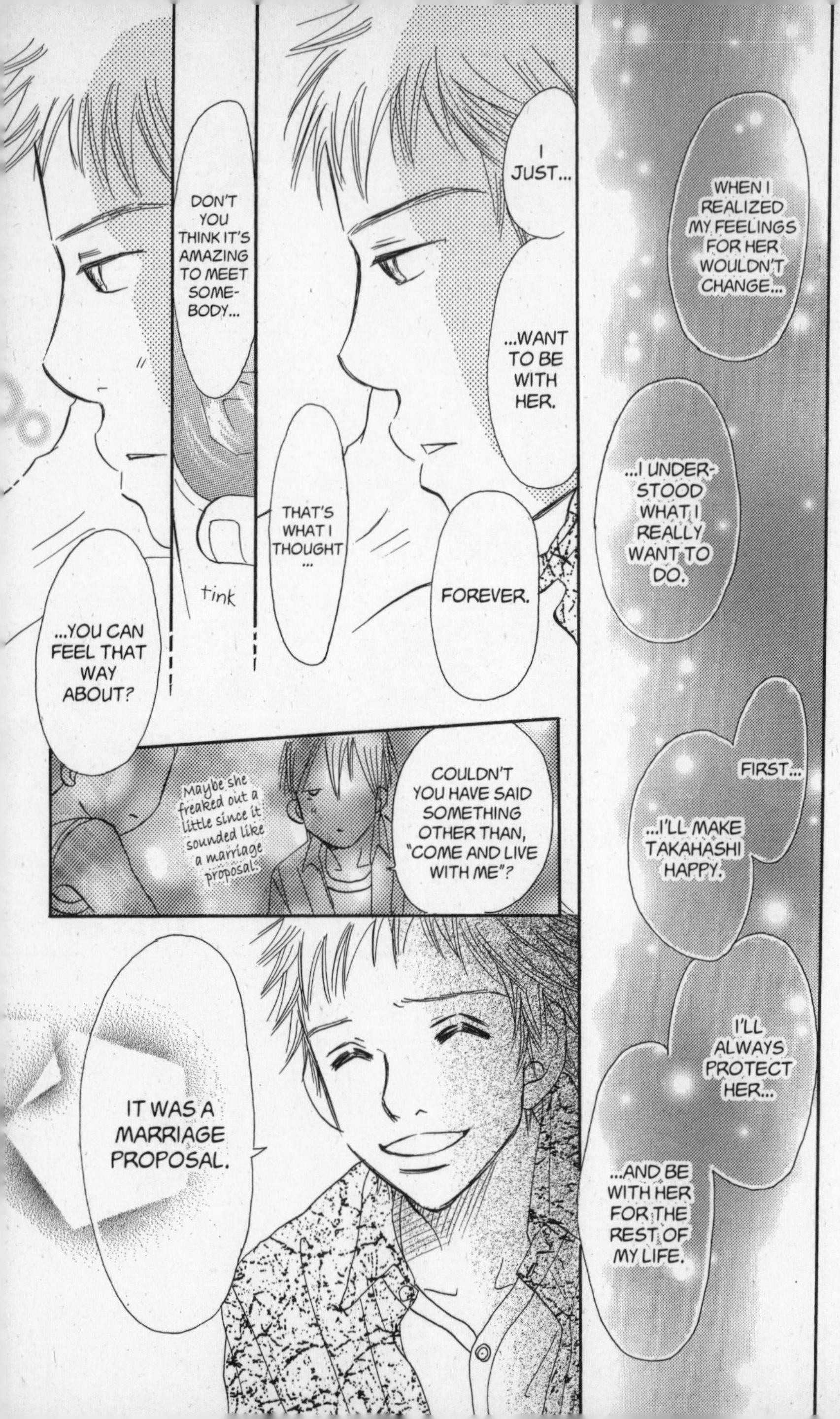
WHEN I REALIZED MY FEELINGS FOR HER WOULDN'T CHANGE...
...I UNDERSTOOD WHAT I REALLY WANT TO DO.
FIRST...
...I'LL MAKE TAKAHASHI HAPPY.
I'LL ALWAYS PROTECT HER...
...AND BE WITH HER FOR THE REST OF MY LIFE.
I JUST...
...WANT TO BE WITH HER.
FOREVER.
THAT'S WHAT I THOUGHT...
DON'T YOU THINK IT'S AMAZING TO MEET SOMEBODY...
tink
...YOU CAN FEEL THAT WAY ABOUT?
COULDN'T YOU HAVE SAID SOMETHING OTHER THAN, "COME AND LIVE WITH ME"?
Maybe she freaked out a little since it sounded like a marriage proposal.
IT WAS A MARRIAGE PROPOSAL.

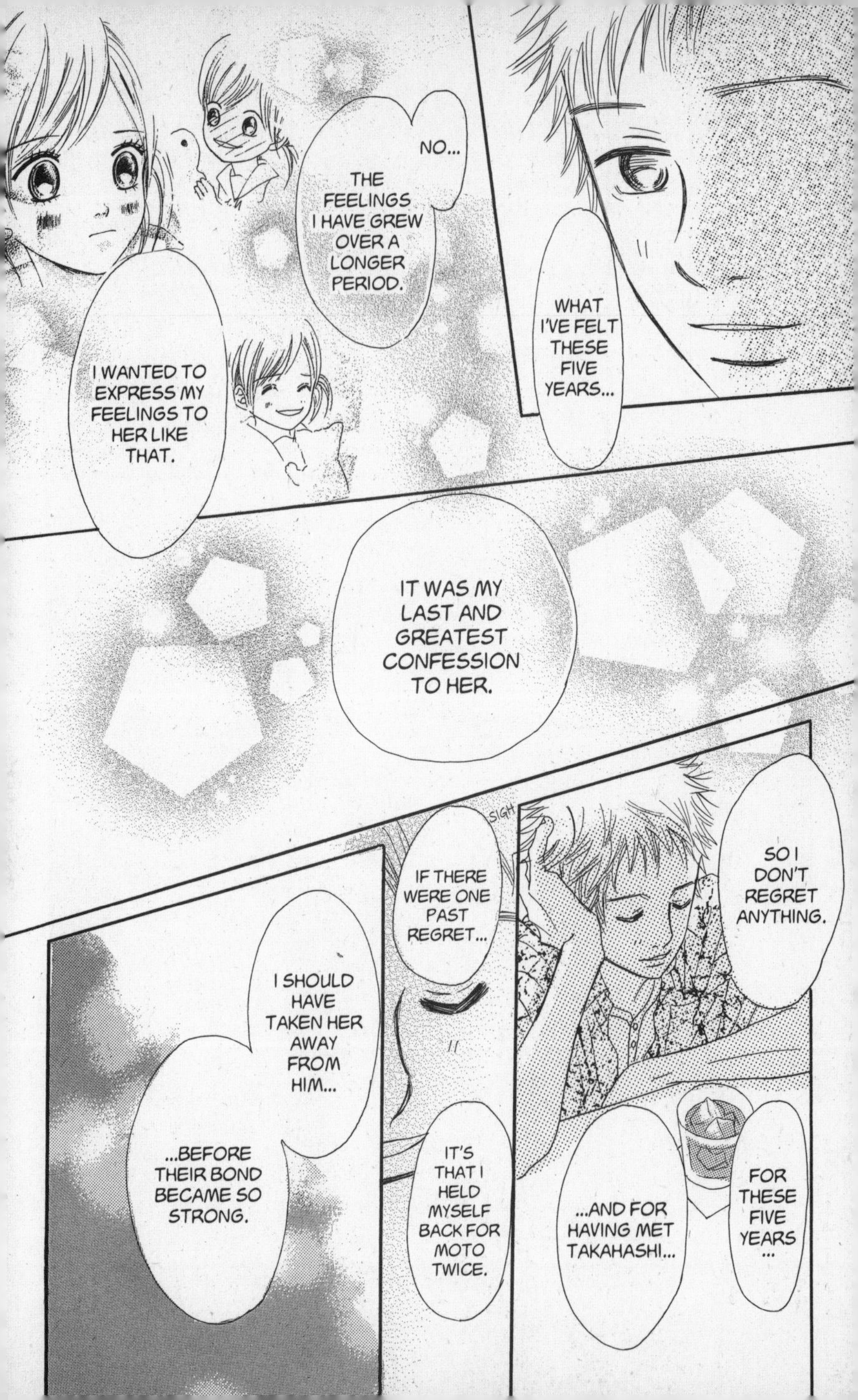
WHAT I'VE FELT THESE FIVE YEARS...
NO...
THE FEELINGS I HAVE GREW OVER A LONGER PERIOD.
I WANTED TO EXPRESS MY FEELINGS TO HER LIKE THAT.
IT WAS MY LAST AND GREATEST CONFESSION TO HER.
SO I DON'T REGRET ANYTHING.
FOR THESE FIVE YEARS ...
...AND FOR HAVING MET TAKAHASHI...
SIGH
IF THERE WERE ONE PAST REGRET...
IT'S THAT I HELD MYSELF BACK FOR MOTO TWICE.
I SHOULD HAVE TAKEN HER AWAY FROM HIM...
...BEFORE THEIR BOND BECAME SO STRONG.

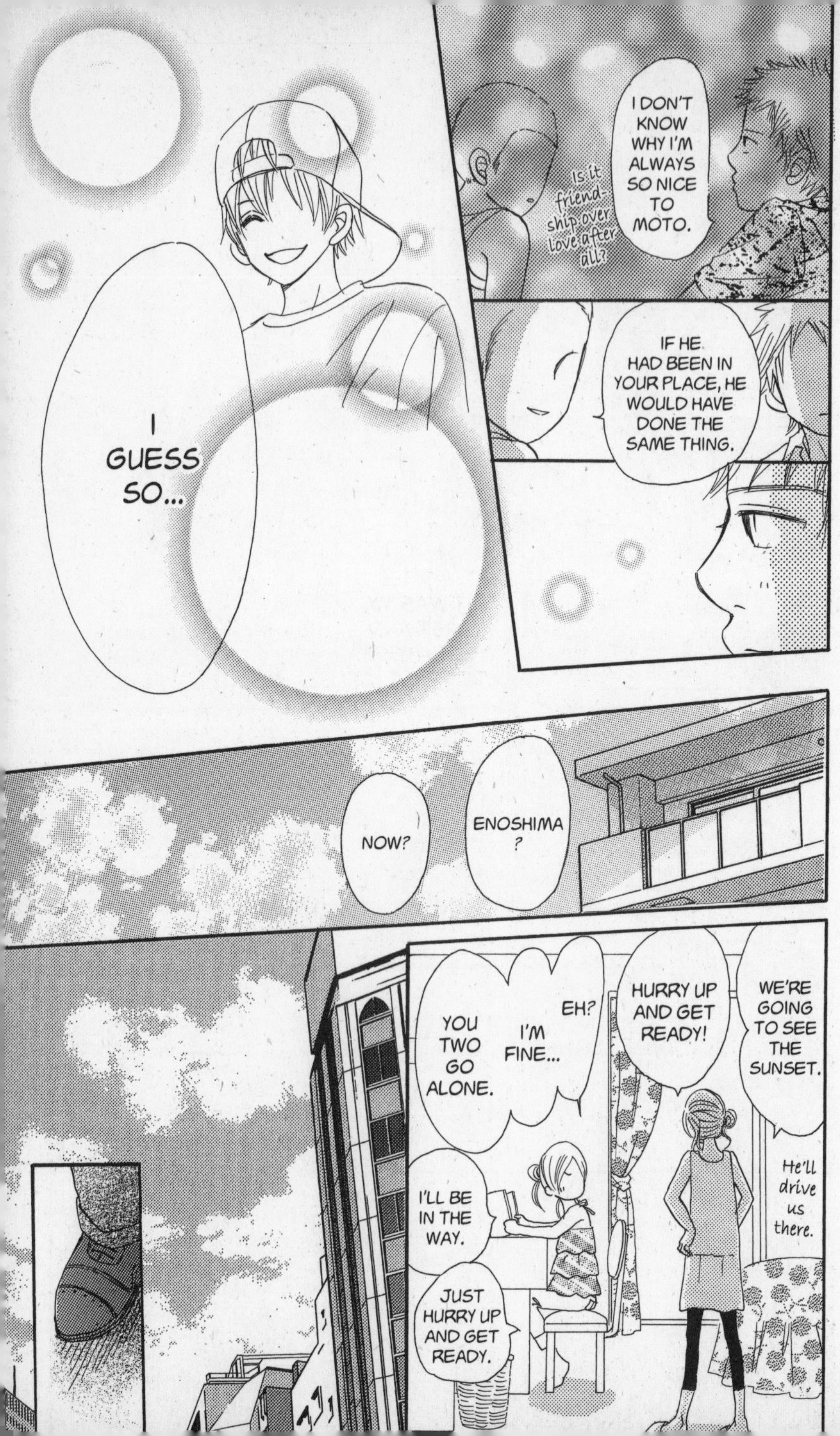
I DON'T KNOW WHY I'M ALWAYS SO NICE TO MOTO.
Is it friendship over love after all?
IF HE HAD BEEN IN YOUR PLACE, HE WOULD HAVE DONE THE SAME THING.
I GUESS SO...
ENOSHIMA?
NOW?
WE'RE GOING TO SEE THE SUNSET.
He'll drive us there.
HURRY UP AND GET READY!
EH? I'M FINE... YOU TWO GO ALONE.
I'LL BE IN THE WAY.
JUST HURRY UP AND GET READY.

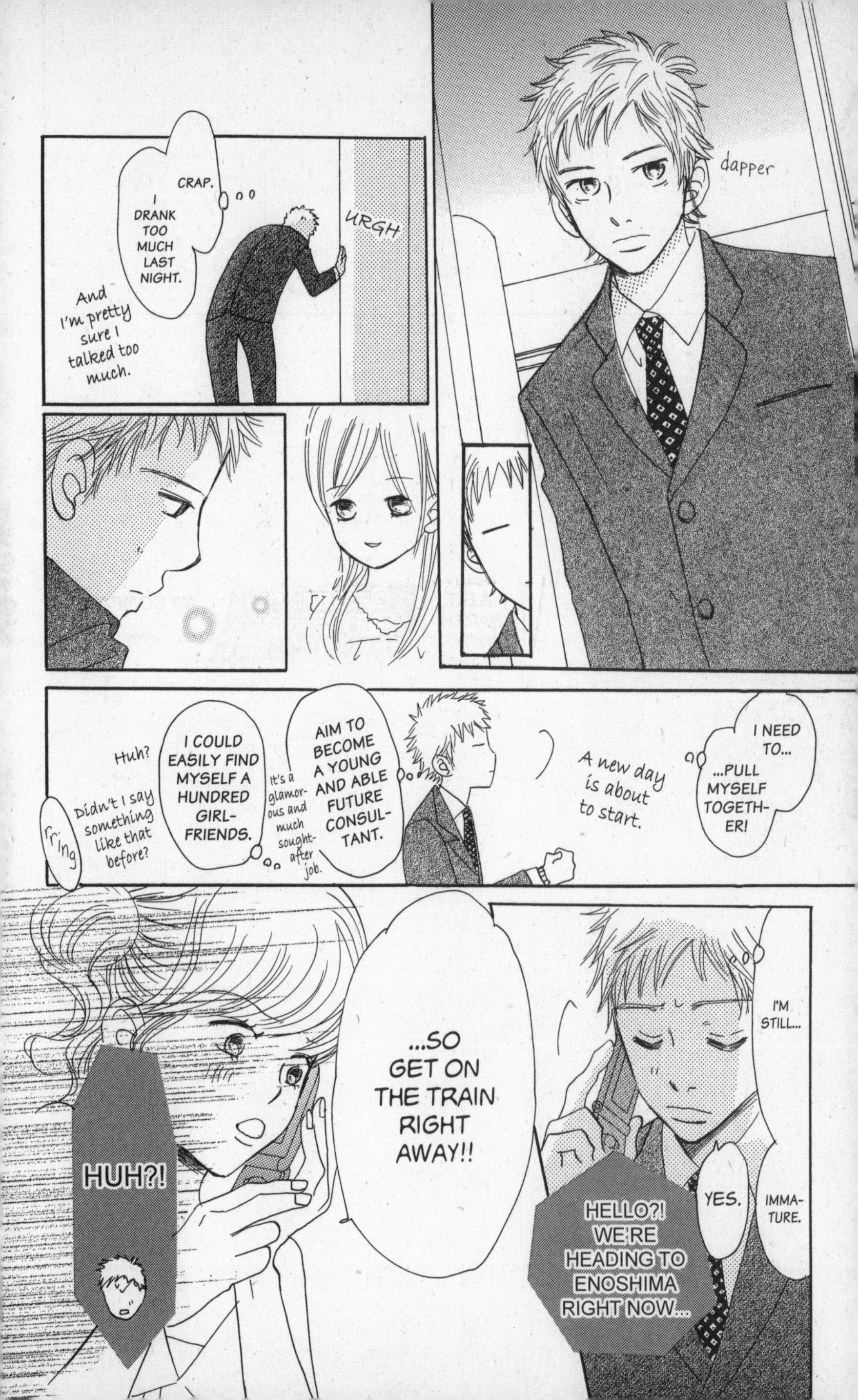
dapper
URGH
CRAP.
I DRANK TOO MUCH LAST NIGHT.
And I'm pretty sure I talked too much.
I NEED TO...
...PULL MYSELF TOGETHER!
A new day is about to start.
AIM TO BECOME A YOUNG AND ABLE FUTURE CONSULTANT.
It's a glamorous and much sought-after job.
I COULD EASILY FIND MYSELF A HUNDRED GIRLFRIENDS.
Huh?
Didn't I say something like that before?
rring
I'M STILL...
IMMATURE.
YES.
HELLO?! WE'RE HEADING TO ENOSHIMA RIGHT NOW...
...SO GET ON THE TRAIN RIGHT AWAY!!
HUH?!

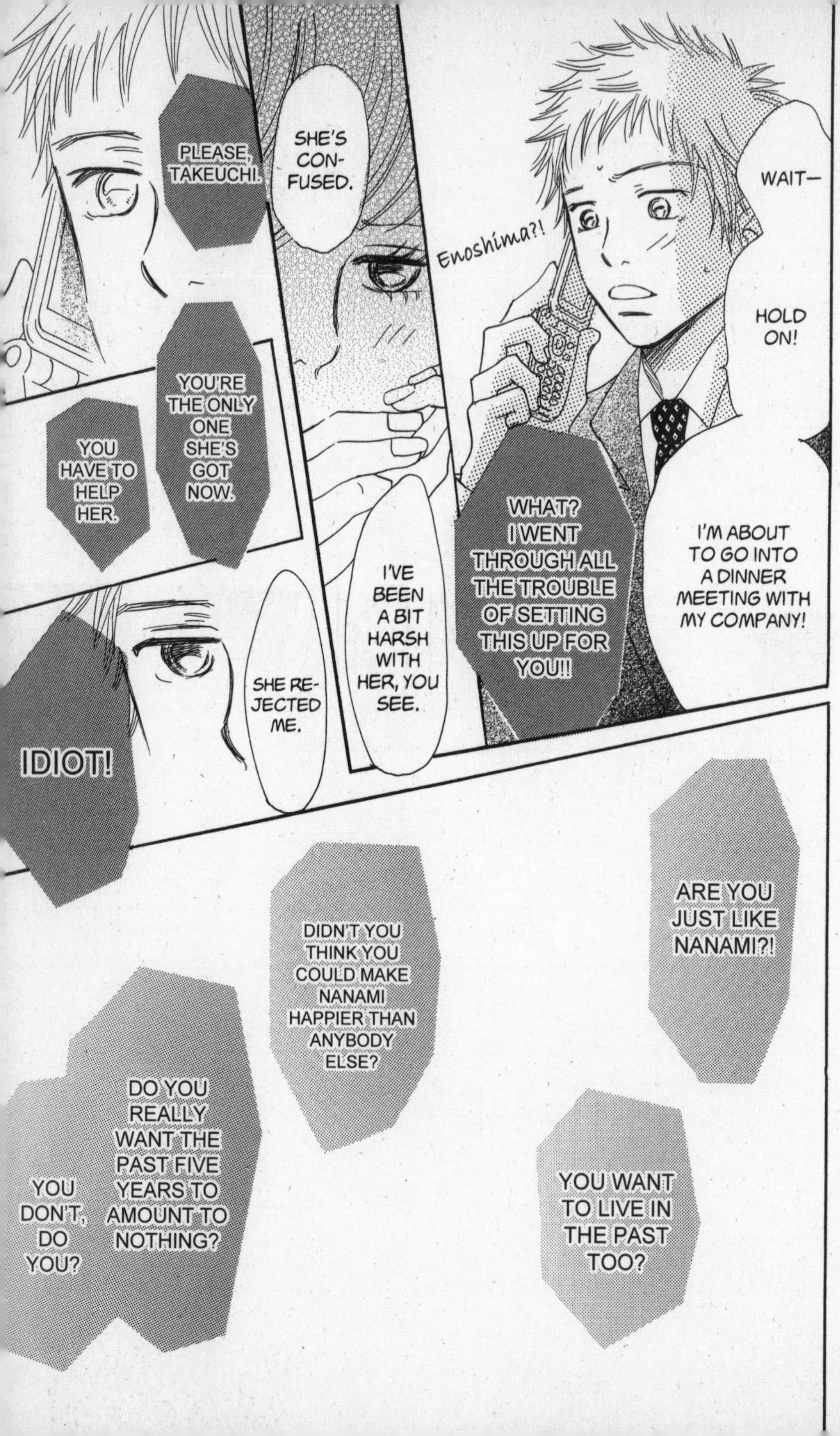
WAIT—
HOLD ON!
I'M ABOUT TO GO INTO A DINNER MEETING WITH MY COMPANY!
Enoshima?!
WHAT? I WENT THROUGH ALL THE TROUBLE OF SETTING THIS UP FOR YOU!!
SHE'S CON-FUSED.
PLEASE, TAKEUCHI.
YOU'RE THE ONLY ONE SHE'S GOT NOW.
YOU HAVE TO HELP HER.
I'VE BEEN A BIT HARSH WITH HER, YOU SEE.
SHE RE-JECTED ME.
IDIOT!
ARE YOU JUST LIKE NANAMI?!
YOU WANT TO LIVE IN THE PAST TOO?
DIDN'T YOU THINK YOU COULD MAKE NANAMI HAPPIER THAN ANYBODY ELSE?
DO YOU REALLY WANT THE PAST FIVE YEARS TO AMOUNT TO NOTHING?
YOU DON'T, DO YOU?

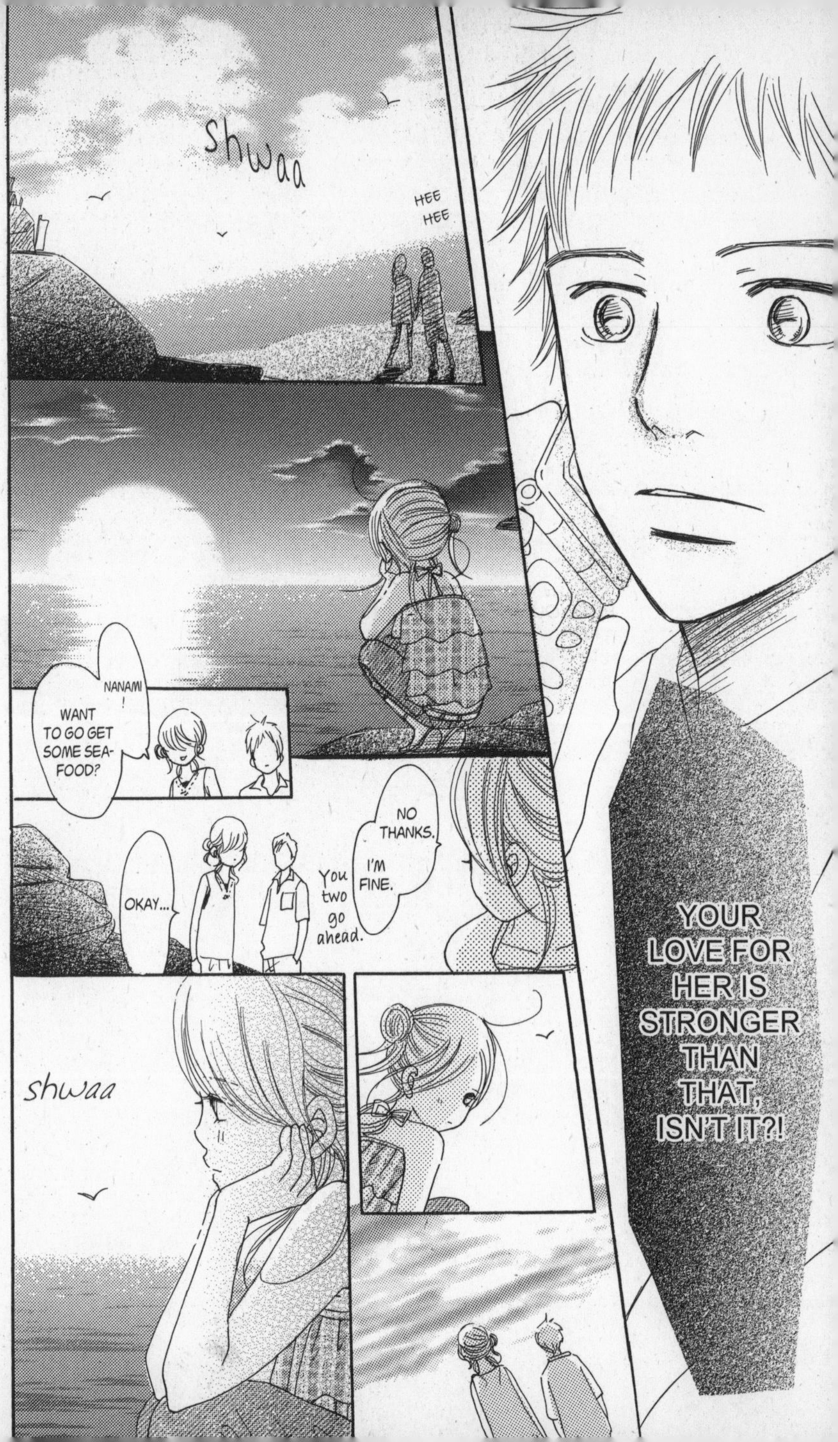
YOUR LOVE FOR HER IS STRONGER THAN THAT, ISN'T IT?!
Shwaa
HEE HEE
NANAMI! WANT TO GO GET SOME SEA-FOOD?
NO THANKS.
I'M FINE.
You two go ahead.
OKAY...
shwaa

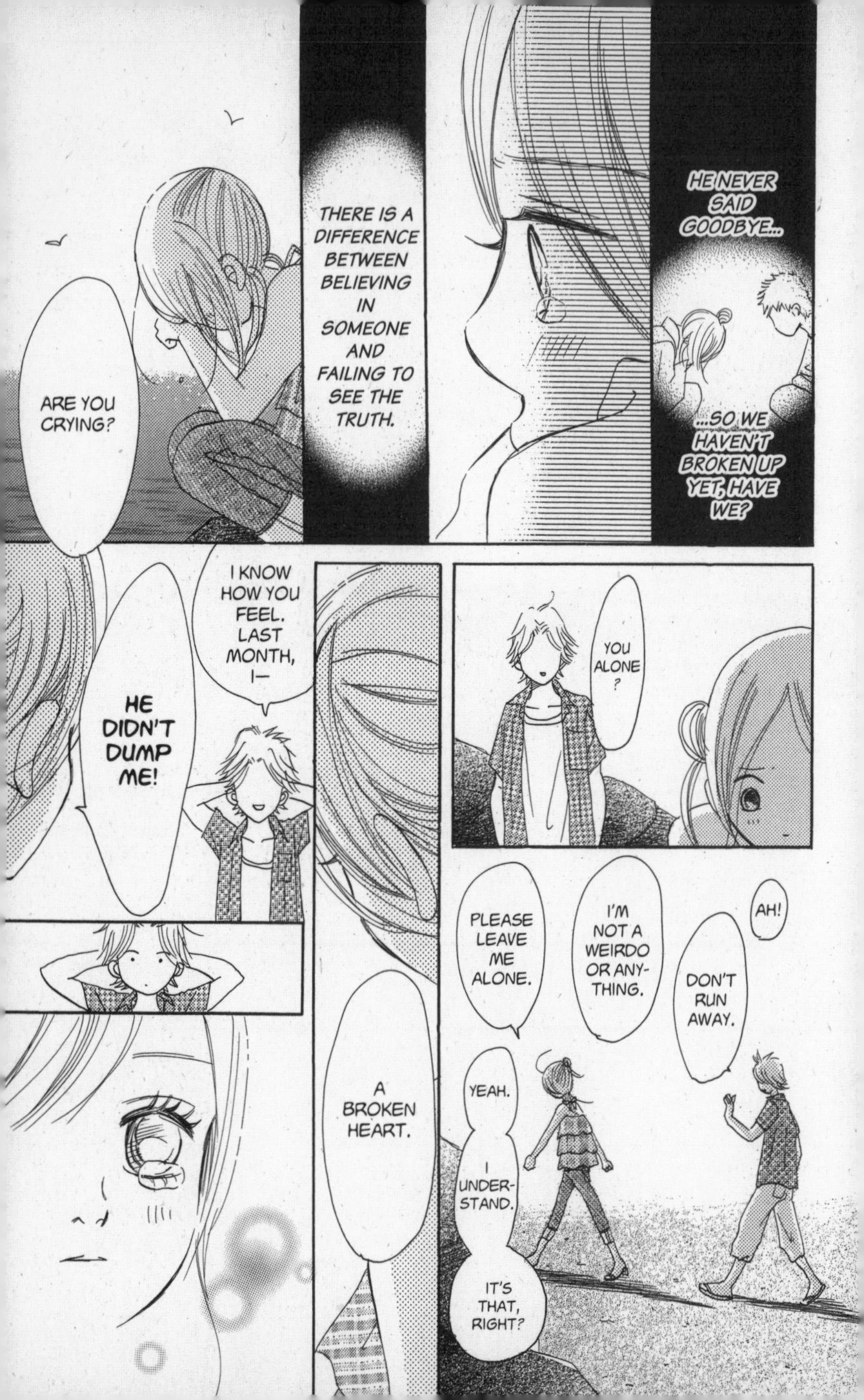
HE NEVER SAID GOODBYE...
...SO WE HAVEN'T BROKEN UP YET, HAVE WE?
THERE IS A DIFFERENCE BETWEEN BELIEVING IN SOMEONE AND FAILING TO SEE THE TRUTH.
ARE YOU CRYING?
YOU ALONE?
AH!
DON'T RUN AWAY.
I'M NOT A WEIRDO OR ANY-THING.
PLEASE LEAVE ME ALONE.
YEAH.
I UNDER-STAND.
IT'S THAT, RIGHT?
A BROKEN HEART.
I KNOW HOW YOU FEEL. LAST MONTH, I—
HE DIDN'T DUMP ME!

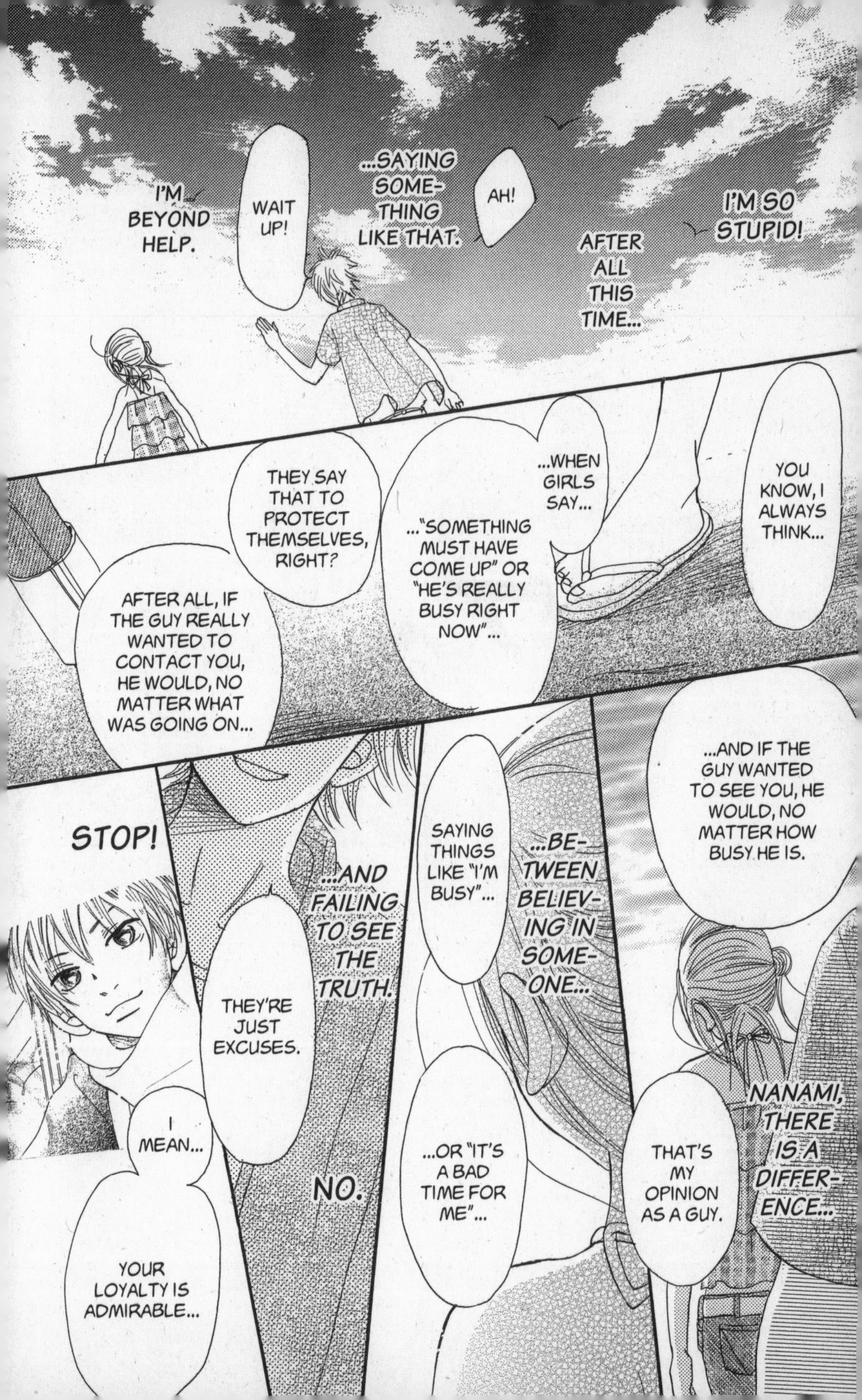
I'M SO STUPID!
AFTER ALL THIS TIME...
AH!
...SAYING SOMETHING LIKE THAT.
WAIT UP!
I'M BEYOND HELP.
YOU KNOW, I ALWAYS THINK...
...WHEN GIRLS SAY...
..."SOMETHING MUST HAVE COME UP" OR "HE'S REALLY BUSY RIGHT NOW"...
THEY SAY THAT TO PROTECT THEMSELVES, RIGHT?
AFTER ALL, IF THE GUY REALLY WANTED TO CONTACT YOU, HE WOULD, NO MATTER WHAT WAS GOING ON...
...AND IF THE GUY WANTED TO SEE YOU, HE WOULD, NO MATTER HOW BUSY HE IS.
NANAMI, THERE IS A DIFFERENCE...
THAT'S MY OPINION AS A GUY.
...BETWEEN BELIEVING IN SOMEONE...
SAYING THINGS LIKE "I'M BUSY"...
...OR "IT'S A BAD TIME FOR ME"...
...AND FAILING TO SEE THE TRUTH.
NO.
THEY'RE JUST EXCUSES.
STOP!
I MEAN...
YOUR LOYALTY IS ADMIRABLE...

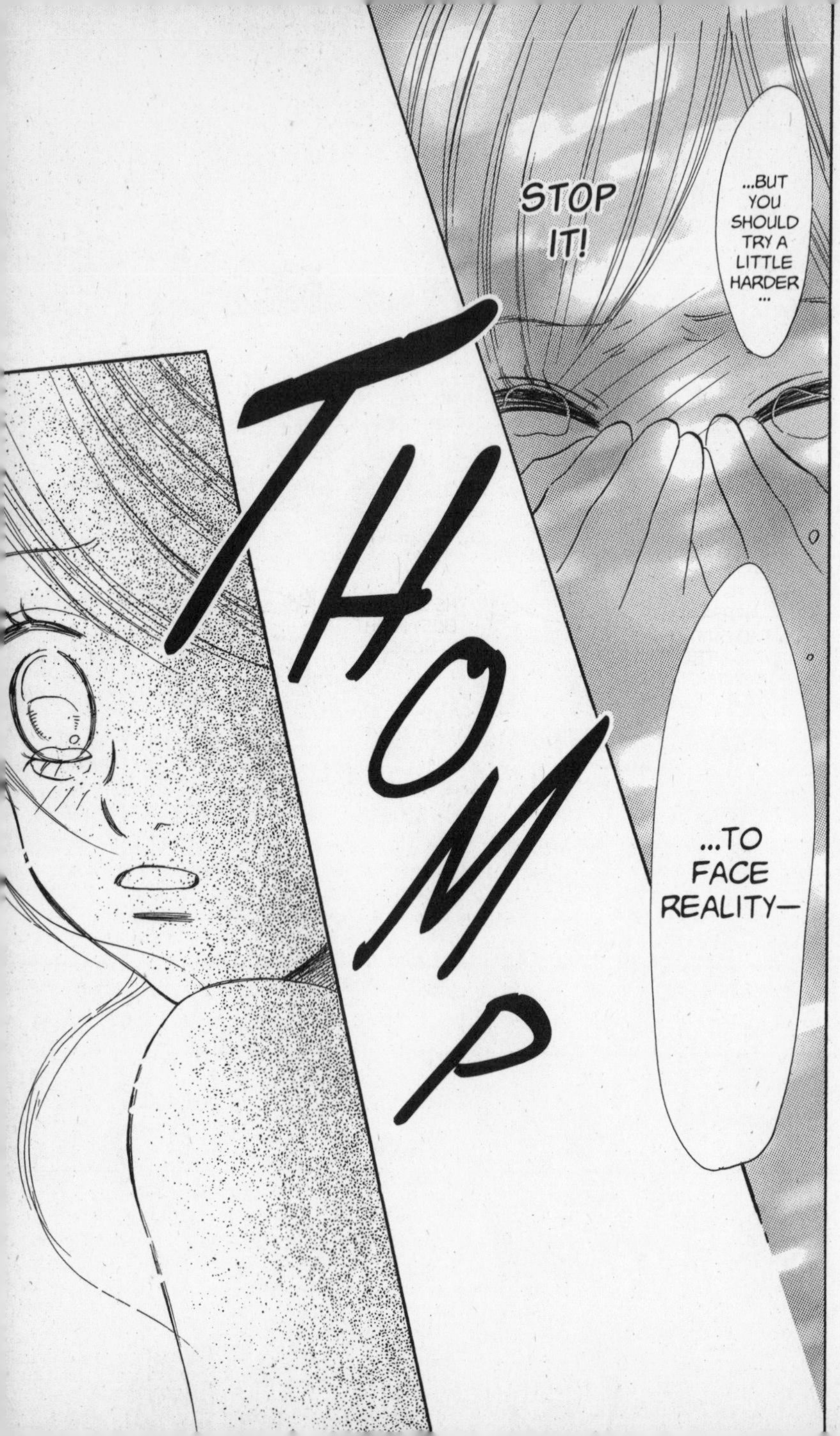
...BUT YOU SHOULD TRY A LITTLE HARDER ...
STOP IT!
...TO FACE REALITY—
THOMP

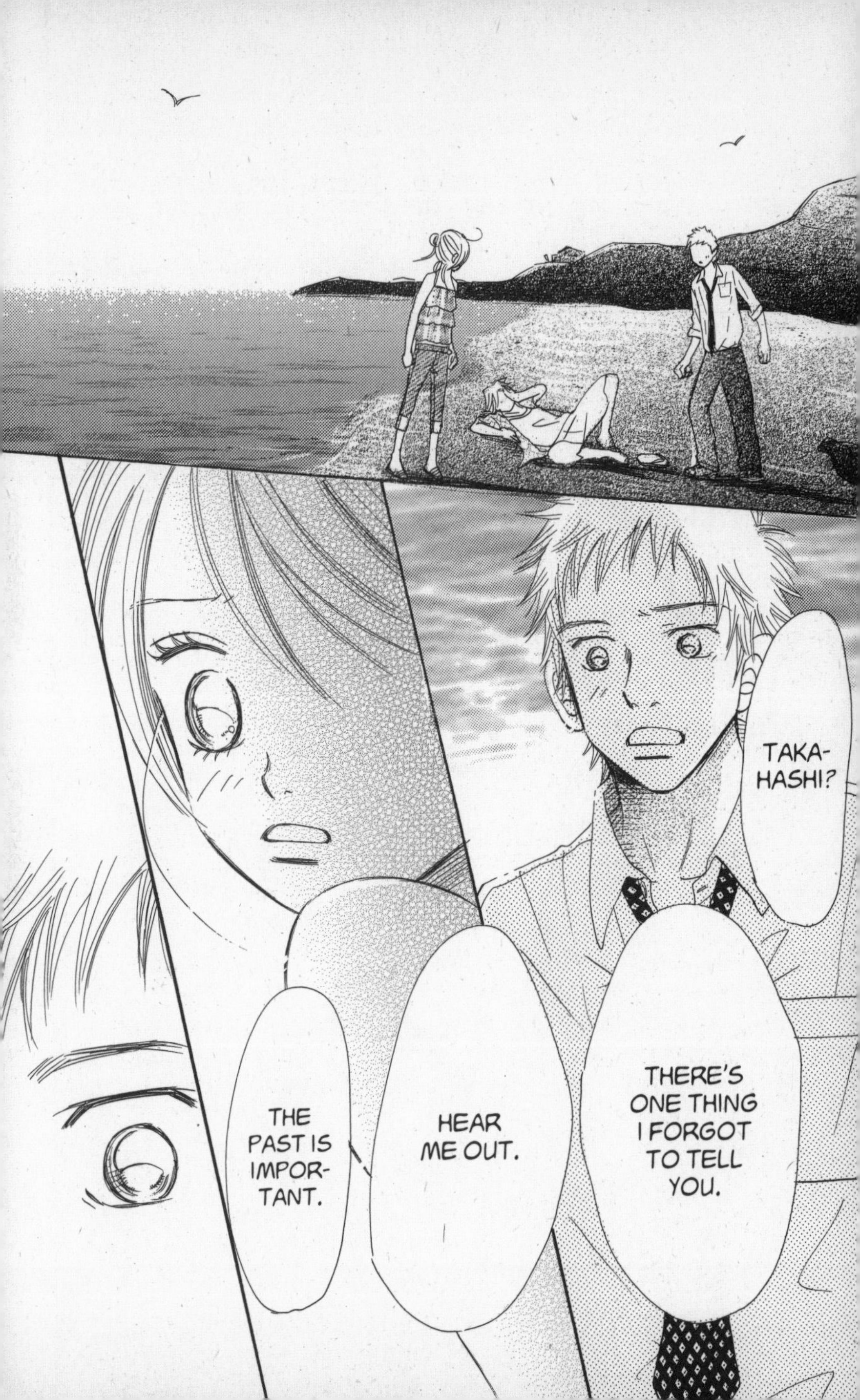
TAKA-HASHI?
THERE'S ONE THING I FORGOT TO TELL YOU.
HEAR ME OUT.
THE PAST IS IMPOR-TANT.

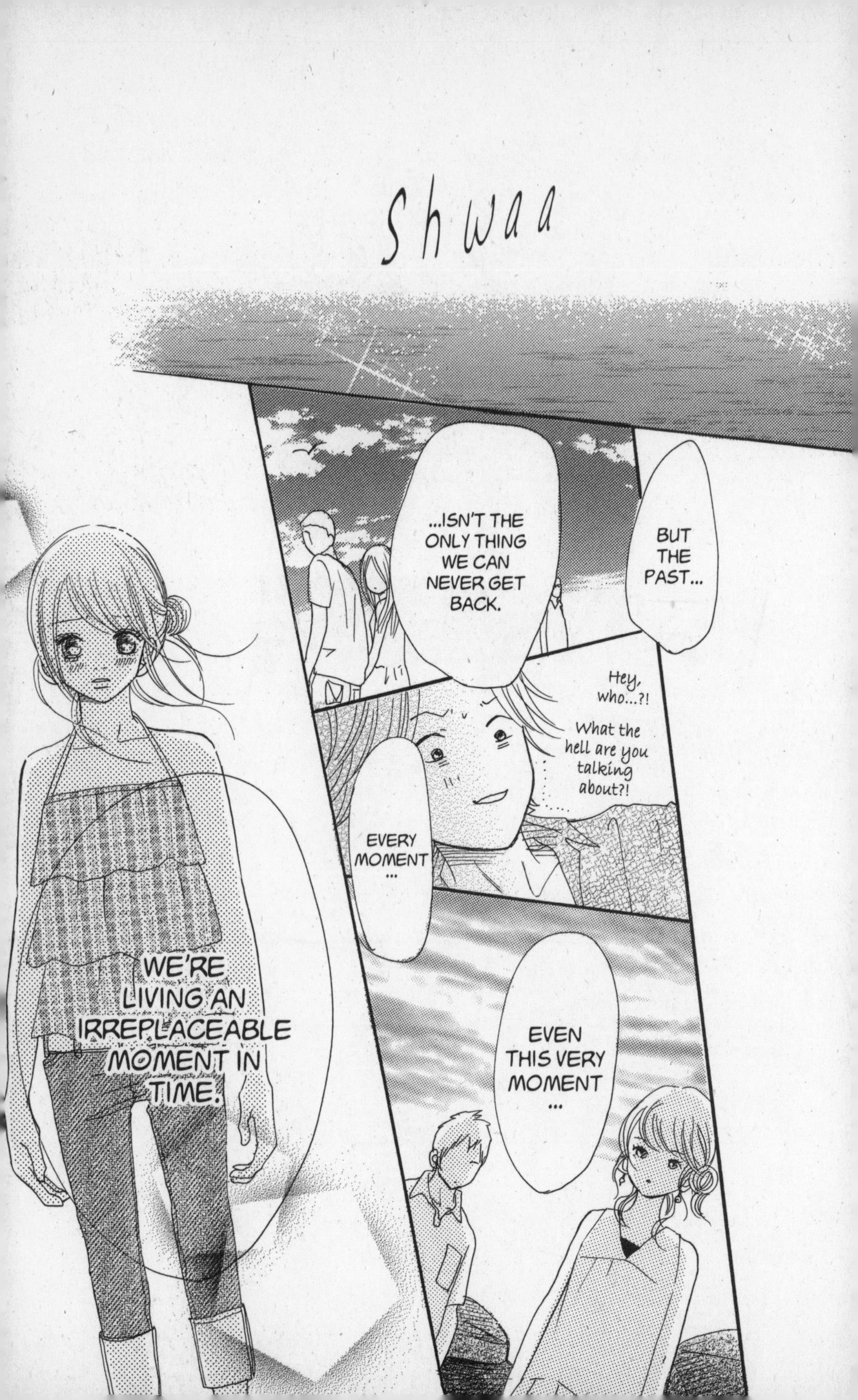
Shwaa
But the past...
...isn't the only thing we can never get back.
Hey, who...?!
What the hell are you talking about?!
Every moment...
Even this very moment...
We're living an irreplaceable moment in time.

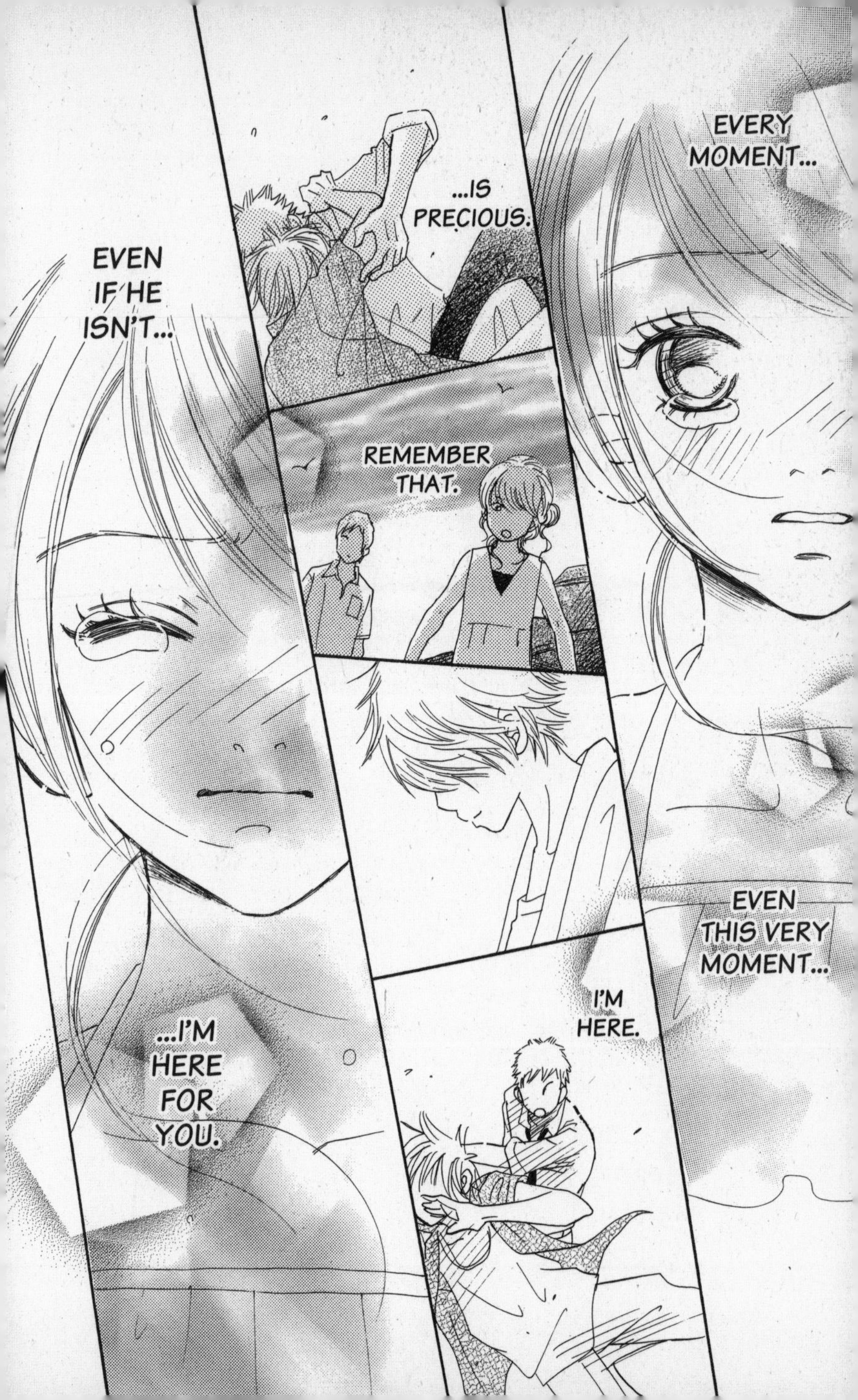
EVERY MOMENT...
EVEN THIS VERY MOMENT...
...IS PRECIOUS.
REMEMBER THAT.
I'M HERE.
EVEN IF HE ISN'T...
...I'M HERE FOR YOU.

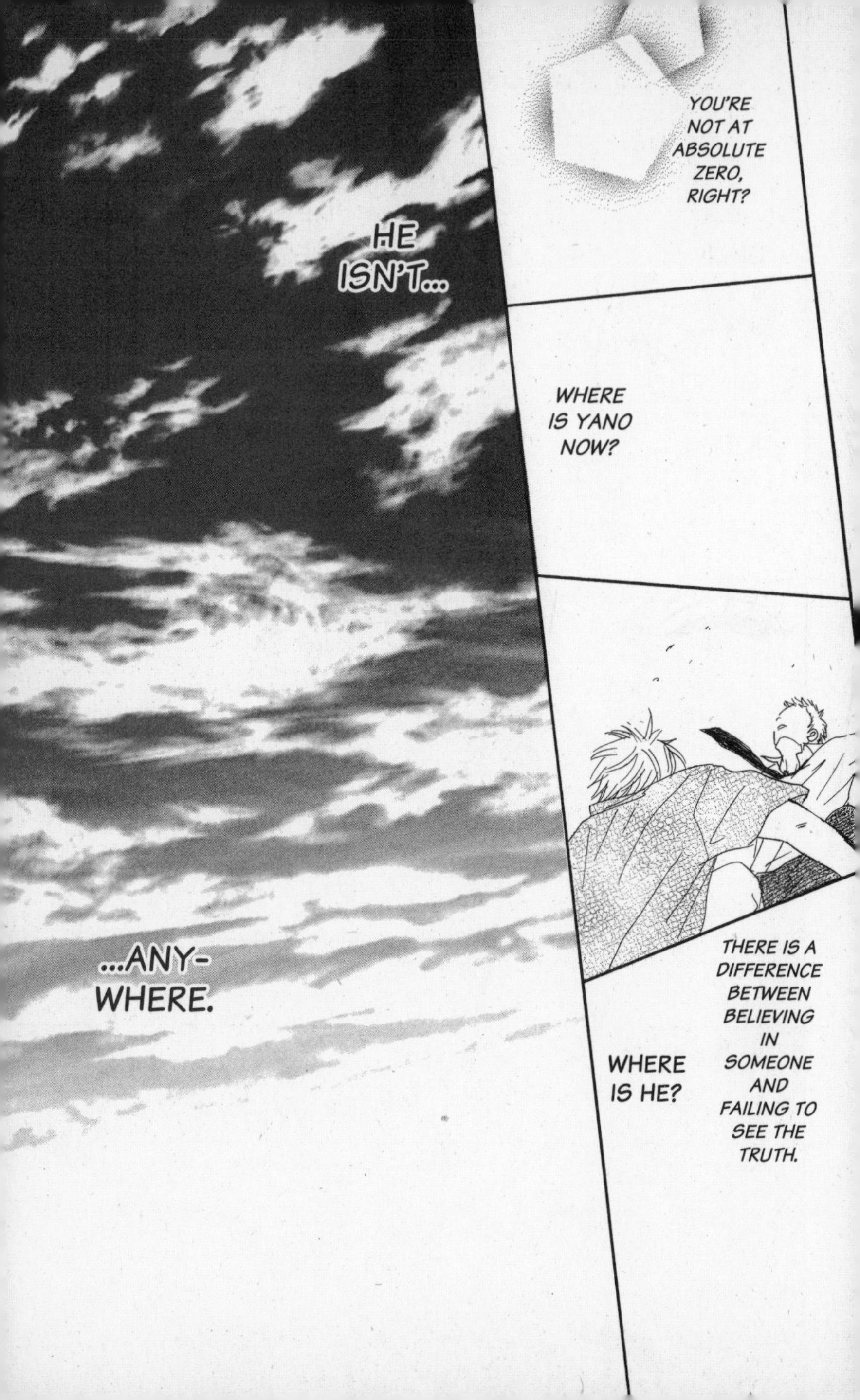
YOU'RE NOT AT ABSOLUTE ZERO, RIGHT?
WHERE IS YANO NOW?
THERE IS A DIFFERENCE BETWEEN BELIEVING IN SOMEONE AND FAILING TO SEE THE TRUTH.
WHERE IS HE?
HE ISN'T...
...ANY-WHERE.

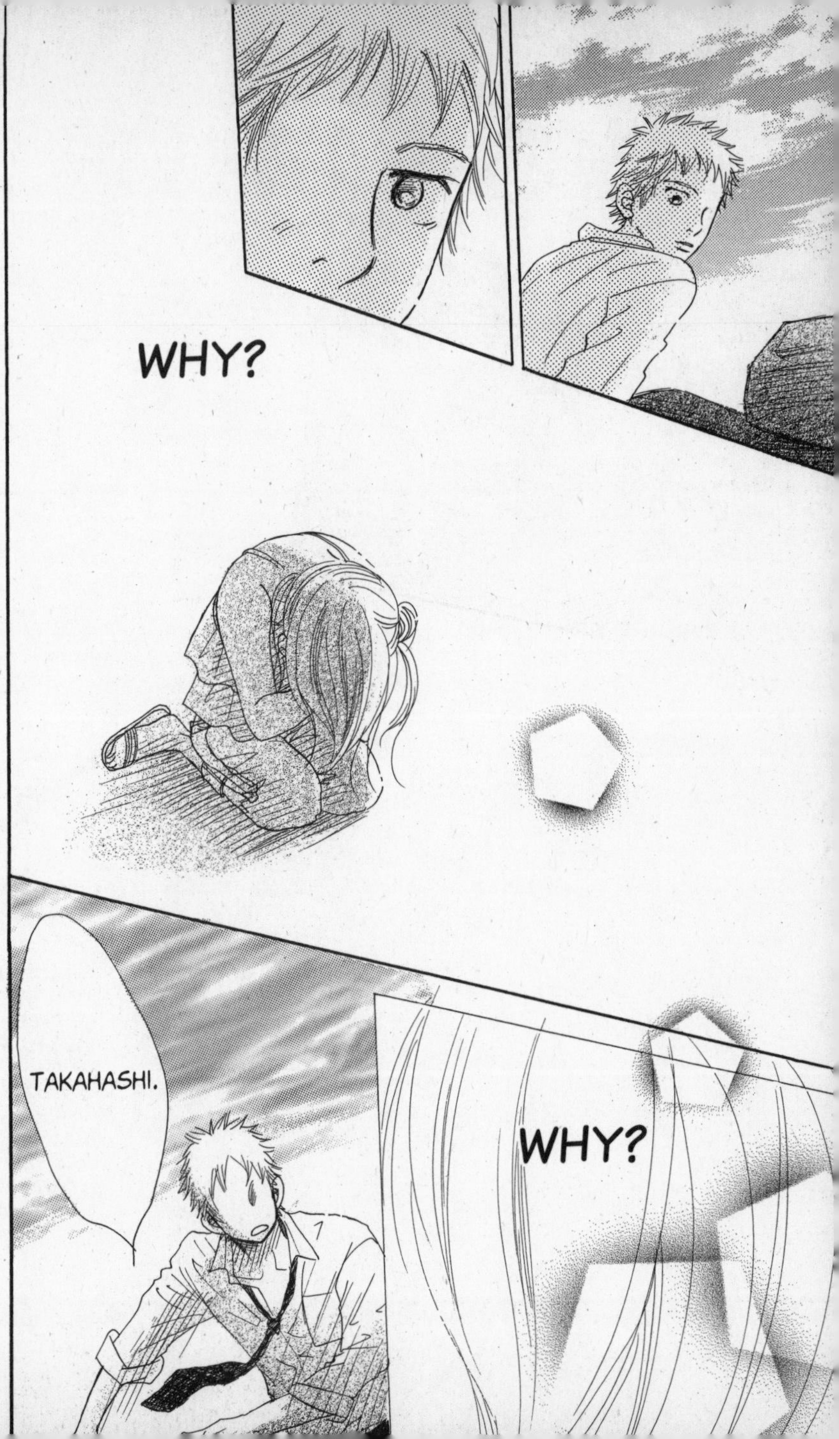
WHY?
WHY?
TAKAHASHI.

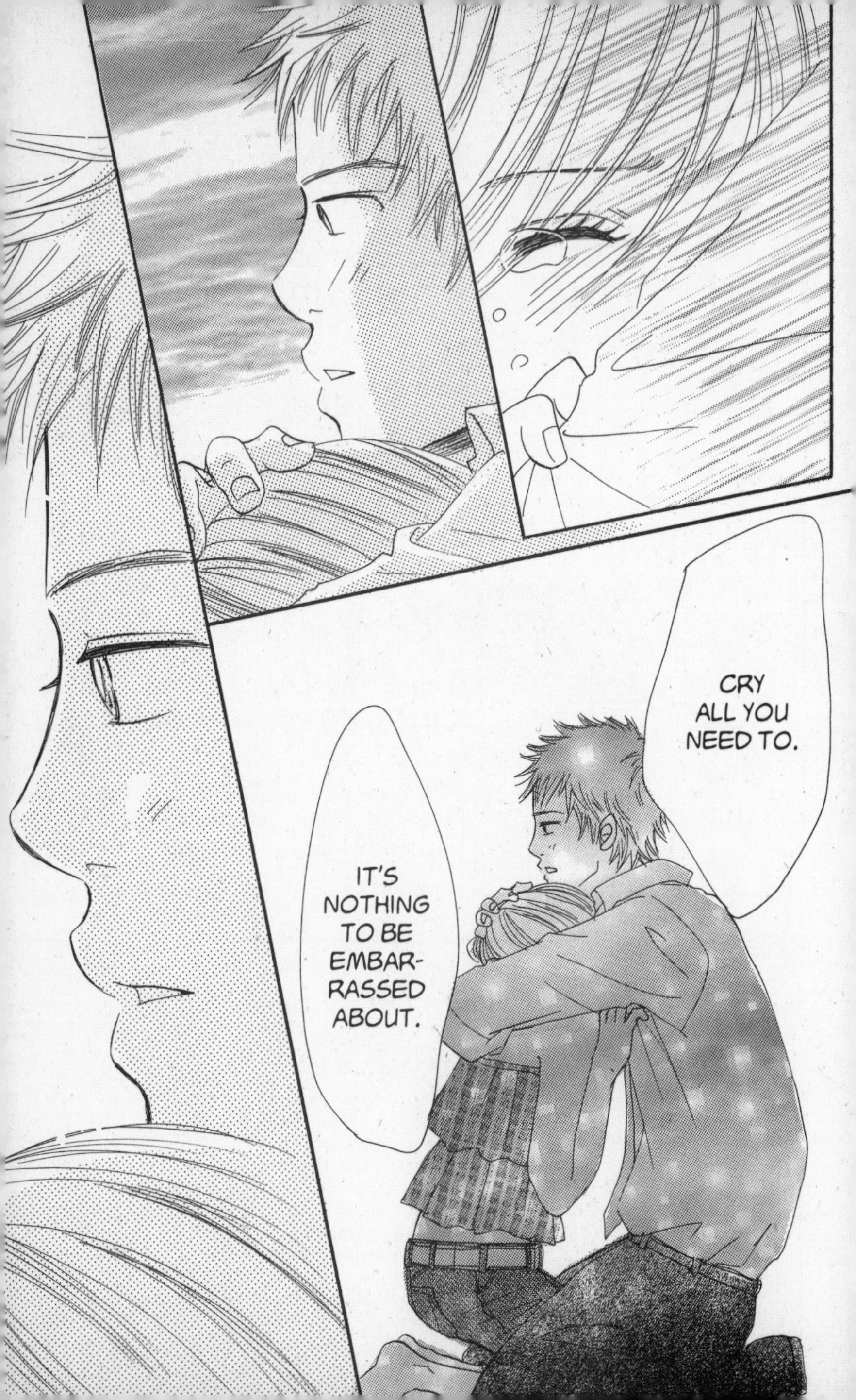
CRY ALL YOU NEED TO.
IT'S NOTHING TO BE EMBARRASSED ABOUT.

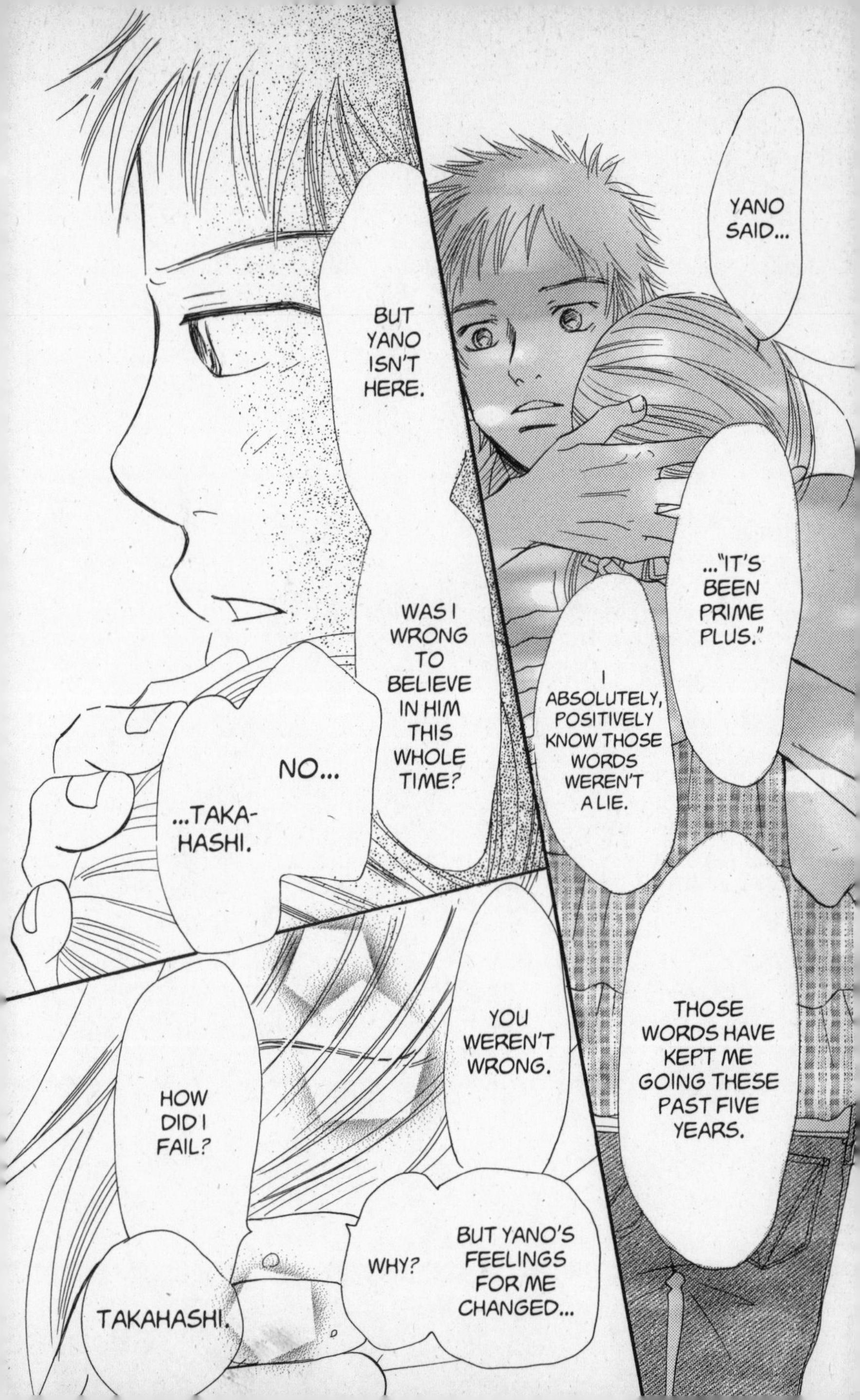
YANO SAID...
..."IT'S BEEN PRIME PLUS."
I ABSOLUTELY, POSITIVELY KNOW THOSE WORDS WEREN'T A LIE.
THOSE WORDS HAVE KEPT ME GOING THESE PAST FIVE YEARS.
BUT YANO ISN'T HERE.
WAS I WRONG TO BELIEVE IN HIM THIS WHOLE TIME?
NO...
...TAKA-HASHI.
YOU WEREN'T WRONG.
BUT YANO'S FEELINGS FOR ME CHANGED...
WHY?
HOW DID I FAIL?
TAKAHASHI.

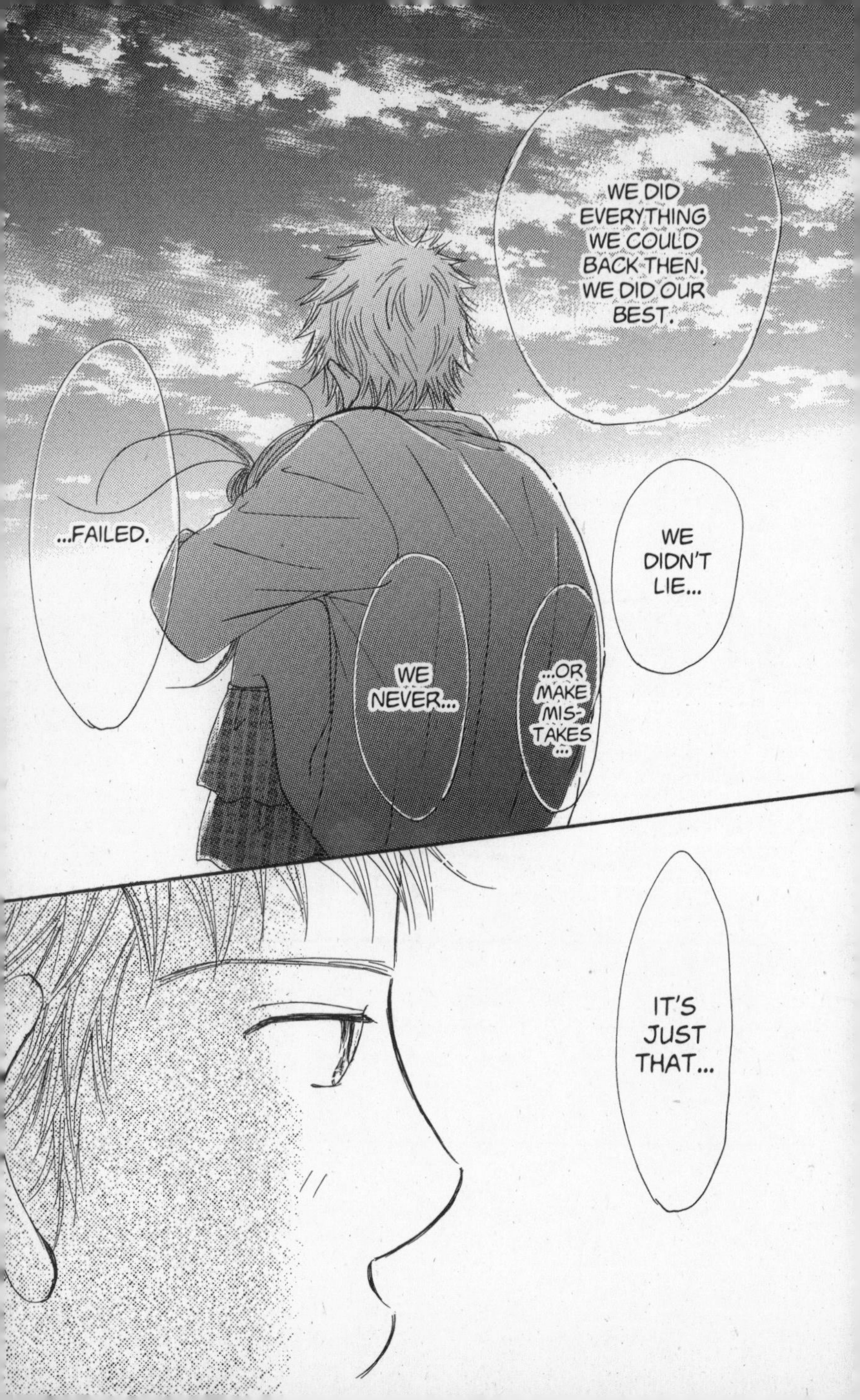
WE DID EVERYTHING WE COULD BACK THEN. WE DID OUR BEST.
WE DIDN'T LIE...
...OR MAKE MIS-TAKES...
WE NEVER...
...FAILED.
IT'S JUST THAT...

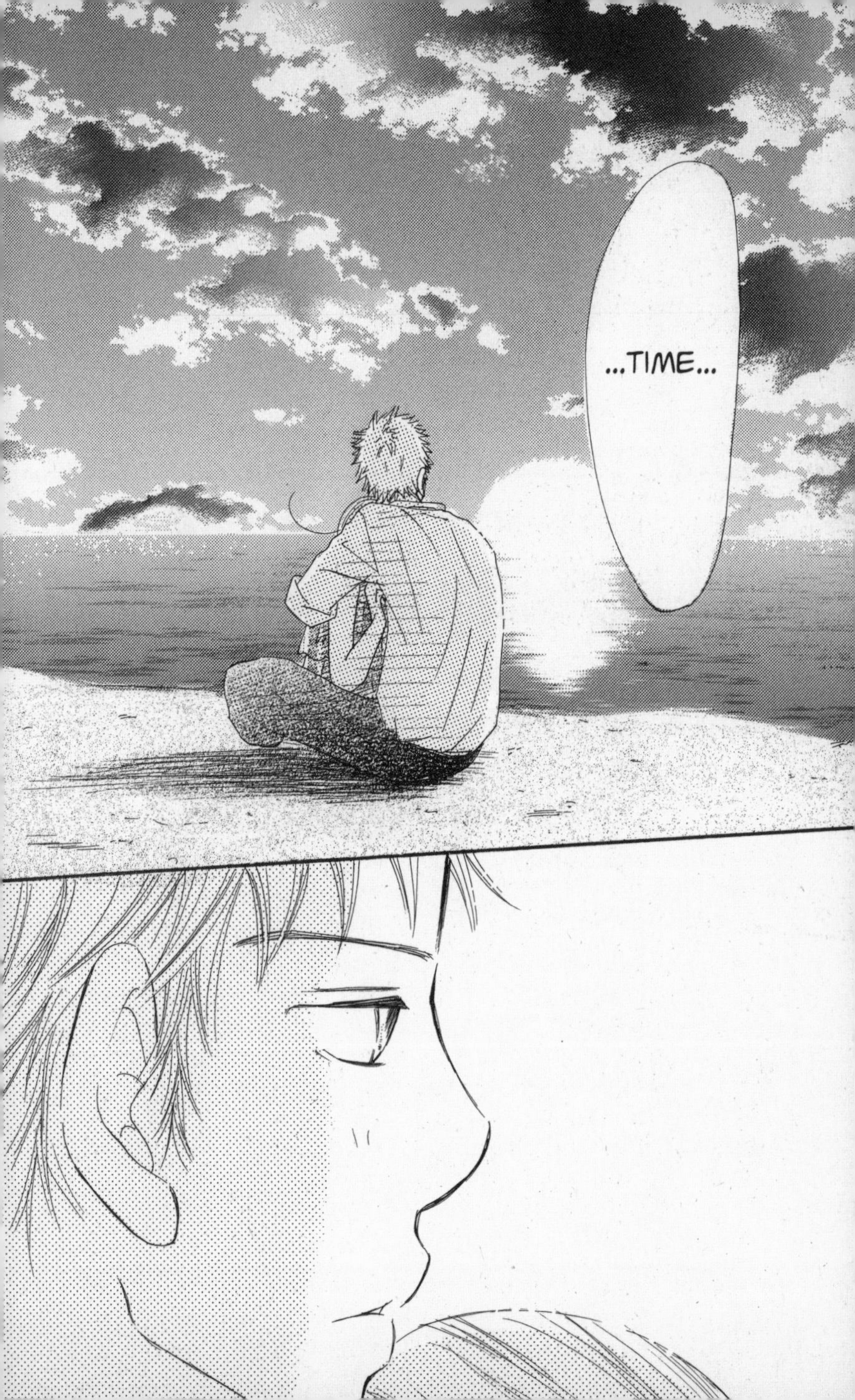
...TIME...

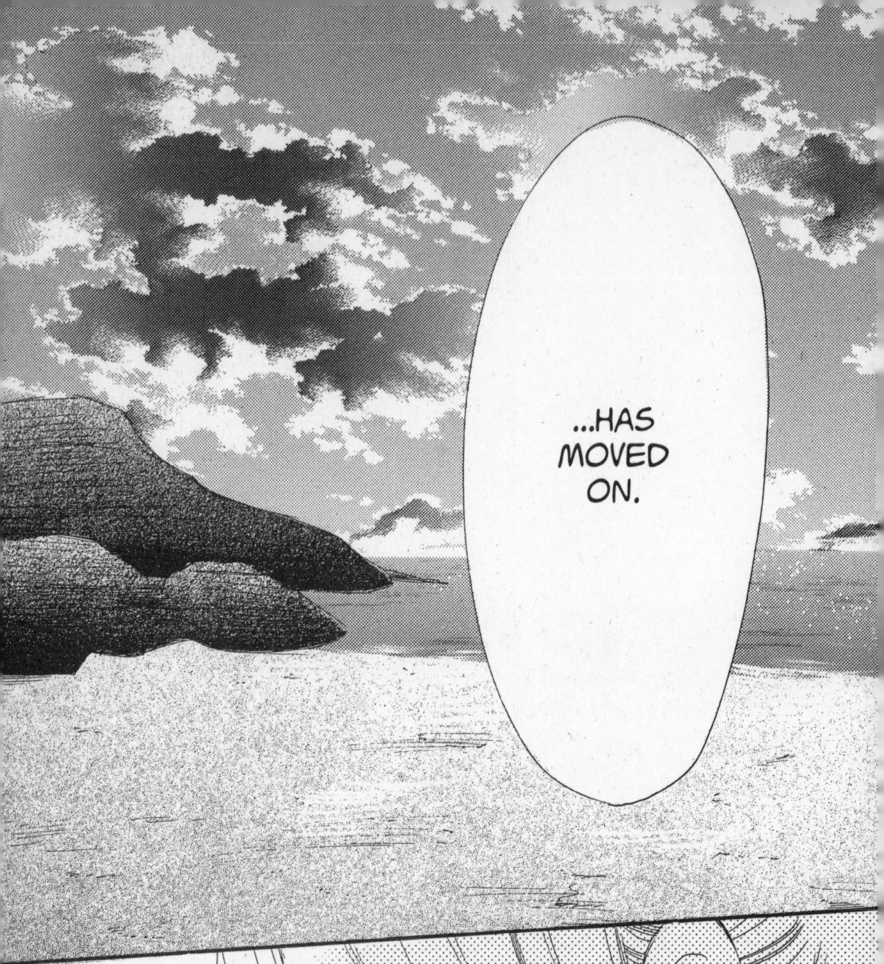
...HAS MOVED ON.
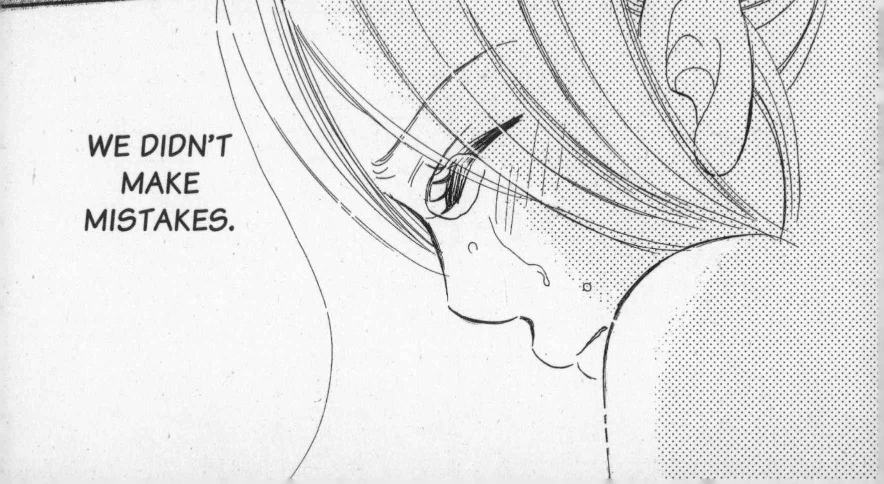
WE DIDN'T MAKE MISTAKES.

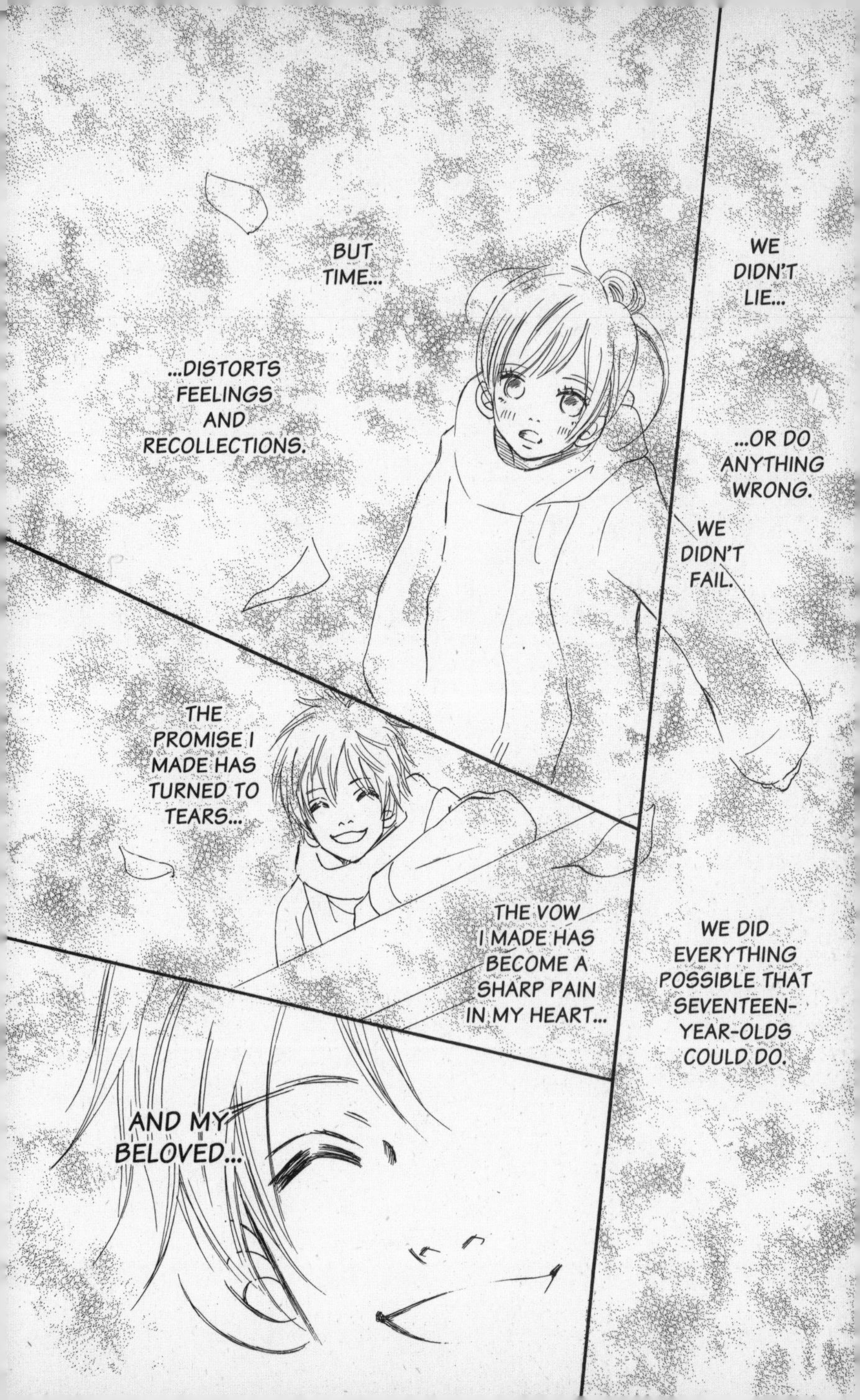
WE DIDN'T LIE...
...OR DO ANYTHING WRONG.
WE DIDN'T FAIL.
WE DID EVERYTHING POSSIBLE THAT SEVENTEEN-YEAR-OLDS COULD DO.
BUT TIME...
...DISTORTS FEELINGS AND RECOLLECTIONS.
THE PROMISE I MADE HAS TURNED TO TEARS...
THE VOW I MADE HAS BECOME A SHARP PAIN IN MY HEART...
AND MY BELOVED...

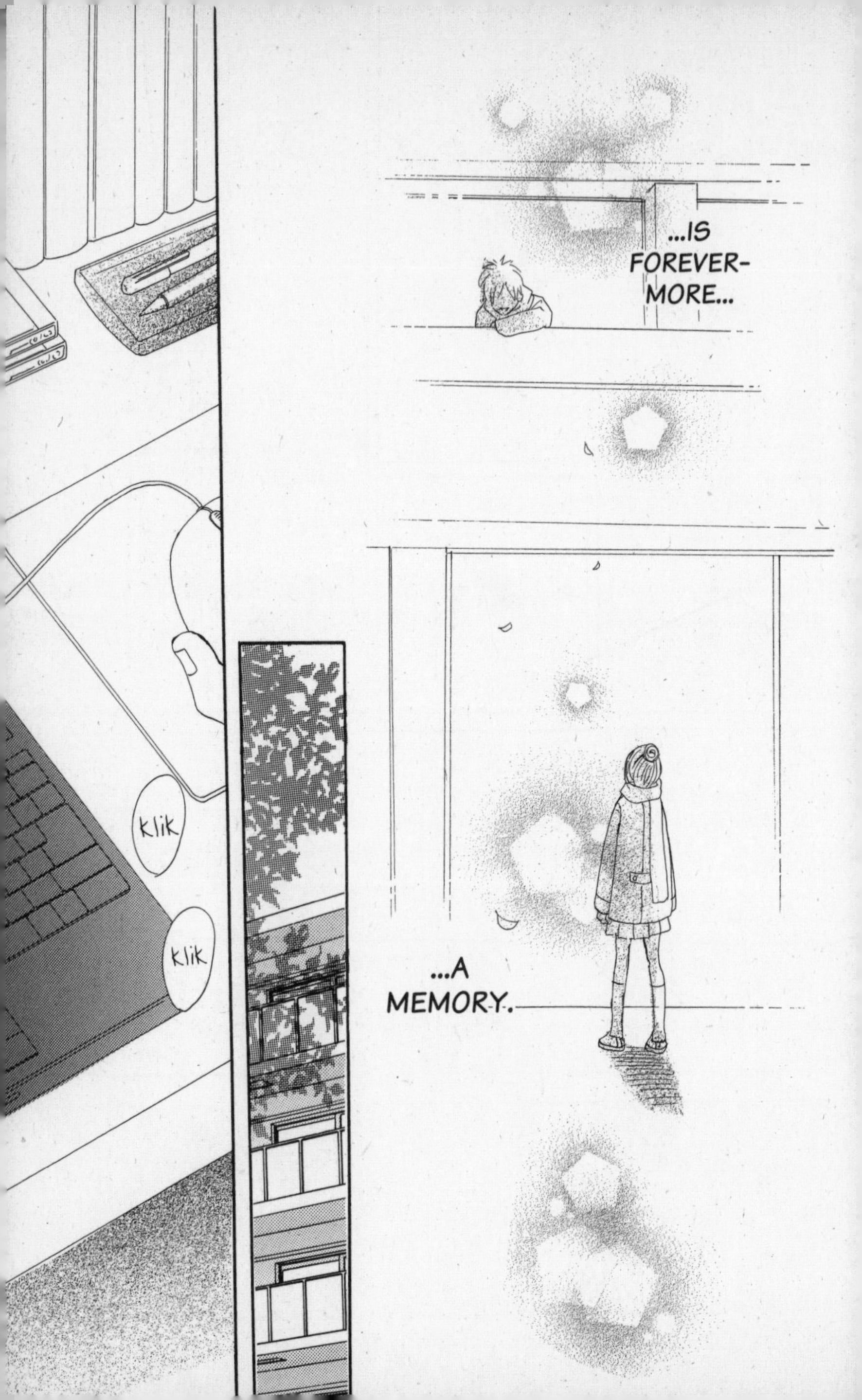
...IS FOREVER-MORE...
...A MEMORY.
klik
klik

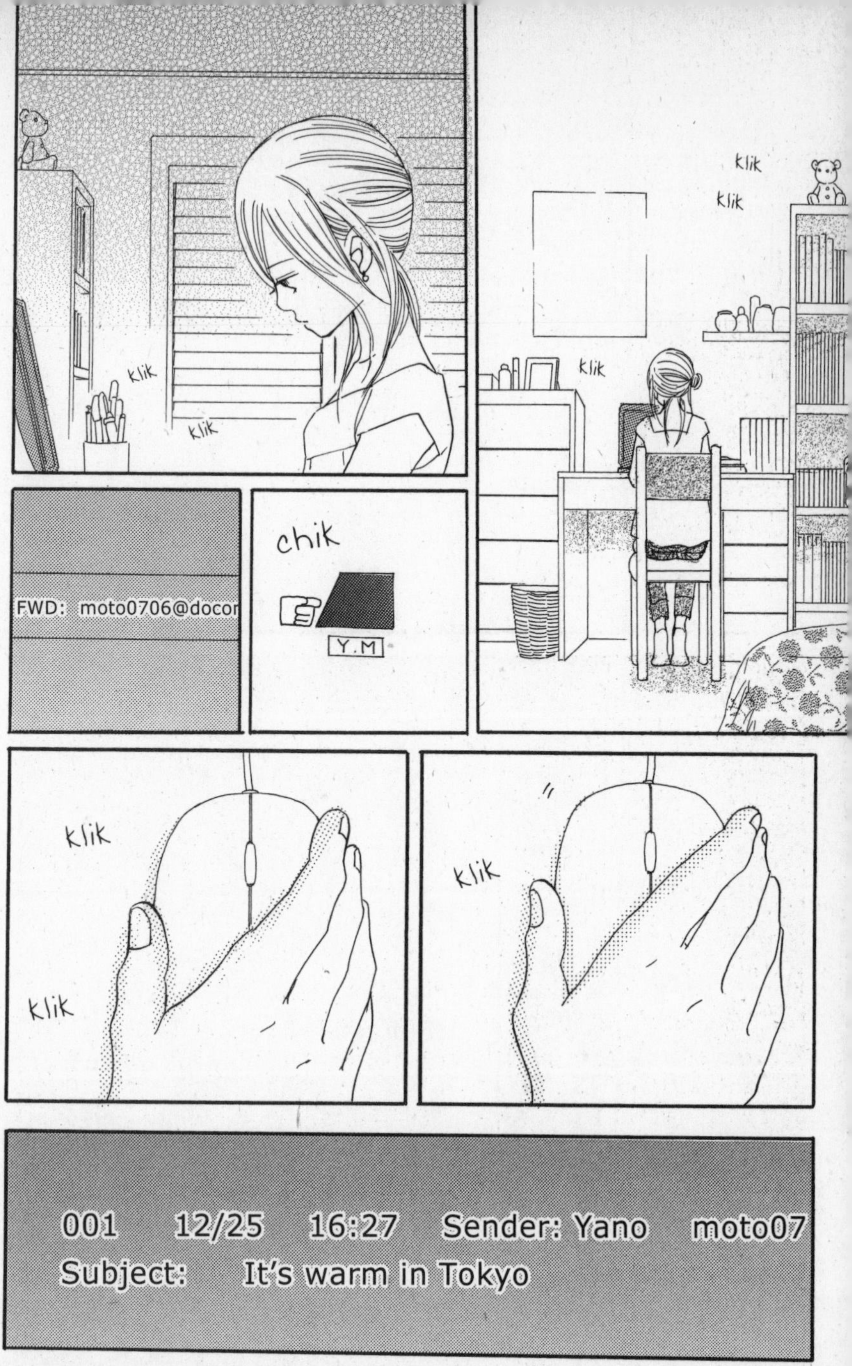
klik
klik
klik
klik
klik
chik
Y.M
FWD: moto0706@docor
klik
klik
klik
001 12/25 16:27 Sender: Yano moto07
Subject: It's warm in Tokyo

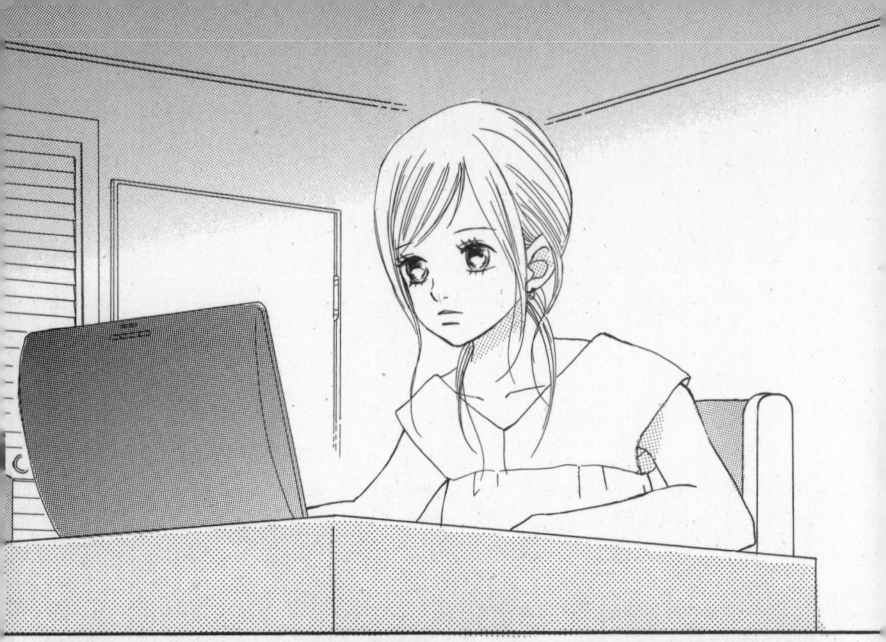

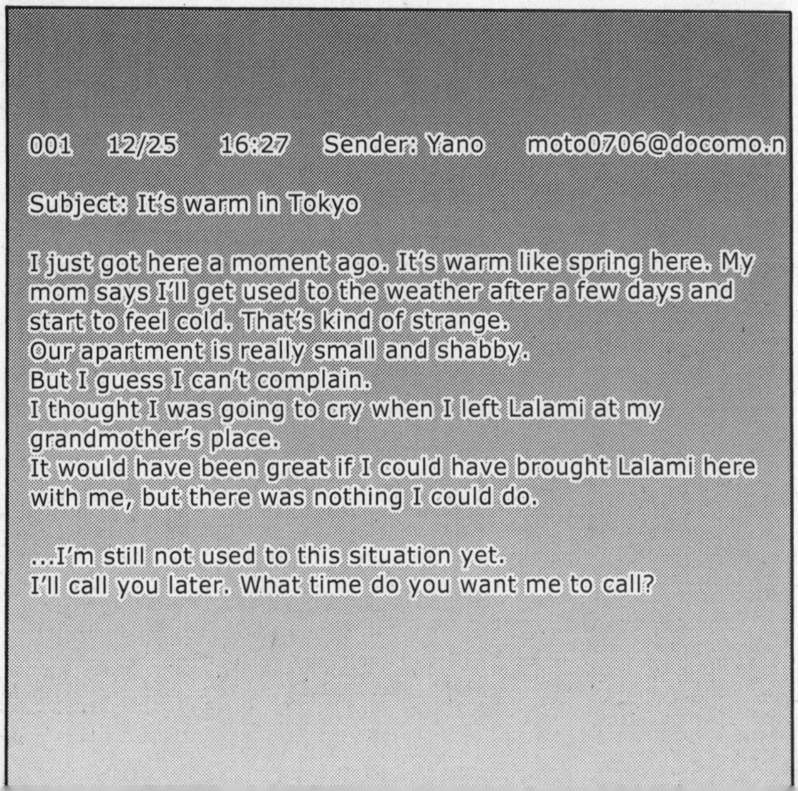
001 12/25 16:27 Sender: Yano moto0706@docomo.n
Subject: It's warm in Tokyo
I just got here a moment ago. It's warm like spring here. My mom says I'll get used to the weather after a few days and start to feel cold. That's kind of strange.
Our apartment is really small and shabby.
But I guess I can't complain.
I thought I was going to cry when I left Lalami at my grandmother's place.
It would have been great if I could have brought Lalami here with me, but there was nothing I could do.
...I'm still not used to this situation yet.
I'll call you later. What time do you want me to call?

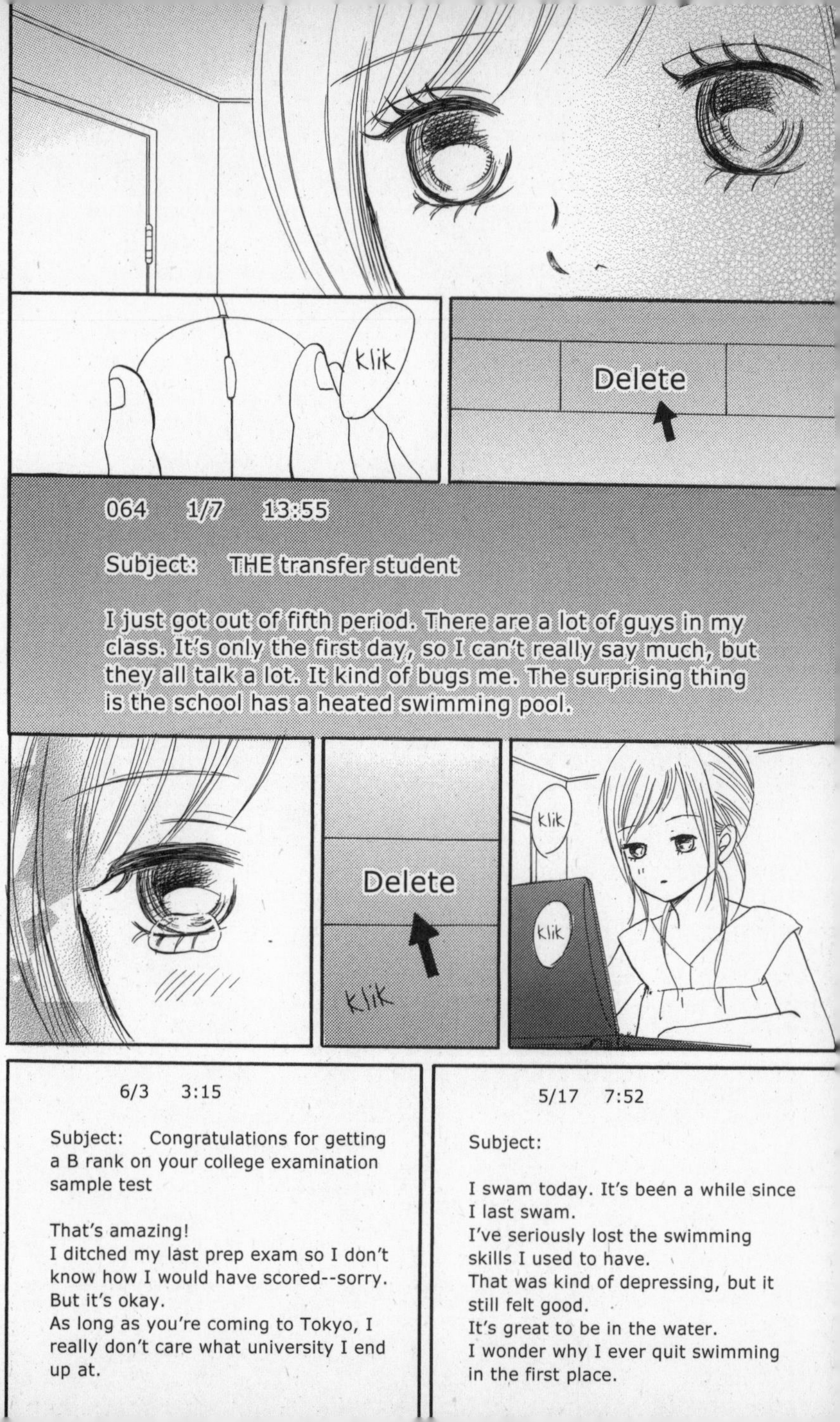
Delete
klik
064 1/7 13:55
Subject: THE transfer student
I just got out of fifth period. There are a lot of guys in my class. It's only the first day, so I can't really say much, but they all talk a lot. It kind of bugs me. The surprising thing is the school has a heated swimming pool.
klik
klik
Delete
klik
5/17 7:52
Subject:
I swam today. It's been a while since I last swam.
I've seriously lost the swimming skills I used to have.
That was kind of depressing, but it still felt good.
It's great to be in the water.
I wonder why I ever quit swimming in the first place.
6/3 3:15
Subject: Congratulations for getting a B rank on your college examination sample test
That's amazing!
I ditched my last prep exam so I don't know how I would have scored--sorry.
But it's okay.
As long as you're coming to Tokyo, I really don't care what university I end up at.

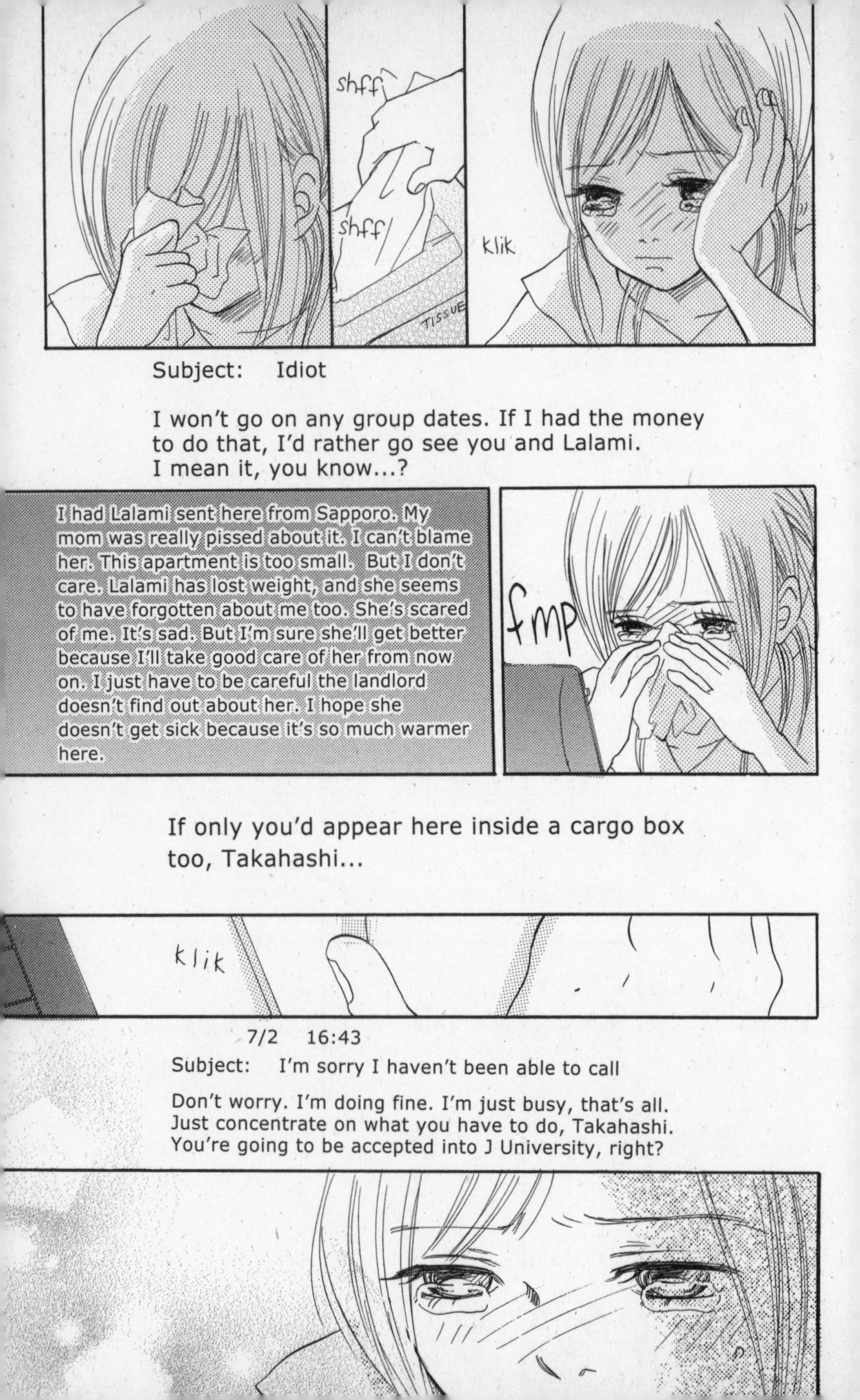
klik
shff
shff
TISSUE
Subject: Idiot
I won't go on any group dates. If I had the money to do that, I'd rather go see you and Lalami. I mean it, you know...?
fmp
I had Lalami sent here from Sapporo. My mom was really pissed about it. I can't blame her. This apartment is too small. But I don't care. Lalami has lost weight, and she seems to have forgotten about me too. She's scared of me. It's sad. But I'm sure she'll get better because I'll take good care of her from now on. I just have to be careful the landlord doesn't find out about her. I hope she doesn't get sick because it's so much warmer here.
If only you'd appear here inside a cargo box too, Takahashi...
klik
7/2 16:43
Subject: I'm sorry I haven't been able to call
Don't worry. I'm doing fine. I'm just busy, that's all. Just concentrate on what you have to do, Takahashi. You're going to be accepted into J University, right?

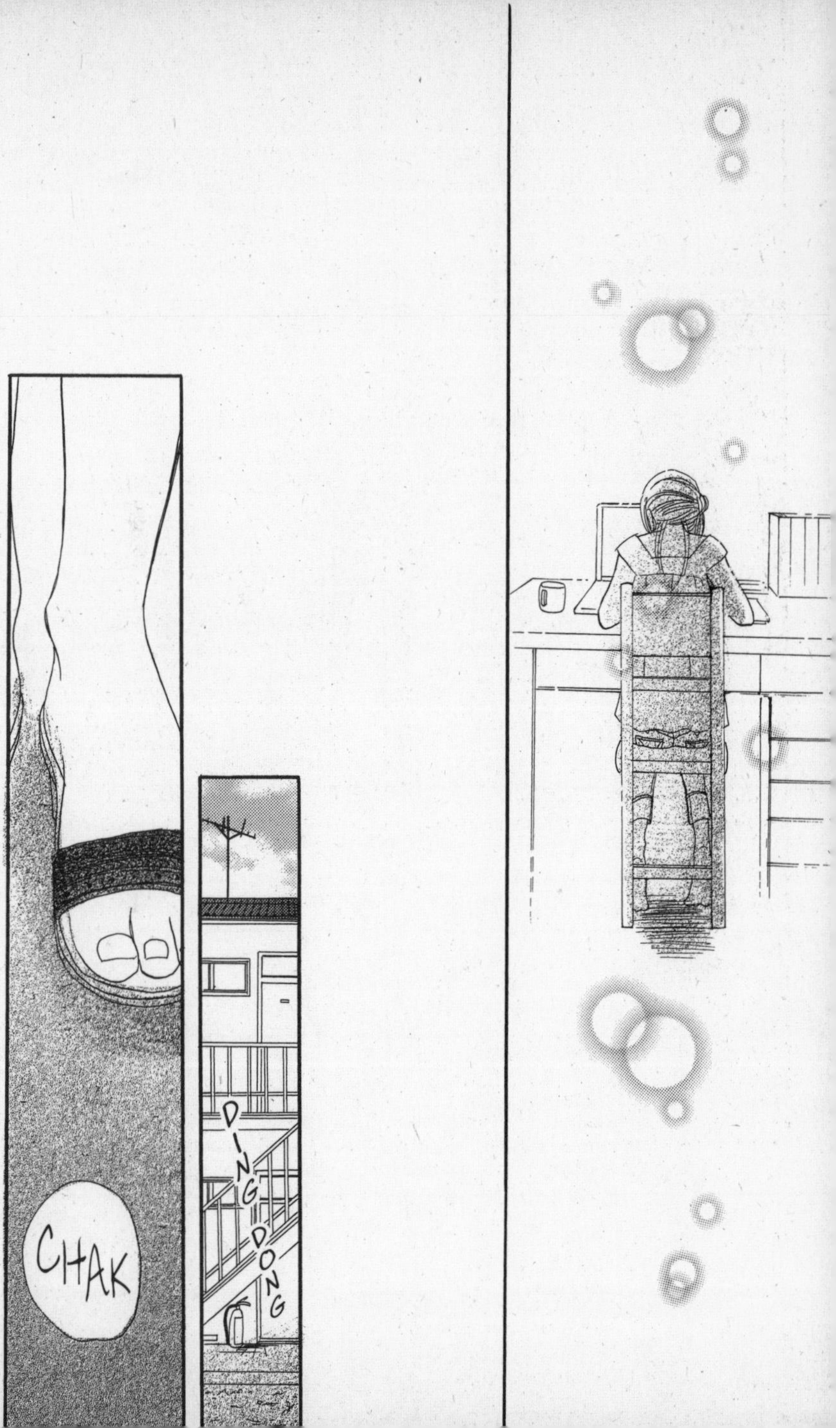
DING DONG
CHAK

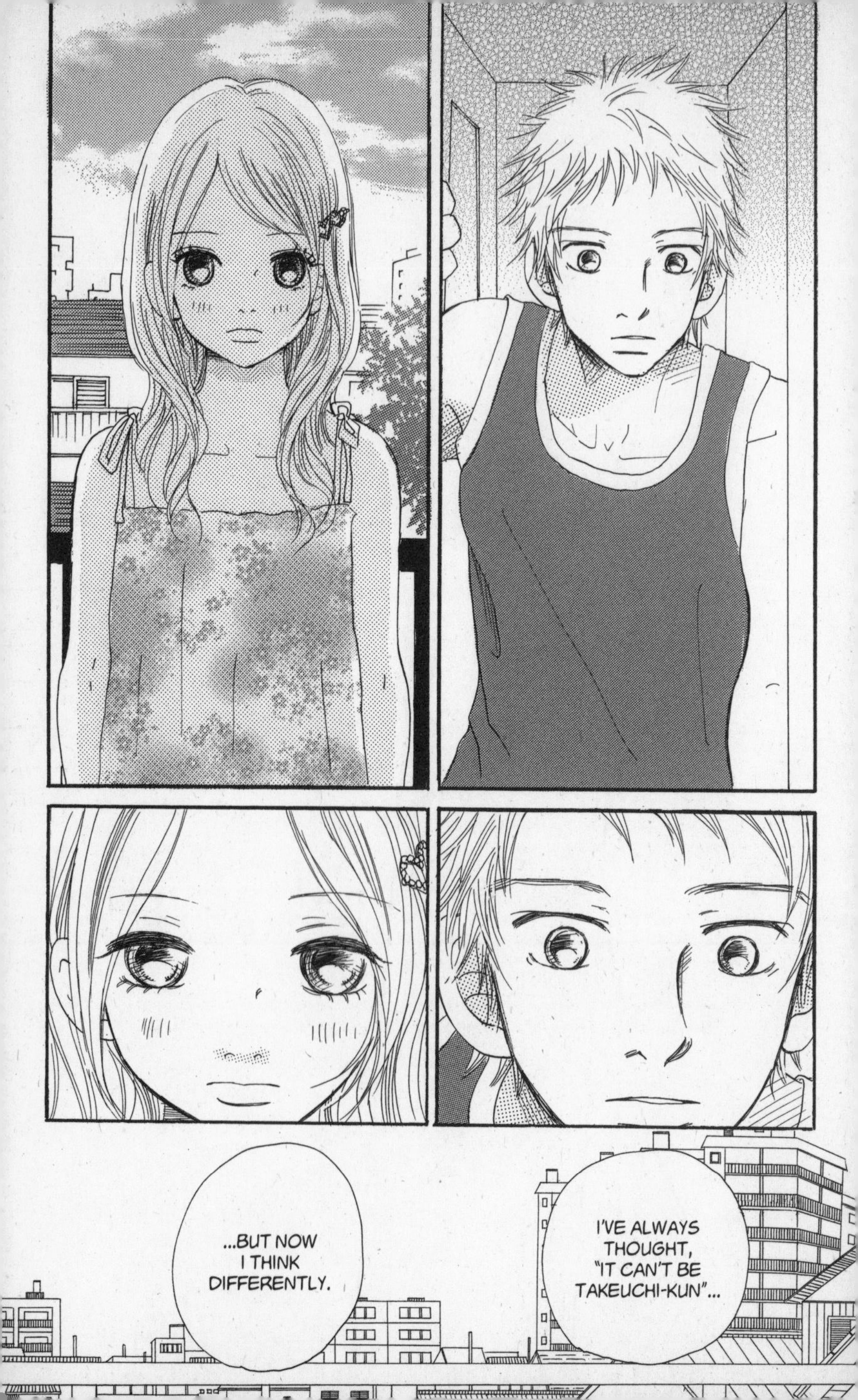
I'VE ALWAYS THOUGHT, "IT CAN'T BE TAKEUCHI-KUN"...
...BUT NOW I THINK DIFFERENTLY.

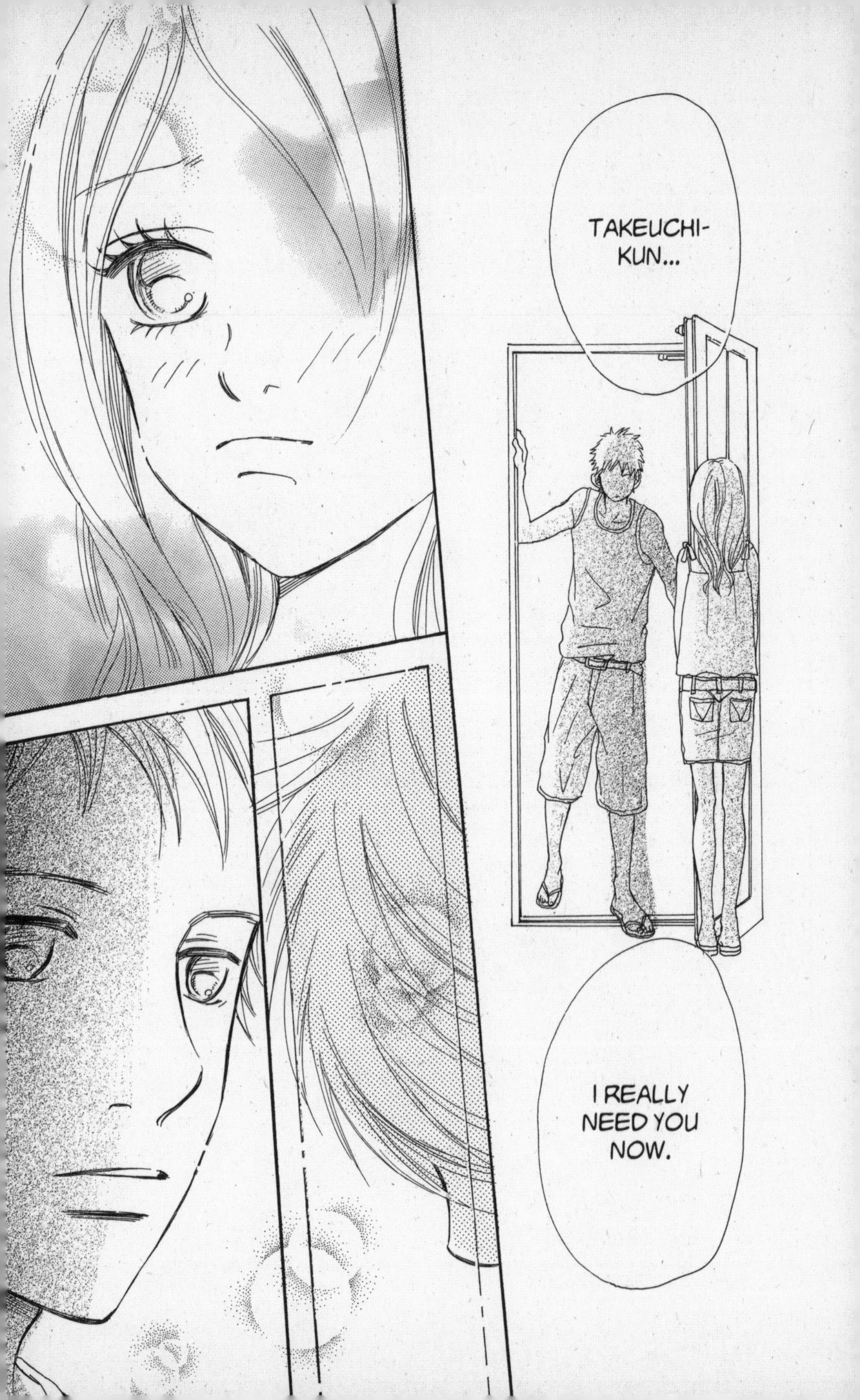
TAKEUCHI-KUN...
I REALLY NEED YOU NOW.

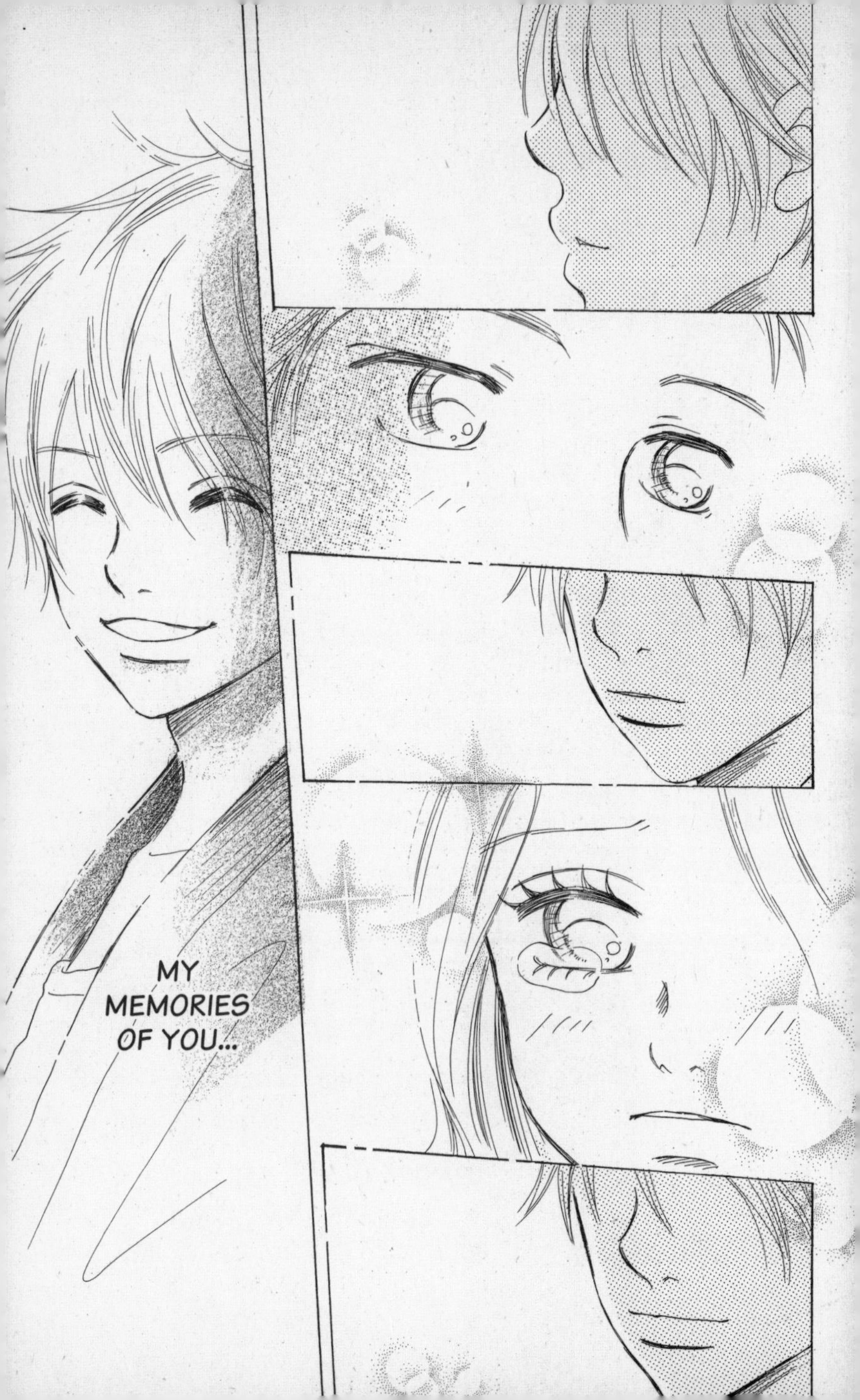
MY MEMORIES OF YOU...

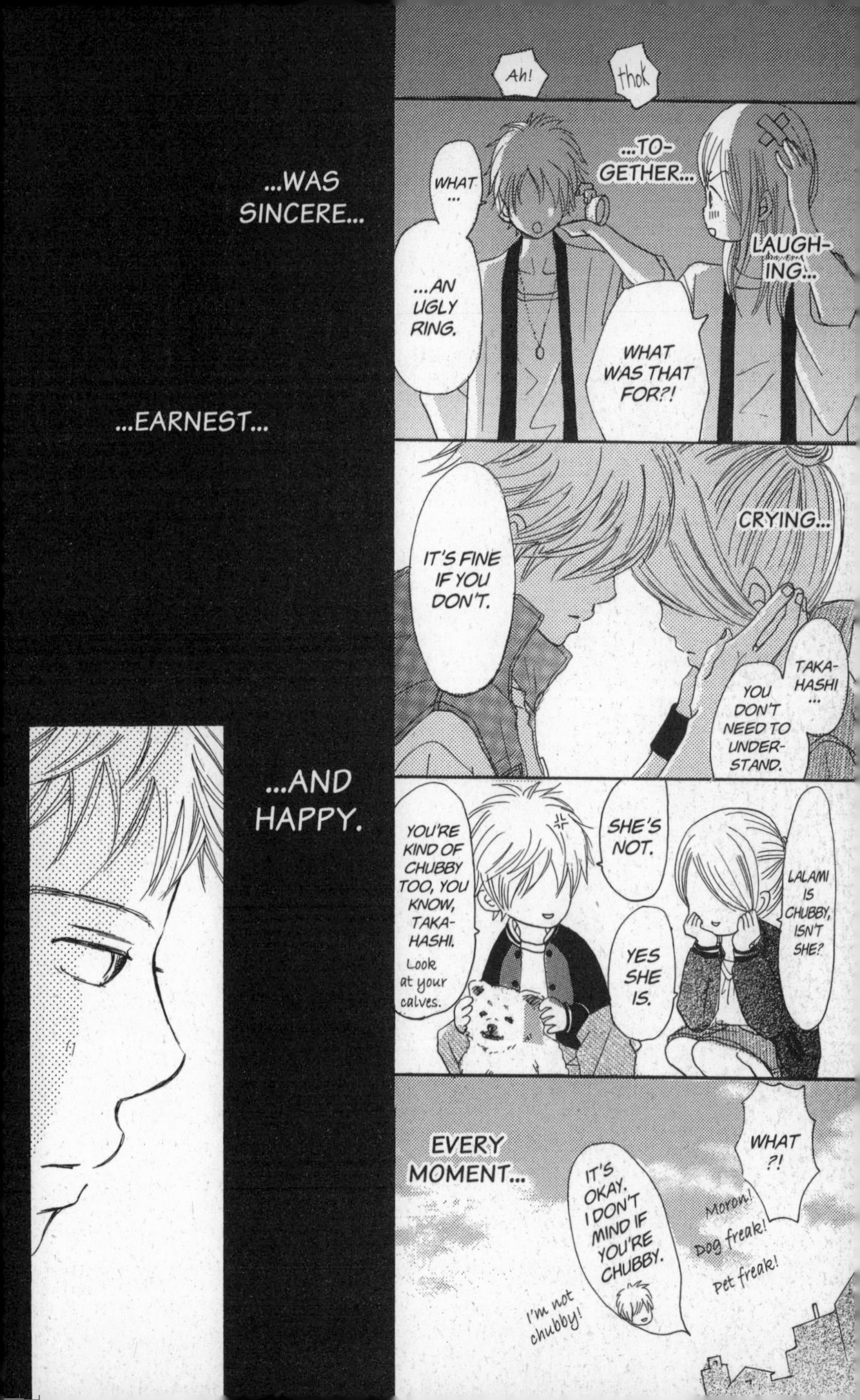
Ah!
thok
...TO-GETHER...
WHAT ...
LAUGH-ING...
...AN UGLY RING.
WHAT WAS THAT FOR?!
...WAS SINCERE...
CRYING...
IT'S FINE IF YOU DON'T.
TAKA-HASHI ...
YOU DON'T NEED TO UNDER-STAND.
...EARNEST...
LALAMI IS CHUBBY, ISN'T SHE?
SHE'S NOT.
YES SHE IS.
YOU'RE KIND OF CHUBBY TOO, YOU KNOW, TAKA-HASHI.
Look at your calves.
...AND HAPPY.
WHAT ?!
Moron!
Dog freak!
Pet freak!
IT'S OKAY. I DON'T MIND IF YOU'RE CHUBBY.
I'm not chubby!
EVERY MOMENT...

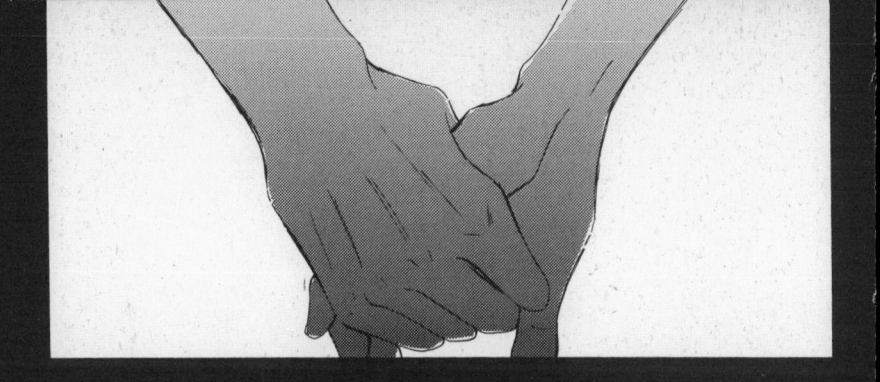

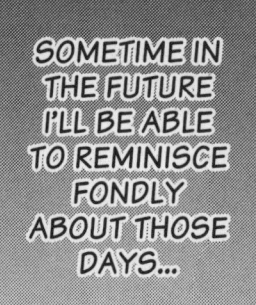

SOMETIME IN
THE FUTURE
I'LL BE ABLE
TO REMINISCE
FONDLY
ABOUT THOSE
DAYS...

# Chapter 34

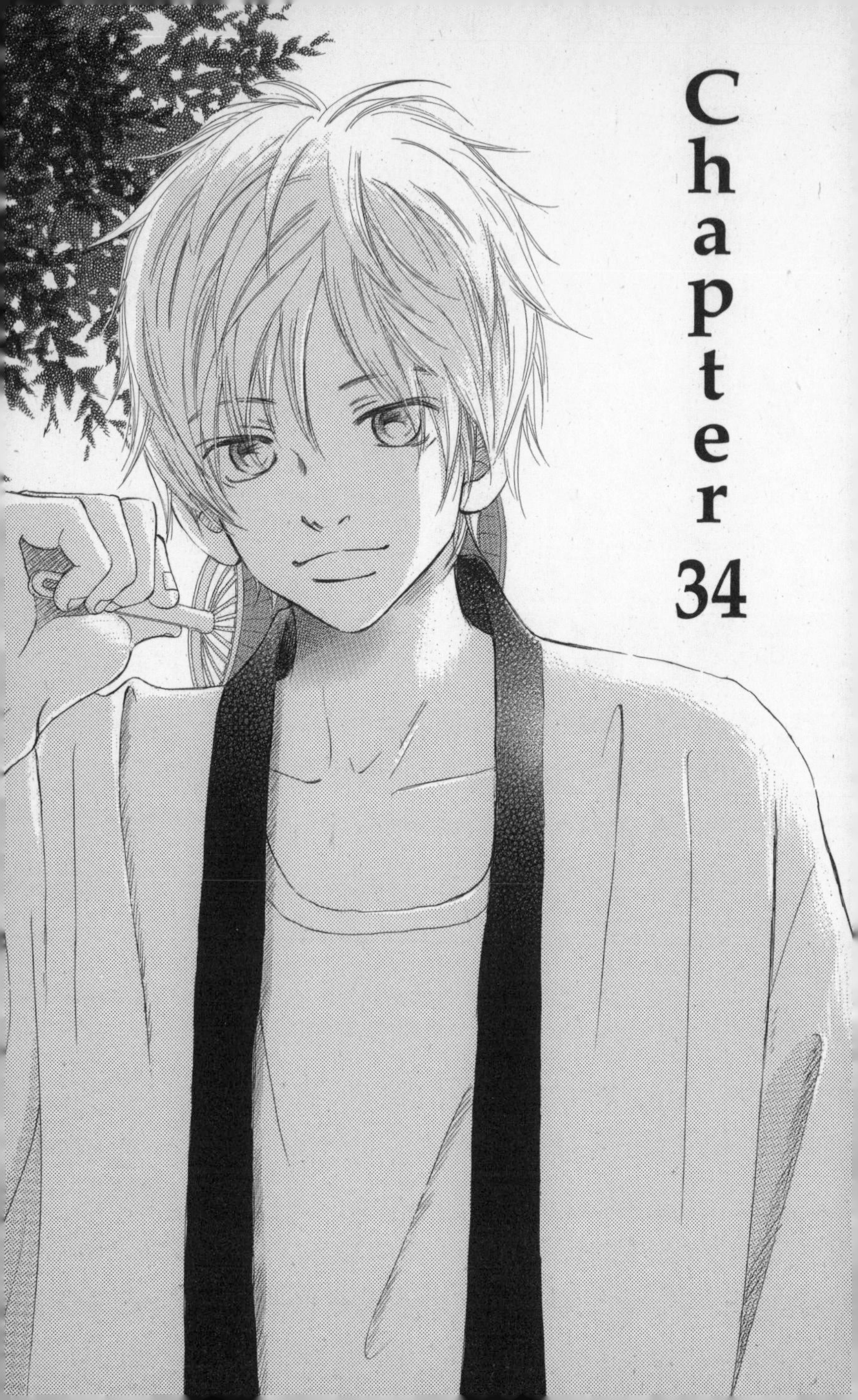

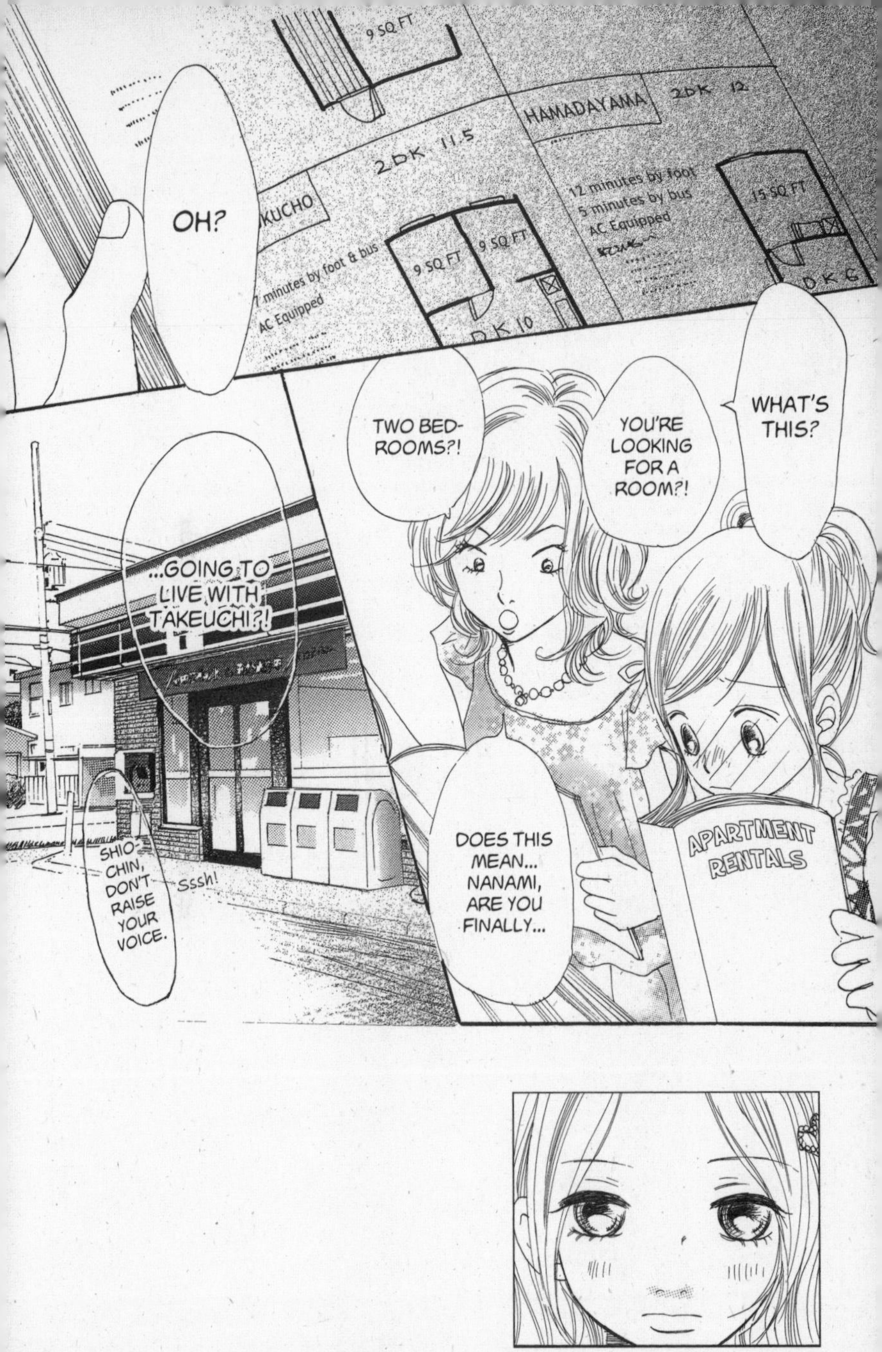
9 SQ FT
HAMADAYAMA
2DK 12
2DK 11.5
12 minutes by foot
5 minutes by bus
AC Equipped
15 SQ FT
DK 6
KUCHO
OH?
9 SQ FT
9 SQ FT
7 minutes by foot & bus
AC Equipped
DK 10
WHAT'S THIS?
YOU'RE LOOKING FOR A ROOM?!
TWO BED-ROOMS?!
APARTMENT RENTALS
DOES THIS MEAN... NANAMI, ARE YOU FINALLY...
...GOING TO LIVE WITH TAKEUCHI?!
SHIO-CHIN, DON'T RAISE YOUR VOICE.
Sssh!

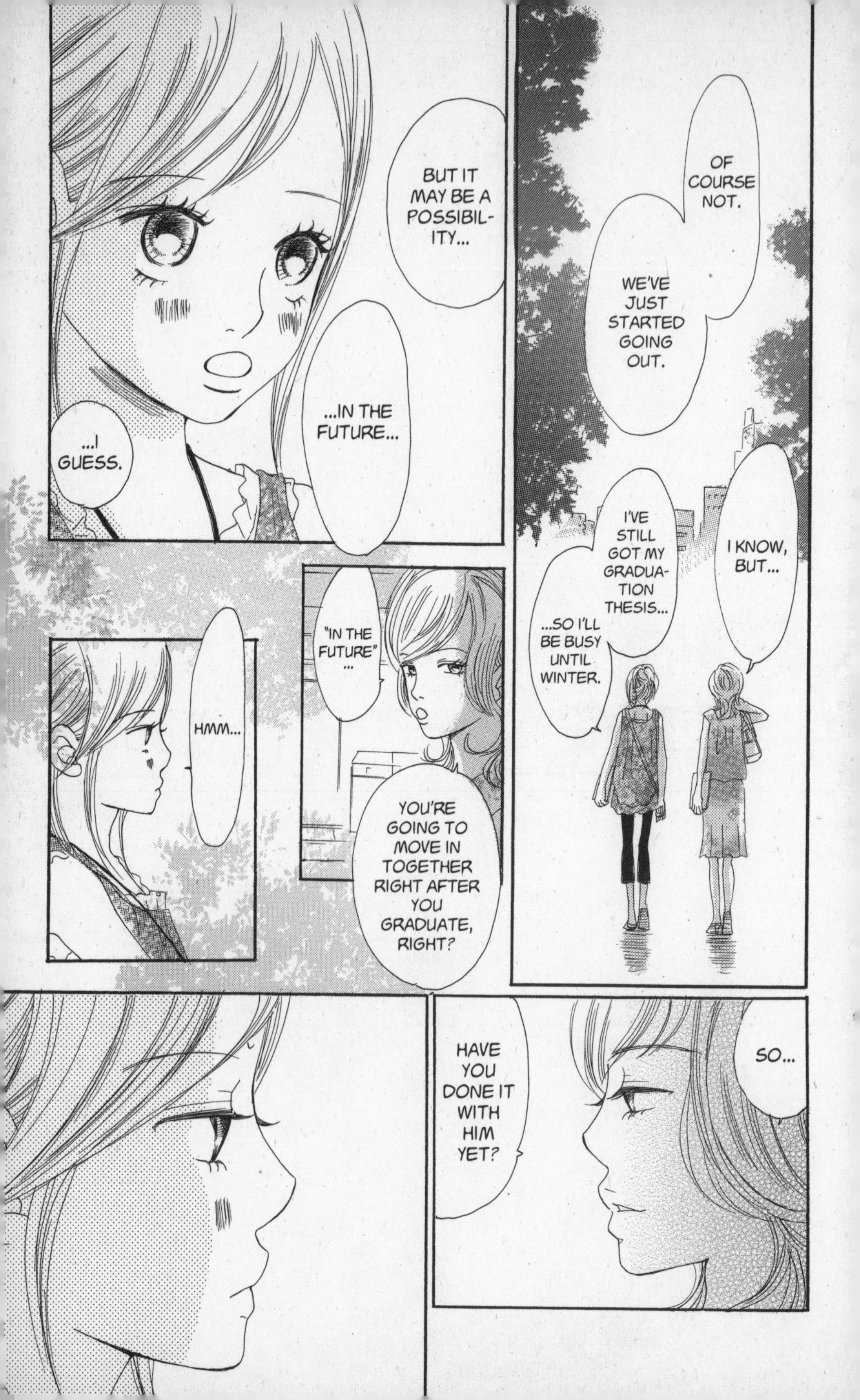
OF COURSE NOT.
WE'VE JUST STARTED GOING OUT.
I KNOW, BUT...
I'VE STILL GOT MY GRADUATION THESIS...
...SO I'LL BE BUSY UNTIL WINTER.
YOU'RE GOING TO MOVE IN TOGETHER RIGHT AFTER YOU GRADUATE, RIGHT?
"IN THE FUTURE"...
HMM...
BUT IT MAY BE A POSSIBILITY...
...IN THE FUTURE...
...I GUESS.
SO...
HAVE YOU DONE IT WITH HIM YET?

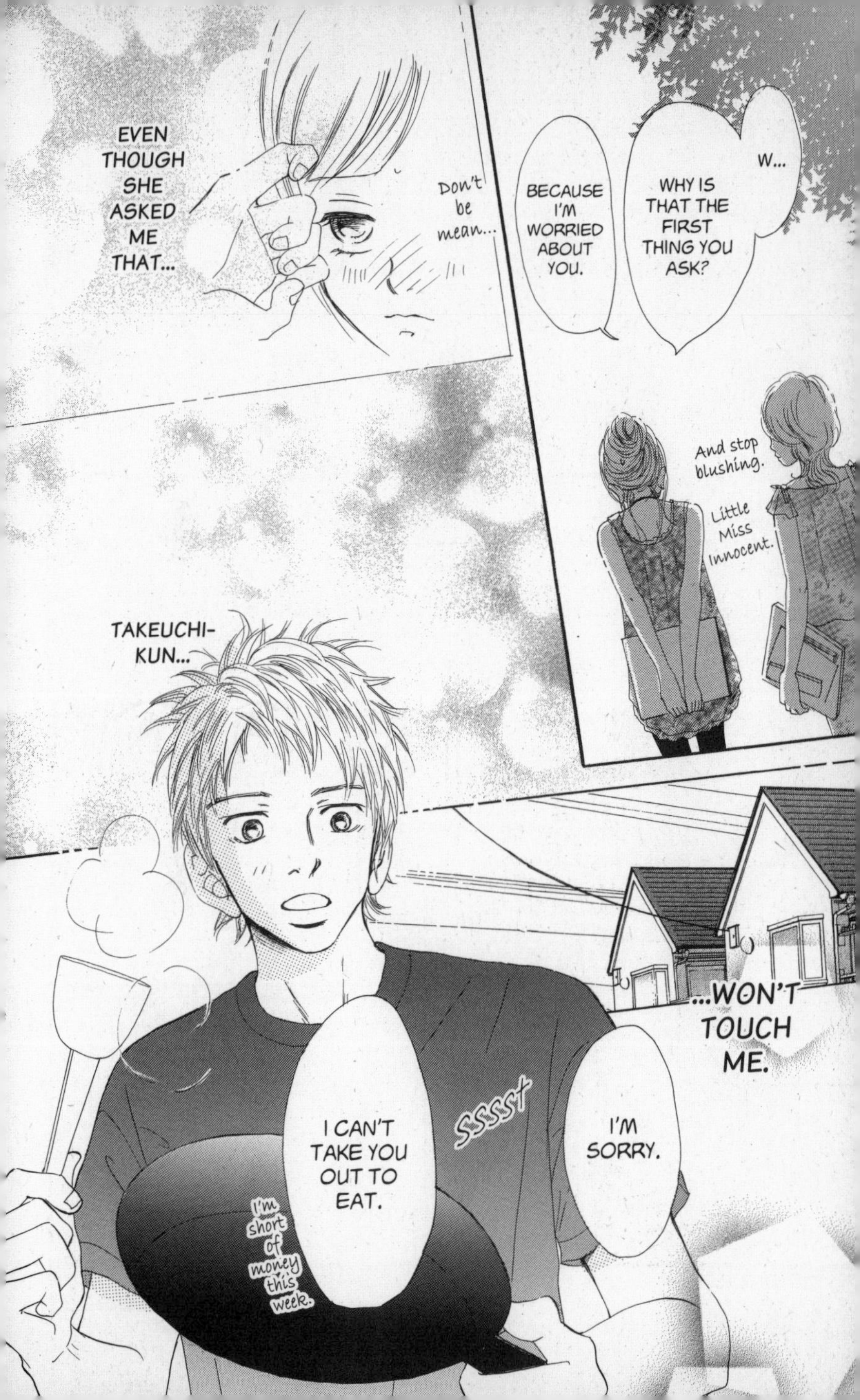
W...
WHY IS THAT THE FIRST THING YOU ASK?
BECAUSE I'M WORRIED ABOUT YOU.
Don't be mean...
EVEN THOUGH SHE ASKED ME THAT...
And stop blushing.
Little Miss Innocent.
TAKEUCHI-KUN...
...WON'T TOUCH ME.
I'M SORRY.
SSSST
I CAN'T TAKE YOU OUT TO EAT.
I'm short of money this week.

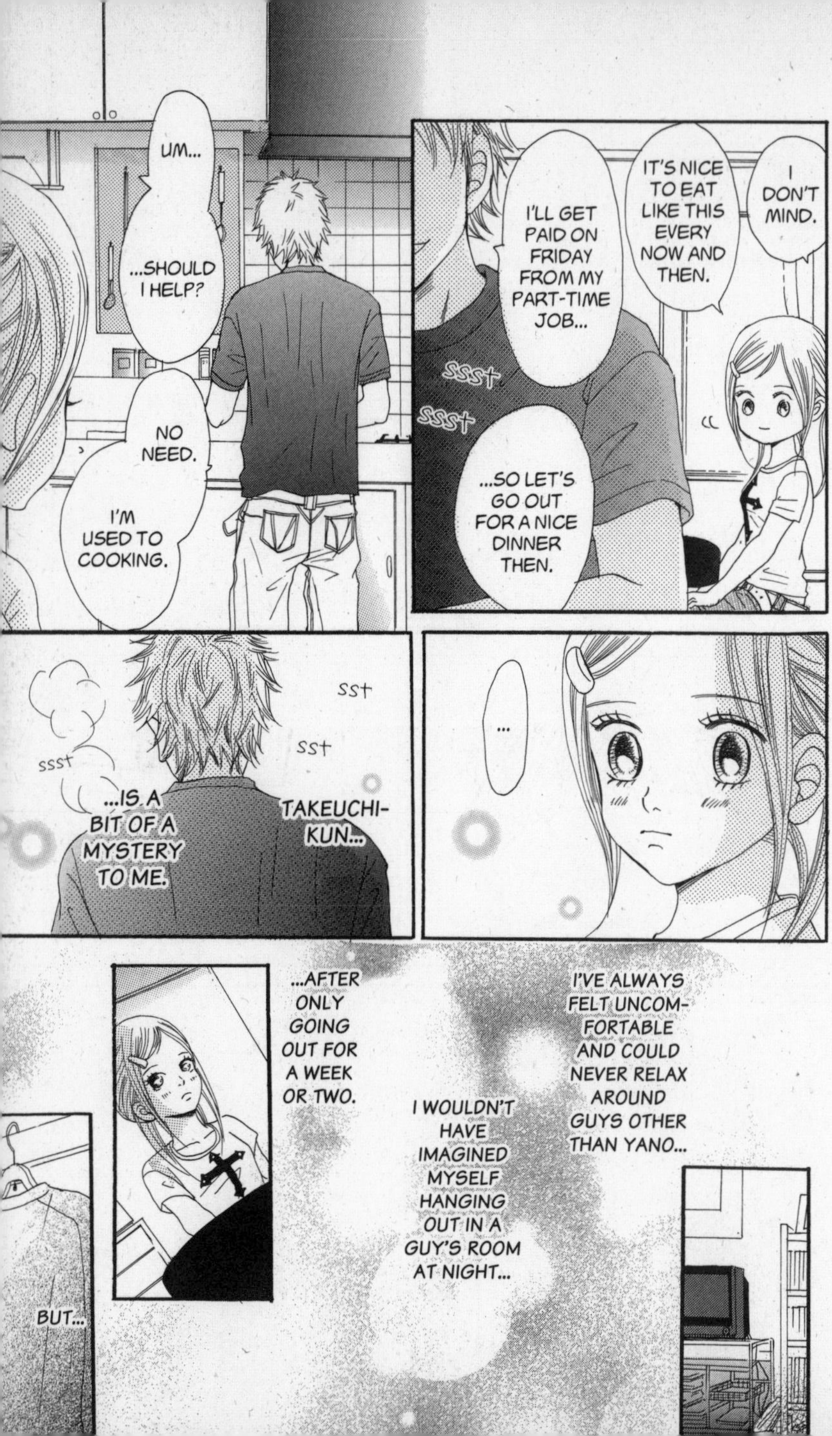
I DON'T MIND.
IT'S NICE TO EAT LIKE THIS EVERY NOW AND THEN.
I'LL GET PAID ON FRIDAY FROM MY PART-TIME JOB...
SSST
SSST
...SO LET'S GO OUT FOR A NICE DINNER THEN.
UM...
...SHOULD I HELP?
NO NEED.
I'M USED TO COOKING.
...
SST
SST
TAKEUCHI-KUN...
SSST
...IS A BIT OF A MYSTERY TO ME.
I'VE ALWAYS FELT UNCOM-FORTABLE AND COULD NEVER RELAX AROUND GUYS OTHER THAN YANO...
I WOULDN'T HAVE IMAGINED MYSELF HANGING OUT IN A GUY'S ROOM AT NIGHT...
...AFTER ONLY GOING OUT FOR A WEEK OR TWO.
BUT...

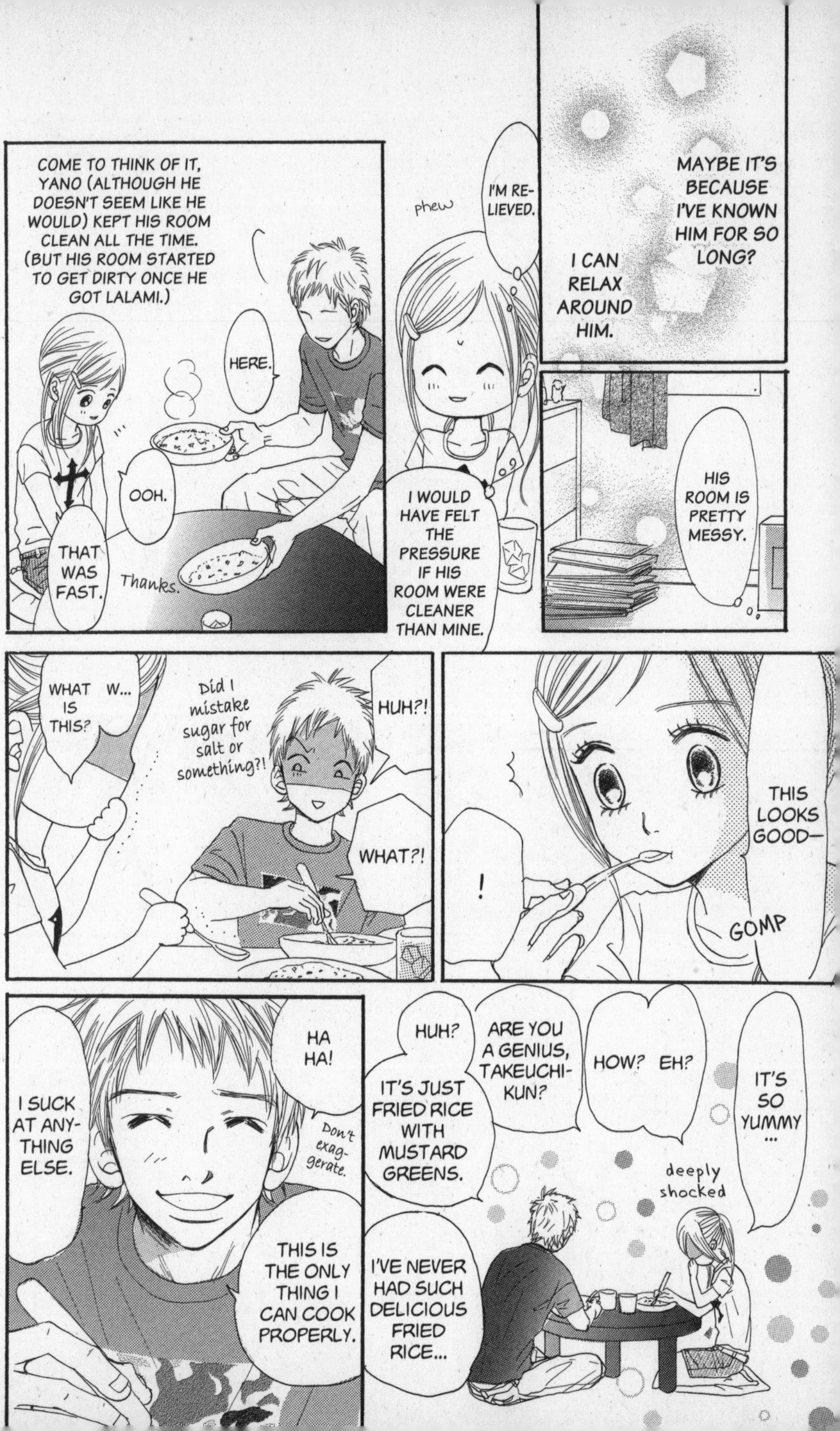
MAYBE IT'S BECAUSE I'VE KNOWN HIM FOR SO LONG?
I CAN RELAX AROUND HIM.
I'M RE-LIEVED.
phew
COME TO THINK OF IT, YANO (ALTHOUGH HE DOESN'T SEEM LIKE HE WOULD) KEPT HIS ROOM CLEAN ALL THE TIME. (BUT HIS ROOM STARTED TO GET DIRTY ONCE HE GOT LALAMI.)
HIS ROOM IS PRETTY MESSY.
I WOULD HAVE FELT THE PRESSURE IF HIS ROOM WERE CLEANER THAN MINE.
HERE.
OOH.
THAT WAS FAST.
Thanks.
THIS LOOKS GOOD—
GOMP
!
HUH?!
WHAT?!
Did I mistake sugar for salt or something?!
W...
WHAT IS THIS?
IT'S SO YUMMY...
deeply shocked
HOW? EH?
HUH?
ARE YOU A GENIUS, TAKEUCHI-KUN?
I'VE NEVER HAD SUCH DELICIOUS FRIED RICE...
IT'S JUST FRIED RICE WITH MUSTARD GREENS.
Don't exag-gerate.
HA HA!
THIS IS THE ONLY THING I CAN COOK PROPERLY.
I SUCK AT ANY-THING ELSE.

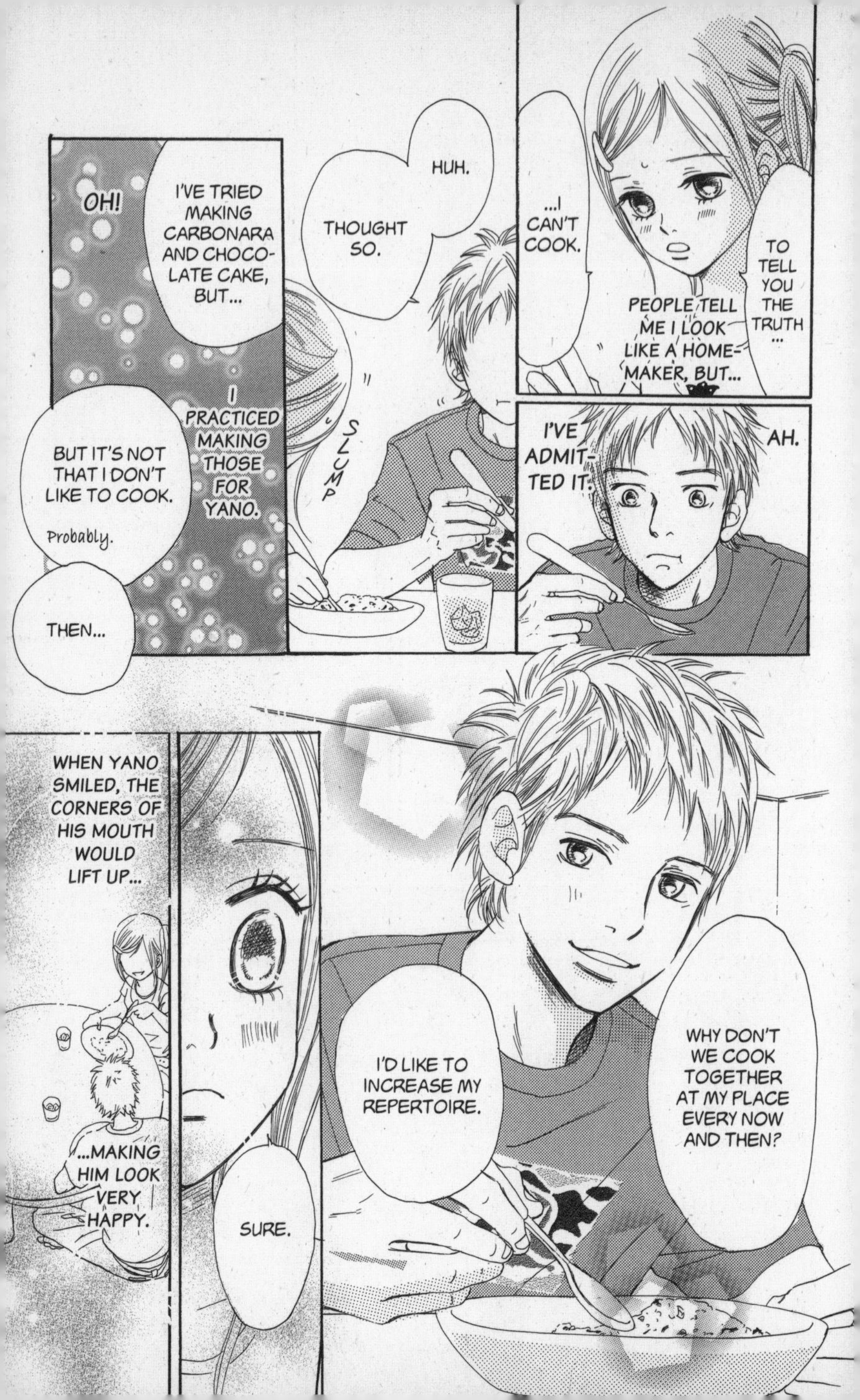
TO TELL YOU THE TRUTH...
PEOPLE TELL ME I LOOK LIKE A HOME-MAKER, BUT...
...I CAN'T COOK.
AH.
I'VE ADMITTED IT.
HUH.
THOUGHT SO.
SLUMP
OH!
I'VE TRIED MAKING CARBONARA AND CHOCOLATE CAKE, BUT...
I PRACTICED MAKING THOSE FOR YANO.
BUT IT'S NOT THAT I DON'T LIKE TO COOK.
Probably.
THEN...
WHY DON'T WE COOK TOGETHER AT MY PLACE EVERY NOW AND THEN?
I'D LIKE TO INCREASE MY REPERTOIRE.
SURE.
WHEN YANO SMILED, THE CORNERS OF HIS MOUTH WOULD LIFT UP...
...MAKING HIM LOOK VERY HAPPY.

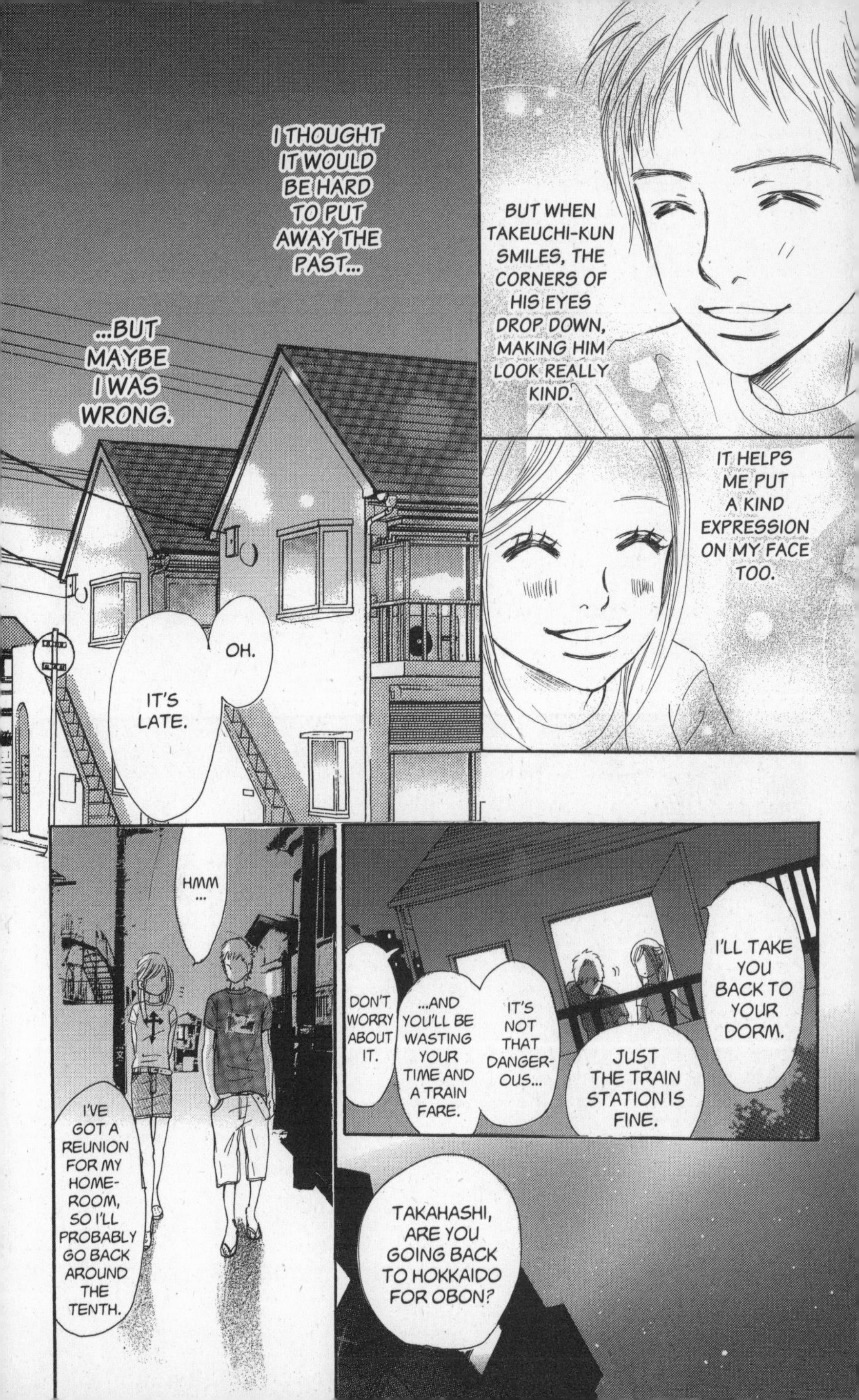
BUT WHEN TAKEUCHI-KUN SMILES, THE CORNERS OF HIS EYES DROP DOWN, MAKING HIM LOOK REALLY KIND.
IT HELPS ME PUT A KIND EXPRESSION ON MY FACE TOO.
I THOUGHT IT WOULD BE HARD TO PUT AWAY THE PAST...
...BUT MAYBE I WAS WRONG.
OH.
IT'S LATE.
I'LL TAKE YOU BACK TO YOUR DORM.
JUST THE TRAIN STATION IS FINE.
IT'S NOT THAT DANGER-OUS...
...AND YOU'LL BE WASTING YOUR TIME AND A TRAIN FARE.
DON'T WORRY ABOUT IT.
TAKAHASHI, ARE YOU GOING BACK TO HOKKAIDO FOR OBON?
HMM ...
I'VE GOT A REUNION FOR MY HOME-ROOM, SO I'LL PROBABLY GO BACK AROUND THE TENTH.

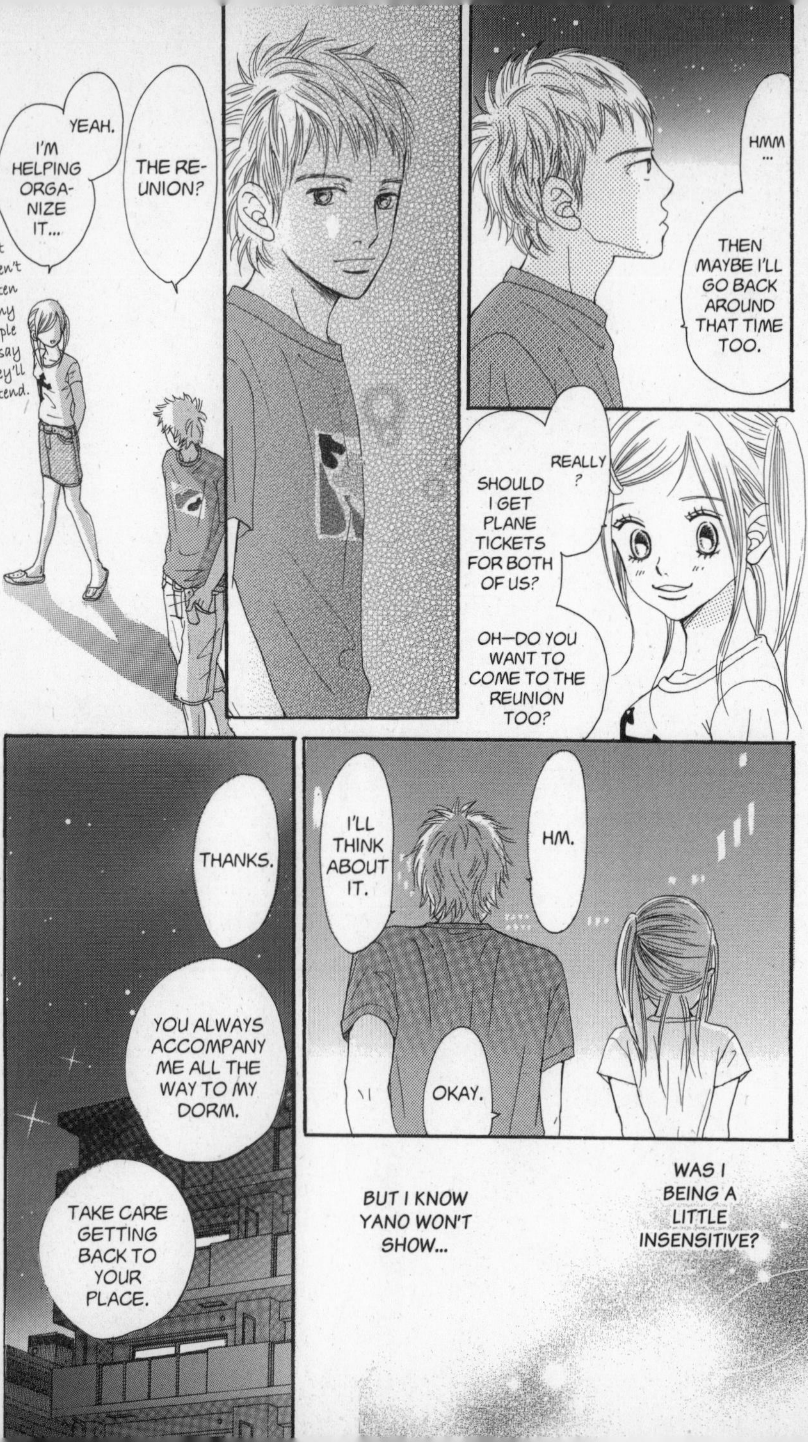
HMM ...
THEN MAYBE I'LL GO BACK AROUND THAT TIME TOO.
REALLY ?
SHOULD I GET PLANE TICKETS FOR BOTH OF US?
OH—DO YOU WANT TO COME TO THE REUNION TOO?
THE RE-UNION?
YEAH. I'M HELPING ORGA-NIZE IT...
...but I haven't gotten many people to say they'll attend.
HM.
I'LL THINK ABOUT IT.
OKAY.
THANKS.
YOU ALWAYS ACCOMPANY ME ALL THE WAY TO MY DORM.
TAKE CARE GETTING BACK TO YOUR PLACE.
WAS I BEING A LITTLE INSENSITIVE?
BUT I KNOW YANO WON'T SHOW...

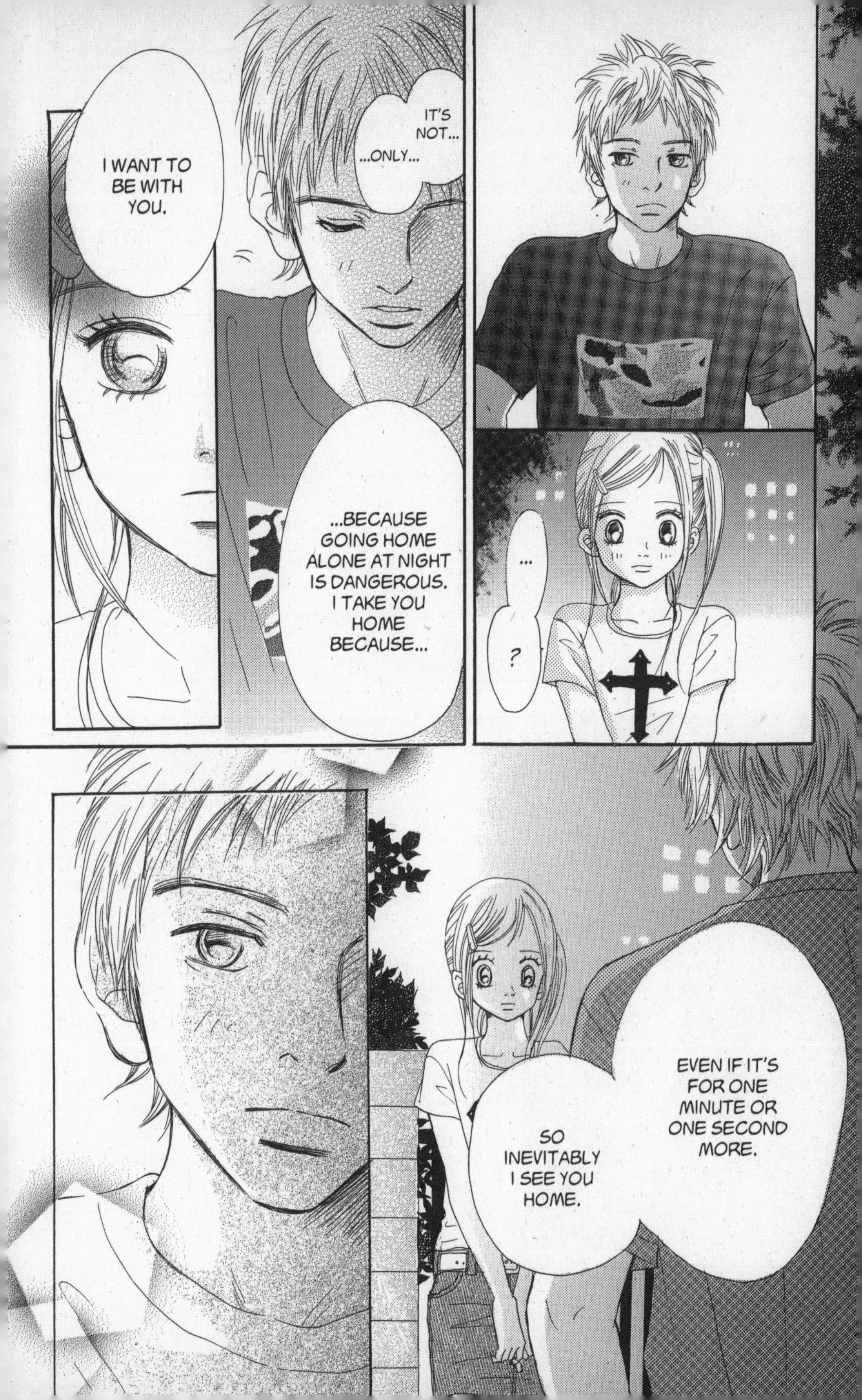
...
?
IT'S NOT...
...ONLY...
...BECAUSE GOING HOME ALONE AT NIGHT IS DANGEROUS. I TAKE YOU HOME BECAUSE...
I WANT TO BE WITH YOU.
EVEN IF IT'S FOR ONE MINUTE OR ONE SECOND MORE.
SO INEVITABLY I SEE YOU HOME.

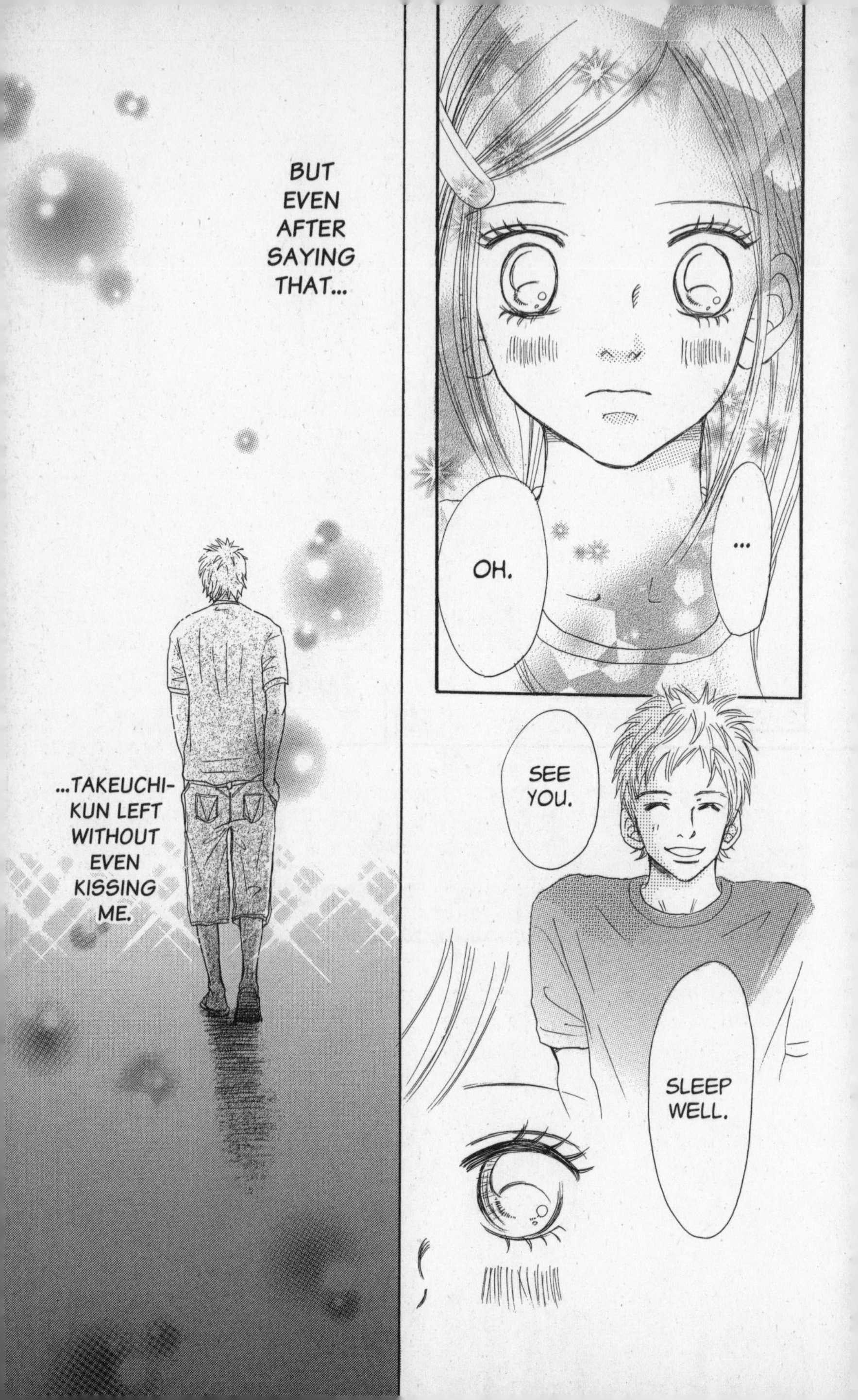
...
OH.
SEE YOU.
SLEEP WELL.
BUT EVEN AFTER SAYING THAT...
...TAKEUCHI-KUN LEFT WITHOUT EVEN KISSING ME.

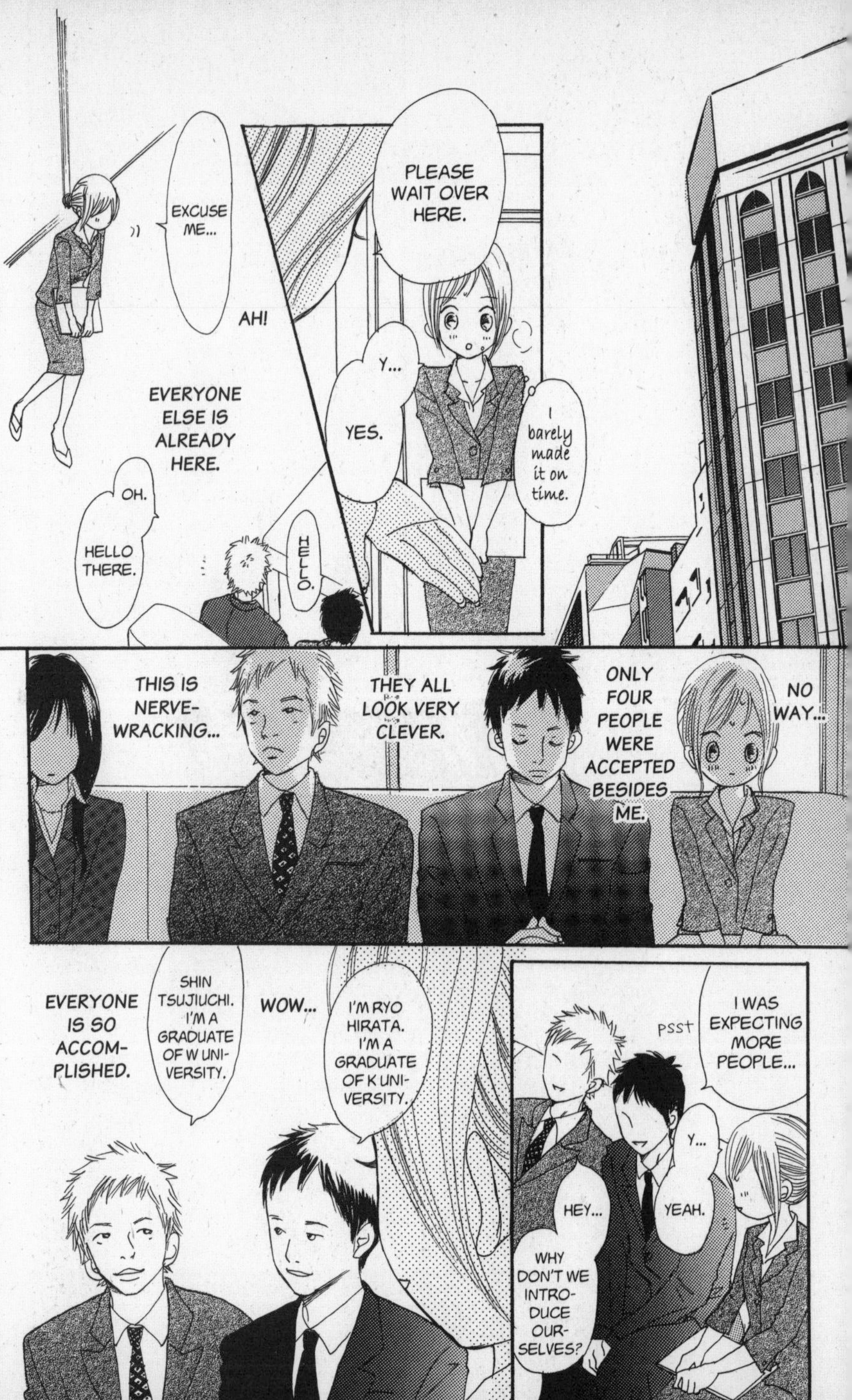
PLEASE WAIT OVER HERE.
Y...
YES.
I barely made it on time.
EXCUSE ME...
AH!
EVERYONE ELSE IS ALREADY HERE.
OH.
HELLO THERE.
HELLO.
NO WAY...
ONLY FOUR PEOPLE WERE ACCEPTED BESIDES ME.
THEY ALL LOOK VERY CLEVER.
THIS IS NERVE-WRACKING...
psst
I WAS EXPECTING MORE PEOPLE...
Y...
YEAH.
HEY...
WHY DON'T WE INTRODUCE OURSELVES?
I'M RYO HIRATA. I'M A GRADUATE OF K UNIVERSITY.
WOW...
SHIN TSUJIUCHI. I'M A GRADUATE OF W UNIVERSITY.
EVERYONE IS SO ACCOMPLISHED.

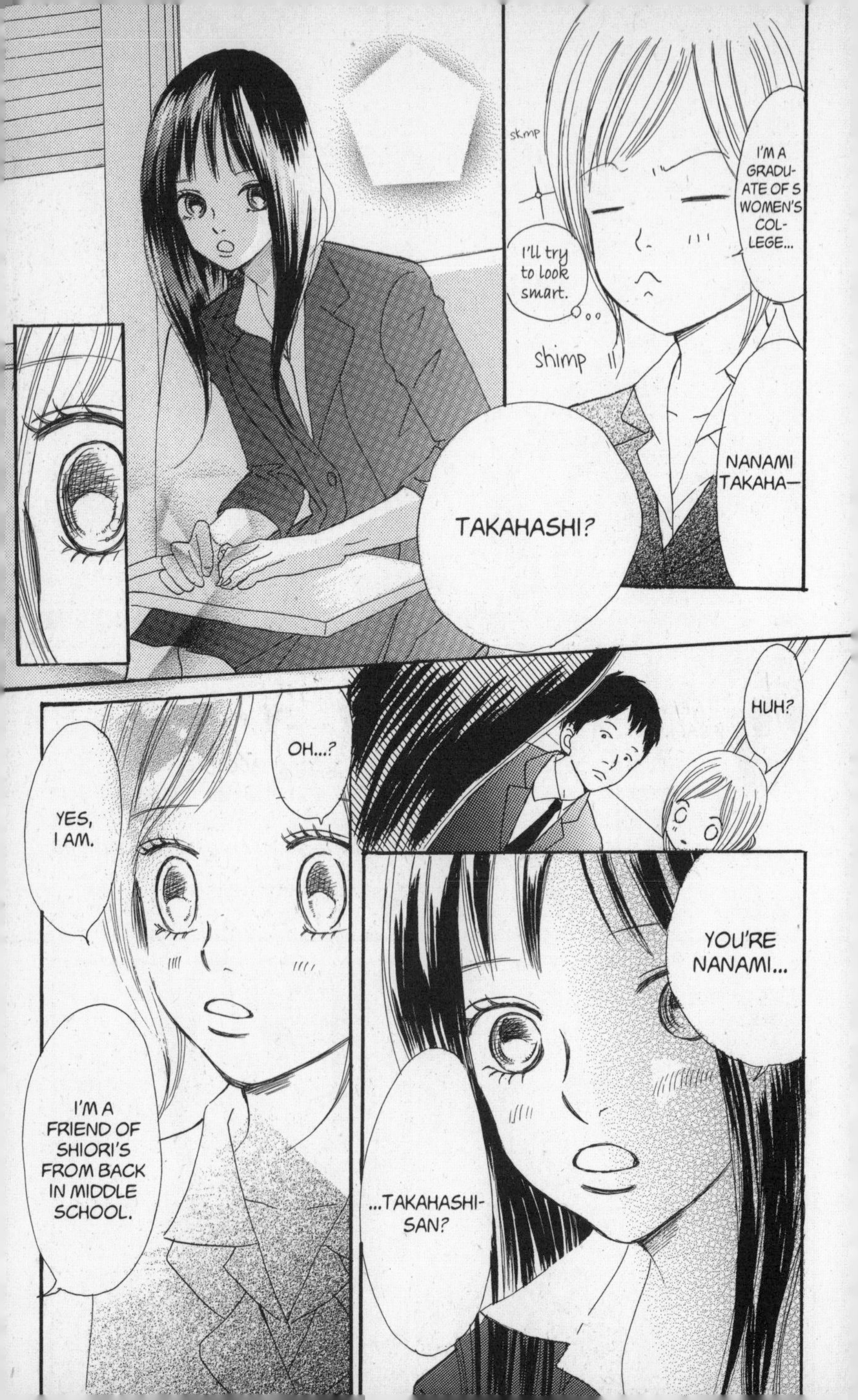
skmp
I'M A GRADUATE OF S WOMEN'S COLLEGE...
I'll try to look smart.
shimp
NANAMI TAKAHA—
TAKAHASHI?
HUH?
YOU'RE NANAMI...
...TAKAHASHI-SAN?
OH...?
YES, I AM.
I'M A FRIEND OF SHIORI'S FROM BACK IN MIDDLE SCHOOL.

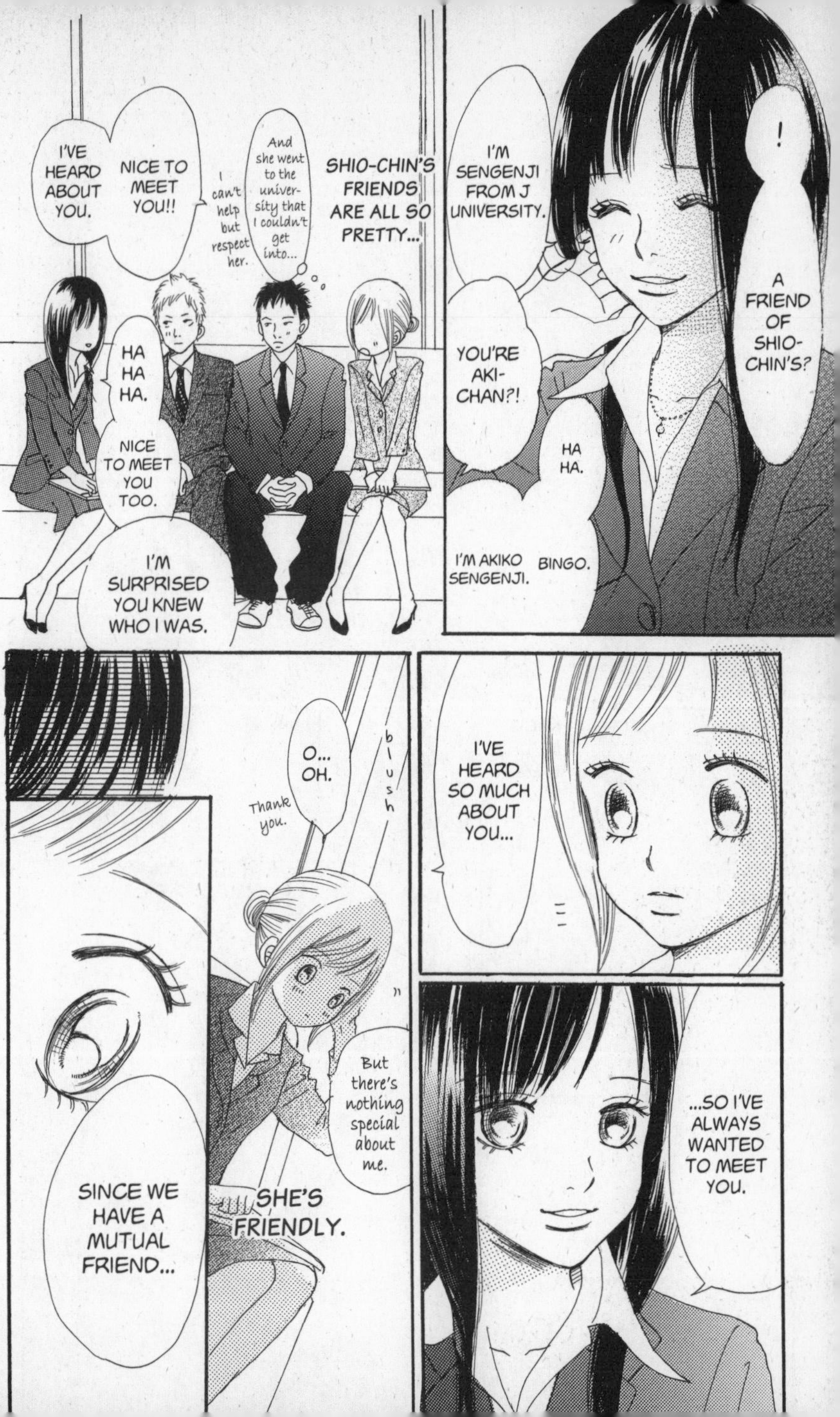
!
A FRIEND OF SHIO-CHIN'S?
I'M SENGENJI FROM J UNIVERSITY.
YOU'RE AKI-CHAN?!
HA HA.
BINGO.
I'M AKIKO SENGENJI.
SHIO-CHIN'S FRIENDS ARE ALL SO PRETTY...
And she went to the univer-sity that I couldn't get into...
I can't help but respect her.
NICE TO MEET YOU!!
I'VE HEARD ABOUT YOU.
HA HA HA.
NICE TO MEET YOU TOO.
I'M SURPRISED YOU KNEW WHO I WAS.
I'VE HEARD SO MUCH ABOUT YOU...
O... OH.
Thank you.
blush
...SO I'VE ALWAYS WANTED TO MEET YOU.
But there's nothing special about me.
SHE'S FRIENDLY.
SINCE WE HAVE A MUTUAL FRIEND...

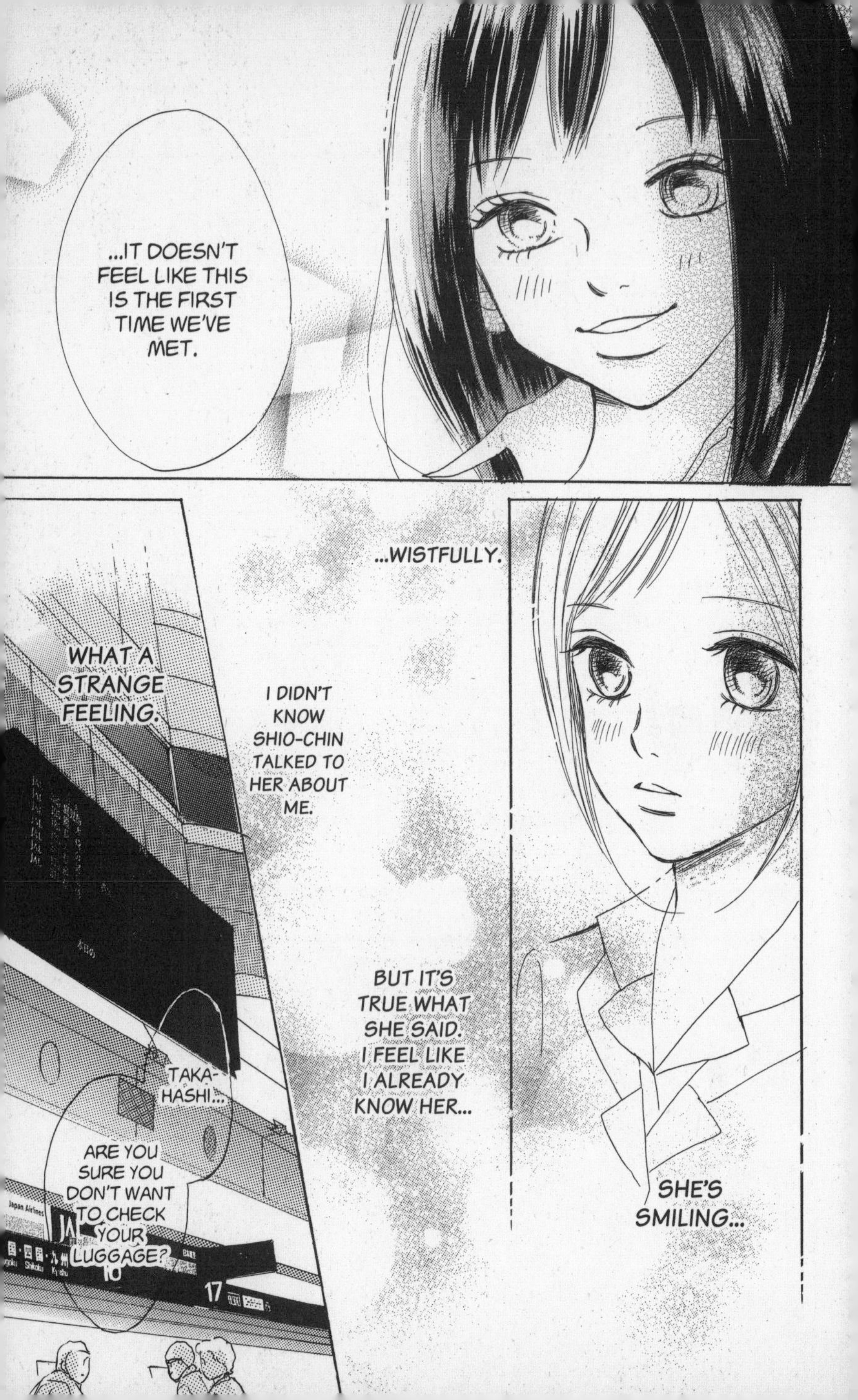
...IT DOESN'T FEEL LIKE THIS IS THE FIRST TIME WE'VE MET.
SHE'S SMILING...
...WISTFULLY.
I DIDN'T KNOW SHIO-CHIN TALKED TO HER ABOUT ME.
BUT IT'S TRUE WHAT SHE SAID. I FEEL LIKE I ALREADY KNOW HER...
WHAT A STRANGE FEELING.
TAKA-HASHI...
ARE YOU SURE YOU DON'T WANT TO CHECK YOUR LUGGAGE?

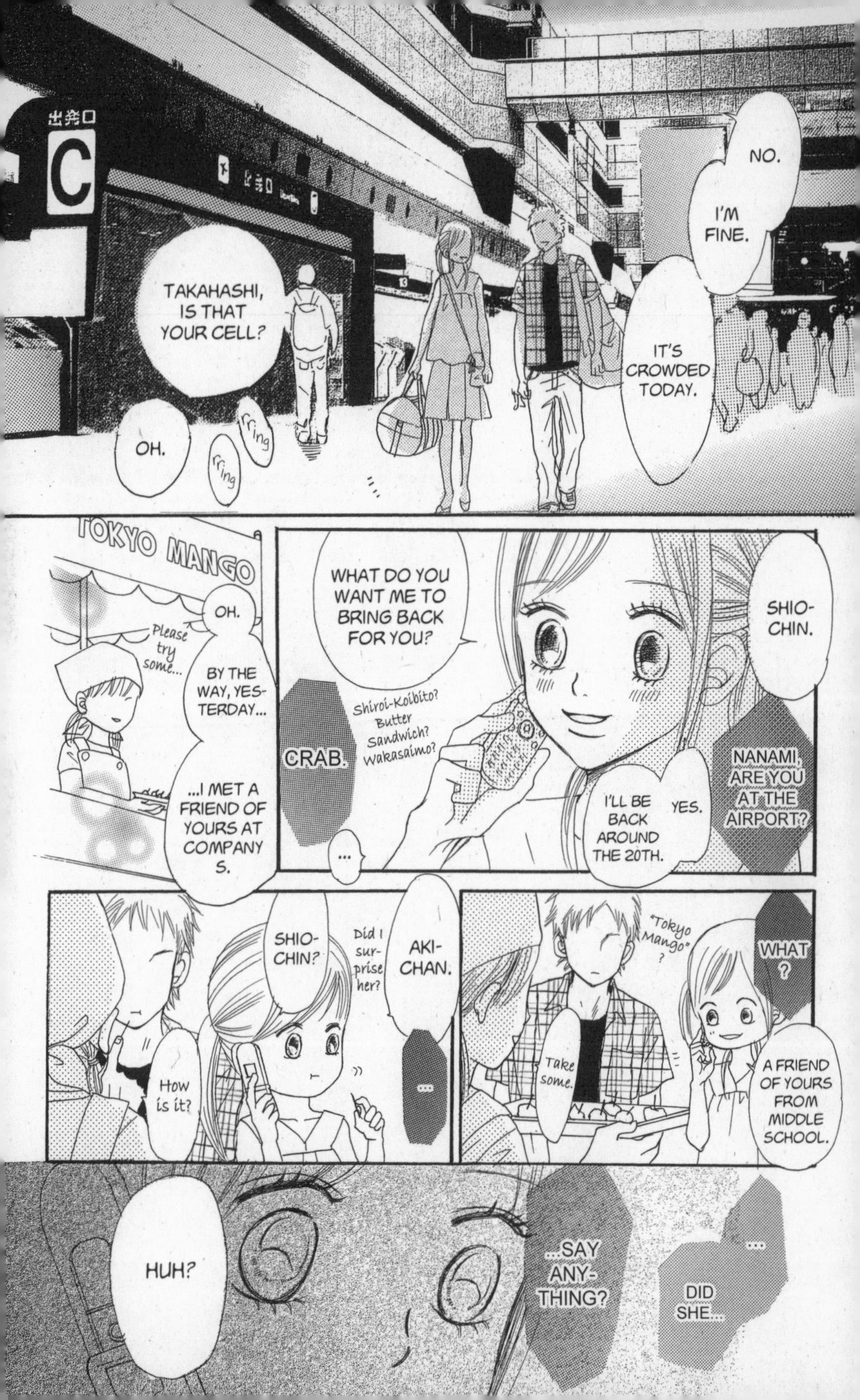
NO.
I'M FINE.
IT'S CROWDED TODAY.
TAKAHASHI, IS THAT YOUR CELL?
rring
rring
OH.
SHIO-CHIN.
NANAMI, ARE YOU AT THE AIRPORT?
YES.
I'LL BE BACK AROUND THE 20TH.
WHAT DO YOU WANT ME TO BRING BACK FOR YOU?
Shiroi-Koibito? Butter Sandwich? Wakasaimo?
CRAB.
...
TOKYO MANGO
OH.
Please try some...
BY THE WAY, YES-TERDAY...
...I MET A FRIEND OF YOURS AT COMPANY S.
WHAT?
"Tokyo Mango"?
A FRIEND OF YOURS FROM MIDDLE SCHOOL.
Take some.
AKI-CHAN.
Did I surprise her?
...
SHIO-CHIN?
How is it?
...SAY ANY-THING?
...
DID SHE...
HUH?

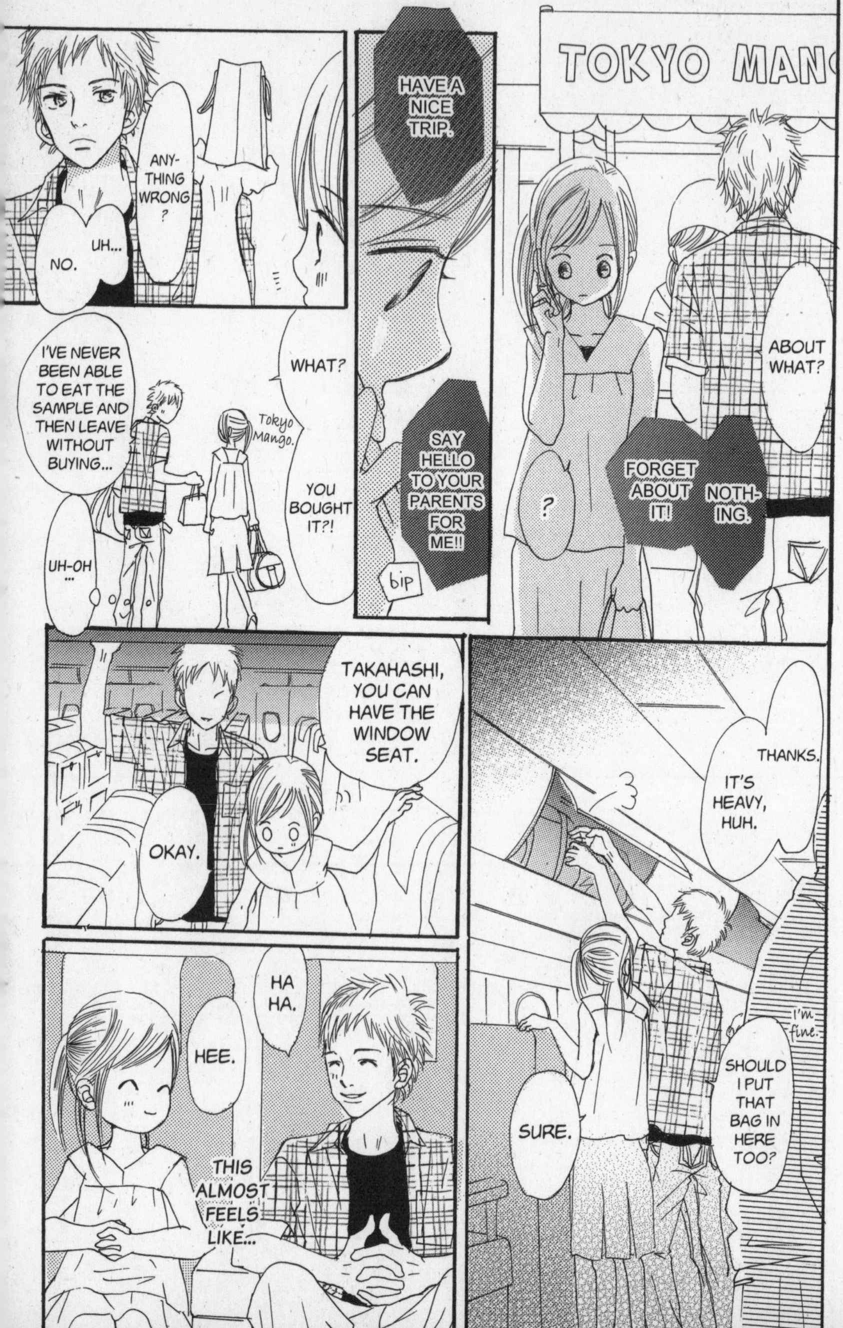
TOKYO MANG
ABOUT WHAT?
NOTH-ING.
FORGET ABOUT IT!
?
HAVE A NICE TRIP.
SAY HELLO TO YOUR PARENTS FOR ME!!
bip
ANY-THING WRONG?
UH... NO.
WHAT?
YOU BOUGHT IT?!
Tokyo Mango.
I'VE NEVER BEEN ABLE TO EAT THE SAMPLE AND THEN LEAVE WITHOUT BUYING...
UH-OH...
THANKS.
IT'S HEAVY, HUH.
I'm fine.
SHOULD I PUT THAT BAG IN HERE TOO?
SURE.
TAKAHASHI, YOU CAN HAVE THE WINDOW SEAT.
OKAY.
HA HA.
HEE.
THIS ALMOST FEELS LIKE...

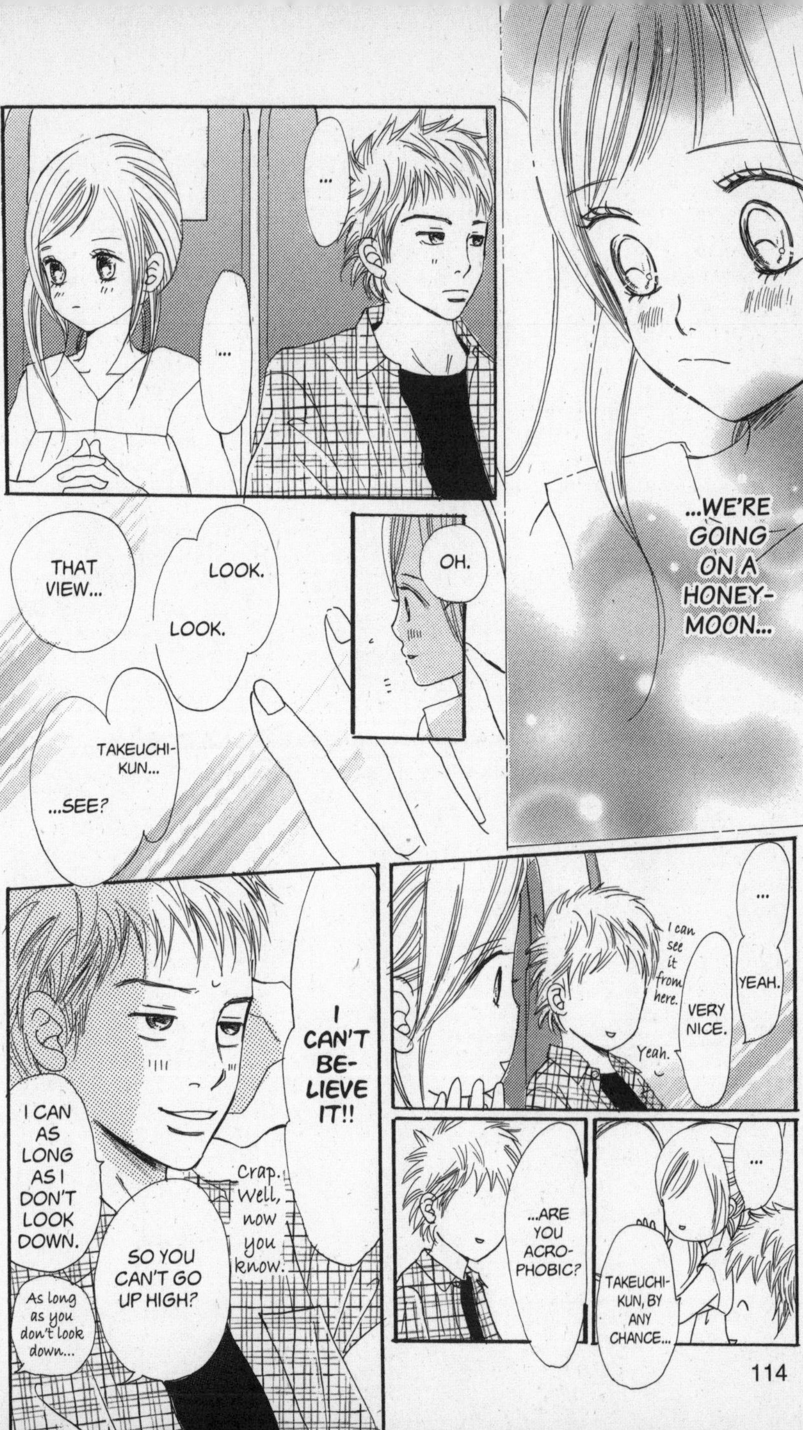
...WE'RE GOING ON A HONEY-MOON...
...
...
OH.
LOOK.
LOOK.
THAT VIEW...
TAKEUCHI-KUN...
...SEE?
...
YEAH.
VERY NICE.
I can see it from here.
Yeah.
...
TAKEUCHI-KUN, BY ANY CHANCE...
...ARE YOU ACRO-PHOBIC?
I CAN'T BE-LIEVE IT!!
Crap. Well, now you know.
I CAN AS LONG AS I DON'T LOOK DOWN.
SO YOU CAN'T GO UP HIGH?
As long as you don't look down...

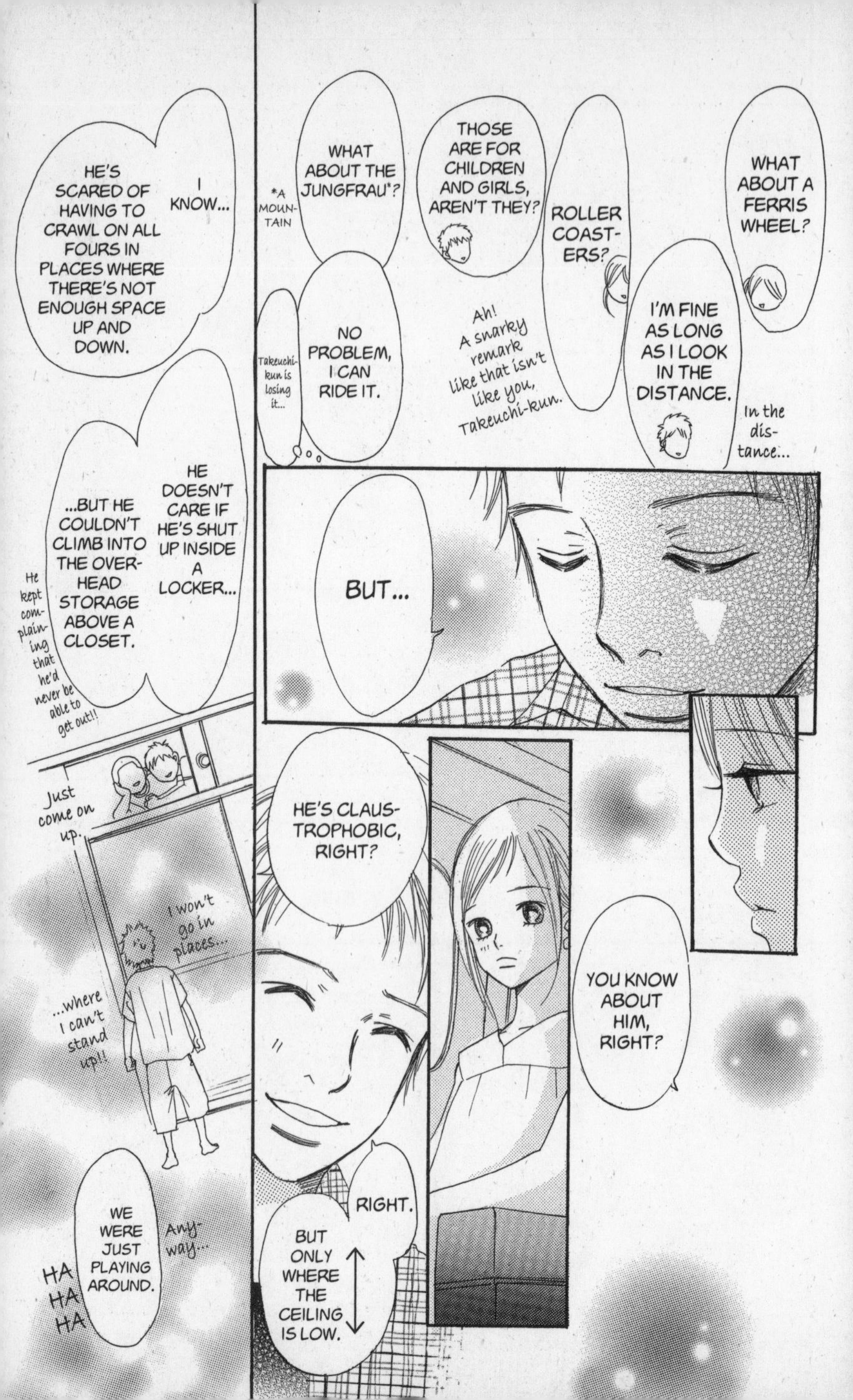
WHAT ABOUT A FERRIS WHEEL?
ROLLER COASTERS?
THOSE ARE FOR CHILDREN AND GIRLS, AREN'T THEY?
WHAT ABOUT THE JUNGFRAU*?
*A MOUNTAIN
I'M FINE AS LONG AS I LOOK IN THE DISTANCE.
In the distance...
Ah! A snarky remark like that isn't like you, Takeuchi-kun.
NO PROBLEM, I CAN RIDE IT.
Takeuchi-kun is losing it...
BUT...
YOU KNOW ABOUT HIM, RIGHT?
HE'S CLAUSTROPHOBIC, RIGHT?
RIGHT.
BUT ONLY WHERE THE CEILING IS LOW.
I KNOW...
HE'S SCARED OF HAVING TO CRAWL ON ALL FOURS IN PLACES WHERE THERE'S NOT ENOUGH SPACE UP AND DOWN.
HE DOESN'T CARE IF HE'S SHUT UP INSIDE A LOCKER...
...BUT HE COULDN'T CLIMB INTO THE OVERHEAD STORAGE ABOVE A CLOSET.
He kept complaining that he'd never be able to get out!!
Just come on up.
I won't go in places...
...where I can't stand up!!
Anyway...
WE WERE JUST PLAYING AROUND.
HA HA HA

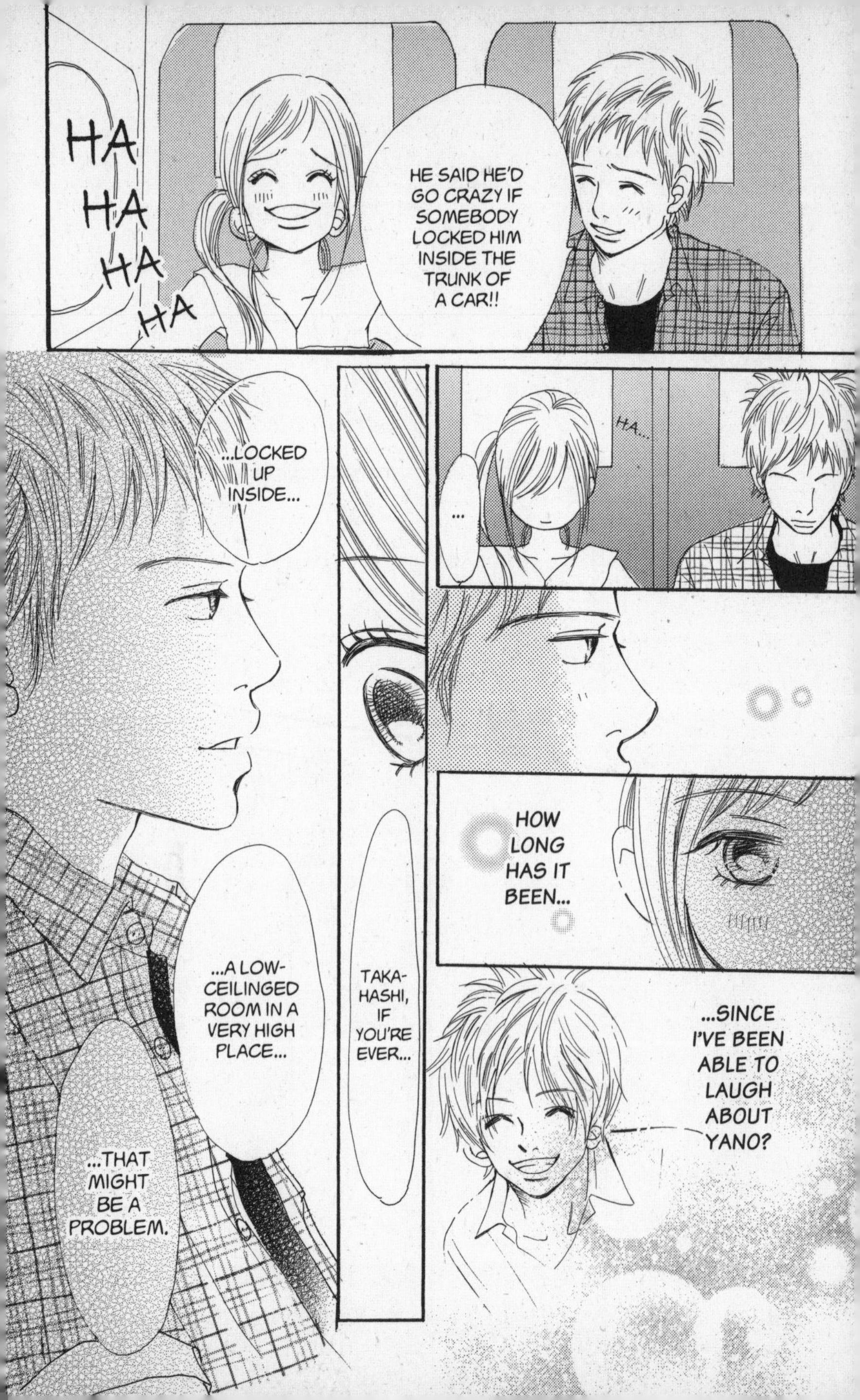
HE SAID HE'D GO CRAZY IF SOMEBODY LOCKED HIM INSIDE THE TRUNK OF A CAR!!
HA HA HA HA
...
HA...
HOW LONG HAS IT BEEN...
...SINCE I'VE BEEN ABLE TO LAUGH ABOUT YANO?
TAKA-HASHI, IF YOU'RE EVER...
...LOCKED UP INSIDE...
...A LOW-CEILINGED ROOM IN A VERY HIGH PLACE...
...THAT MIGHT BE A PROBLEM.

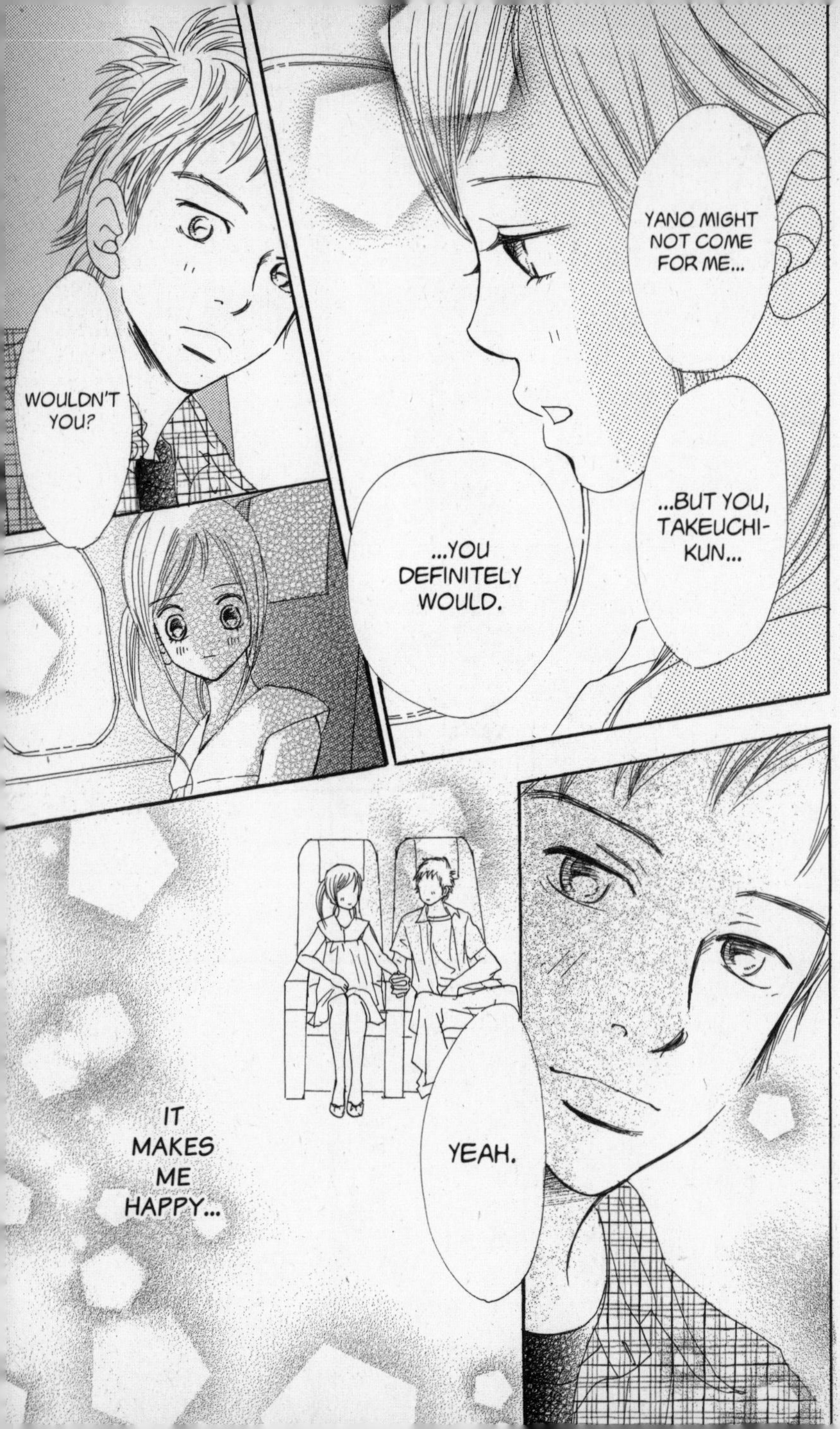
YANO MIGHT NOT COME FOR ME...
...BUT YOU, TAKEUCHI-KUN...
...YOU DEFINITELY WOULD.
WOULDN'T YOU?
YEAH.
IT MAKES ME HAPPY...

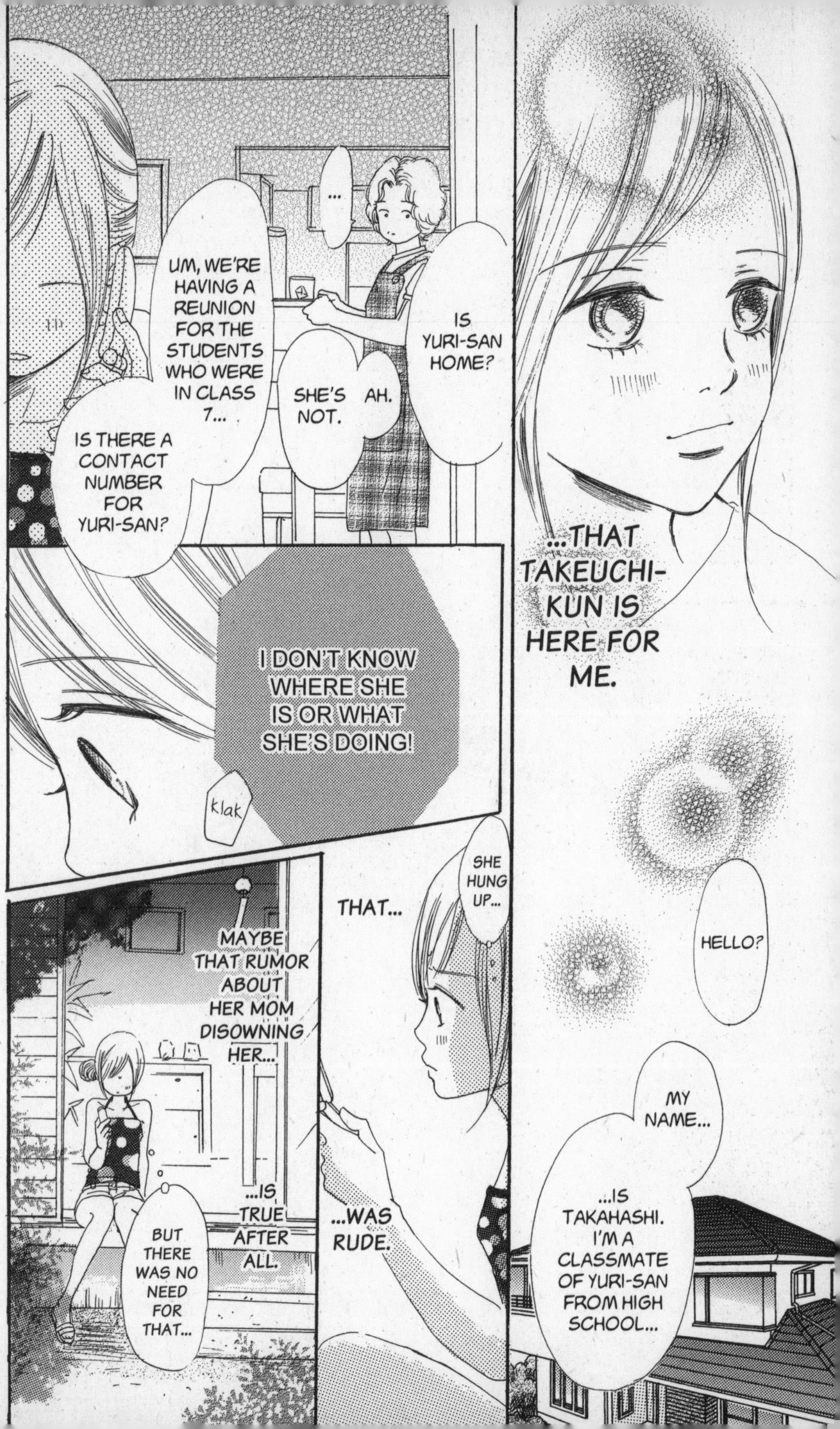
...THAT TAKEUCHI-KUN IS HERE FOR ME.
HELLO?
MY NAME...
...IS TAKAHASHI. I'M A CLASSMATE OF YURI-SAN FROM HIGH SCHOOL...
IS YURI-SAN HOME?
...
AH.
SHE'S NOT.
UM, WE'RE HAVING A REUNION FOR THE STUDENTS WHO WERE IN CLASS 7...
IS THERE A CONTACT NUMBER FOR YURI-SAN?
I DON'T KNOW WHERE SHE IS OR WHAT SHE'S DOING!
klak
SHE HUNG UP...
THAT...
...WAS RUDE.
MAYBE THAT RUMOR ABOUT HER MOM DISOWNING HER...
...IS TRUE AFTER ALL.
BUT THERE WAS NO NEED FOR THAT...

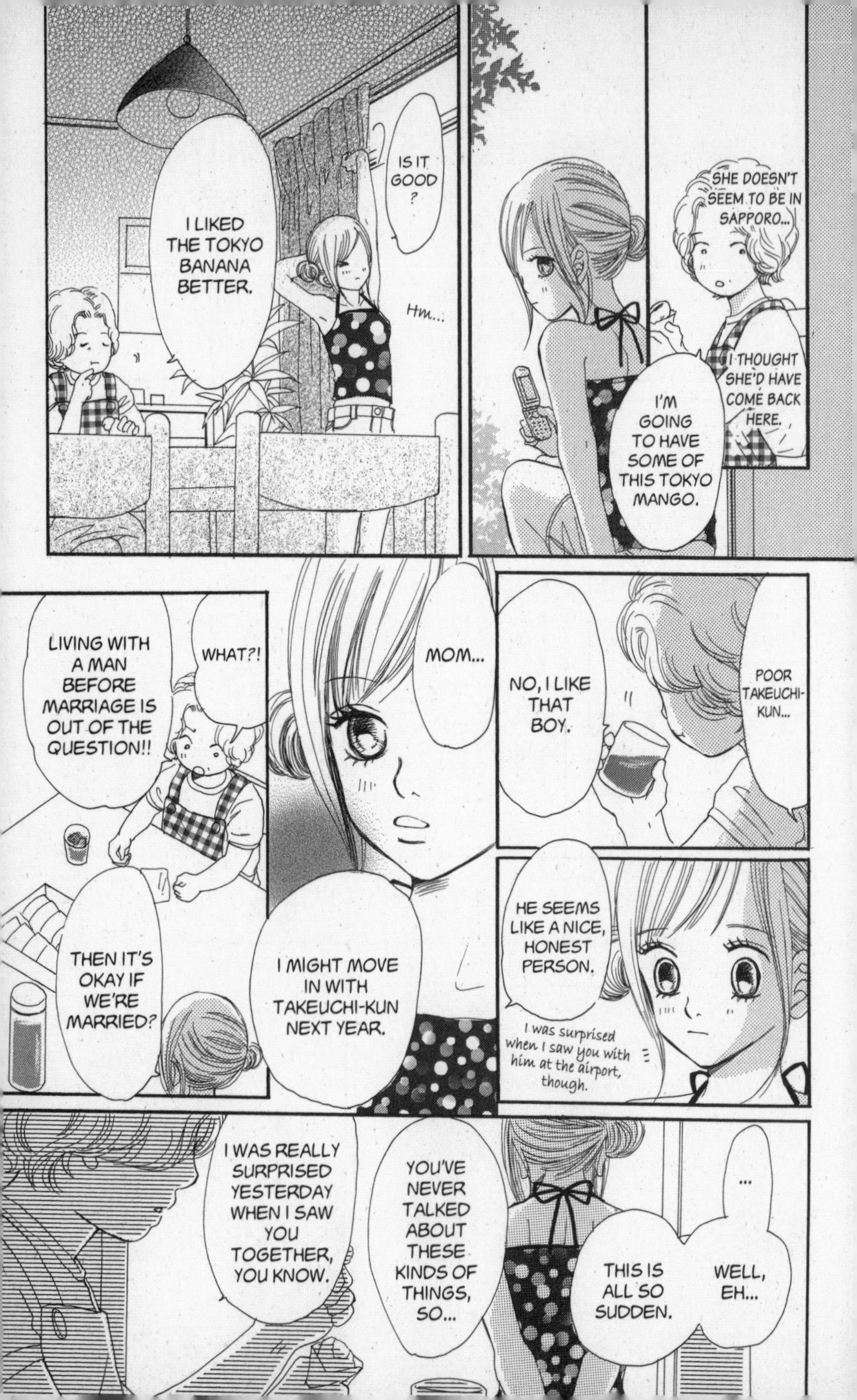
SHE DOESN'T SEEM TO BE IN SAPPORO...
I THOUGHT SHE'D HAVE COME BACK HERE.
I'M GOING TO HAVE SOME OF THIS TOKYO MANGO.
IS IT GOOD?
Hm...
I LIKED THE TOKYO BANANA BETTER.
POOR TAKEUCHI-KUN...
NO, I LIKE THAT BOY.
HE SEEMS LIKE A NICE, HONEST PERSON.
I was surprised when I saw you with him at the airport, though.
MOM...
I MIGHT MOVE IN WITH TAKEUCHI-KUN NEXT YEAR.
WHAT?!
LIVING WITH A MAN BEFORE MARRIAGE IS OUT OF THE QUESTION!!
THEN IT'S OKAY IF WE'RE MARRIED?
...
WELL, EH...
THIS IS ALL SO SUDDEN.
YOU'VE NEVER TALKED ABOUT THESE KINDS OF THINGS, SO...
I WAS REALLY SURPRISED YESTERDAY WHEN I SAW YOU TOGETHER, YOU KNOW.

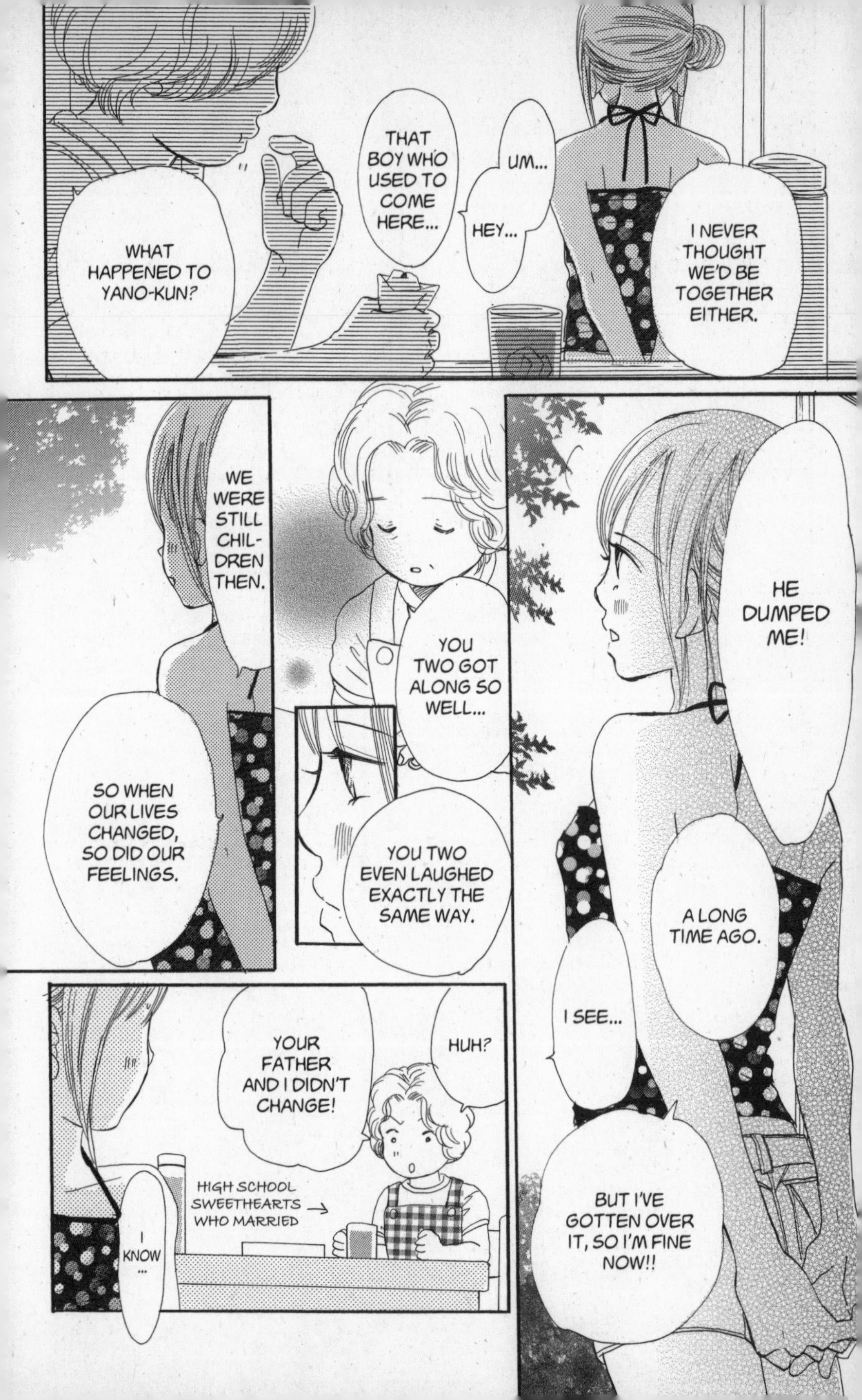
I NEVER THOUGHT WE'D BE TOGETHER EITHER.
UM...
HEY...
THAT BOY WHO USED TO COME HERE...
WHAT HAPPENED TO YANO-KUN?
HE DUMPED ME!
A LONG TIME AGO.
I SEE...
BUT I'VE GOTTEN OVER IT, SO I'M FINE NOW!!
YOU TWO GOT ALONG SO WELL...
YOU TWO EVEN LAUGHED EXACTLY THE SAME WAY.
WE WERE STILL CHIL-DREN THEN.
SO WHEN OUR LIVES CHANGED, SO DID OUR FEELINGS.
HUH?
YOUR FATHER AND I DIDN'T CHANGE!
HIGH SCHOOL SWEETHEARTS WHO MARRIED →
I KNOW ...

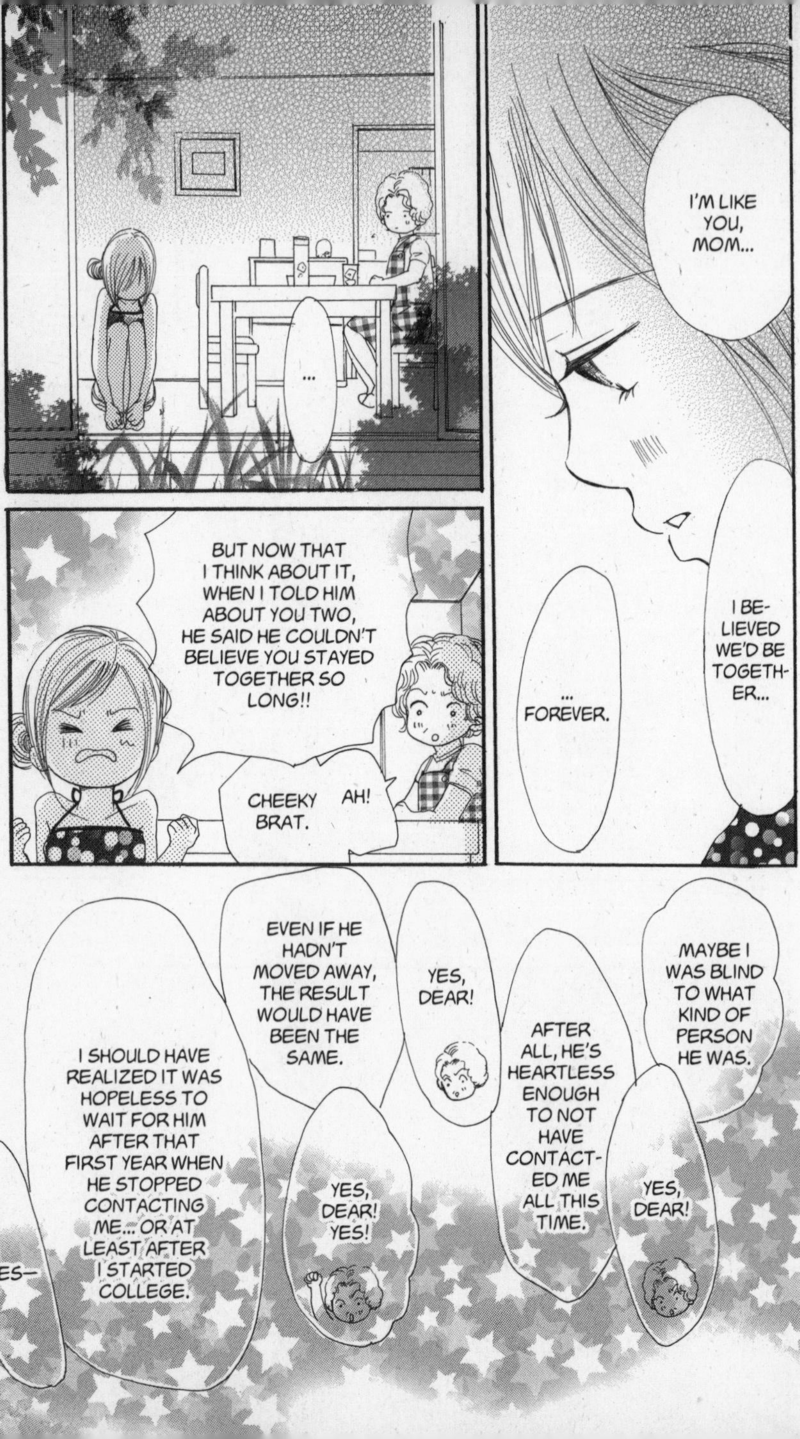
I'M LIKE YOU, MOM...
I BE-LIEVED WE'D BE TOGETH-ER...
... FOREVER.
...
BUT NOW THAT I THINK ABOUT IT, WHEN I TOLD HIM ABOUT YOU TWO, HE SAID HE COULDN'T BELIEVE YOU STAYED TOGETHER SO LONG!!
AH!
CHEEKY BRAT.
MAYBE I WAS BLIND TO WHAT KIND OF PERSON HE WAS.
YES, DEAR!
AFTER ALL, HE'S HEARTLESS ENOUGH TO NOT HAVE CONTACT-ED ME ALL THIS TIME.
YES, DEAR!
EVEN IF HE HADN'T MOVED AWAY, THE RESULT WOULD HAVE BEEN THE SAME.
YES, DEAR! YES!
I SHOULD HAVE REALIZED IT WAS HOPELESS TO WAIT FOR HIM AFTER THAT FIRST YEAR WHEN HE STOPPED CONTACTING ME... OR AT LEAST AFTER I STARTED COLLEGE.
YES—

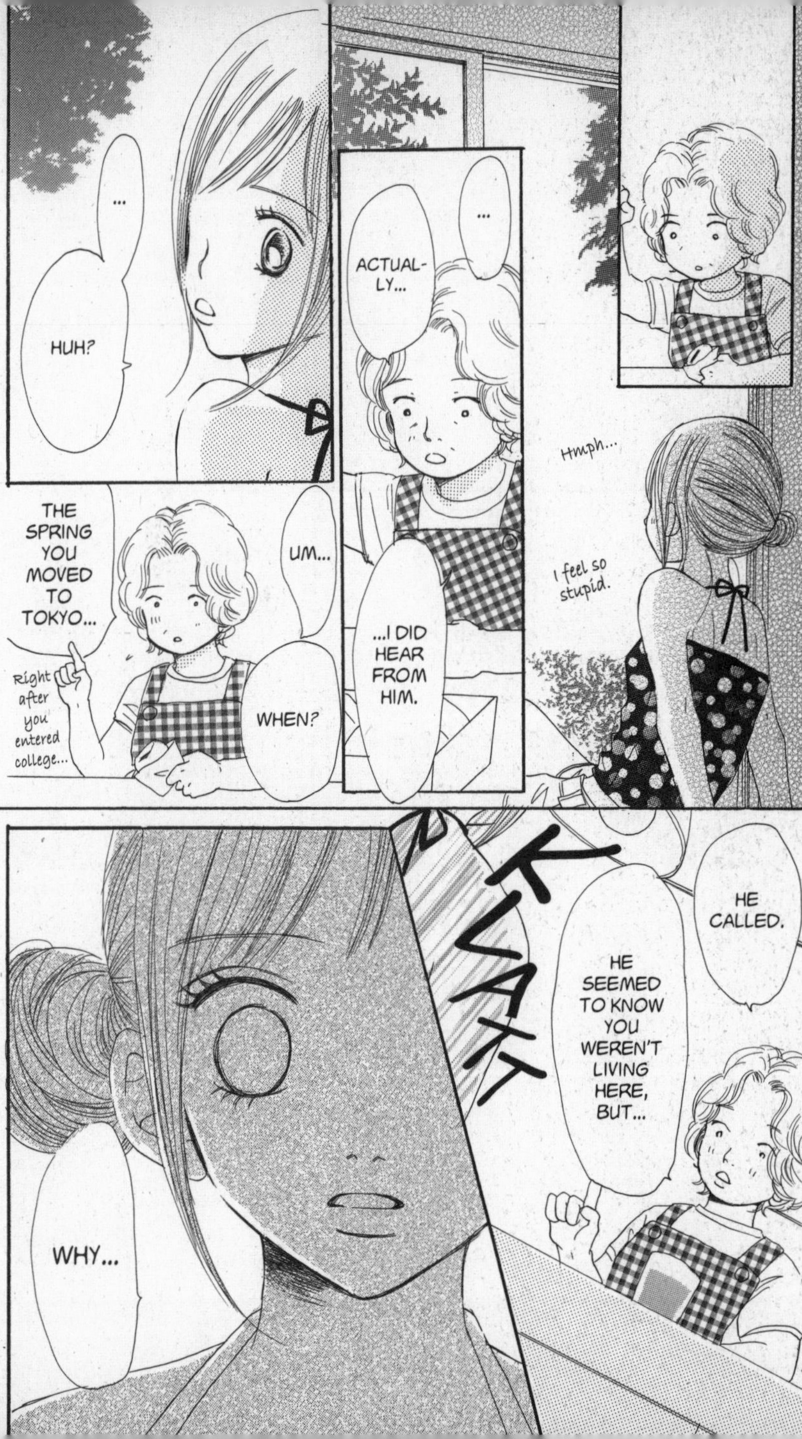
Hmph...
I feel so stupid.
...
ACTUAL-LY...
...I DID HEAR FROM HIM.
...
HUH?
WHEN?
UM...
THE SPRING YOU MOVED TO TOKYO...
Right after you entered college...
HE CALLED.
HE SEEMED TO KNOW YOU WEREN'T LIVING HERE, BUT...
WHY...

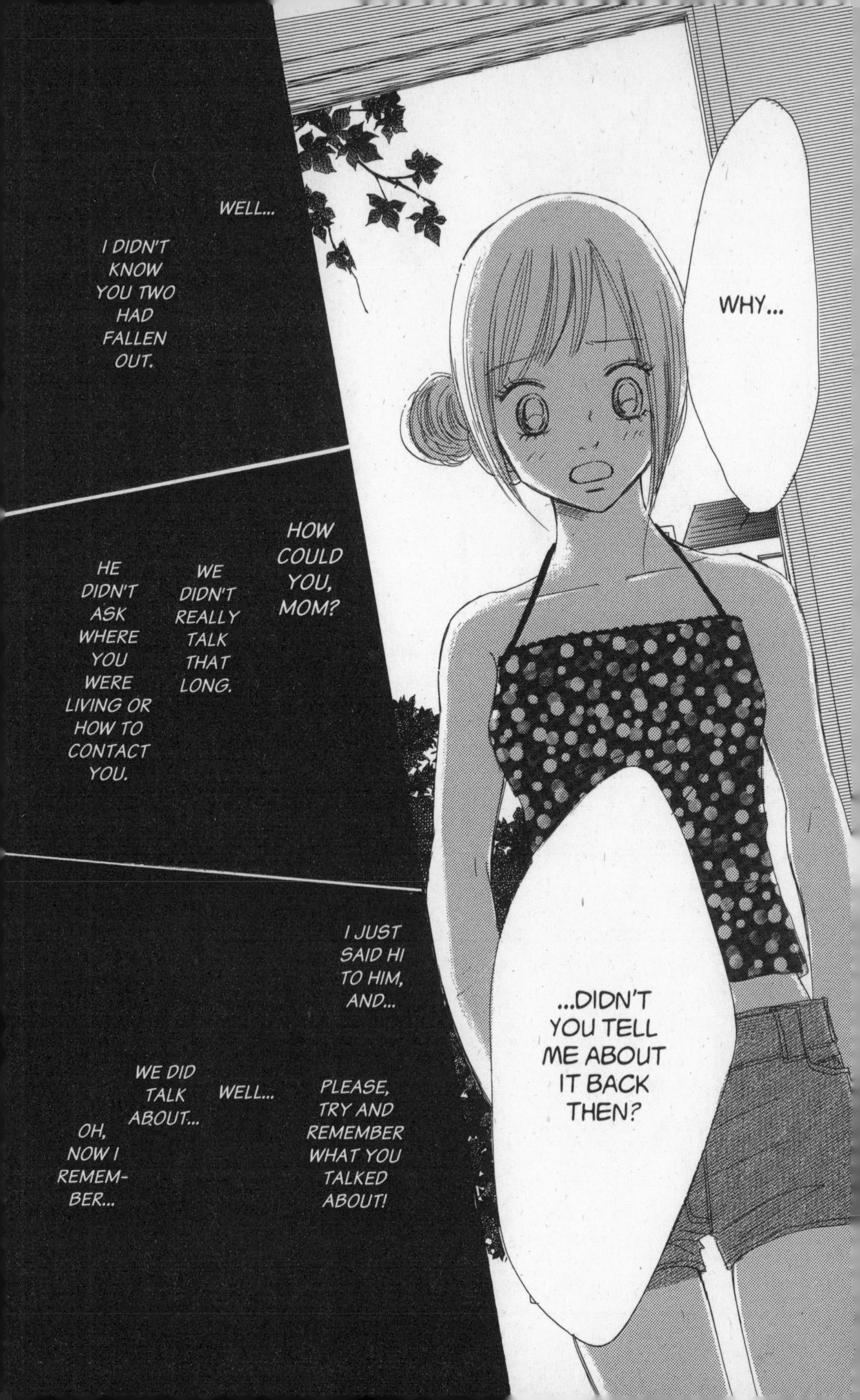
WHY...
...DIDN'T YOU TELL ME ABOUT IT BACK THEN?
WELL...
I DIDN'T KNOW YOU TWO HAD FALLEN OUT.
HOW COULD YOU, MOM?
WE DIDN'T REALLY TALK THAT LONG.
HE DIDN'T ASK WHERE YOU WERE LIVING OR HOW TO CONTACT YOU.
I JUST SAID HI TO HIM, AND...
PLEASE, TRY AND REMEMBER WHAT YOU TALKED ABOUT!
WELL...
WE DID TALK ABOUT...
OH, NOW I REMEMBER...

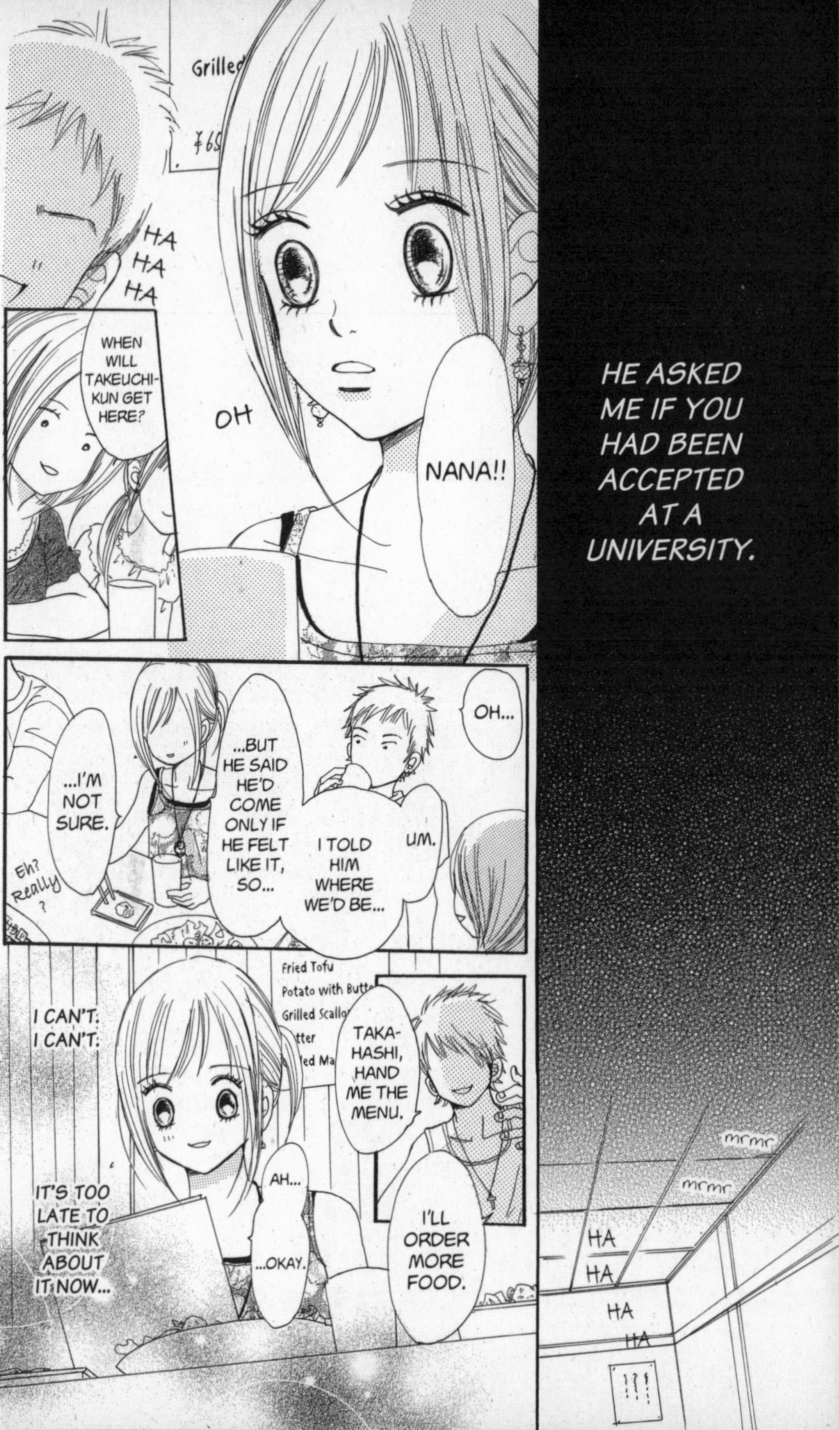
HE ASKED ME IF YOU HAD BEEN ACCEPTED AT A UNIVERSITY.
mrmr
mrmr
HA
HA
HA
HA
NANA!!
OH
HA
HA
HA
WHEN WILL TAKEUCHI-KUN GET HERE?
Grilled
OH...
UM.
I TOLD HIM WHERE WE'D BE...
...BUT HE SAID HE'D COME ONLY IF HE FELT LIKE IT, SO...
...I'M NOT SURE.
Eh? Really?
TAKA-HASHI, HAND ME THE MENU.
I'LL ORDER MORE FOOD.
Fried Tofu
Potato with Butter
Grilled Scallop
AH...
...OKAY.
I CAN'T. I CAN'T.
IT'S TOO LATE TO THINK ABOUT IT NOW...

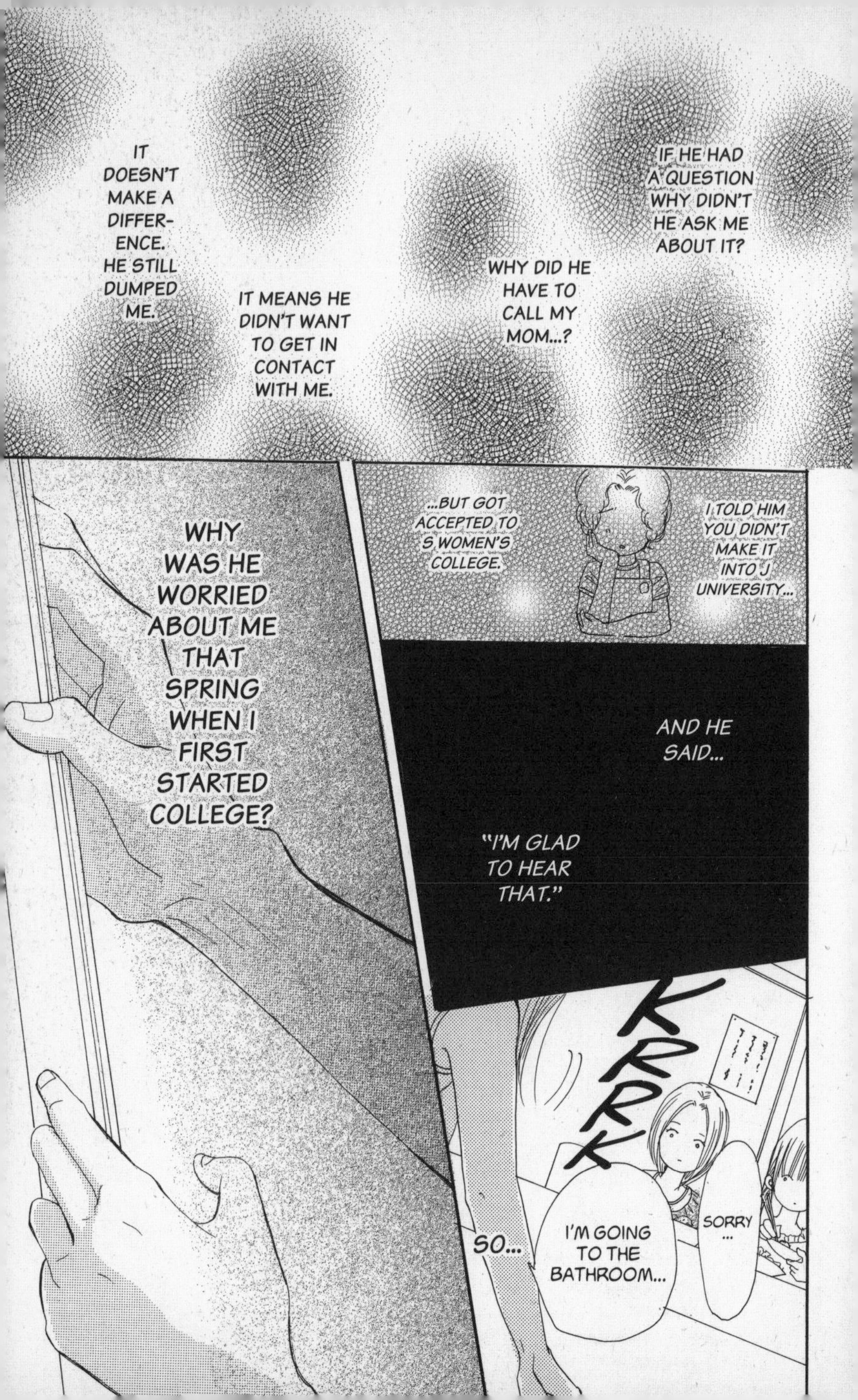
IF HE HAD A QUESTION WHY DIDN'T HE ASK ME ABOUT IT?
WHY DID HE HAVE TO CALL MY MOM...?
IT MEANS HE DIDN'T WANT TO GET IN CONTACT WITH ME.
IT DOESN'T MAKE A DIFFER-ENCE. HE STILL DUMPED ME.
I TOLD HIM YOU DIDN'T MAKE IT INTO J UNIVERSITY...
...BUT GOT ACCEPTED TO S WOMEN'S COLLEGE.
AND HE SAID...
"I'M GLAD TO HEAR THAT."
KRRK
SORRY ...
I'M GOING TO THE BATHROOM...
SO...
WHY WAS HE WORRIED ABOUT ME THAT SPRING WHEN I FIRST STARTED COLLEGE?

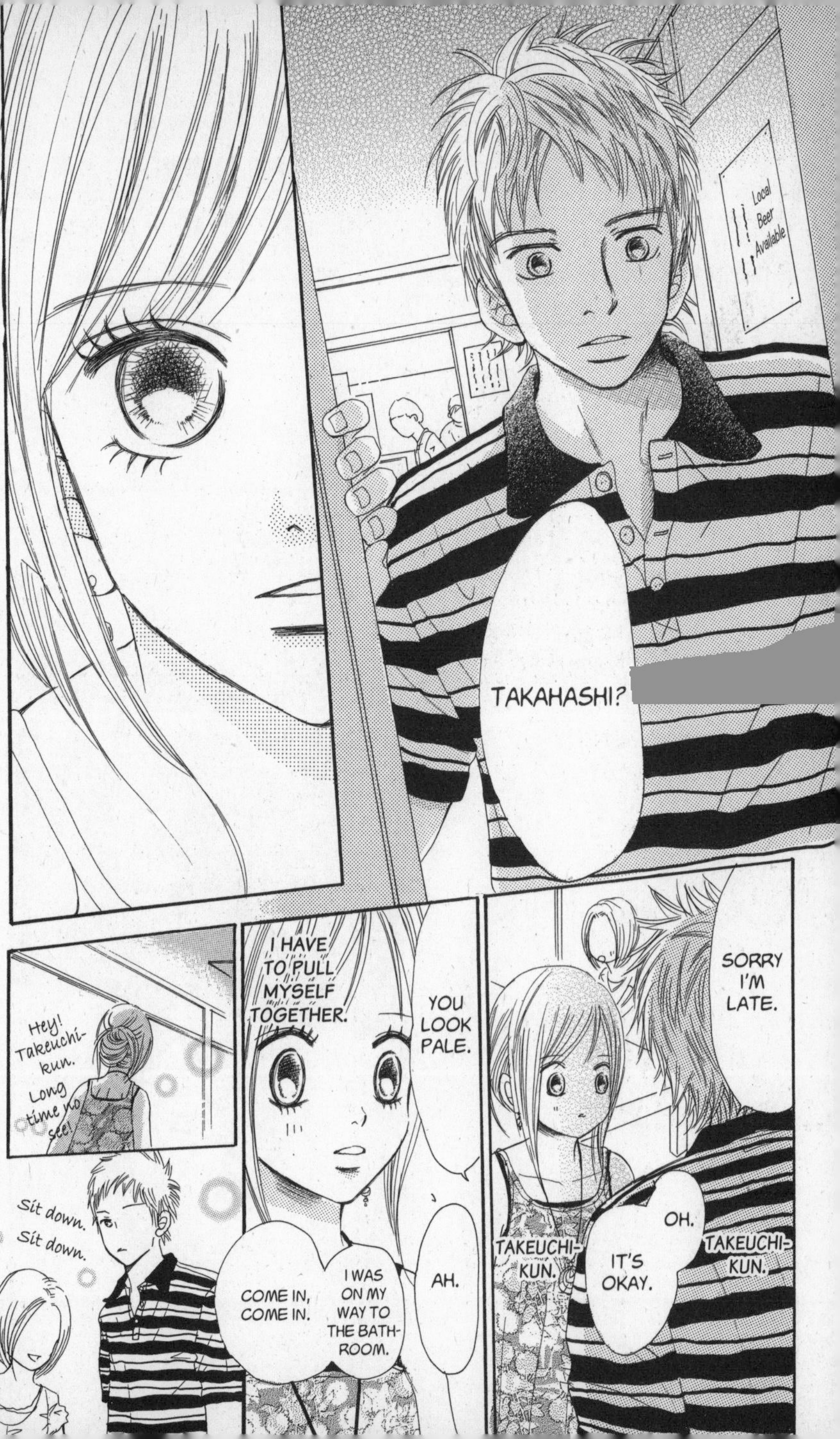

Local Beer Available
TAKAHASHI?
SORRY I'M LATE.
OH.
TAKEUCHI-KUN.
IT'S OKAY.
TAKEUCHI-KUN.
YOU LOOK PALE.
AH.
I HAVE TO PULL MYSELF TOGETHER.
I WAS ON MY WAY TO THE BATH-ROOM.
COME IN, COME IN.
Hey! Takeuchi-kun. Long time no see!
Sit down. Sit down.

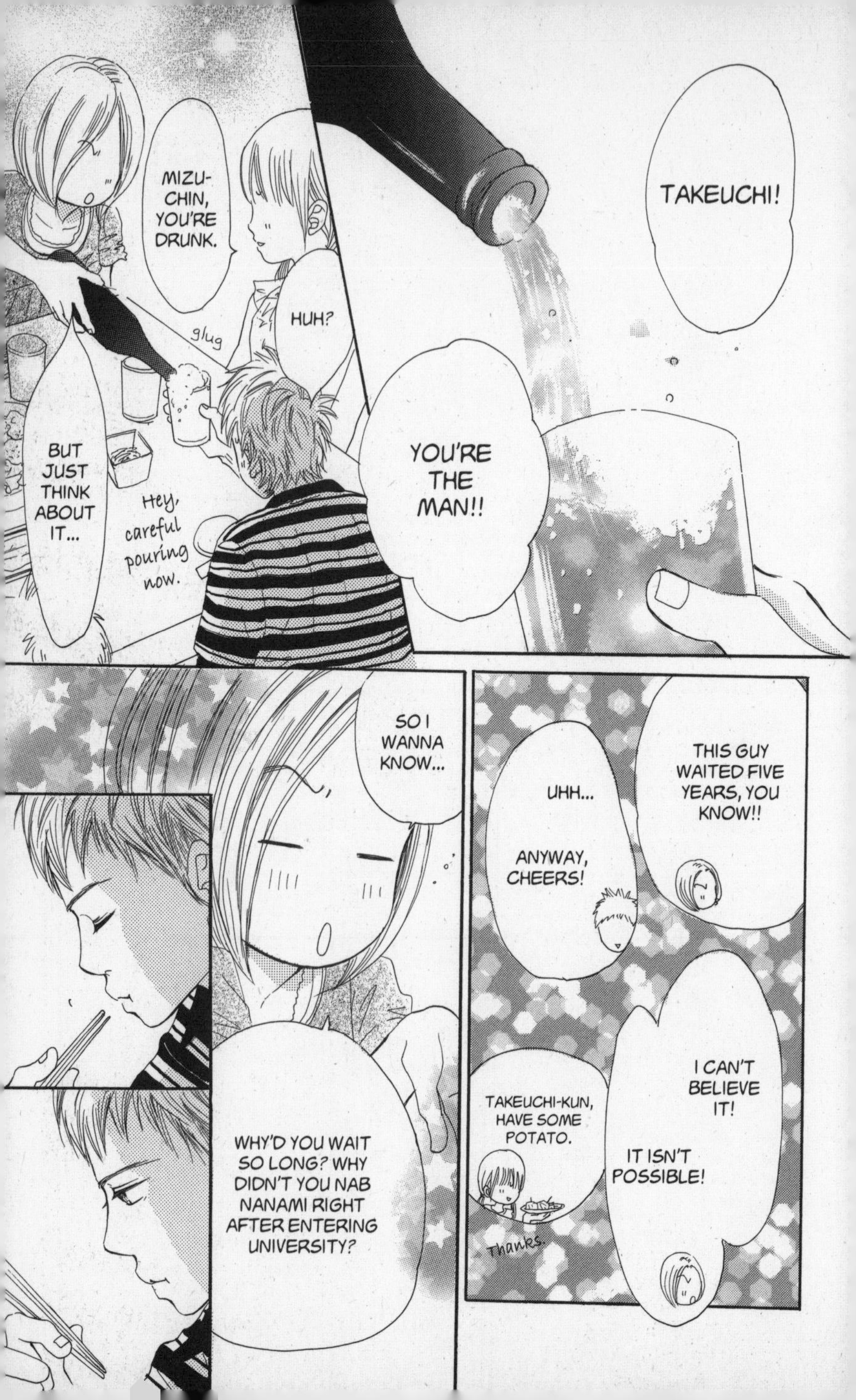
TAKEUCHI!
YOU'RE THE MAN!!
HUH?
glug
MIZU-CHIN, YOU'RE DRUNK.
Hey, careful pouring now.
BUT JUST THINK ABOUT IT...
THIS GUY WAITED FIVE YEARS, YOU KNOW!!
UHH...
ANYWAY, CHEERS!
I CAN'T BELIEVE IT!
IT ISN'T POSSIBLE!
TAKEUCHI-KUN, HAVE SOME POTATO.
Thanks.
SO I WANNA KNOW...
WHY'D YOU WAIT SO LONG? WHY DIDN'T YOU NAB NANAMI RIGHT AFTER ENTERING UNIVERSITY?

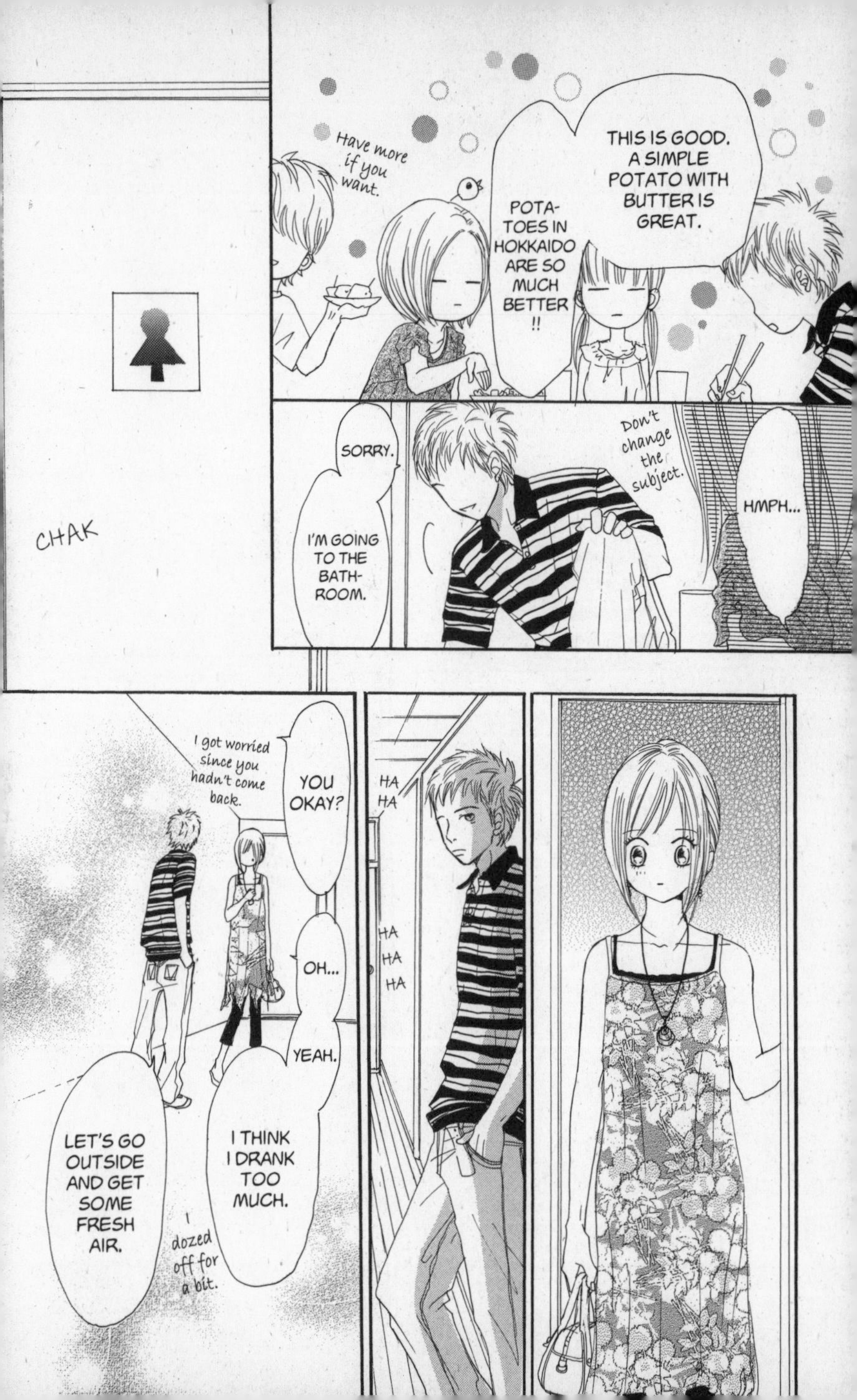
THIS IS GOOD. A SIMPLE POTATO WITH BUTTER IS GREAT.
POTATOES IN HOKKAIDO ARE SO MUCH BETTER !!
Have more if you want.
HMPH...
Don't change the subject.
SORRY.
I'M GOING TO THE BATHROOM.
CHAK
HA HA
HA HA HA
YOU OKAY?
I got worried since you hadn't come back.
OH...
YEAH.
I THINK I DRANK TOO MUCH.
I dozed off for a bit.
LET'S GO OUTSIDE AND GET SOME FRESH AIR.

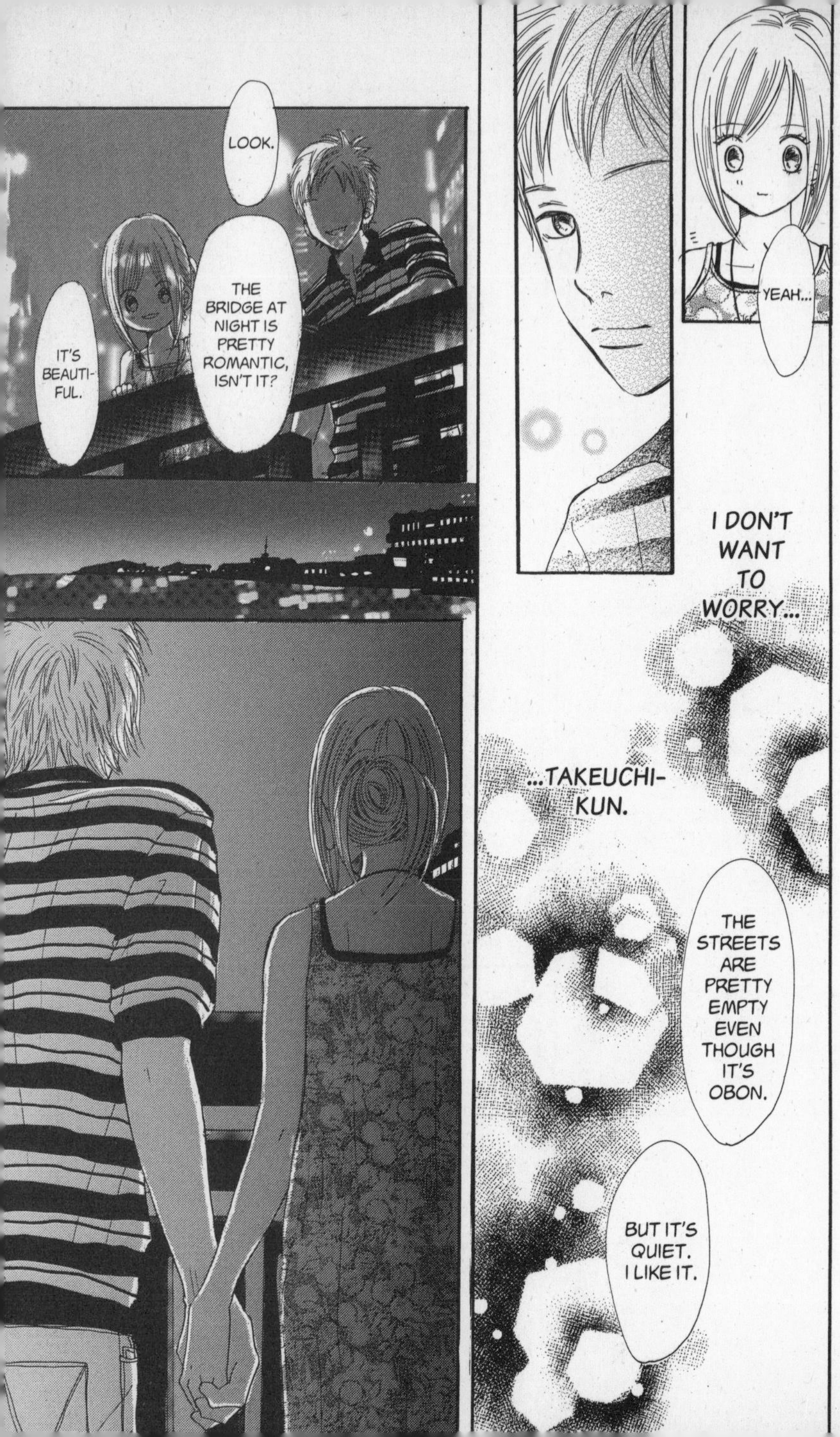
YEAH...
I DON'T WANT TO WORRY...
...TAKEUCHI-KUN.
THE STREETS ARE PRETTY EMPTY EVEN THOUGH IT'S OBON.
BUT IT'S QUIET. I LIKE IT.
LOOK.
THE BRIDGE AT NIGHT IS PRETTY ROMANTIC, ISN'T IT?
IT'S BEAUTI-FUL.

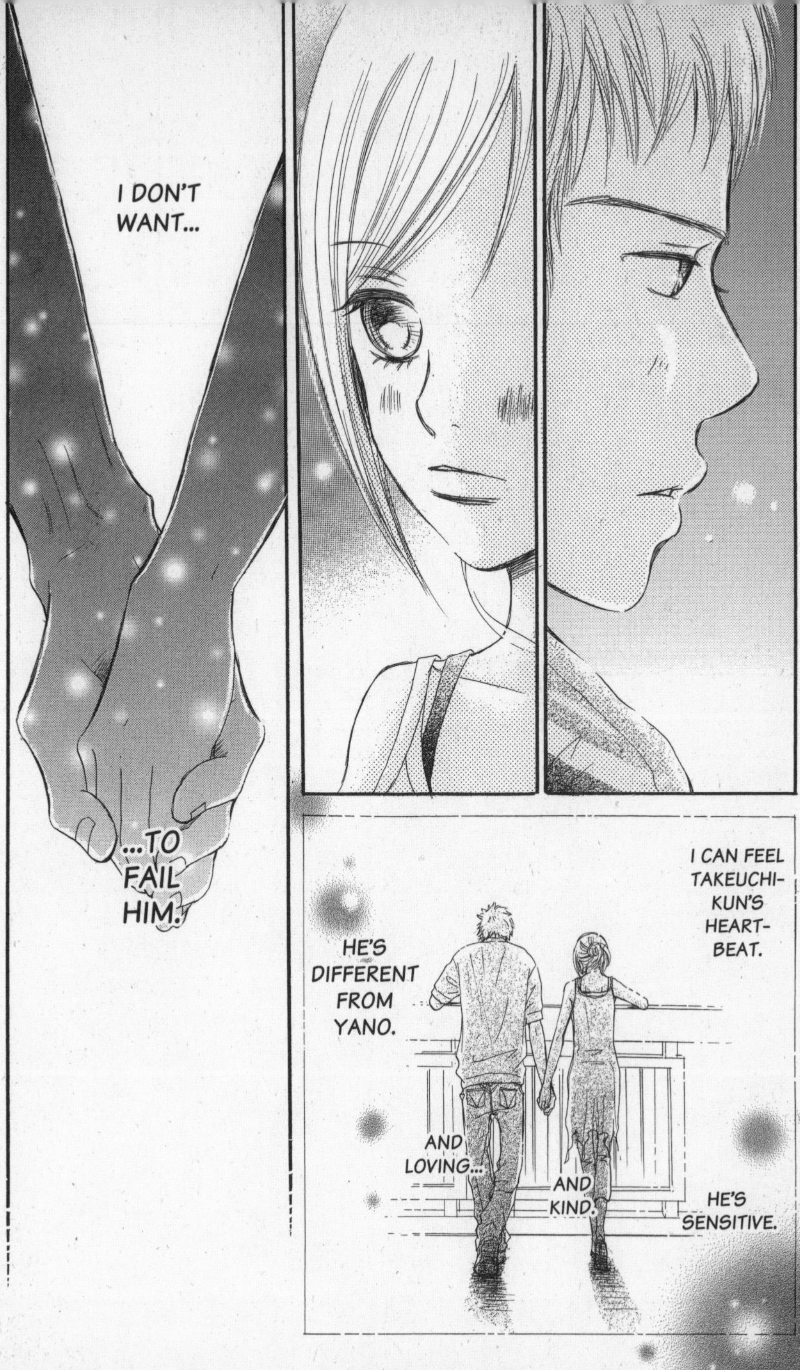
I CAN FEEL TAKEUCHI-KUN'S HEART-BEAT.
HE'S DIFFERENT FROM YANO.
HE'S SENSITIVE.
AND KIND.
AND LOVING...
I DON'T WANT...
...TO FAIL HIM.

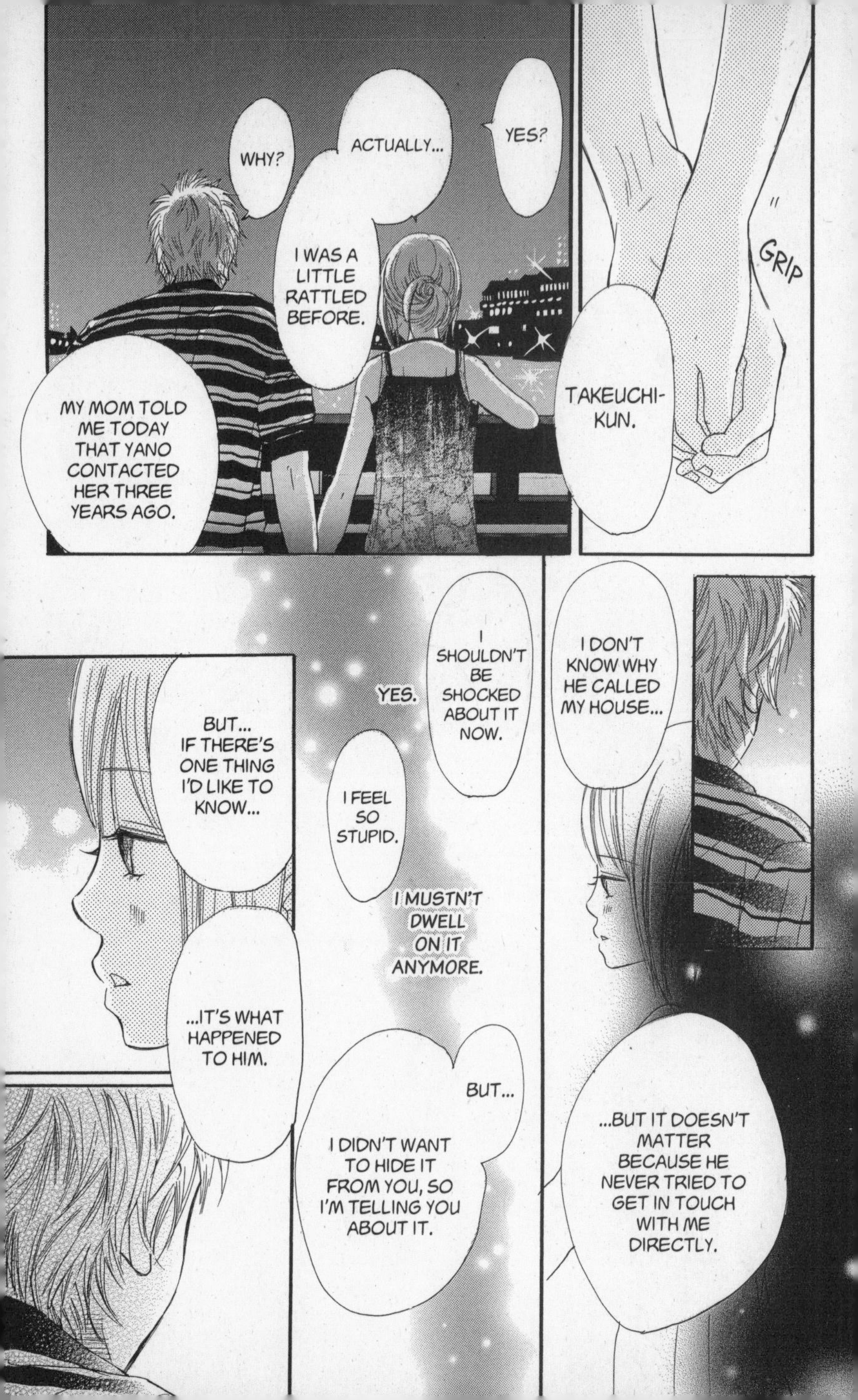
TAKEUCHI-KUN.
GRIP
YES?
ACTUALLY...
I WAS A LITTLE RATTLED BEFORE.
WHY?
MY MOM TOLD ME TODAY THAT YANO CONTACTED HER THREE YEARS AGO.
I DON'T KNOW WHY HE CALLED MY HOUSE...
...BUT IT DOESN'T MATTER BECAUSE HE NEVER TRIED TO GET IN TOUCH WITH ME DIRECTLY.
I SHOULDN'T BE SHOCKED ABOUT IT NOW.
YES.
I FEEL SO STUPID.
I MUSTN'T DWELL ON IT ANYMORE.
BUT...
I DIDN'T WANT TO HIDE IT FROM YOU, SO I'M TELLING YOU ABOUT IT.
BUT... IF THERE'S ONE THING I'D LIKE TO KNOW...
...IT'S WHAT HAPPENED TO HIM.

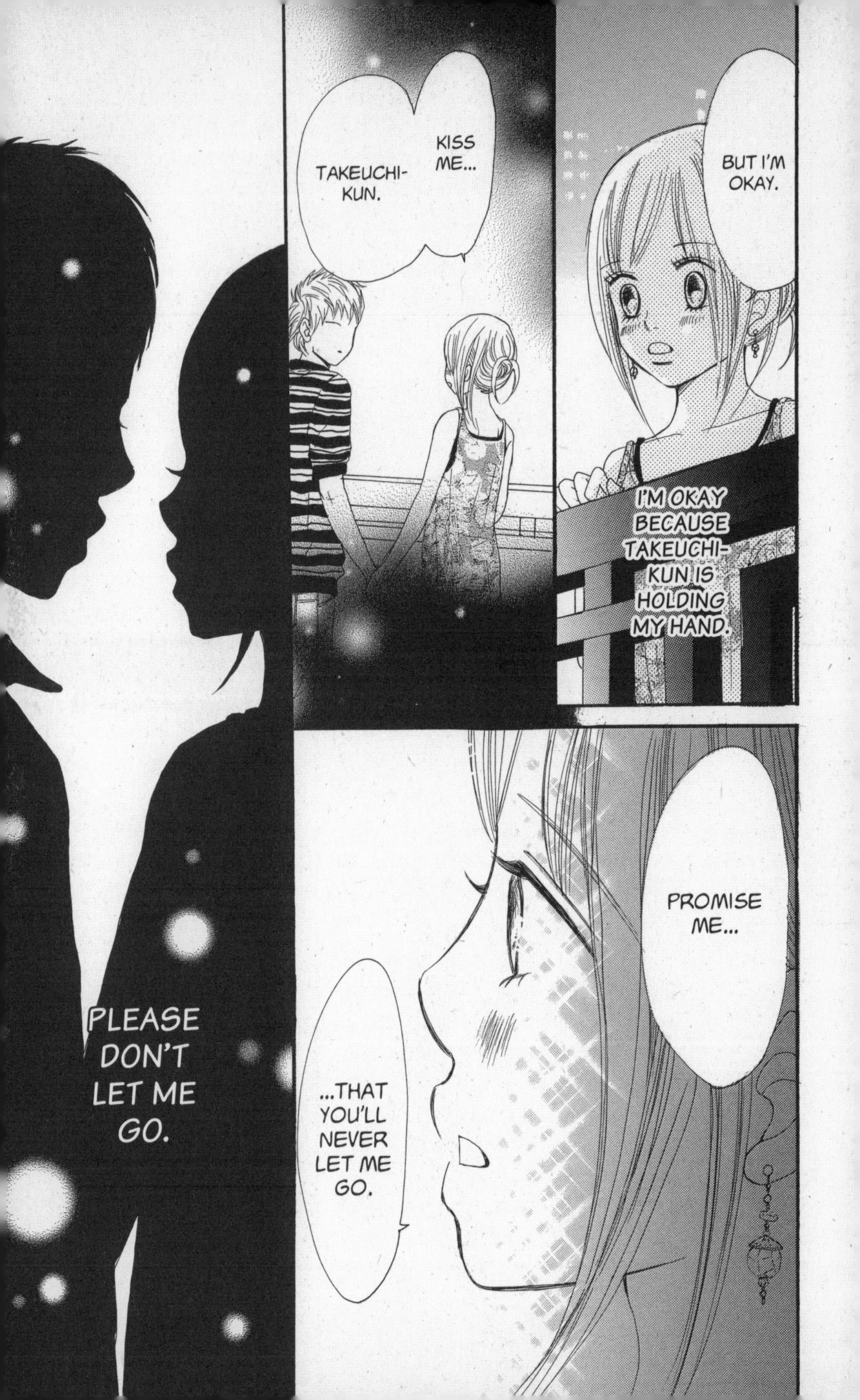
BUT I'M OKAY.
I'M OKAY BECAUSE TAKEUCHI-KUN IS HOLDING MY HAND.
KISS ME...
TAKEUCHI-KUN.
PROMISE ME...
...THAT YOU'LL NEVER LET ME GO.
PLEASE DON'T LET ME GO.

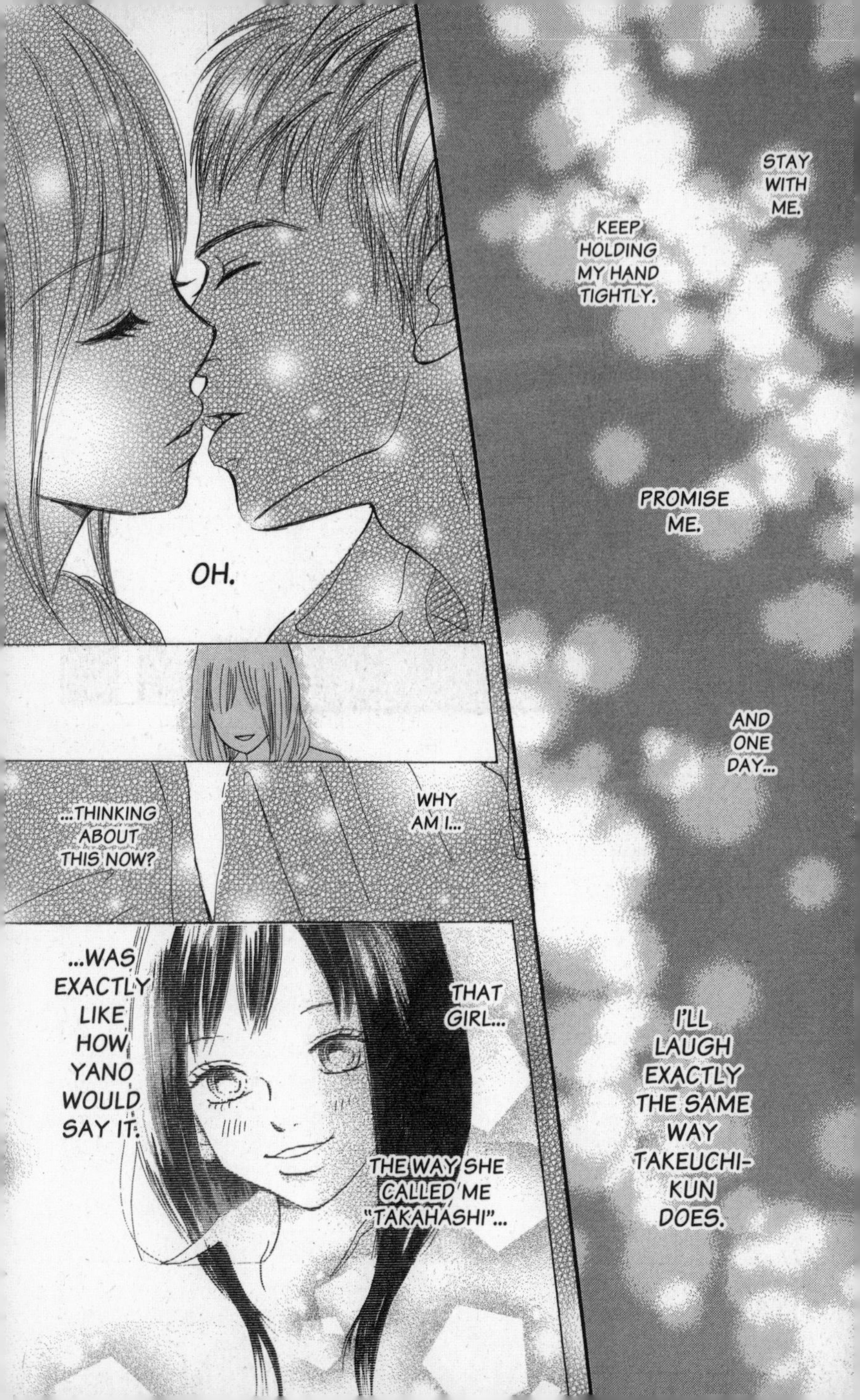
STAY WITH ME.
KEEP HOLDING MY HAND TIGHTLY.
PROMISE ME.
AND ONE DAY...
I'LL LAUGH EXACTLY THE SAME WAY TAKEUCHI-KUN DOES.
OH.
WHY AM I...
...THINKING ABOUT THIS NOW?
THAT GIRL...
THE WAY SHE CALLED ME "TAKAHASHI"...
...WAS EXACTLY LIKE HOW YANO WOULD SAY IT.

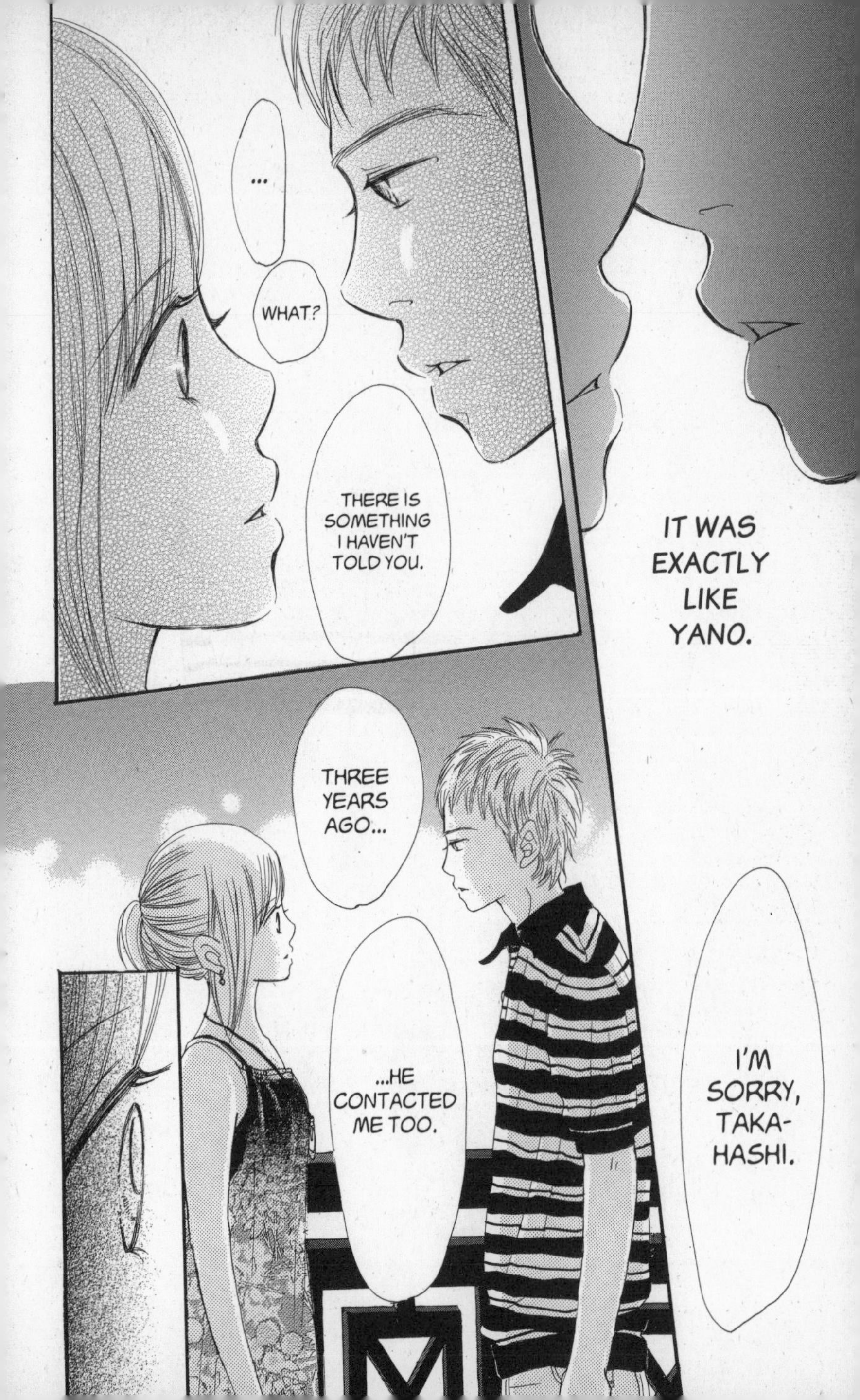
...
WHAT?
THERE IS SOMETHING I HAVEN'T TOLD YOU.
IT WAS EXACTLY LIKE YANO.
THREE YEARS AGO...
...HE CONTACTED ME TOO.
I'M SORRY, TAKA-HASHI.

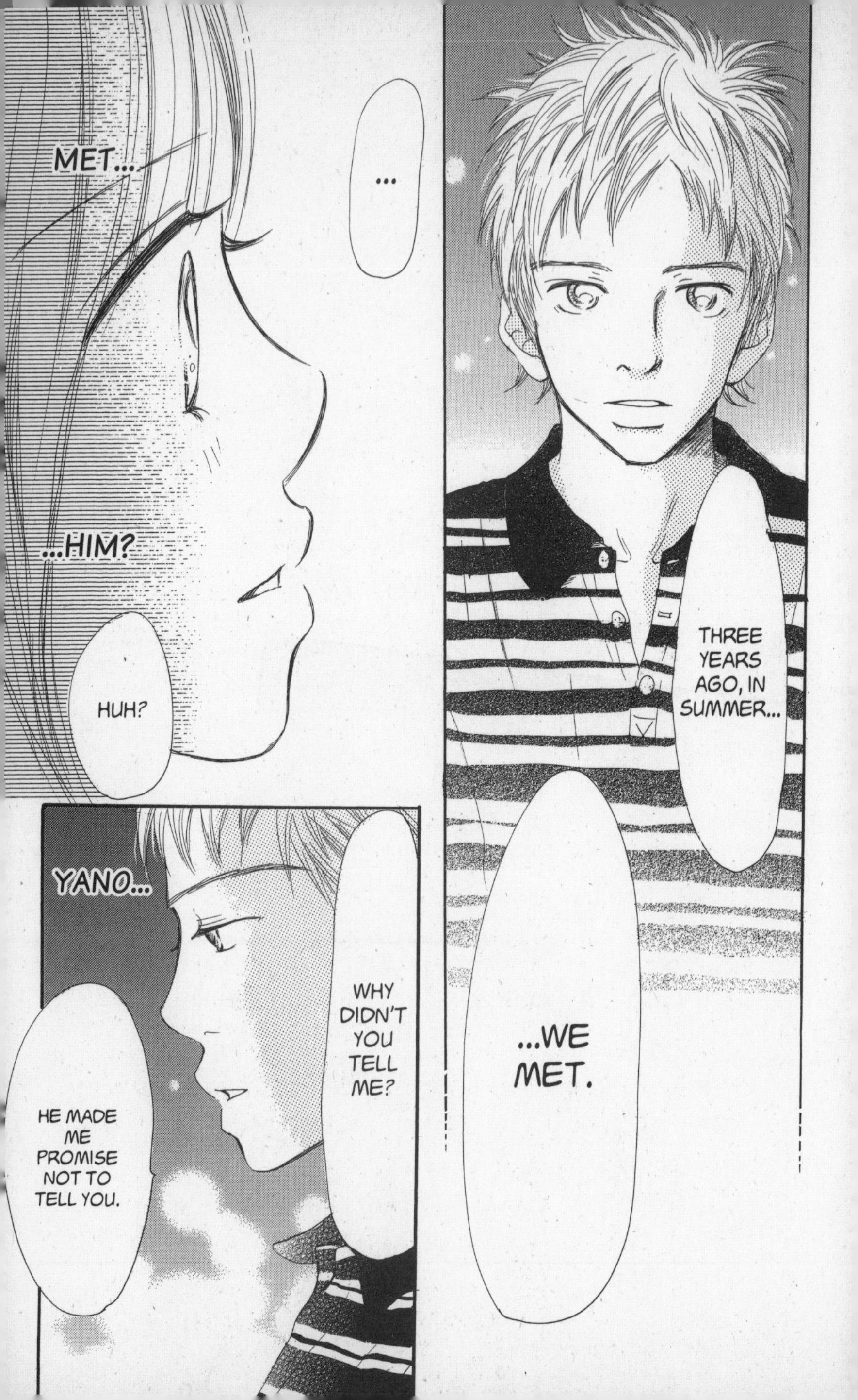
THREE YEARS AGO, IN SUMMER...
...WE MET.
...
MET...
...HIM?
HUH?
WHY DIDN'T YOU TELL ME?
YANO...
HE MADE ME PROMISE NOT TO TELL YOU.

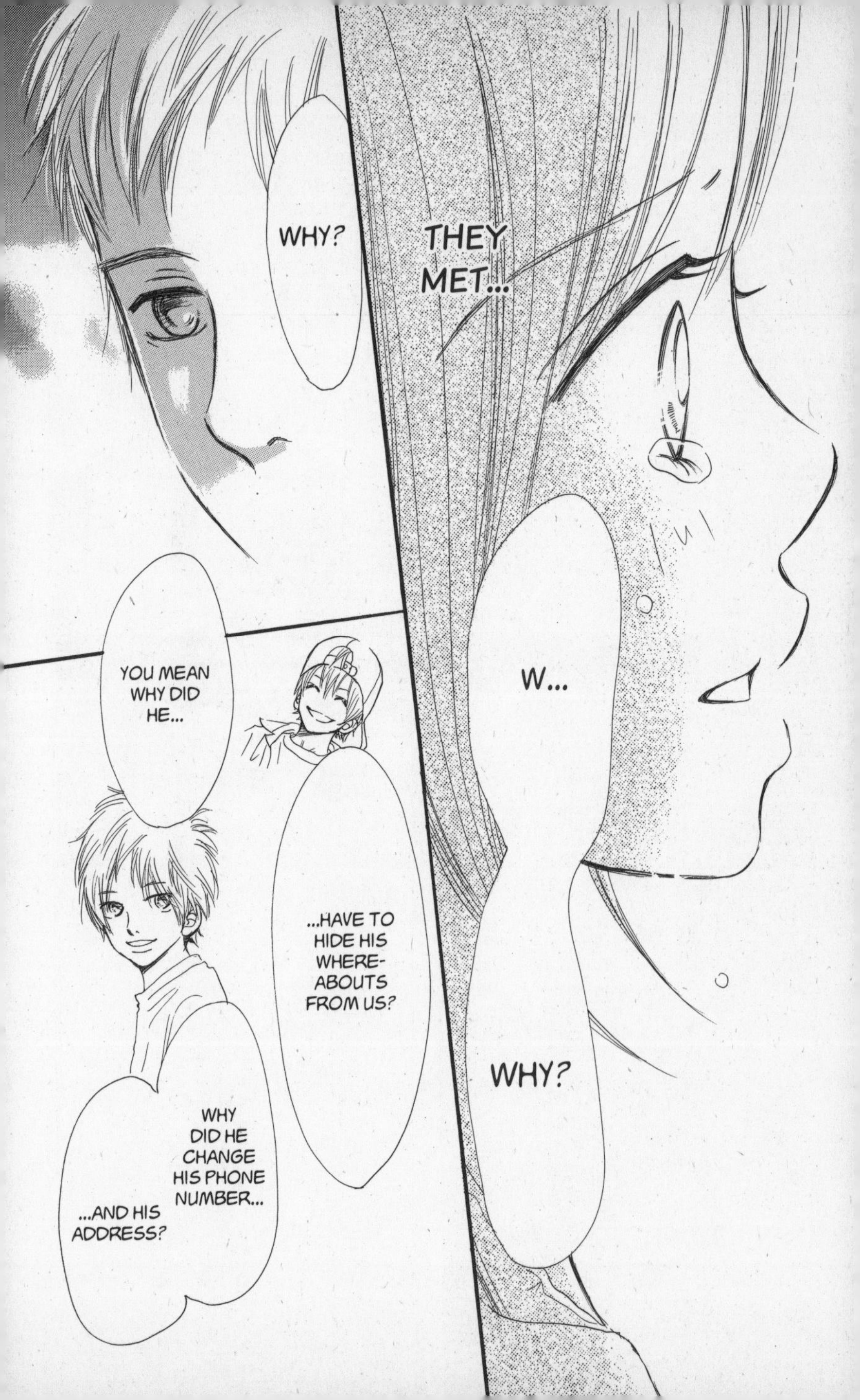
THEY MET...
W...
WHY?
WHY?
YOU MEAN WHY DID HE...
...HAVE TO HIDE HIS WHERE-ABOUTS FROM US?
WHY DID HE CHANGE HIS PHONE NUMBER...
...AND HIS ADDRESS?

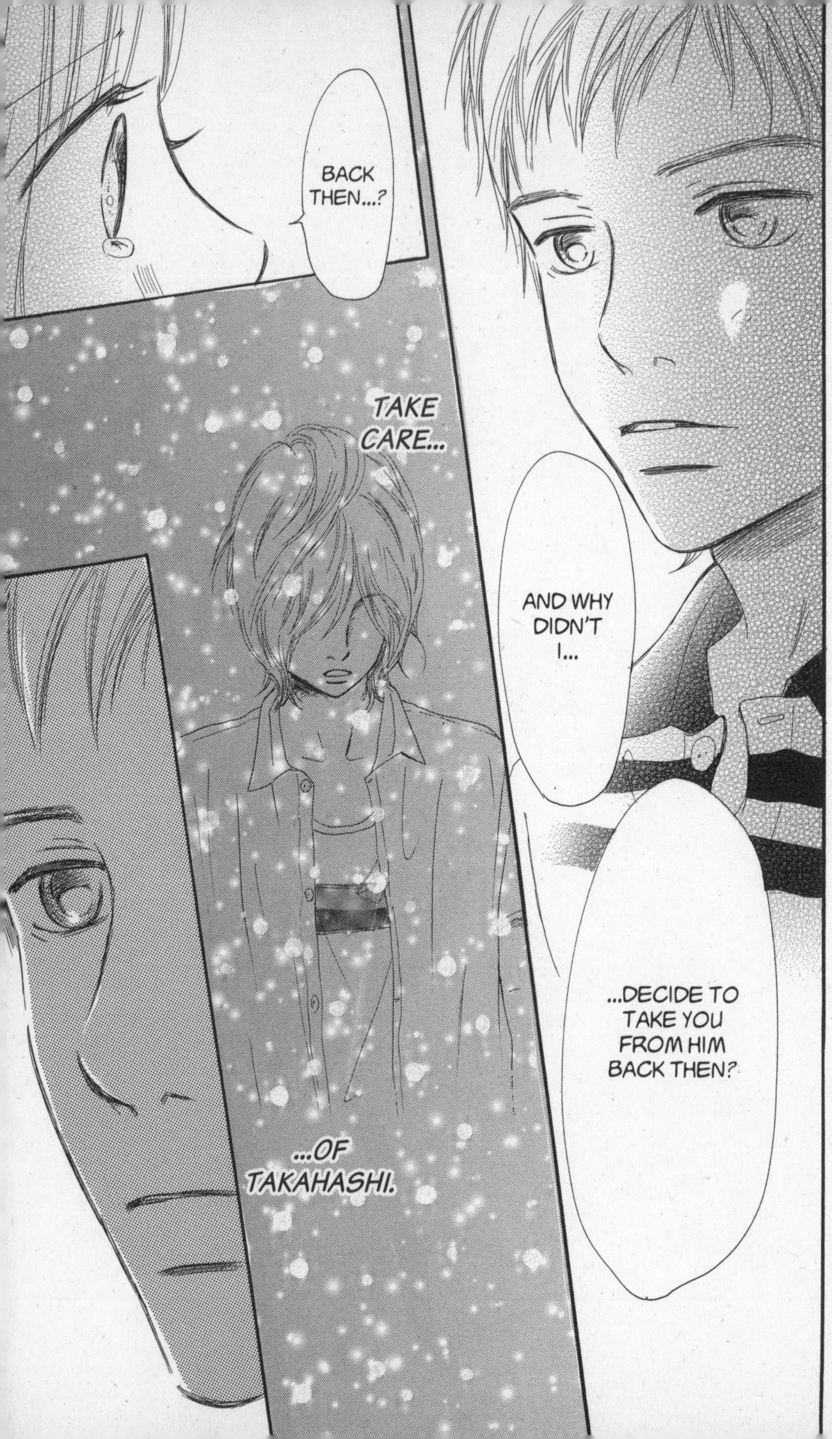
AND WHY DIDN'T I...
...DECIDE TO TAKE YOU FROM HIM BACK THEN?
BACK THEN...?
TAKE CARE...
...OF TAKAHASHI.

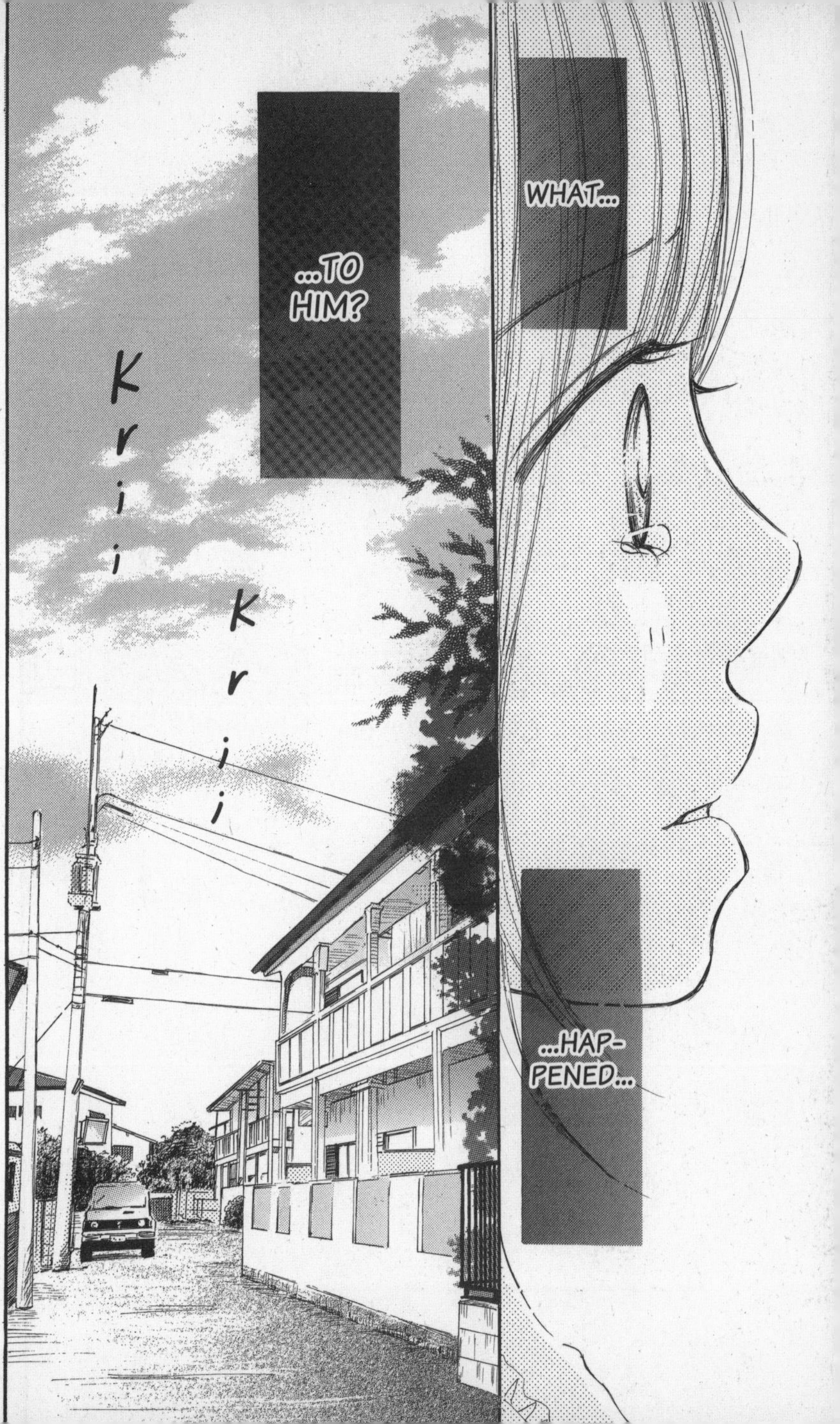
WHAT...
...HAP-PENED...
...TO HIM?
Kri
Kri

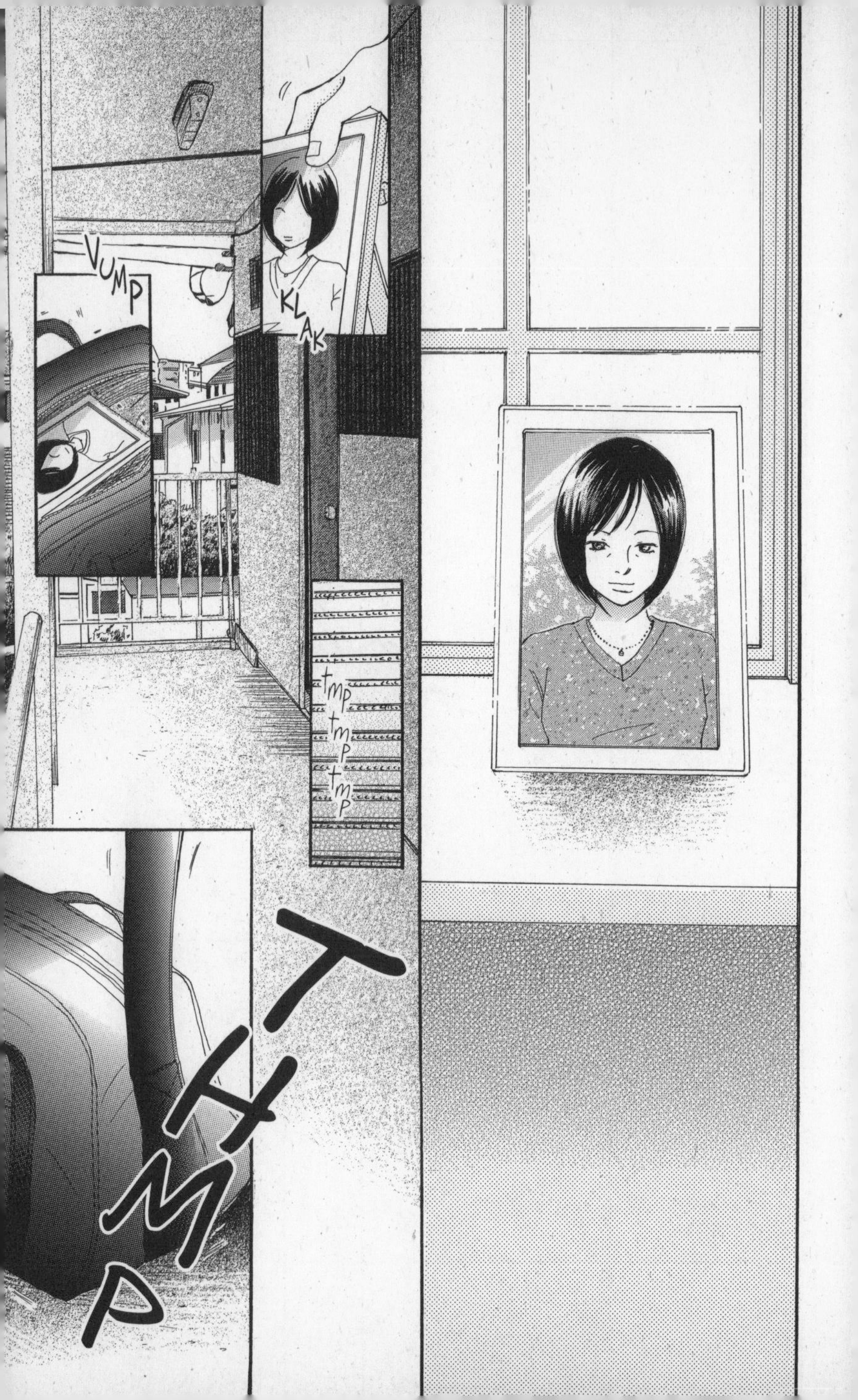
KLAK
VUMP
tmp tmp tmp
THMP

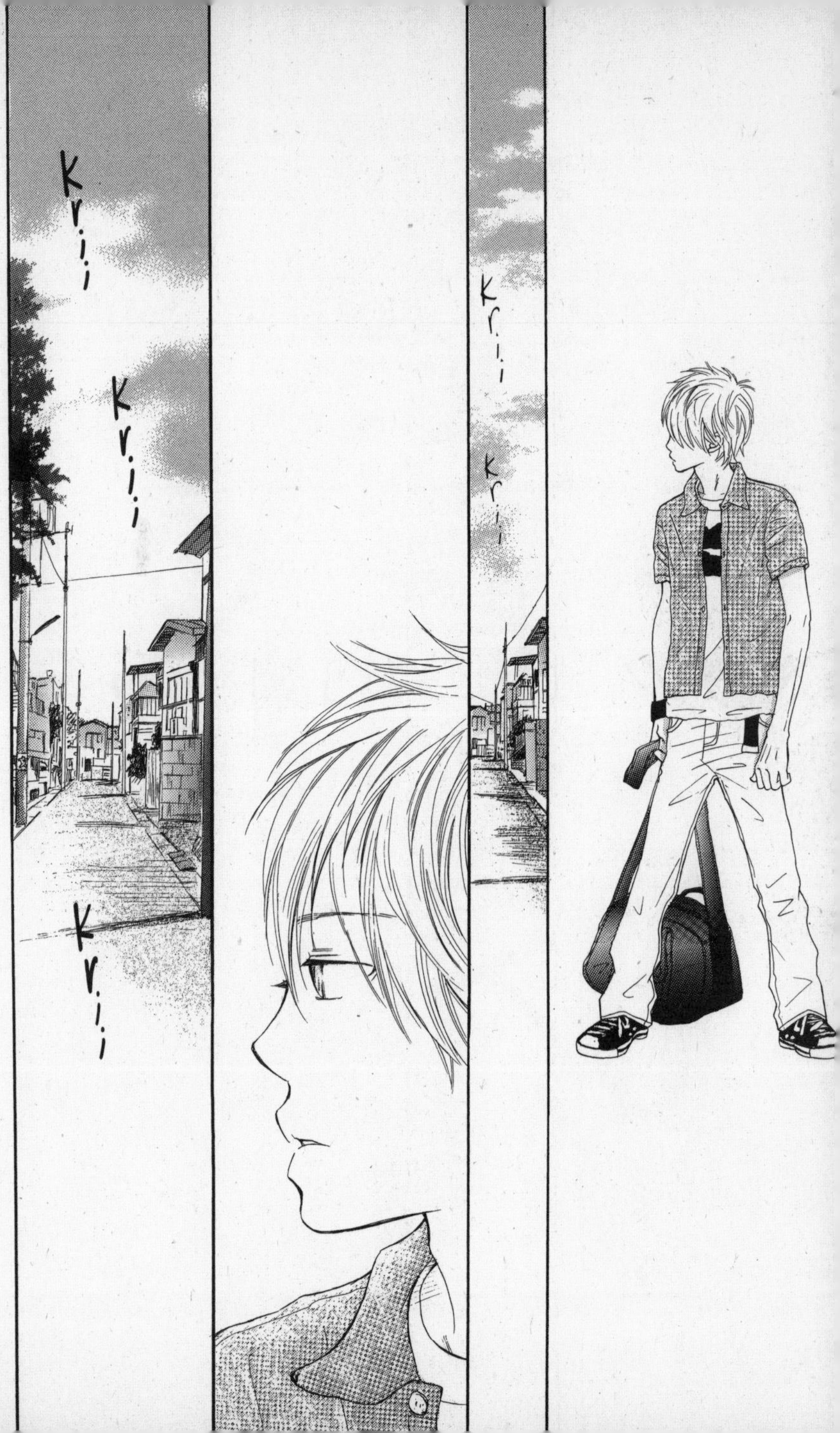
Krii
Krii
Krii
Krii
Krii

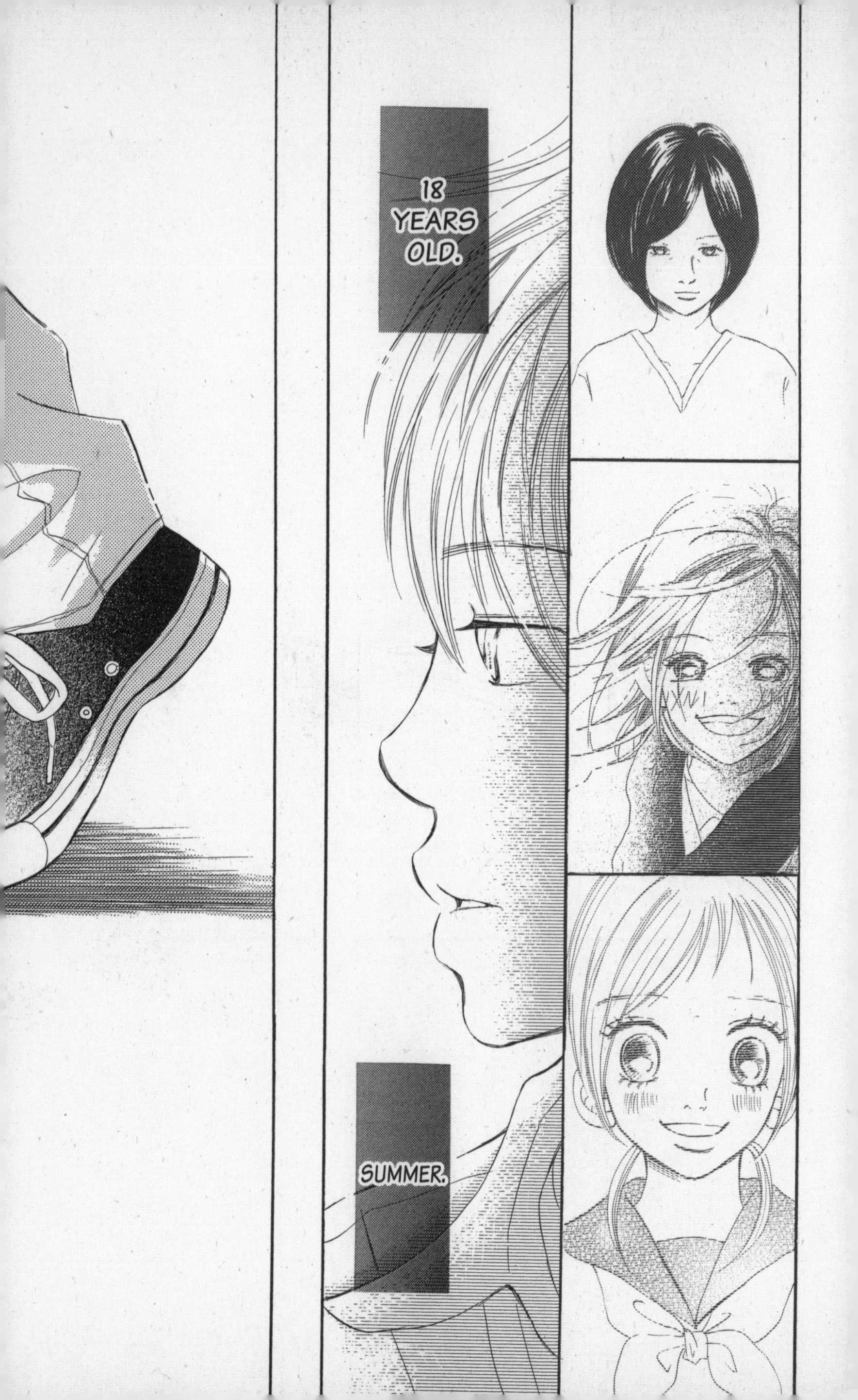
18 YEARS OLD.
SUMMER.

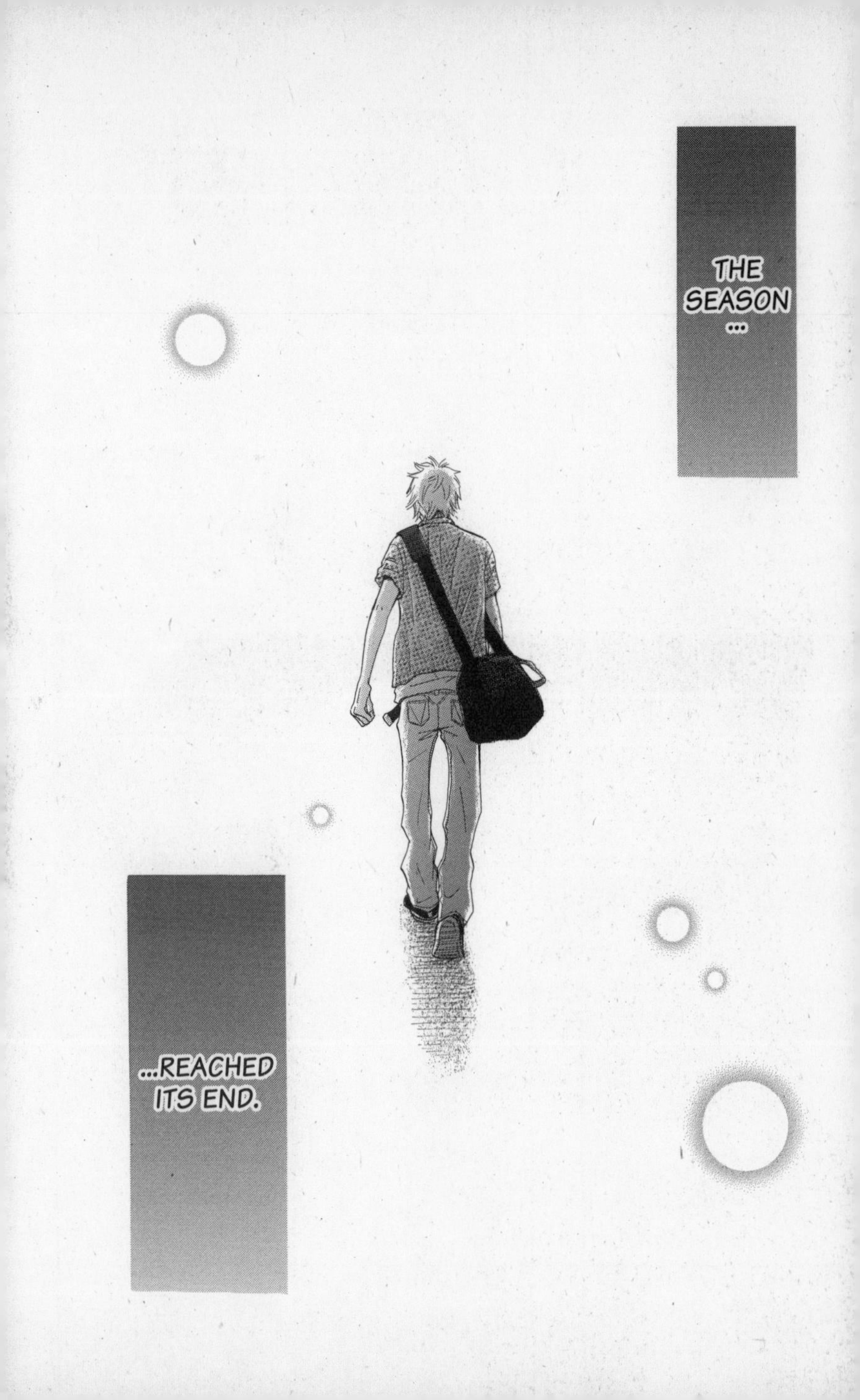
THE SEASON ...
...REACHED ITS END.

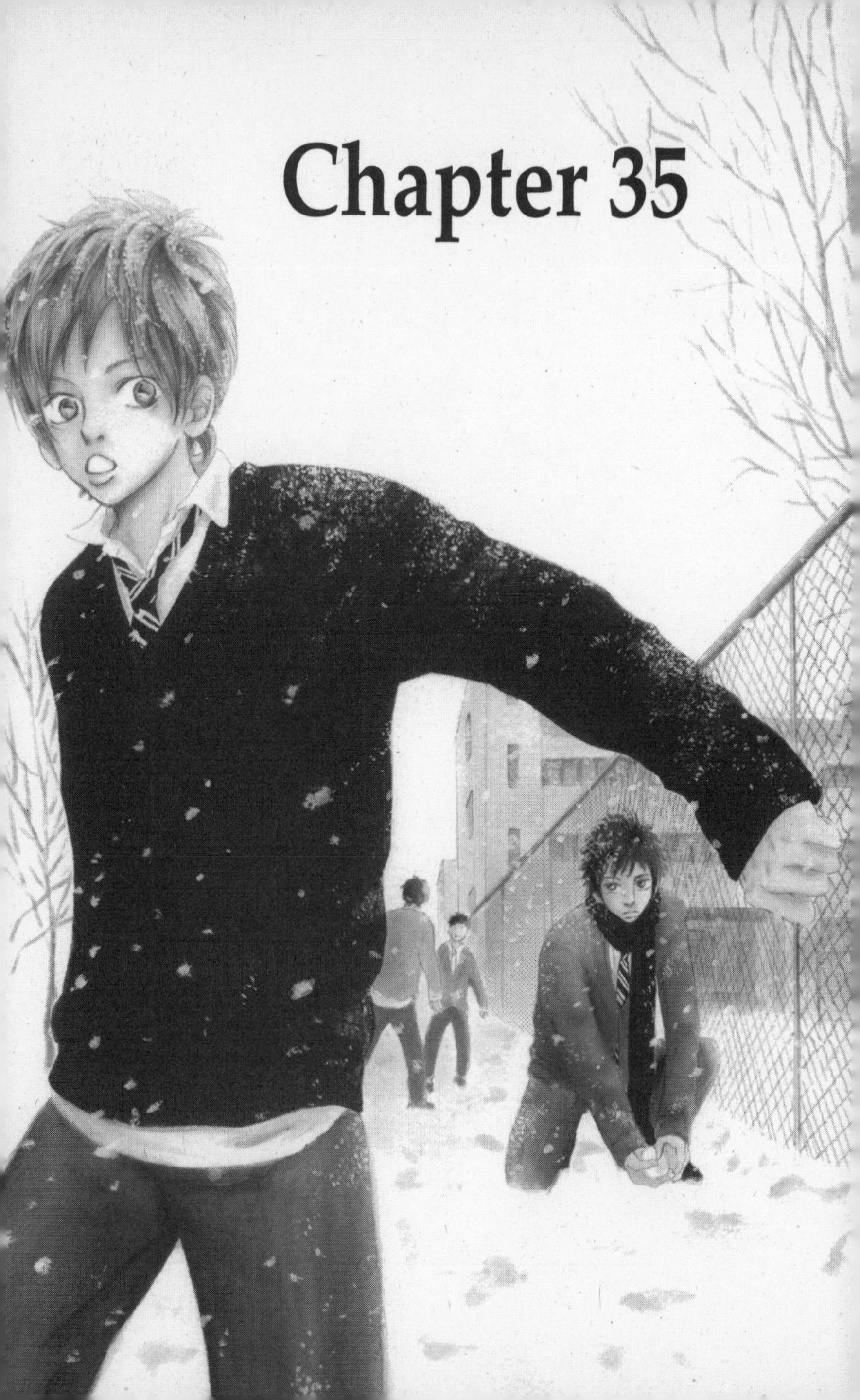
Chapter 35

SOMEONE ONCE SAID...

MEMORIES...

...ARE SIMPLY A PRODUCT OF ONE'S IMAGINATION, CREATED FROM THE FRAGMENTS OF THE PAST.

REMEMBERING...

...IS THE SAME AS SEEING AN ILLUSION.

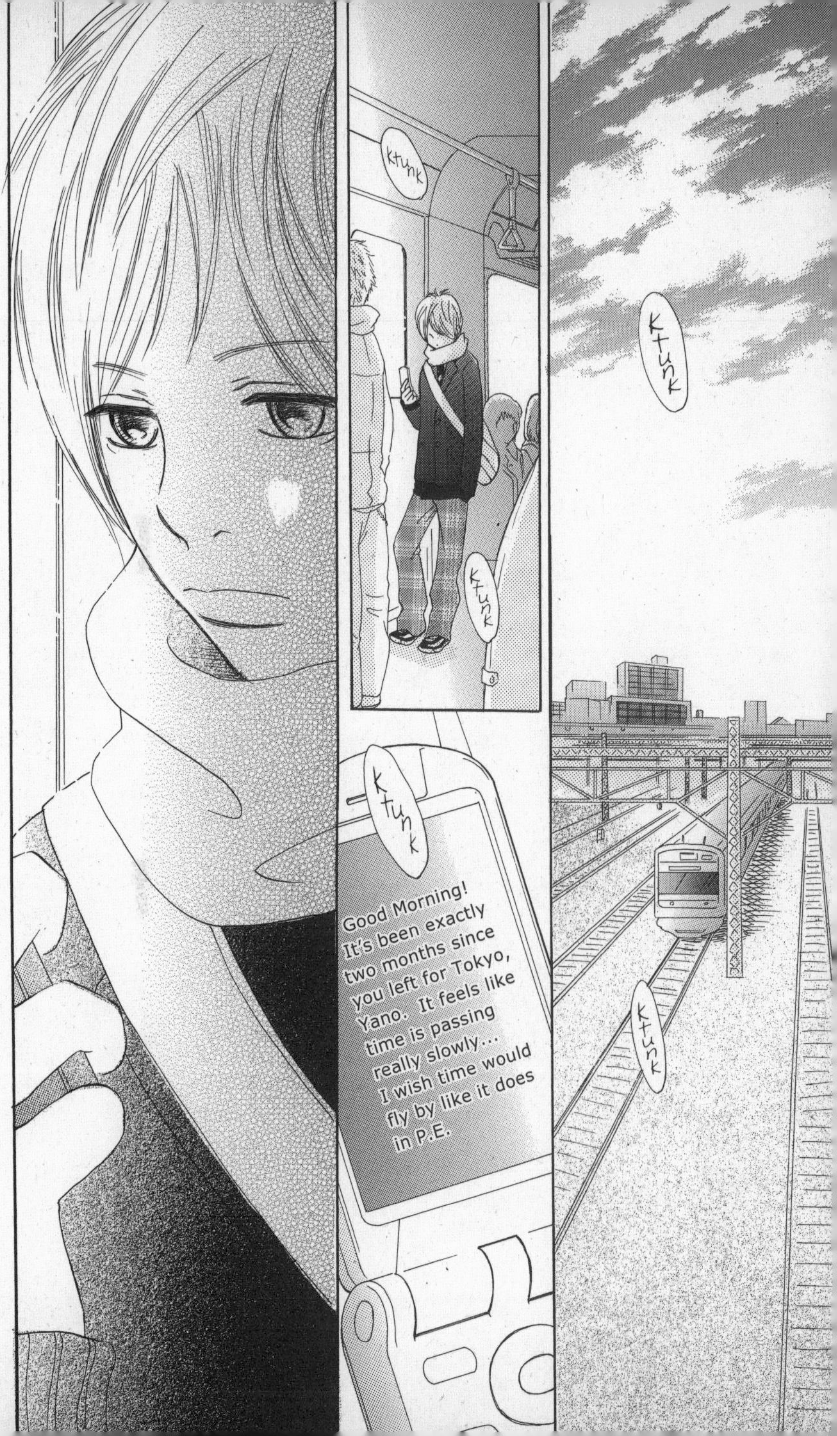
Ktunk
Ktunk
ktunk
Ktunk
Ktunk
Good Morning!
It's been exactly two months since you left for Tokyo, Yano. It feels like time is passing really slowly... I wish time would fly by like it does in P.E.

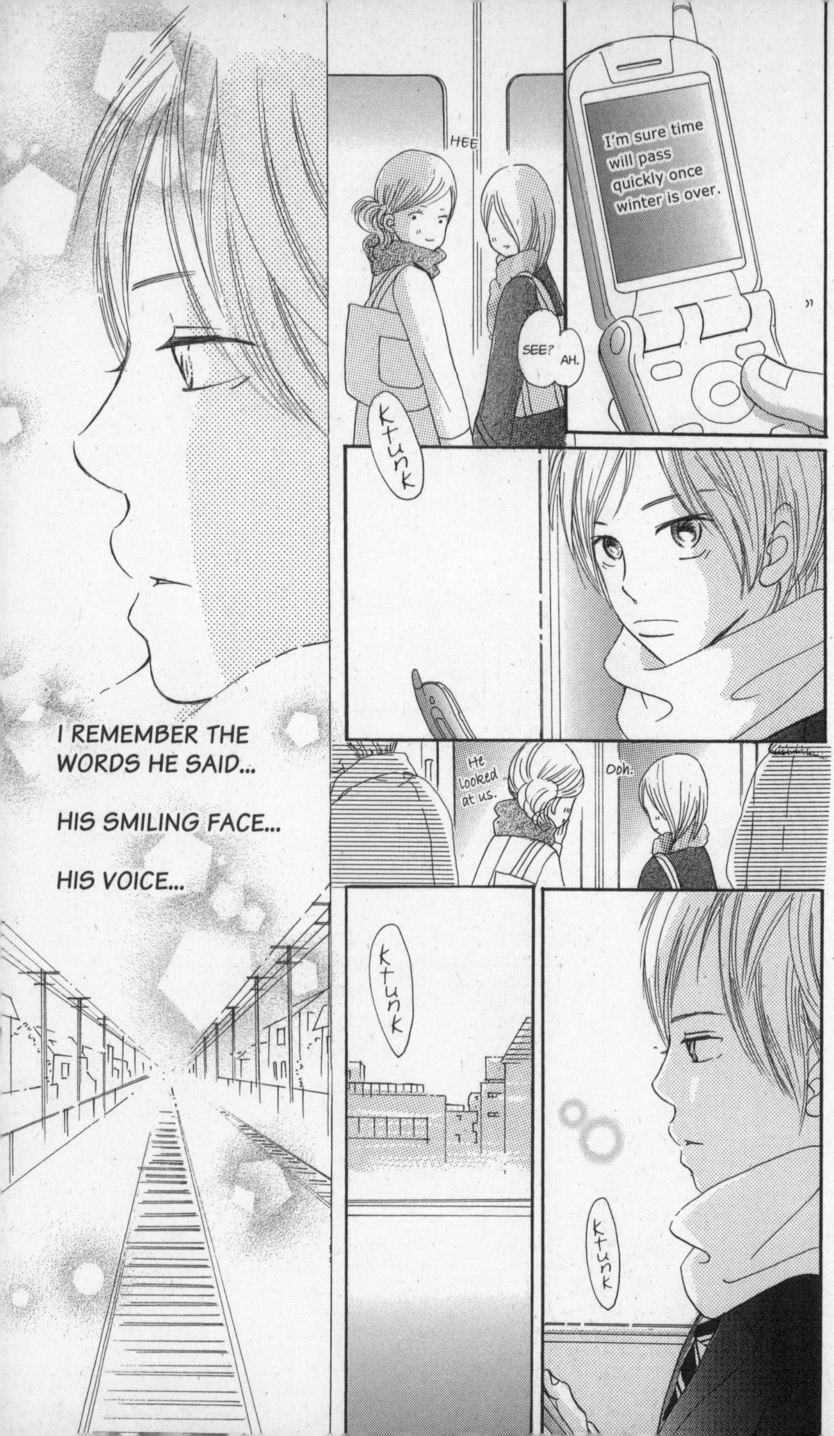
I'm sure time will pass quickly once winter is over.
HEE
SEE?
AH.
ktunk
Ooh.
He looked at us.
ktunk
ktunk
I REMEMBER THE WORDS HE SAID...
HIS SMILING FACE...
HIS VOICE...

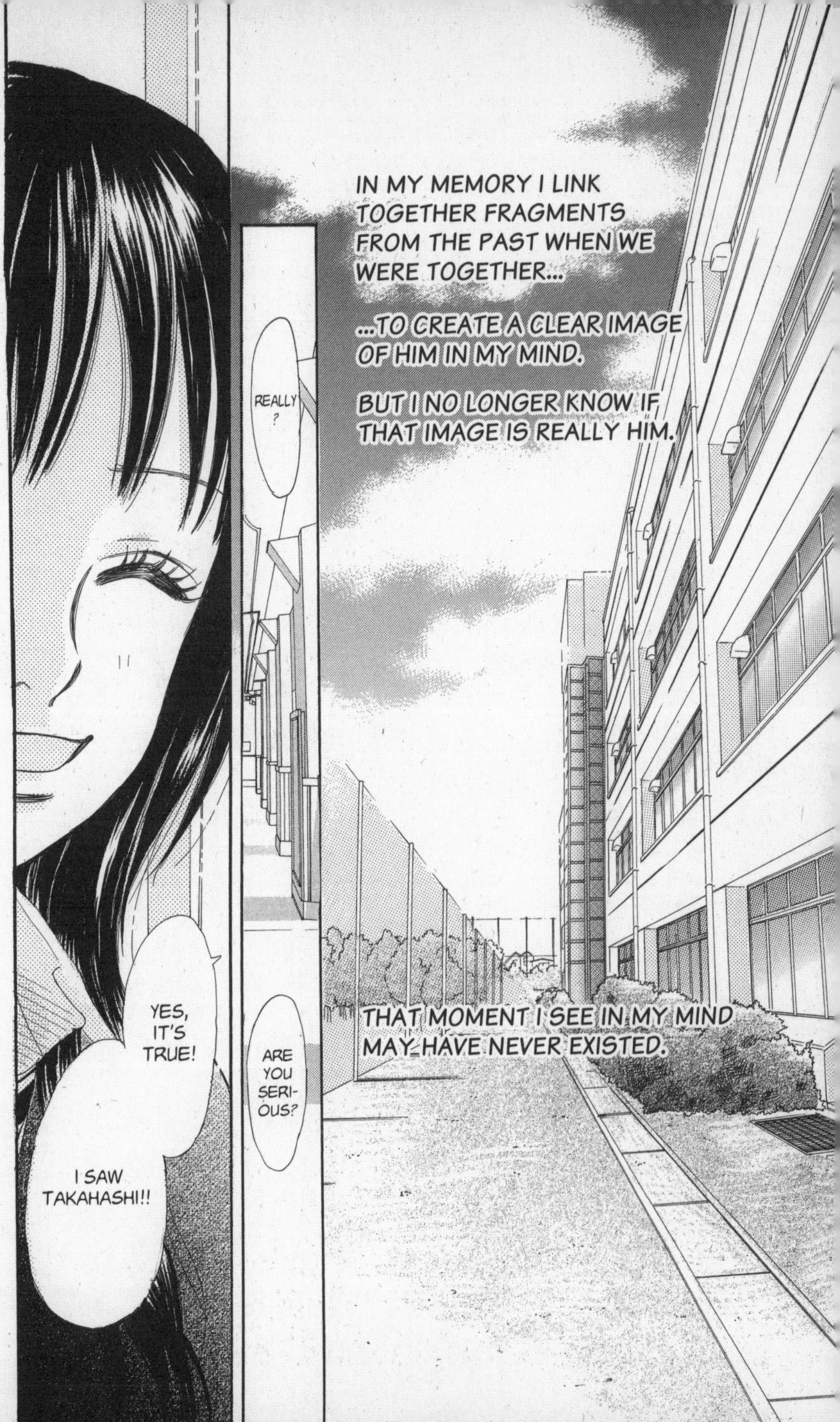
IN MY MEMORY I LINK TOGETHER FRAGMENTS FROM THE PAST WHEN WE WERE TOGETHER...
...TO CREATE A CLEAR IMAGE OF HIM IN MY MIND.
BUT I NO LONGER KNOW IF THAT IMAGE IS REALLY HIM.
THAT MOMENT I SEE IN MY MIND MAY HAVE NEVER EXISTED.
REALLY?
ARE YOU SERIOUS?
YES, IT'S TRUE!
I SAW TAKAHASHI!!

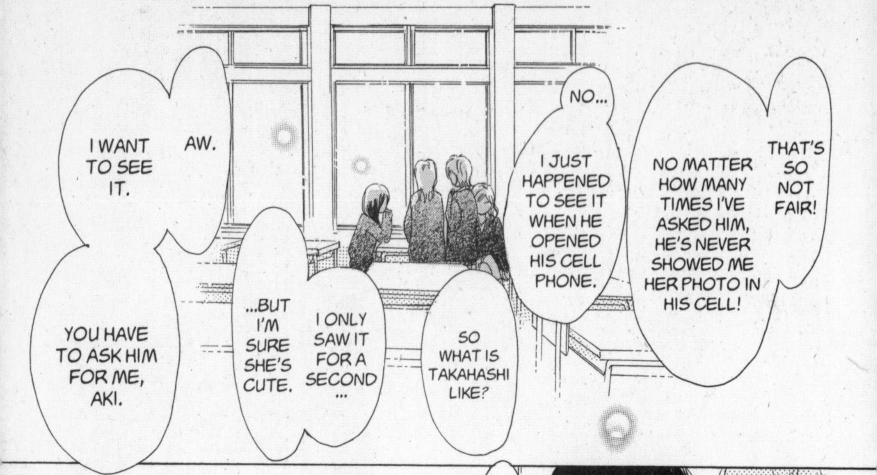
THAT'S SO NOT FAIR!
NO MATTER HOW MANY TIMES I'VE ASKED HIM, HE'S NEVER SHOWED ME HER PHOTO IN HIS CELL!
NO...
I JUST HAPPENED TO SEE IT WHEN HE OPENED HIS CELL PHONE.
SO WHAT IS TAKAHASHI LIKE?
I ONLY SAW IT FOR A SECOND...
...BUT I'M SURE SHE'S CUTE.
AW.
I WANT TO SEE IT.
YOU HAVE TO ASK HIM FOR ME, AKI.

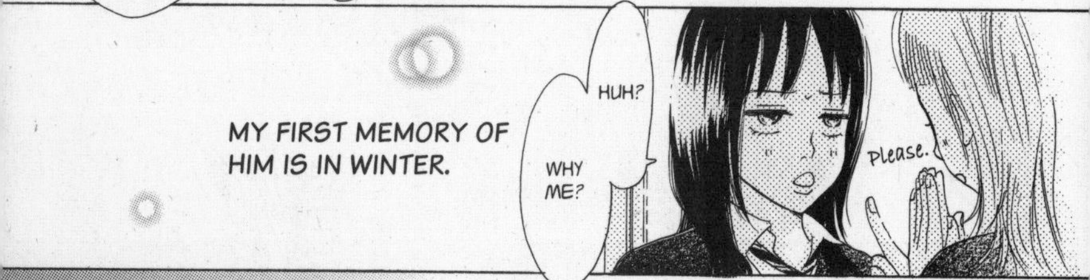
Please.
HUH?
WHY ME?
MY FIRST MEMORY OF HIM IS IN WINTER.

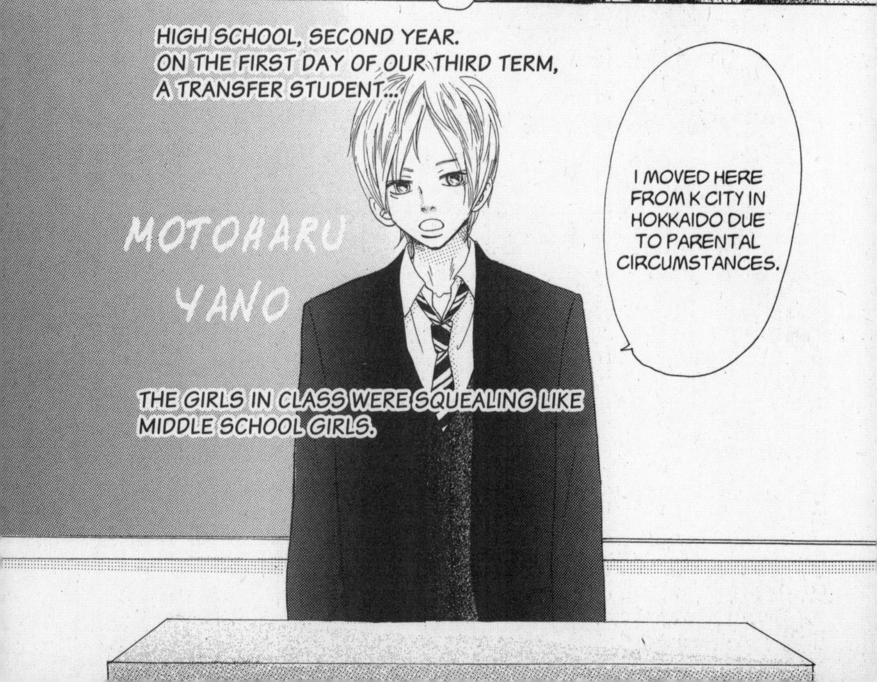
HIGH SCHOOL, SECOND YEAR. ON THE FIRST DAY OF OUR THIRD TERM, A TRANSFER STUDENT...
I MOVED HERE FROM K CITY IN HOKKAIDO DUE TO PARENTAL CIRCUMSTANCES.
MOTOHARU YANO
THE GIRLS IN CLASS WERE SQUEALING LIKE MIDDLE SCHOOL GIRLS.

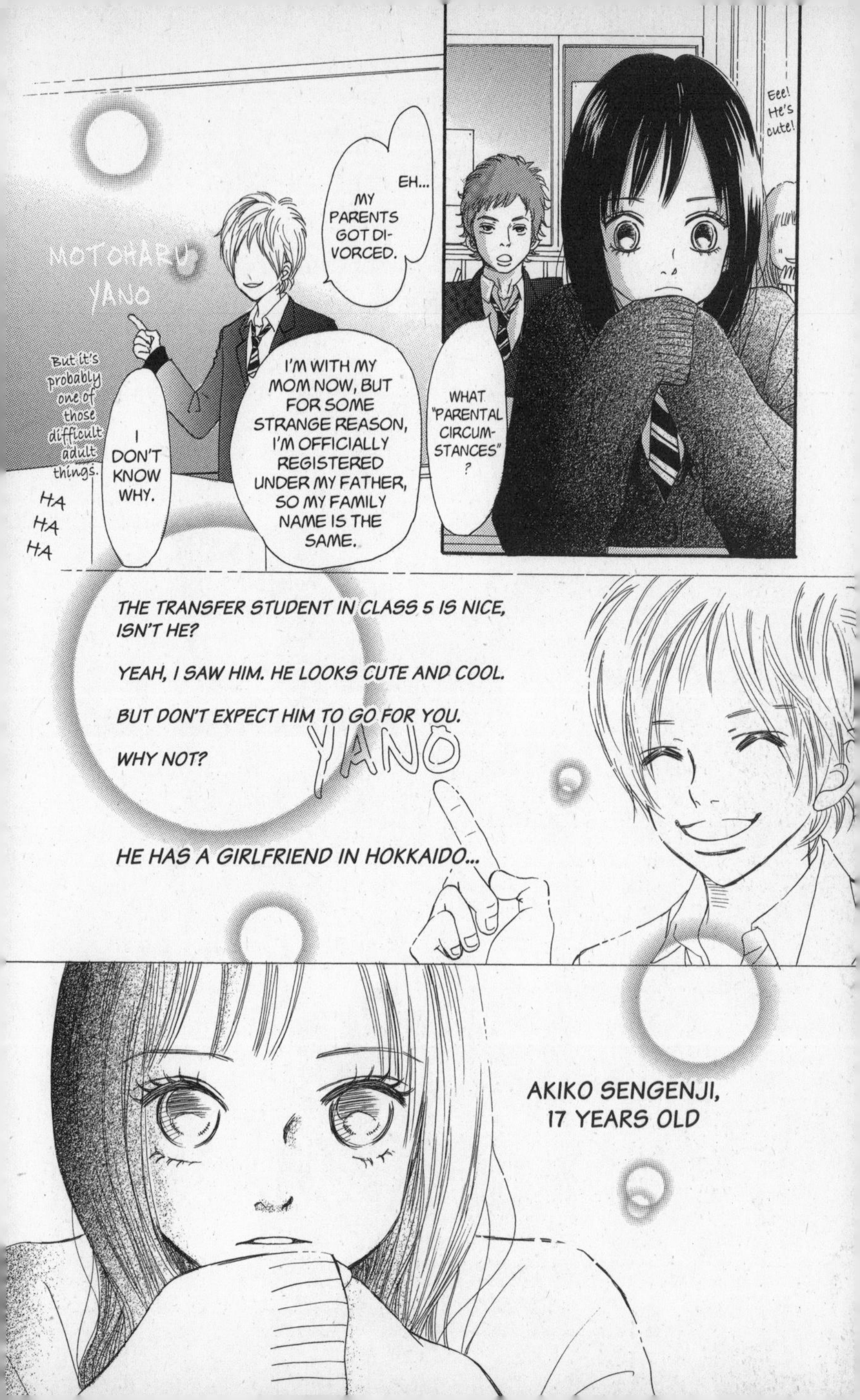
Eee! He's cute!
WHAT "PARENTAL CIRCUMSTANCES"?
EH... MY PARENTS GOT DIVORCED.
I'M WITH MY MOM NOW, BUT FOR SOME STRANGE REASON, I'M OFFICIALLY REGISTERED UNDER MY FATHER, SO MY FAMILY NAME IS THE SAME.
MOTOHARU YANO
I DON'T KNOW WHY.
But it's probably one of those difficult adult things.
HA HA HA
THE TRANSFER STUDENT IN CLASS 5 IS NICE, ISN'T HE?
YEAH, I SAW HIM. HE LOOKS CUTE AND COOL.
BUT DON'T EXPECT HIM TO GO FOR YOU.
WHY NOT?
YANO
HE HAS A GIRLFRIEND IN HOKKAIDO...
AKIKO SENGENJI, 17 YEARS OLD

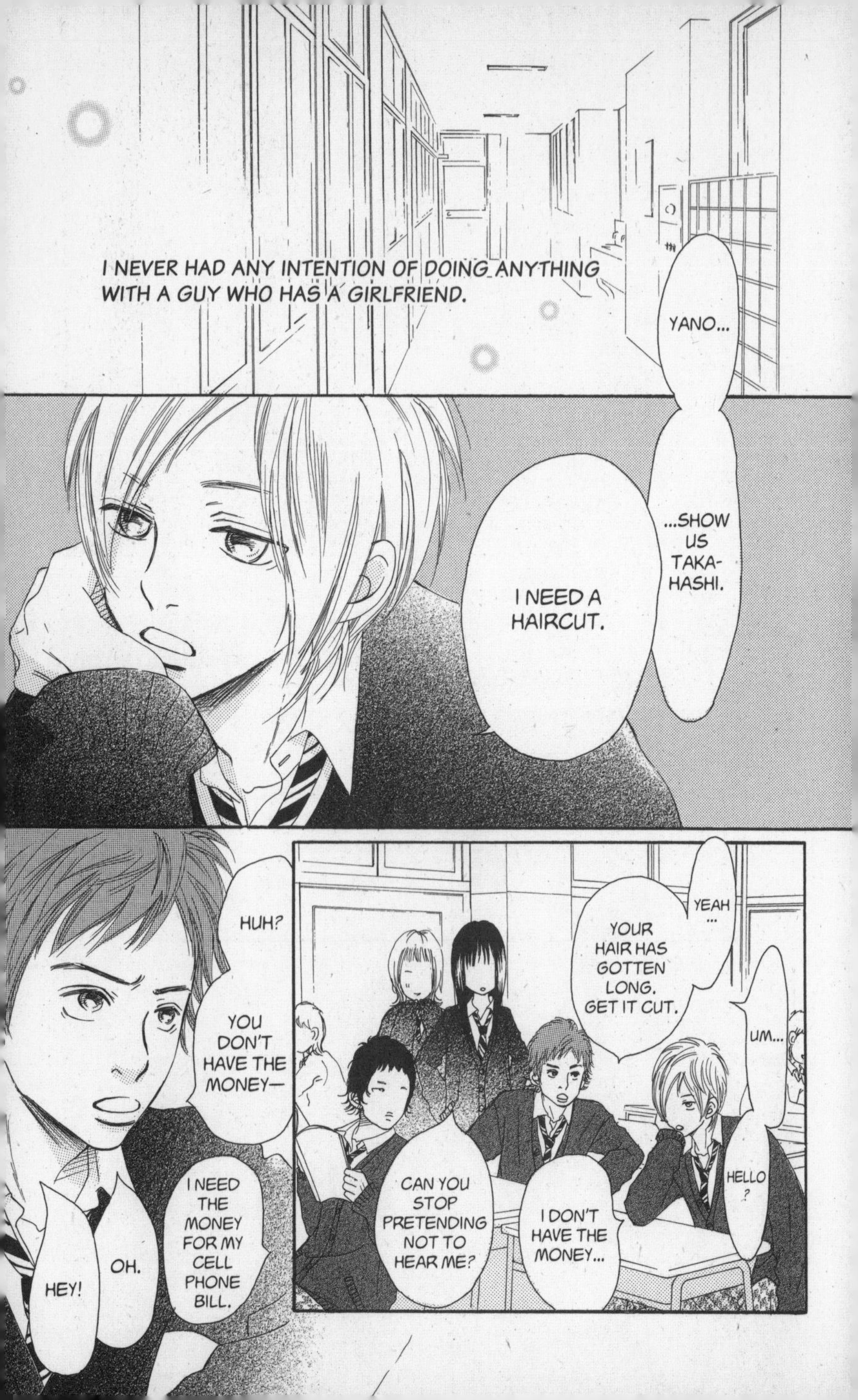
I NEVER HAD ANY INTENTION OF DOING ANYTHING WITH A GUY WHO HAS A GIRLFRIEND.
YANO...
...SHOW US TAKA-HASHI.
I NEED A HAIRCUT.
YEAH ...
YOUR HAIR HAS GOTTEN LONG. GET IT CUT.
UM...
HELLO ?
I DON'T HAVE THE MONEY...
CAN YOU STOP PRETENDING NOT TO HEAR ME?
HUH?
YOU DON'T HAVE THE MONEY—
I NEED THE MONEY FOR MY CELL PHONE BILL.
OH.
HEY!

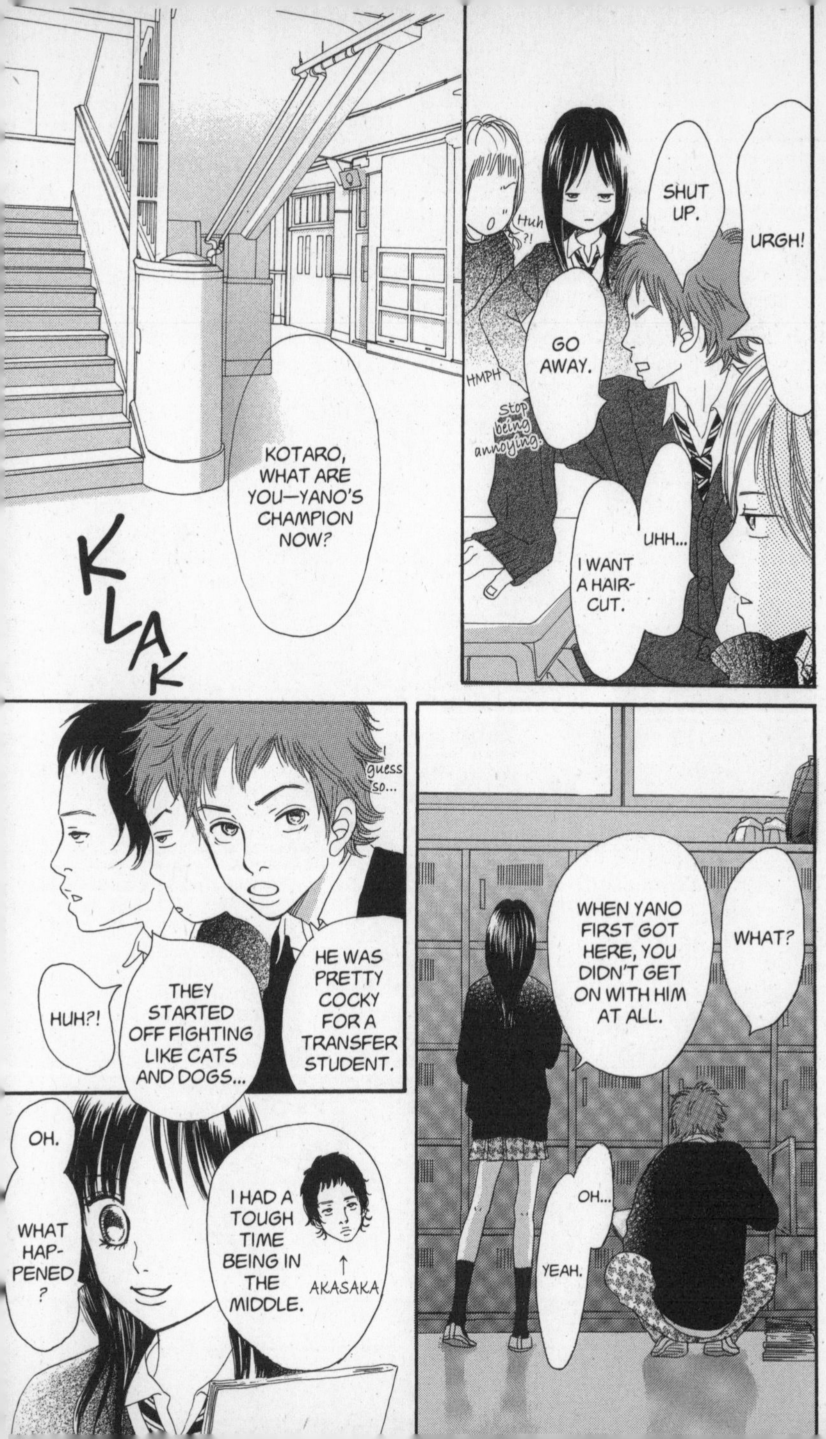
URGH!
SHUT UP.
Huh ?!
GO AWAY.
HMPH
Stop being annoying.
UHH...
I WANT A HAIR-CUT.
KOTARO, WHAT ARE YOU—YANO'S CHAMPION NOW?
KLAK
WHAT?
WHEN YANO FIRST GOT HERE, YOU DIDN'T GET ON WITH HIM AT ALL.
OH...
YEAH.
I guess so...
HE WAS PRETTY COCKY FOR A TRANSFER STUDENT.
THEY STARTED OFF FIGHTING LIKE CATS AND DOGS...
HUH?!
I HAD A TOUGH TIME BEING IN THE MIDDLE.
↑ AKASAKA
OH.
WHAT HAP-PENED ?

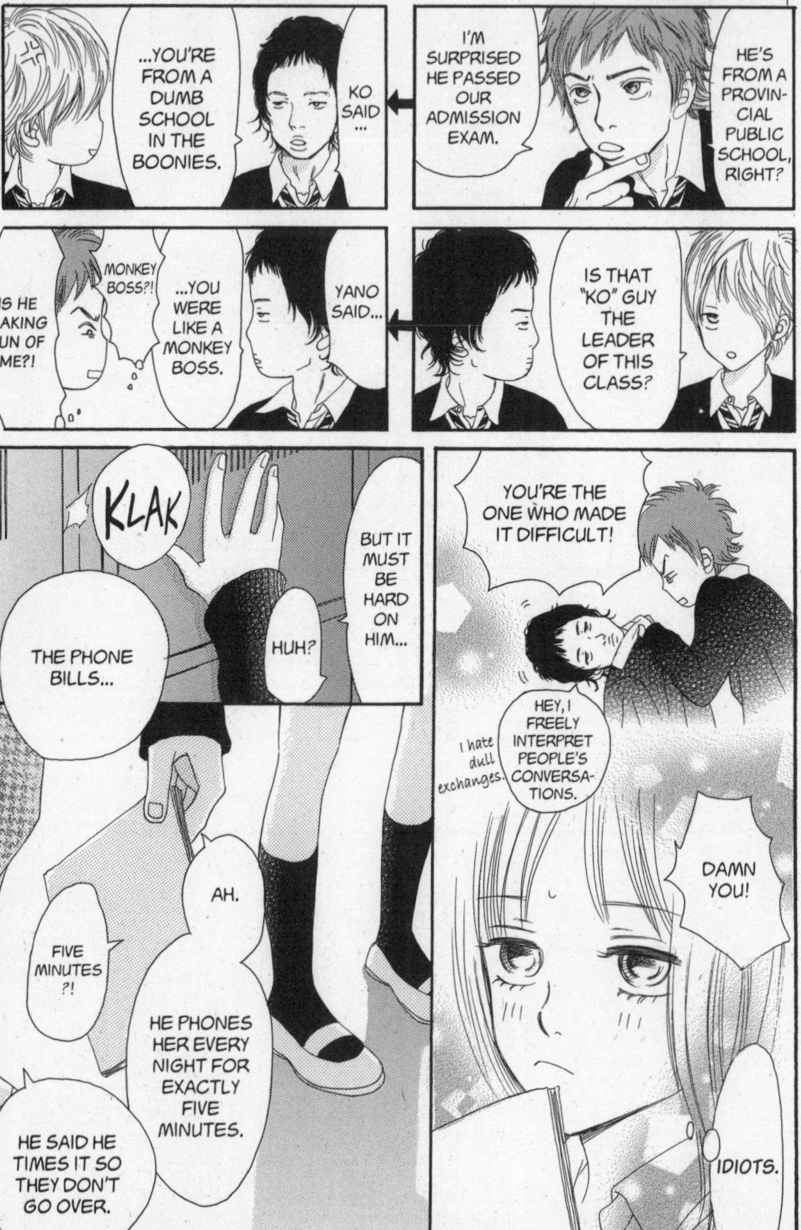
HE'S FROM A PROVIN-CIAL PUBLIC SCHOOL, RIGHT?
I'M SURPRISED HE PASSED OUR ADMISSION EXAM.
KO SAID ...
...YOU'RE FROM A DUMB SCHOOL IN THE BOONIES.
IS THAT "KO" GUY THE LEADER OF THIS CLASS?
YANO SAID...
...YOU WERE LIKE A MONKEY BOSS.
MONKEY BOSS?!
IS HE MAKING FUN OF ME?!
YOU'RE THE ONE WHO MADE IT DIFFICULT!
HEY, I FREELY INTERPRET PEOPLE'S CONVERSA-TIONS.
I hate dull exchanges.
DAMN YOU!
IDIOTS.
KLAK
BUT IT MUST BE HARD ON HIM...
HUH?
THE PHONE BILLS...
AH.
FIVE MINUTES ?!
HE PHONES HER EVERY NIGHT FOR EXACTLY FIVE MINUTES.
HE SAID HE TIMES IT SO THEY DON'T GO OVER.

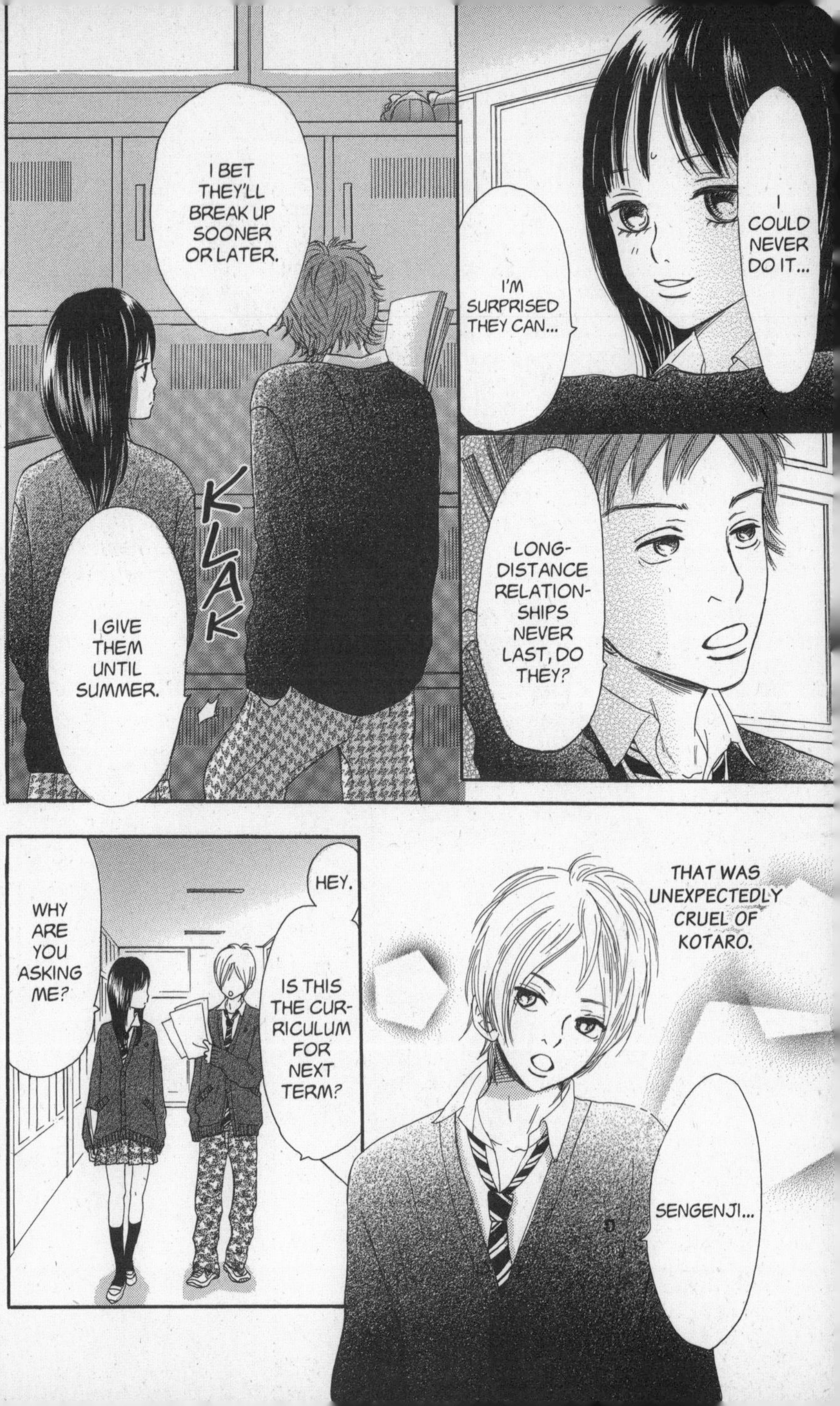
I COULD NEVER DO IT...
I'M SURPRISED THEY CAN...
LONG-DISTANCE RELATION-SHIPS NEVER LAST, DO THEY?
I BET THEY'LL BREAK UP SOONER OR LATER.
KLAK
I GIVE THEM UNTIL SUMMER.
THAT WAS UNEXPECTEDLY CRUEL OF KOTARO.
SENGENJI...
HEY.
IS THIS THE CUR-RICULUM FOR NEXT TERM?
WHY ARE YOU ASKING ME?

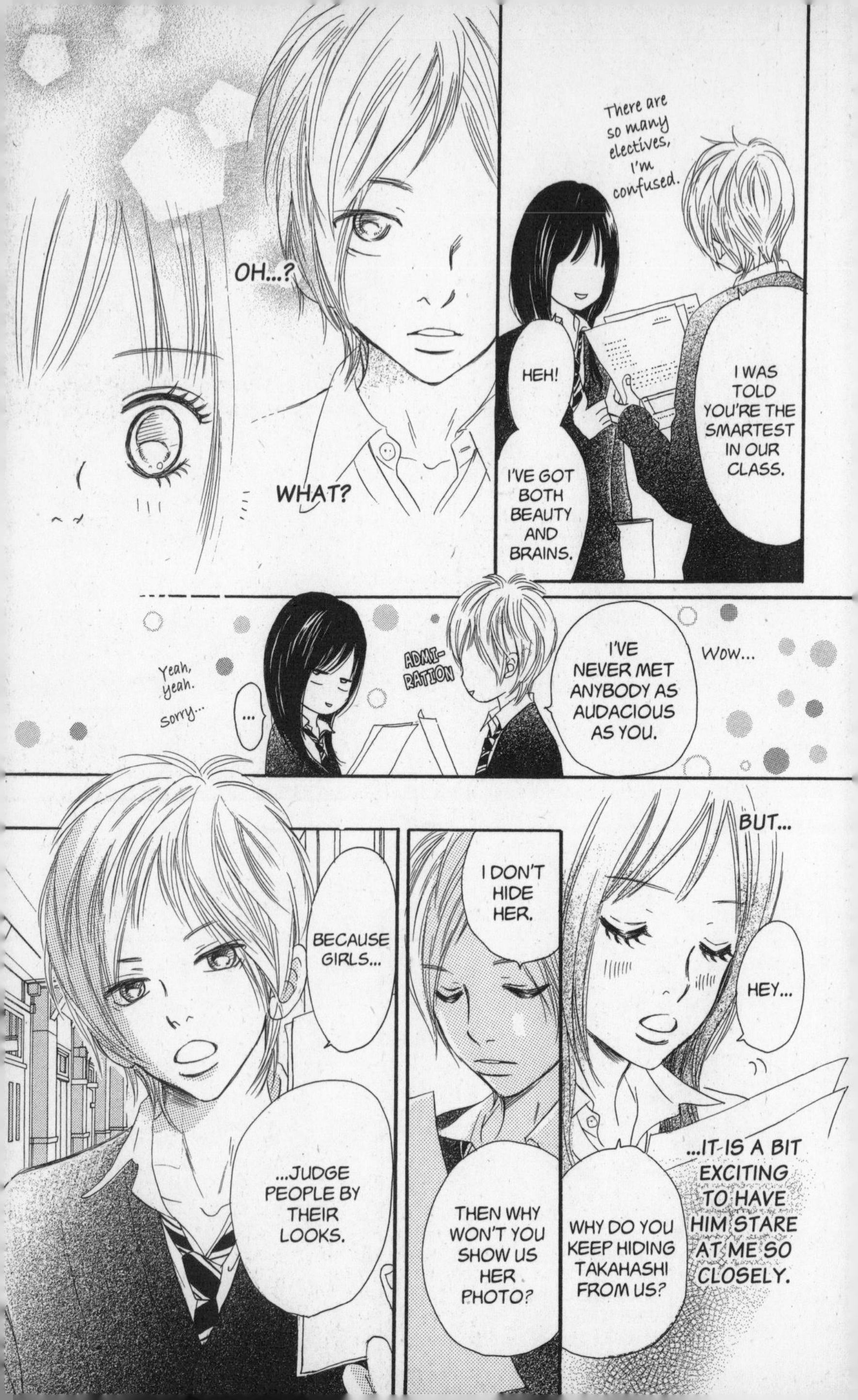
There are so many electives, I'm confused.
I WAS TOLD YOU'RE THE SMARTEST IN OUR CLASS.
HEH!
I'VE GOT BOTH BEAUTY AND BRAINS.
OH...?
WHAT?
Wow...
I'VE NEVER MET ANYBODY AS AUDACIOUS AS YOU.
ADMI-RATION
...
Yeah, yeah. Sorry...
BUT...
HEY...
...IT IS A BIT EXCITING TO HAVE HIM STARE AT ME SO CLOSELY.
WHY DO YOU KEEP HIDING TAKAHASHI FROM US?
I DON'T HIDE HER.
THEN WHY WON'T YOU SHOW US HER PHOTO?
BECAUSE GIRLS...
...JUDGE PEOPLE BY THEIR LOOKS.

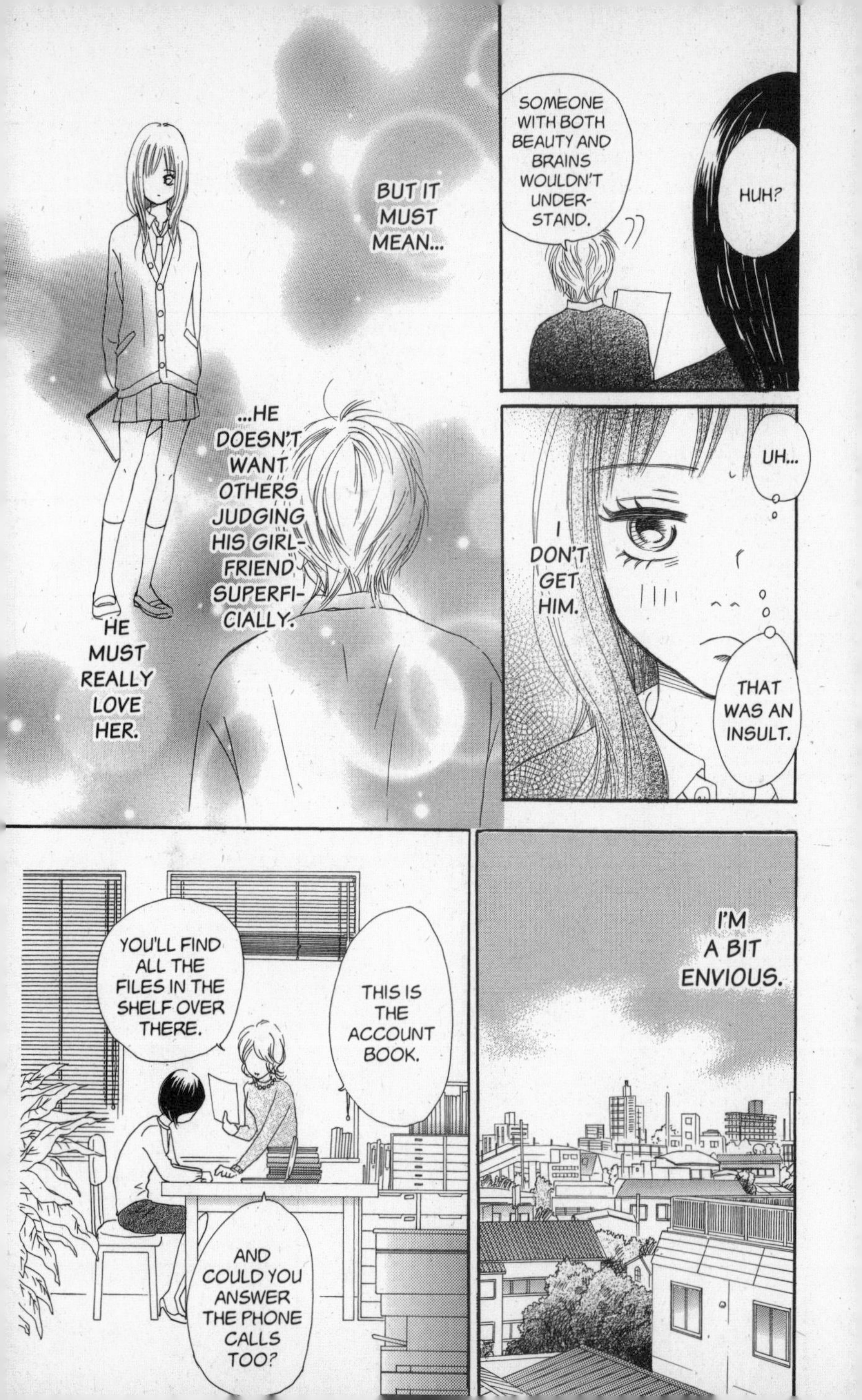
HUH?
SOMEONE WITH BOTH BEAUTY AND BRAINS WOULDN'T UNDER-STAND.
UH...
I DON'T GET HIM.
THAT WAS AN INSULT.
BUT IT MUST MEAN...
...HE DOESN'T WANT OTHERS JUDGING HIS GIRL-FRIEND SUPERFI-CIALLY.
HE MUST REALLY LOVE HER.
I'M A BIT ENVIOUS.
THIS IS THE ACCOUNT BOOK.
YOU'LL FIND ALL THE FILES IN THE SHELF OVER THERE.
AND COULD YOU ANSWER THE PHONE CALLS TOO?

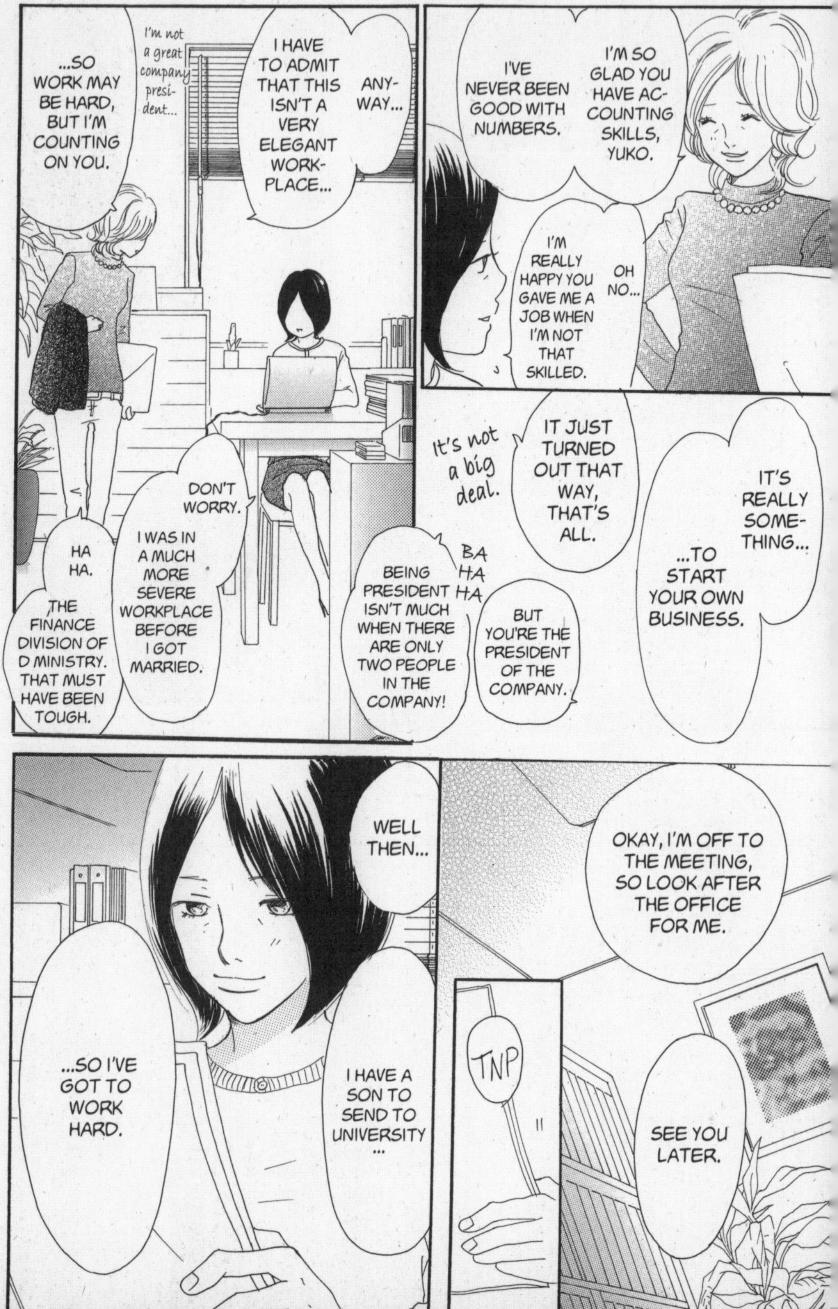
I'M SO GLAD YOU HAVE AC-COUNTING SKILLS, YUKO.
I'VE NEVER BEEN GOOD WITH NUMBERS.
OH NO...
I'M REALLY HAPPY YOU GAVE ME A JOB WHEN I'M NOT THAT SKILLED.
IT'S REALLY SOME-THING...
...TO START YOUR OWN BUSINESS.
IT JUST TURNED OUT THAT WAY, THAT'S ALL.
It's not a big deal.
BUT YOU'RE THE PRESIDENT OF THE COMPANY.
BA HA HA
BEING PRESIDENT ISN'T MUCH WHEN THERE ARE ONLY TWO PEOPLE IN THE COMPANY!
ANY-WAY...
I HAVE TO ADMIT THAT THIS ISN'T A VERY ELEGANT WORK-PLACE...
I'm not a great company presi-dent...
...SO WORK MAY BE HARD, BUT I'M COUNTING ON YOU.
DON'T WORRY.
I WAS IN A MUCH MORE SEVERE WORKPLACE BEFORE I GOT MARRIED.
HA HA.
THE FINANCE DIVISION OF D MINISTRY. THAT MUST HAVE BEEN TOUGH.
OKAY, I'M OFF TO THE MEETING, SO LOOK AFTER THE OFFICE FOR ME.
TNP
SEE YOU LATER.
WELL THEN...
I HAVE A SON TO SEND TO UNIVERSITY ...
...SO I'VE GOT TO WORK HARD.

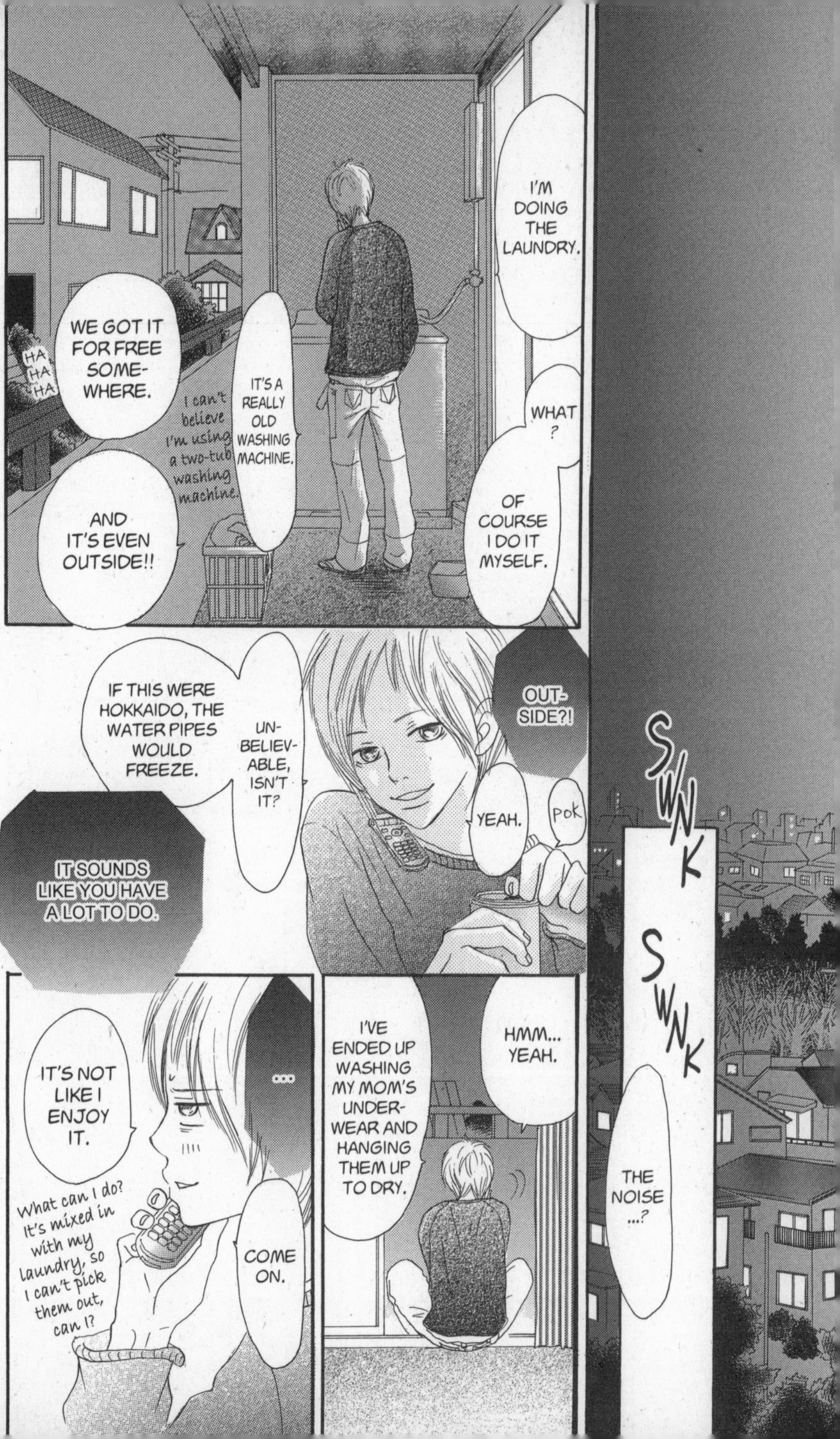
SWNK
SWNK
THE NOISE ...?
I'M DOING THE LAUNDRY.
WHAT?
OF COURSE I DO IT MYSELF.
IT'S A REALLY OLD WASHING MACHINE.
I can't believe I'm using a two-tub washing machine.
WE GOT IT FOR FREE SOME-WHERE.
HA HA HA
AND IT'S EVEN OUTSIDE!!
OUT-SIDE?!
YEAH.
pok
IF THIS WERE HOKKAIDO, THE WATER PIPES WOULD FREEZE.
UN-BELIEV-ABLE, ISN'T IT?
IT SOUNDS LIKE YOU HAVE A LOT TO DO.
HMM... YEAH.
I'VE ENDED UP WASHING MY MOM'S UNDER-WEAR AND HANGING THEM UP TO DRY.
COME ON.
...
IT'S NOT LIKE I ENJOY IT.
What can I do? It's mixed in with my laundry, so I can't pick them out, can I?

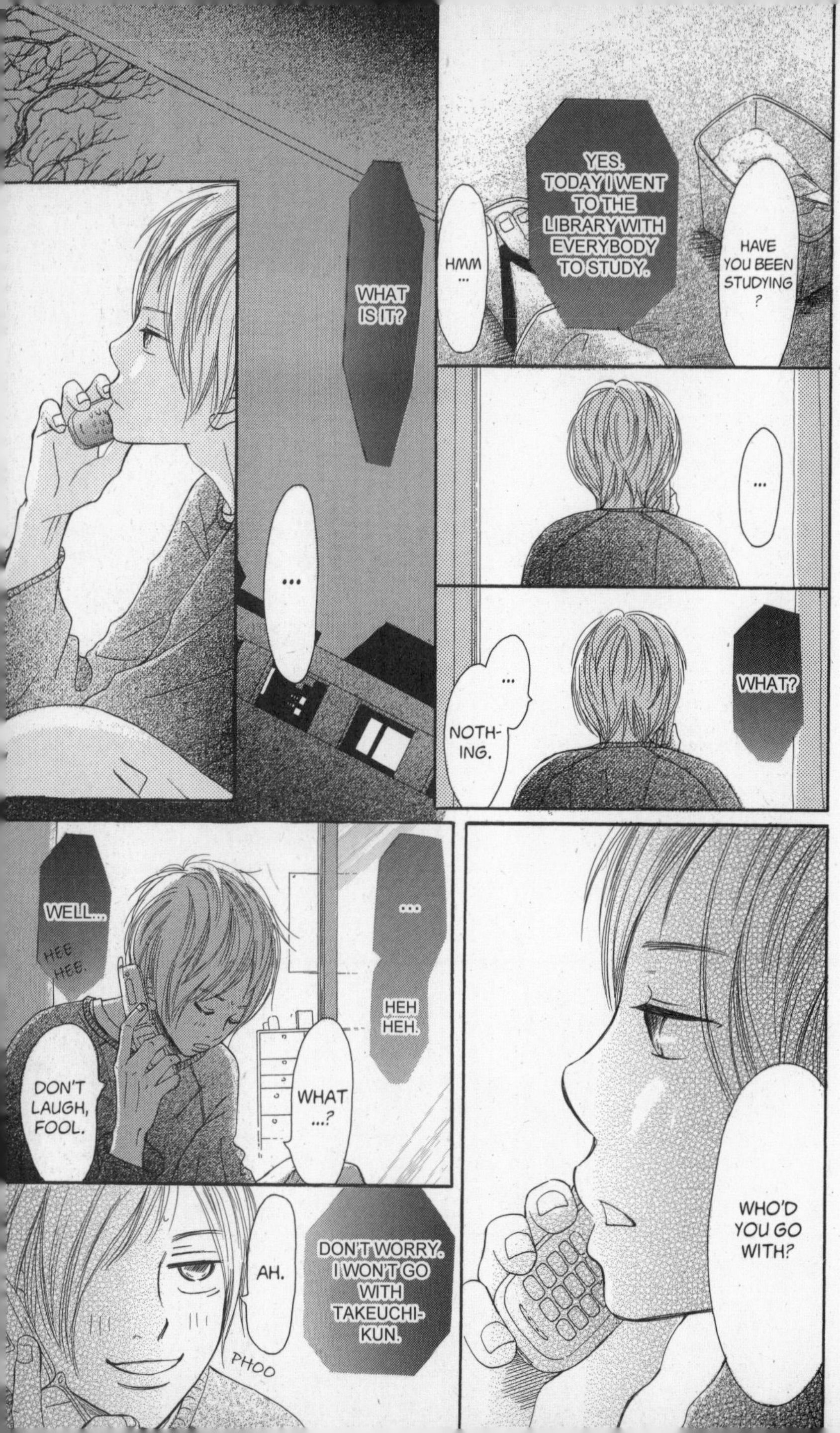
HAVE YOU BEEN STUDYING?
YES. TODAY I WENT TO THE LIBRARY WITH EVERYBODY TO STUDY.
HMM ...
...
WHAT?
...
NOTHING.
WHAT IS IT?
...
WHO'D YOU GO WITH?
...
HEH HEH.
WHAT ...?
WELL...
HEE HEE.
DON'T LAUGH, FOOL.
DON'T WORRY. I WON'T GO WITH TAKEUCHI-KUN.
AH.
PHOO

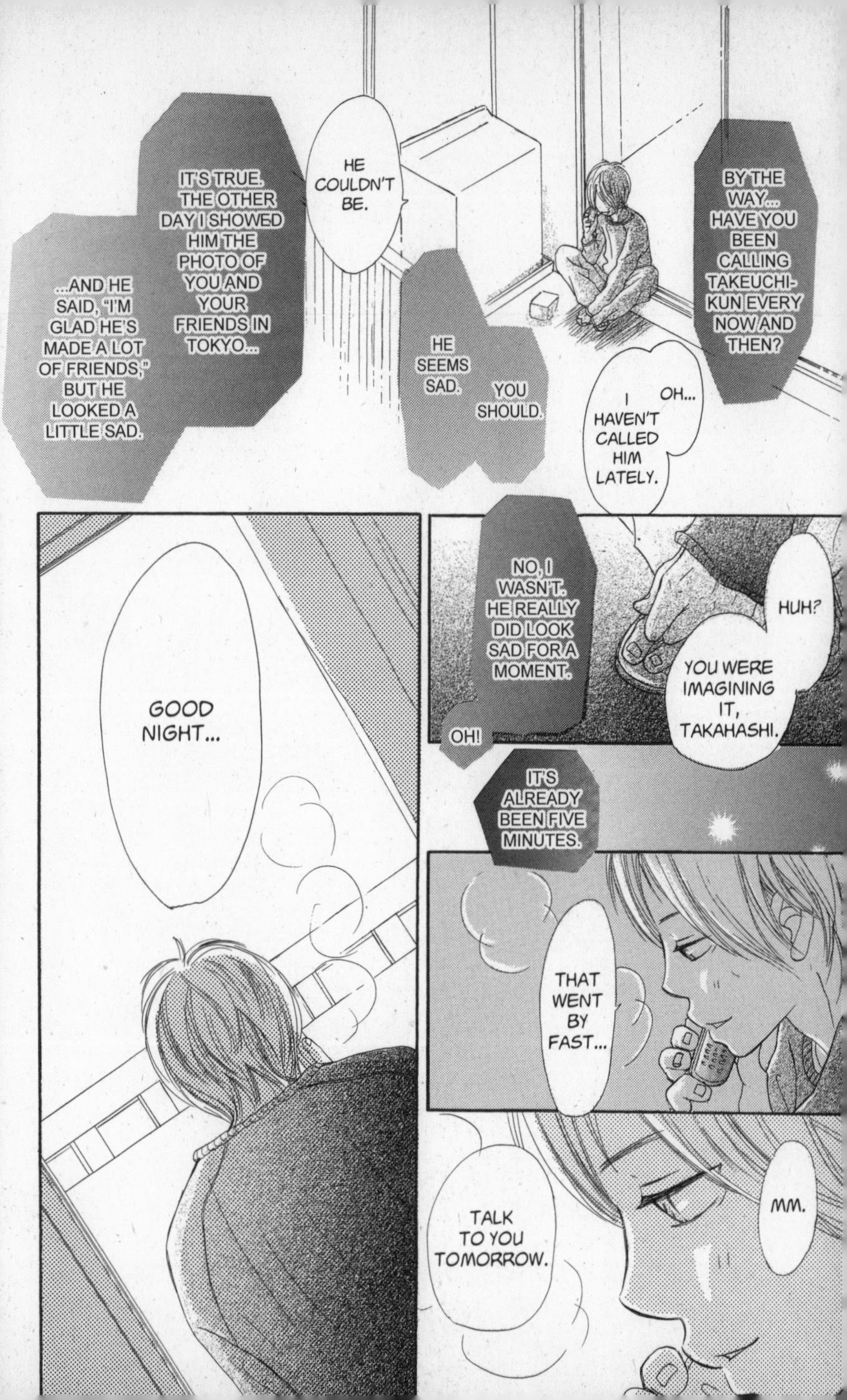
BY THE WAY... HAVE YOU BEEN CALLING TAKEUCHI-KUN EVERY NOW AND THEN?
OH... I HAVEN'T CALLED HIM LATELY.
YOU SHOULD.
HE SEEMS SAD.
HE COULDN'T BE.
IT'S TRUE. THE OTHER DAY I SHOWED HIM THE PHOTO OF YOU AND YOUR FRIENDS IN TOKYO...
...AND HE SAID, "I'M GLAD HE'S MADE A LOT OF FRIENDS," BUT HE LOOKED A LITTLE SAD.
HUH?
YOU WERE IMAGINING IT, TAKAHASHI.
NO, I WASN'T. HE REALLY DID LOOK SAD FOR A MOMENT.
OH!
IT'S ALREADY BEEN FIVE MINUTES.
THAT WENT BY FAST...
MM.
TALK TO YOU TOMORROW.
GOOD NIGHT...

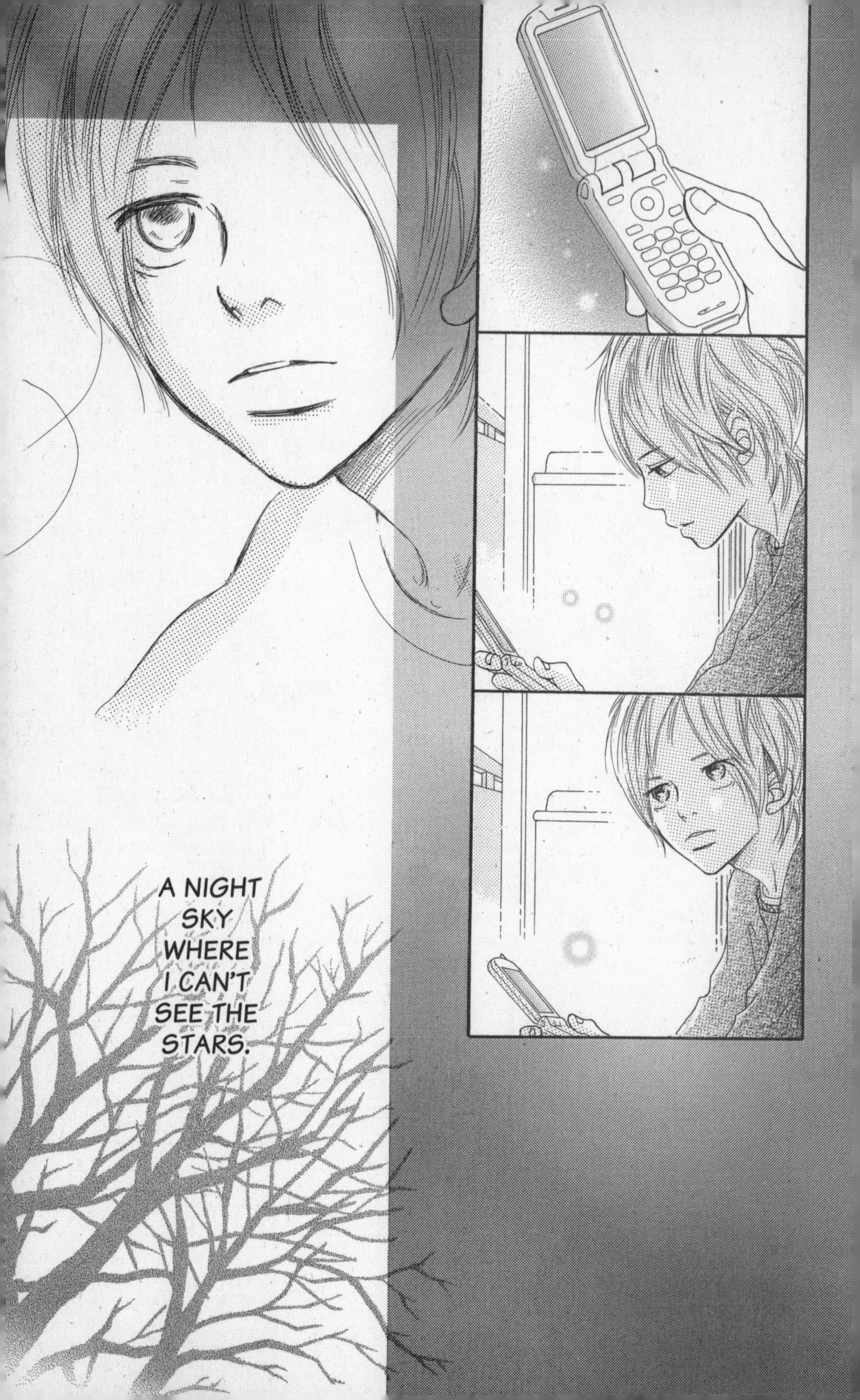
A NIGHT SKY WHERE I CAN'T SEE THE STARS.

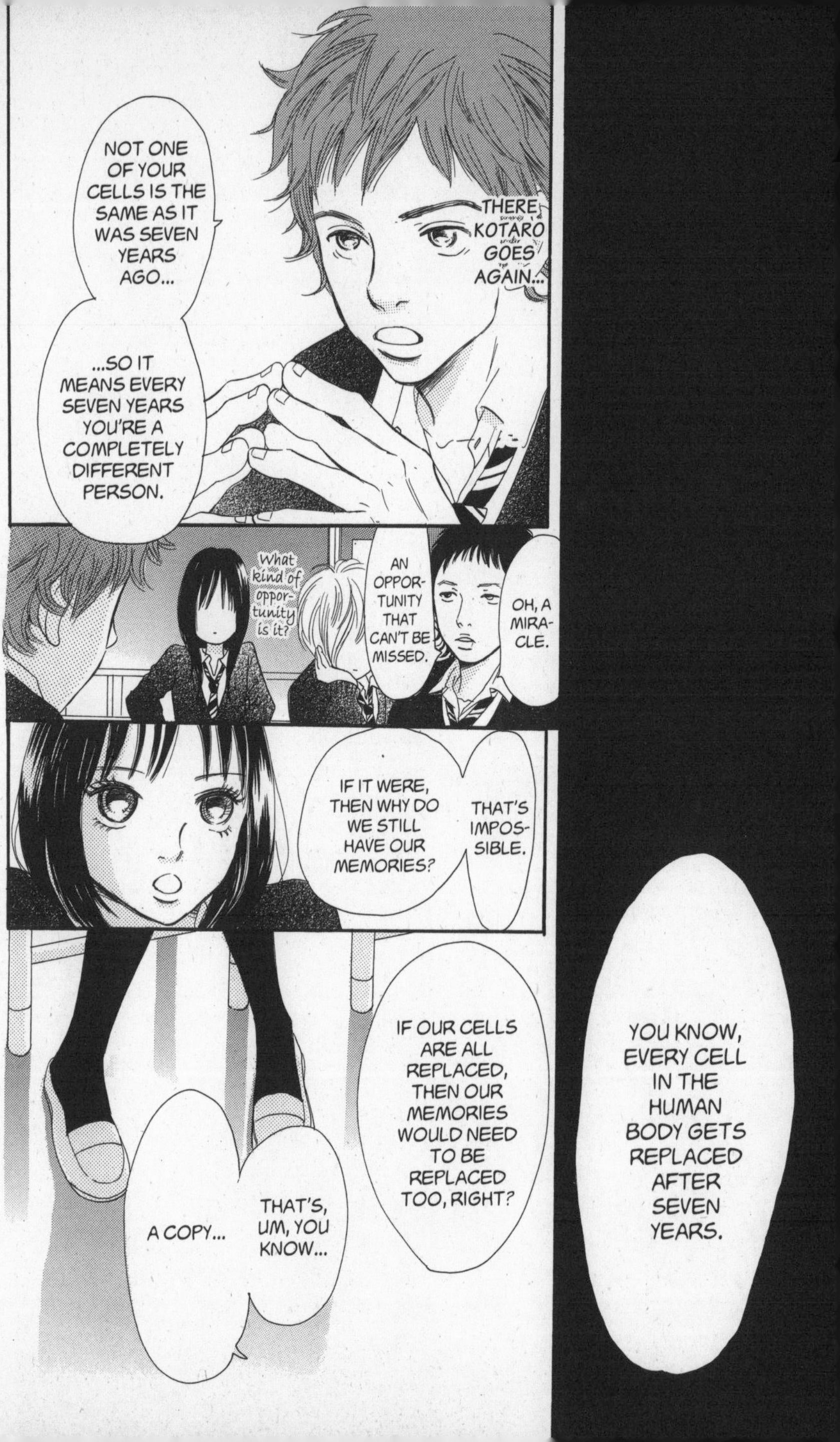
YOU KNOW, EVERY CELL IN THE HUMAN BODY GETS REPLACED AFTER SEVEN YEARS.
NOT ONE OF YOUR CELLS IS THE SAME AS IT WAS SEVEN YEARS AGO...
THERE KOTARO GOES AGAIN...
...SO IT MEANS EVERY SEVEN YEARS YOU'RE A COMPLETELY DIFFERENT PERSON.
OH, A MIRACLE.
AN OPPORTUNITY THAT CAN'T BE MISSED.
What kind of opportunity is it?
THAT'S IMPOSSIBLE.
IF IT WERE, THEN WHY DO WE STILL HAVE OUR MEMORIES?
IF OUR CELLS ARE ALL REPLACED, THEN OUR MEMORIES WOULD NEED TO BE REPLACED TOO, RIGHT?
THAT'S, UM, YOU KNOW...
A COPY...

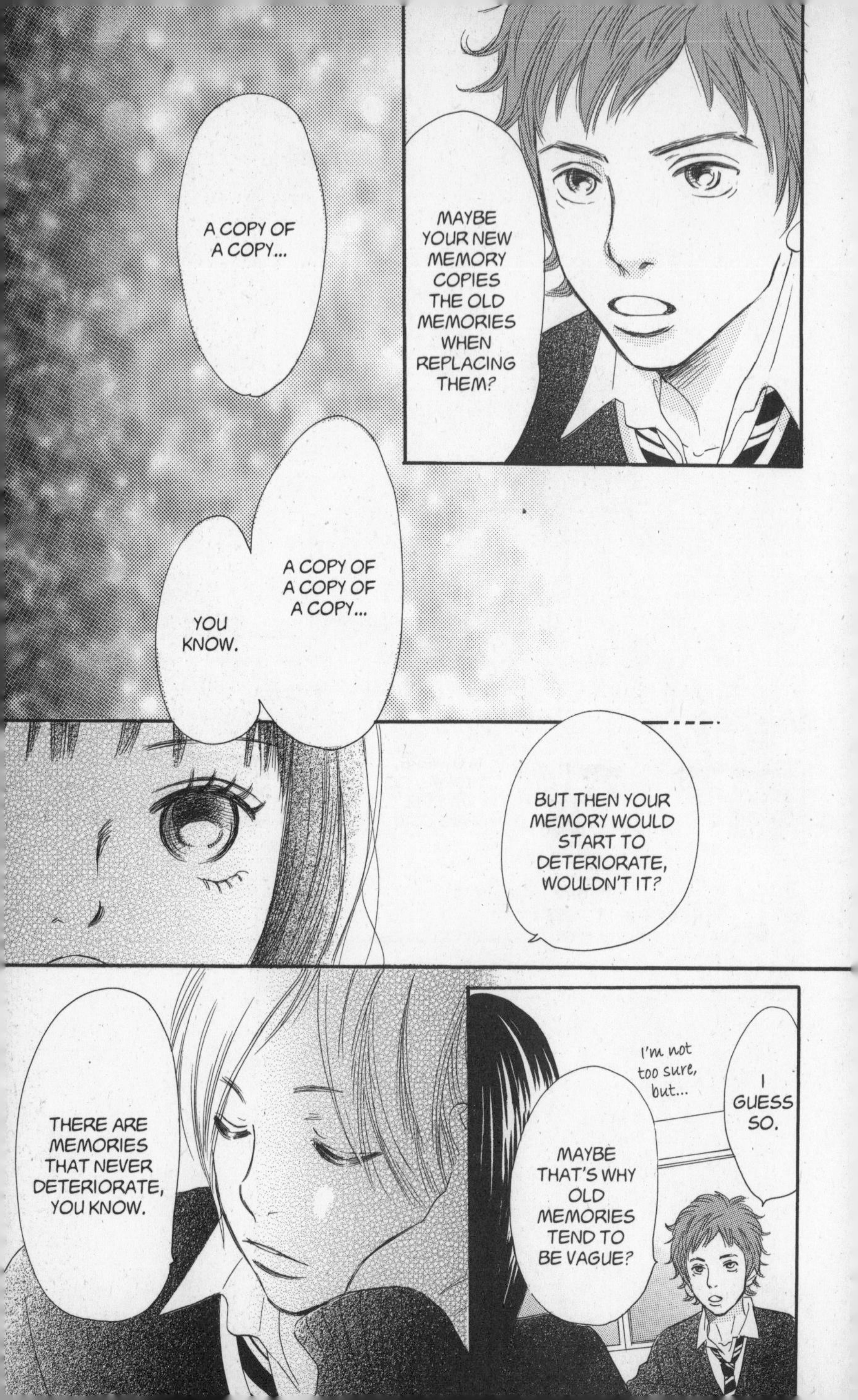
MAYBE YOUR NEW MEMORY COPIES THE OLD MEMORIES WHEN REPLACING THEM?
A COPY OF A COPY...
A COPY OF A COPY OF A COPY...
YOU KNOW.
BUT THEN YOUR MEMORY WOULD START TO DETERIORATE, WOULDN'T IT?
I GUESS SO.
I'm not too sure, but...
MAYBE THAT'S WHY OLD MEMORIES TEND TO BE VAGUE?
THERE ARE MEMORIES THAT NEVER DETERIORATE, YOU KNOW.

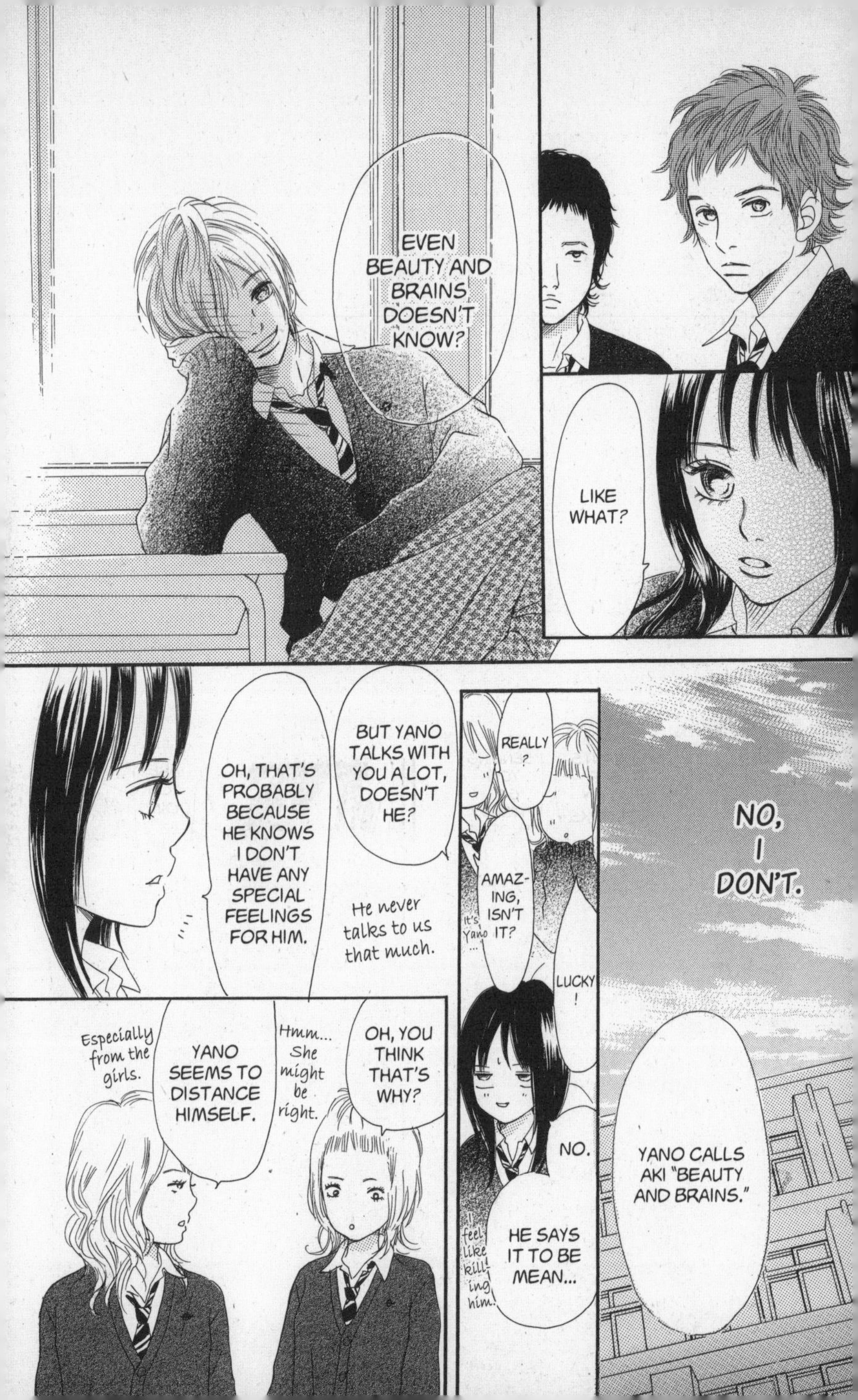
LIKE WHAT?
EVEN BEAUTY AND BRAINS DOESN'T KNOW?
NO, I DON'T.
YANO CALLS AKI "BEAUTY AND BRAINS."
REALLY?
AMAZING, ISN'T IT?
It's Yano...
LUCKY!
NO.
HE SAYS IT TO BE MEAN...
I feel like killing him.
BUT YANO TALKS WITH YOU A LOT, DOESN'T HE?
OH, THAT'S PROBABLY BECAUSE HE KNOWS I DON'T HAVE ANY SPECIAL FEELINGS FOR HIM.
...
He never talks to us that much.
YANO SEEMS TO DISTANCE HIMSELF.
Especially from the girls.
OH, YOU THINK THAT'S WHY?
Hmm... She might be right.

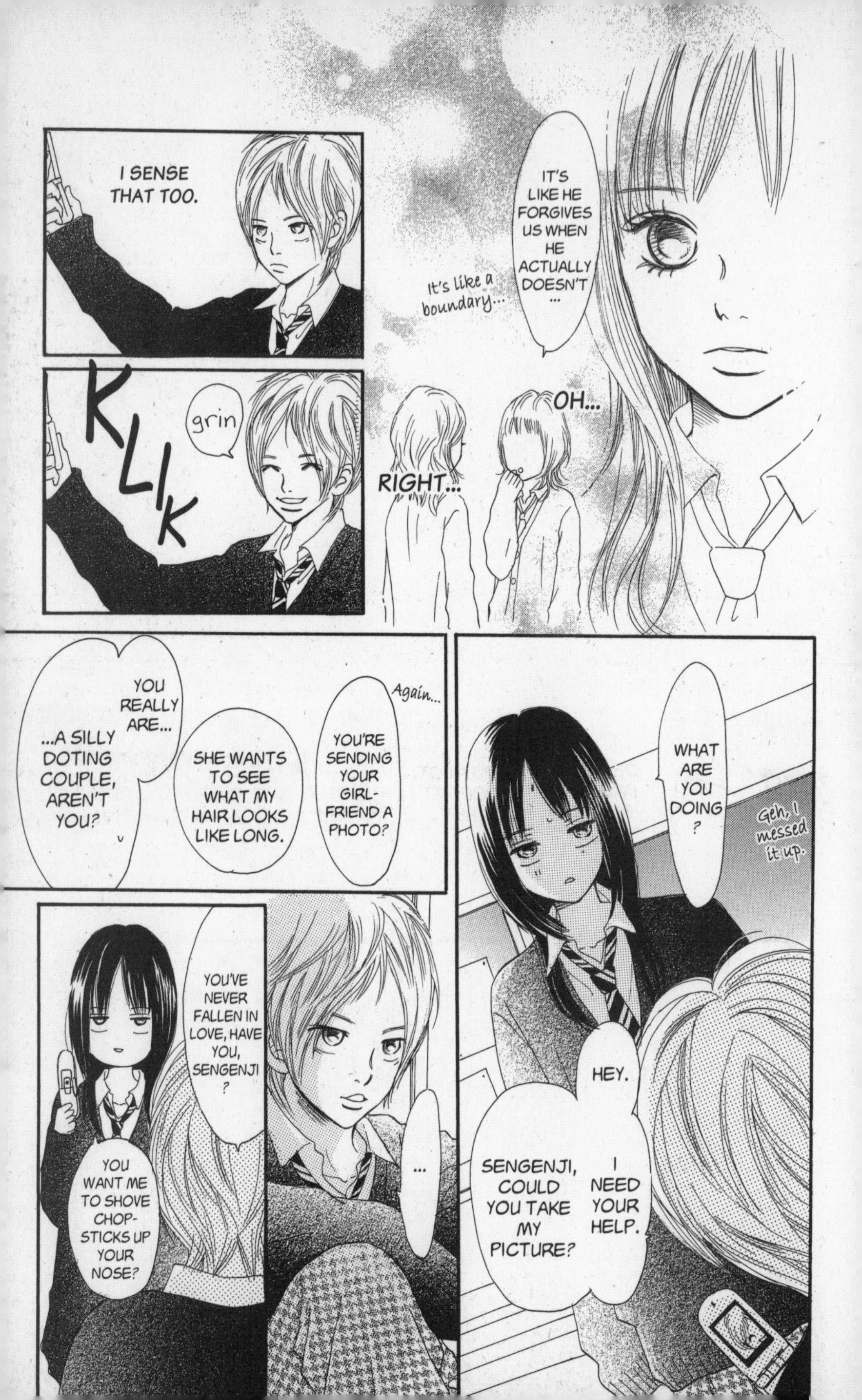
IT'S LIKE HE FORGIVES US WHEN HE ACTUALLY DOESN'T ...
It's like a boundary...
OH...
RIGHT...
I SENSE THAT TOO.
grin
KLIK
WHAT ARE YOU DOING ?
Geh, I messed it up.
HEY.
I NEED YOUR HELP.
SENGENJI, COULD YOU TAKE MY PICTURE?
Again...
YOU'RE SENDING YOUR GIRL-FRIEND A PHOTO?
SHE WANTS TO SEE WHAT MY HAIR LOOKS LIKE LONG.
YOU REALLY ARE...
...A SILLY DOTING COUPLE, AREN'T YOU?
YOU'VE NEVER FALLEN IN LOVE, HAVE YOU, SENGENJI ?
...
YOU WANT ME TO SHOVE CHOP-STICKS UP YOUR NOSE?

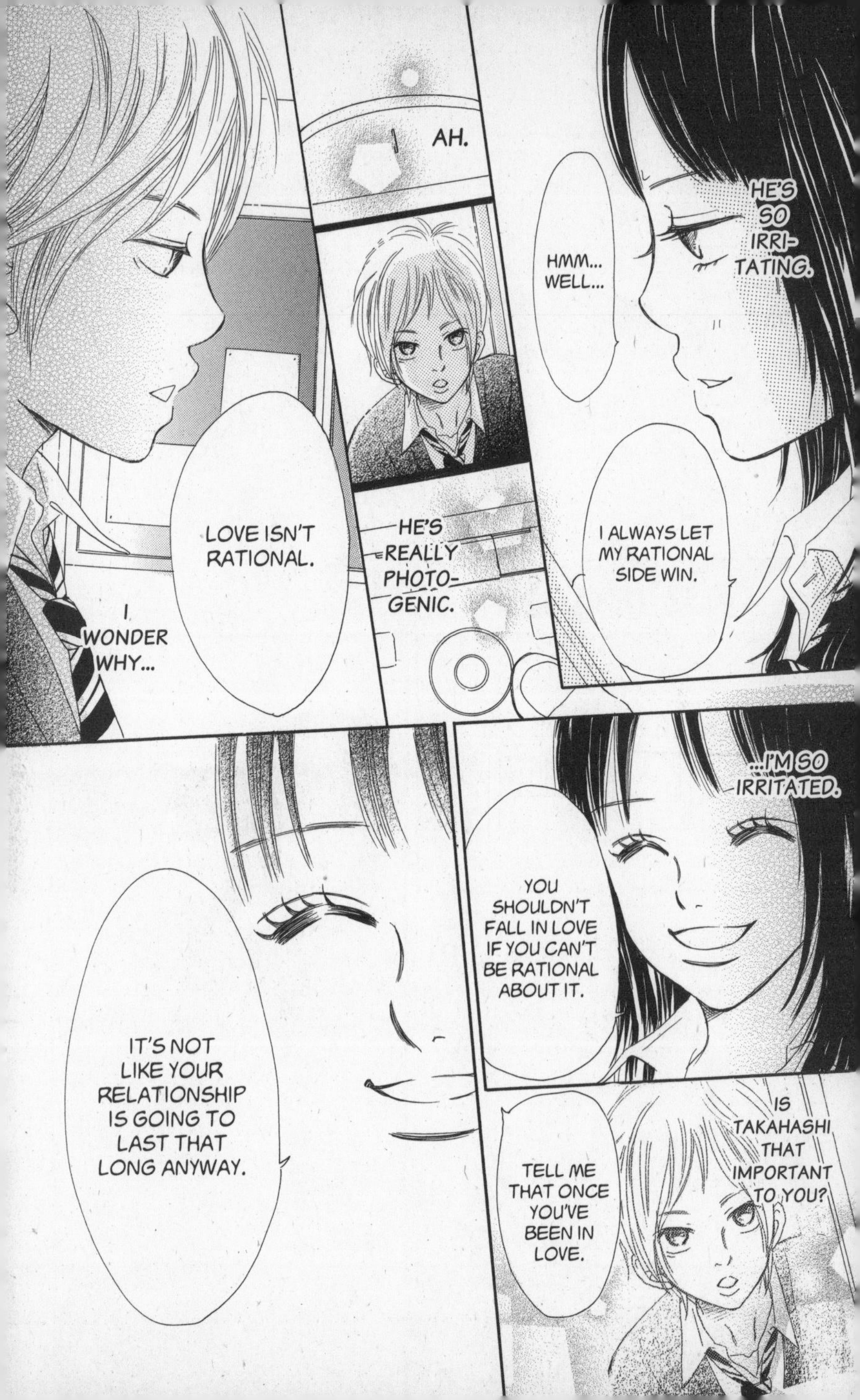
HE'S SO IRRI-TATING.
HMM... WELL...
I ALWAYS LET MY RATIONAL SIDE WIN.
AH.
HE'S REALLY PHOTO-GENIC.
LOVE ISN'T RATIONAL.
I WONDER WHY...
...I'M SO IRRITATED.
YOU SHOULDN'T FALL IN LOVE IF YOU CAN'T BE RATIONAL ABOUT IT.
IS TAKAHASHI THAT IMPORTANT TO YOU?
TELL ME THAT ONCE YOU'VE BEEN IN LOVE.
IT'S NOT LIKE YOUR RELATIONSHIP IS GOING TO LAST THAT LONG ANYWAY.

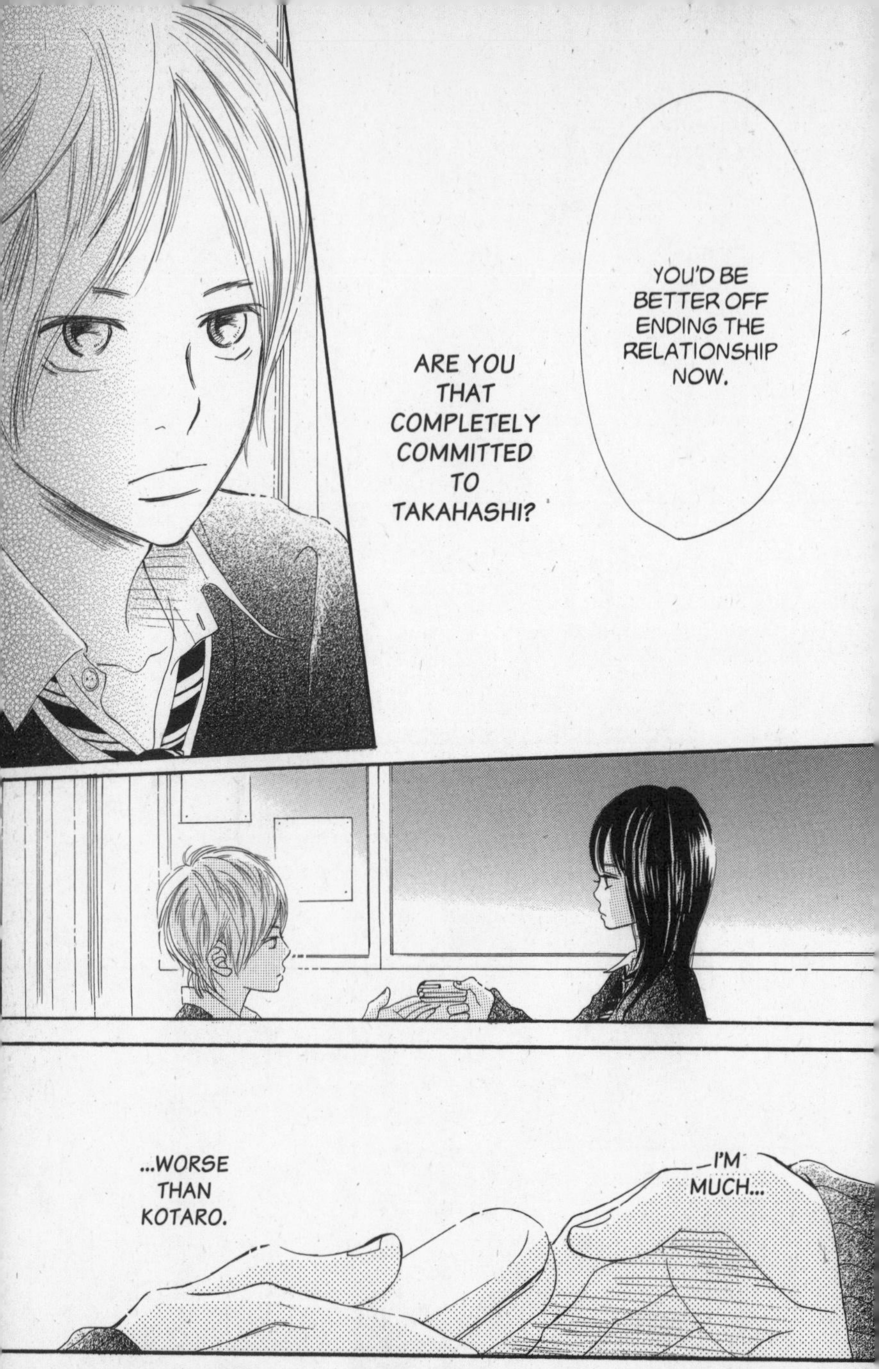
YOU'D BE BETTER OFF ENDING THE RELATIONSHIP NOW.
ARE YOU THAT COMPLETELY COMMITTED TO TAKAHASHI?
I'M MUCH...
...WORSE THAN KOTARO.

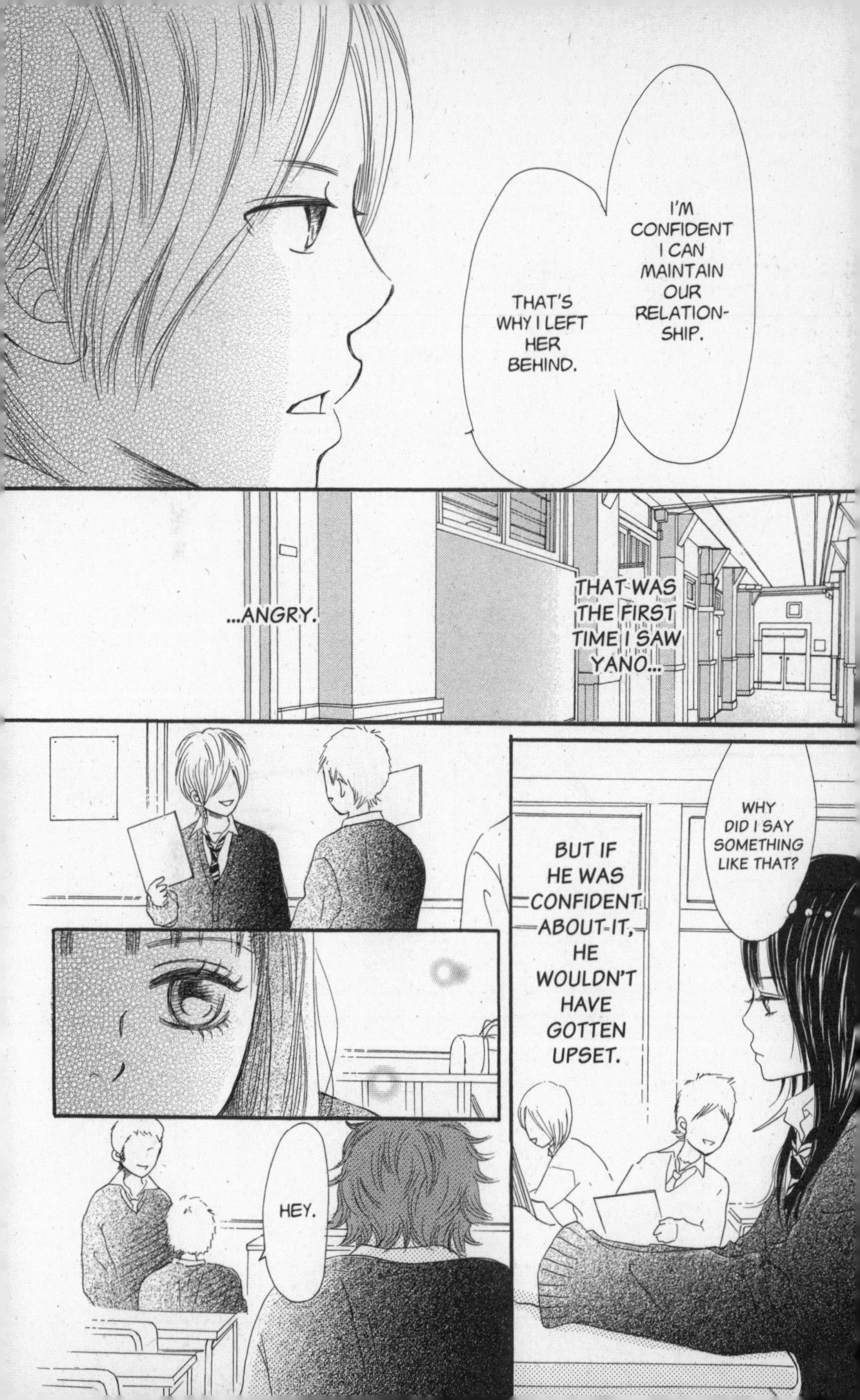
I'M CONFIDENT I CAN MAINTAIN OUR RELATION-SHIP.
THAT'S WHY I LEFT HER BEHIND.
THAT WAS THE FIRST TIME I SAW YANO...
...ANGRY.
WHY DID I SAY SOMETHING LIKE THAT?
BUT IF HE WAS CONFIDENT ABOUT IT, HE WOULDN'T HAVE GOTTEN UPSET.
HEY.

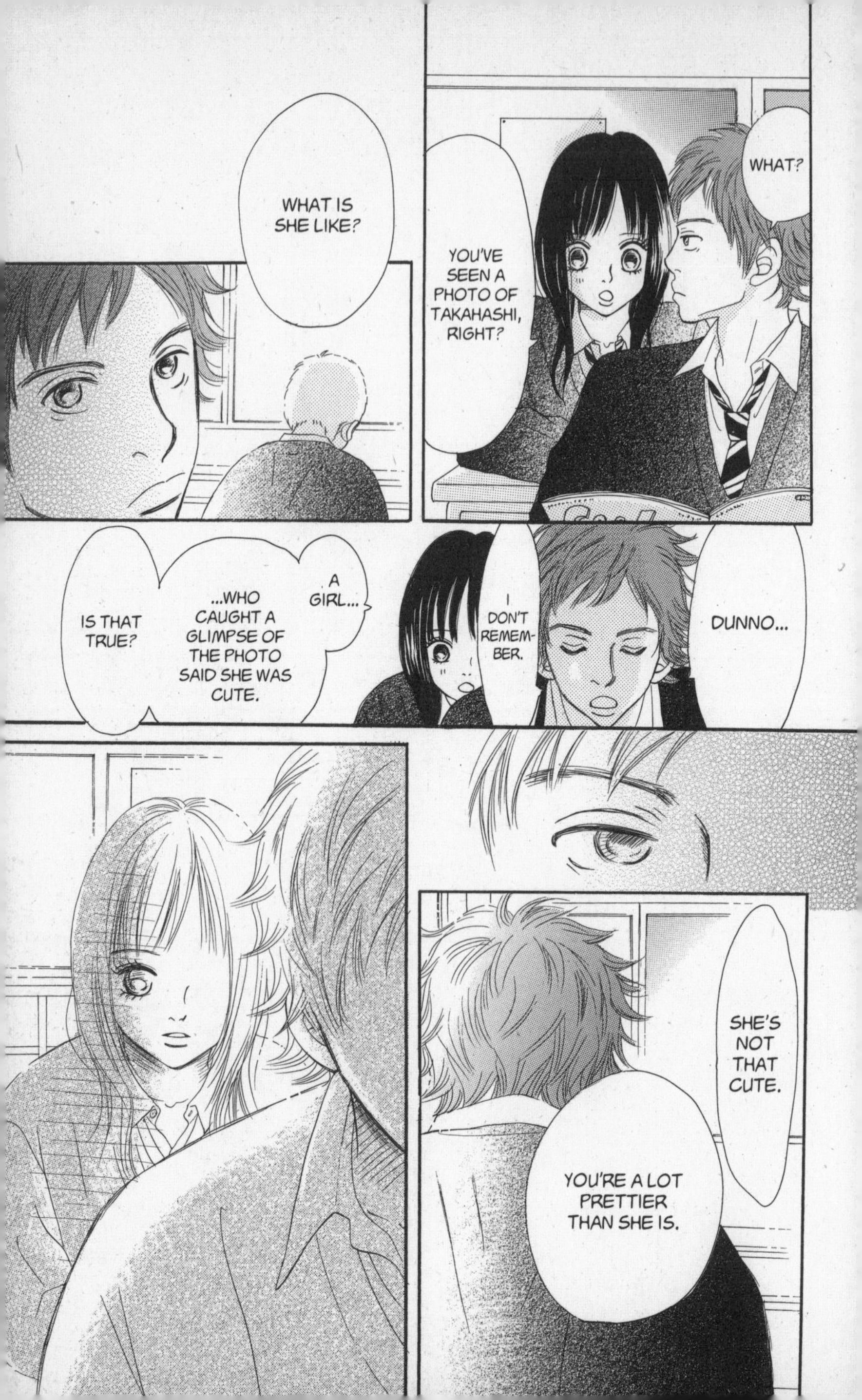
WHAT?
YOU'VE SEEN A PHOTO OF TAKAHASHI, RIGHT?
WHAT IS SHE LIKE?
DUNNO...
I DON'T REMEMBER.
A GIRL...
...WHO CAUGHT A GLIMPSE OF THE PHOTO SAID SHE WAS CUTE.
IS THAT TRUE?
SHE'S NOT THAT CUTE.
YOU'RE A LOT PRETTIER THAN SHE IS.

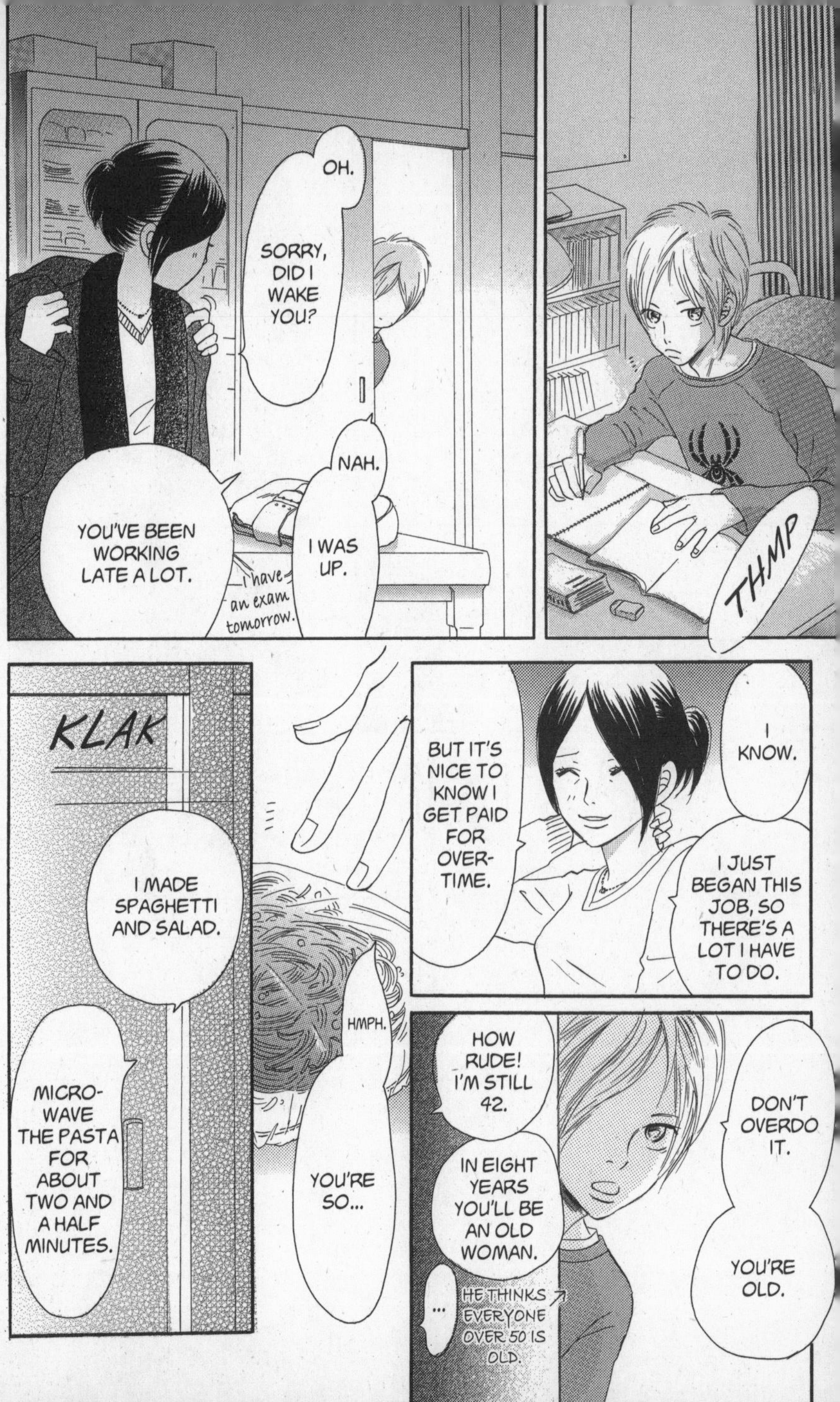
THMP
OH.
SORRY, DID I WAKE YOU?
NAH.
I WAS UP.
I have an exam tomorrow.
YOU'VE BEEN WORKING LATE A LOT.
I KNOW.
I JUST BEGAN THIS JOB, SO THERE'S A LOT I HAVE TO DO.
BUT IT'S NICE TO KNOW I GET PAID FOR OVER-TIME.
DON'T OVERDO IT.
YOU'RE OLD.
HOW RUDE! I'M STILL 42.
IN EIGHT YEARS YOU'LL BE AN OLD WOMAN.
...
HE THINKS EVERYONE OVER 50 IS OLD.
KLAK
I MADE SPAGHETTI AND SALAD.
MICRO-WAVE THE PASTA FOR ABOUT TWO AND A HALF MINUTES.
HMPH.
YOU'RE SO...

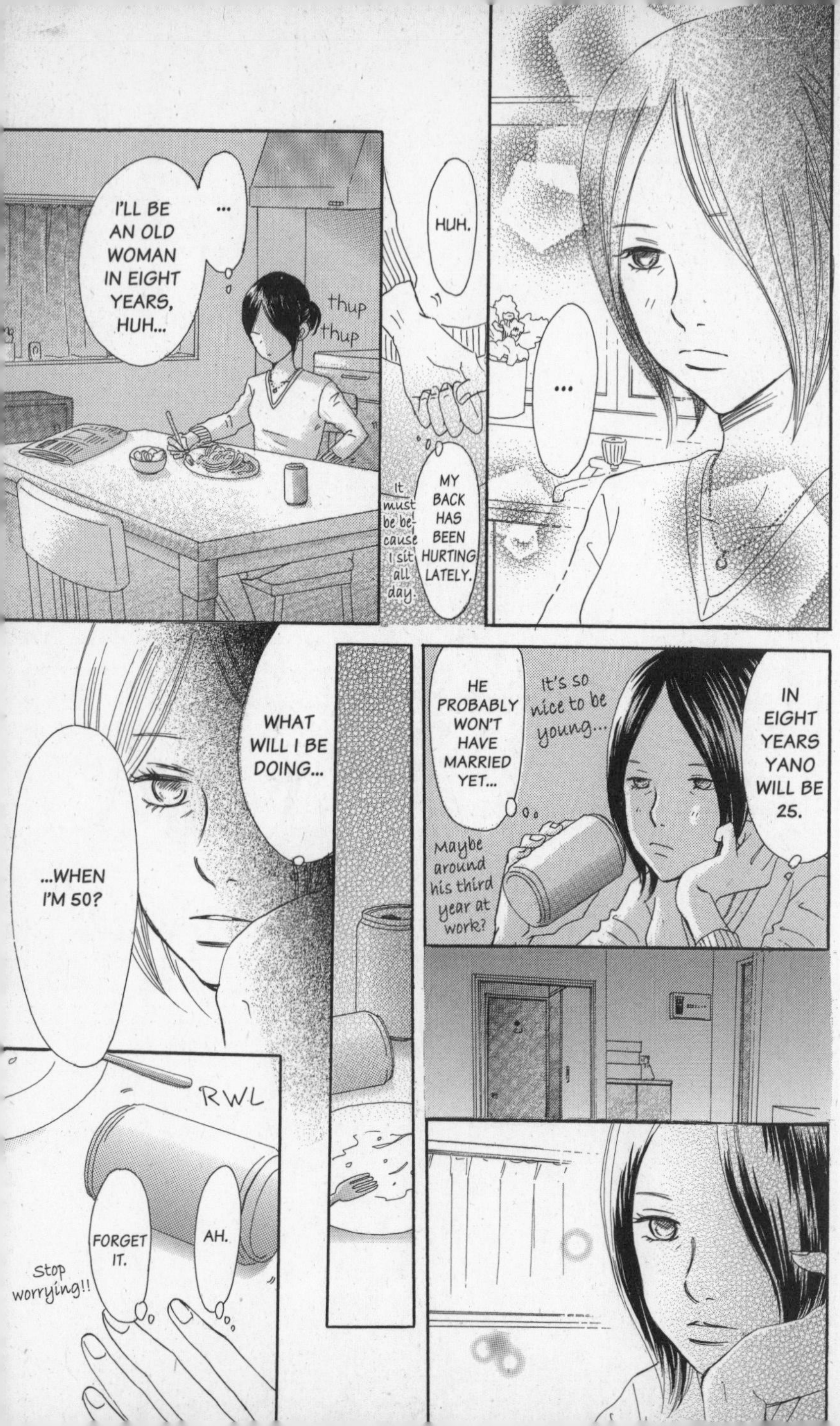
...
HUH.
MY BACK HAS BEEN HURTING LATELY.
It must be because I sit all day.
...
I'LL BE AN OLD WOMAN IN EIGHT YEARS, HUH...
thup thup
IN EIGHT YEARS YANO WILL BE 25.
It's so nice to be young...
HE PROBABLY WON'T HAVE MARRIED YET...
Maybe around his third year at work?
WHAT WILL I BE DOING...
...WHEN I'M 50?
RWL
AH.
FORGET IT.
Stop worrying!!

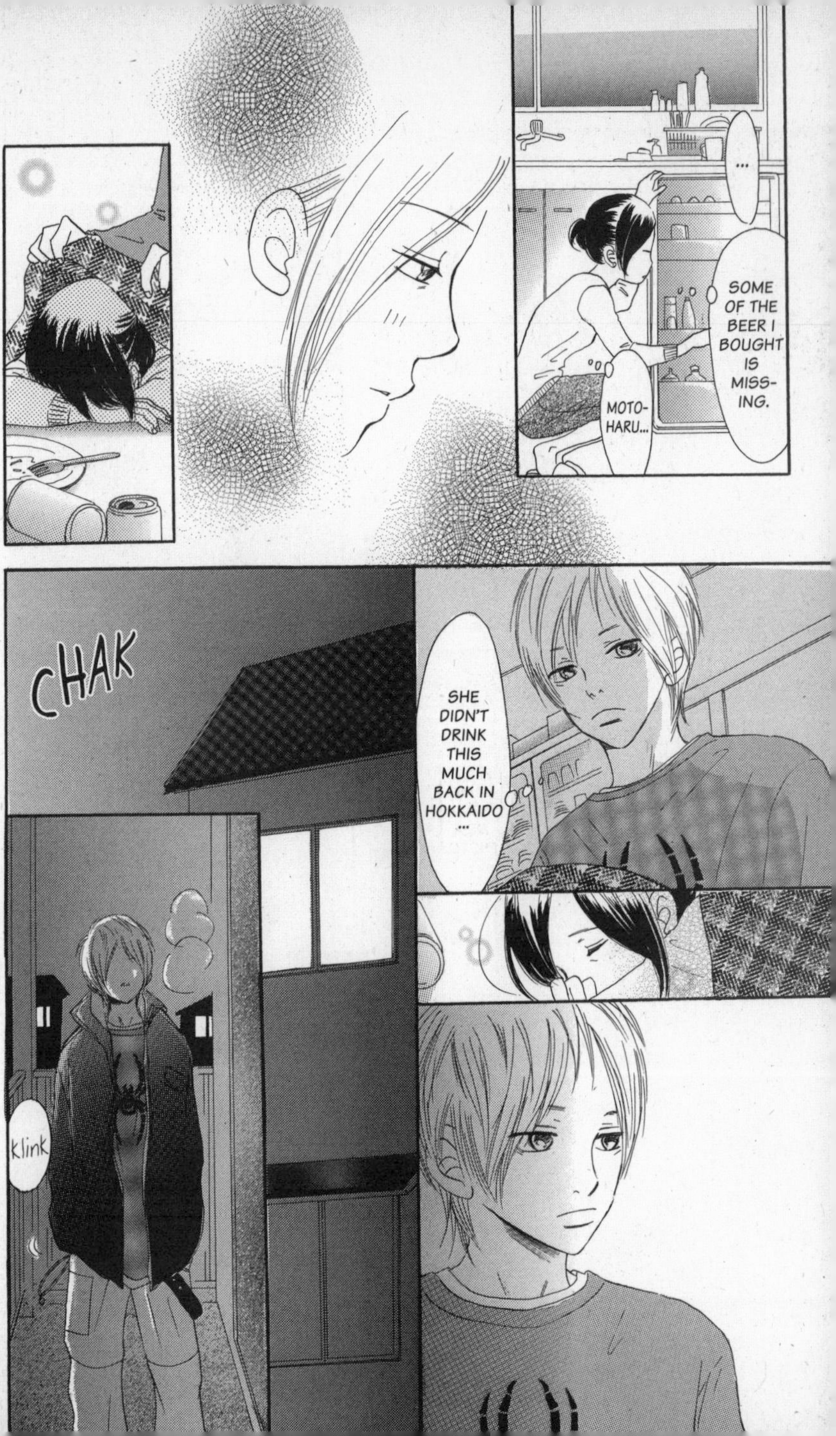
...
SOME OF THE BEER I BOUGHT IS MISS-ING.
MOTO-HARU...
SHE DIDN'T DRINK THIS MUCH BACK IN HOKKAIDO...
CHAK
klink

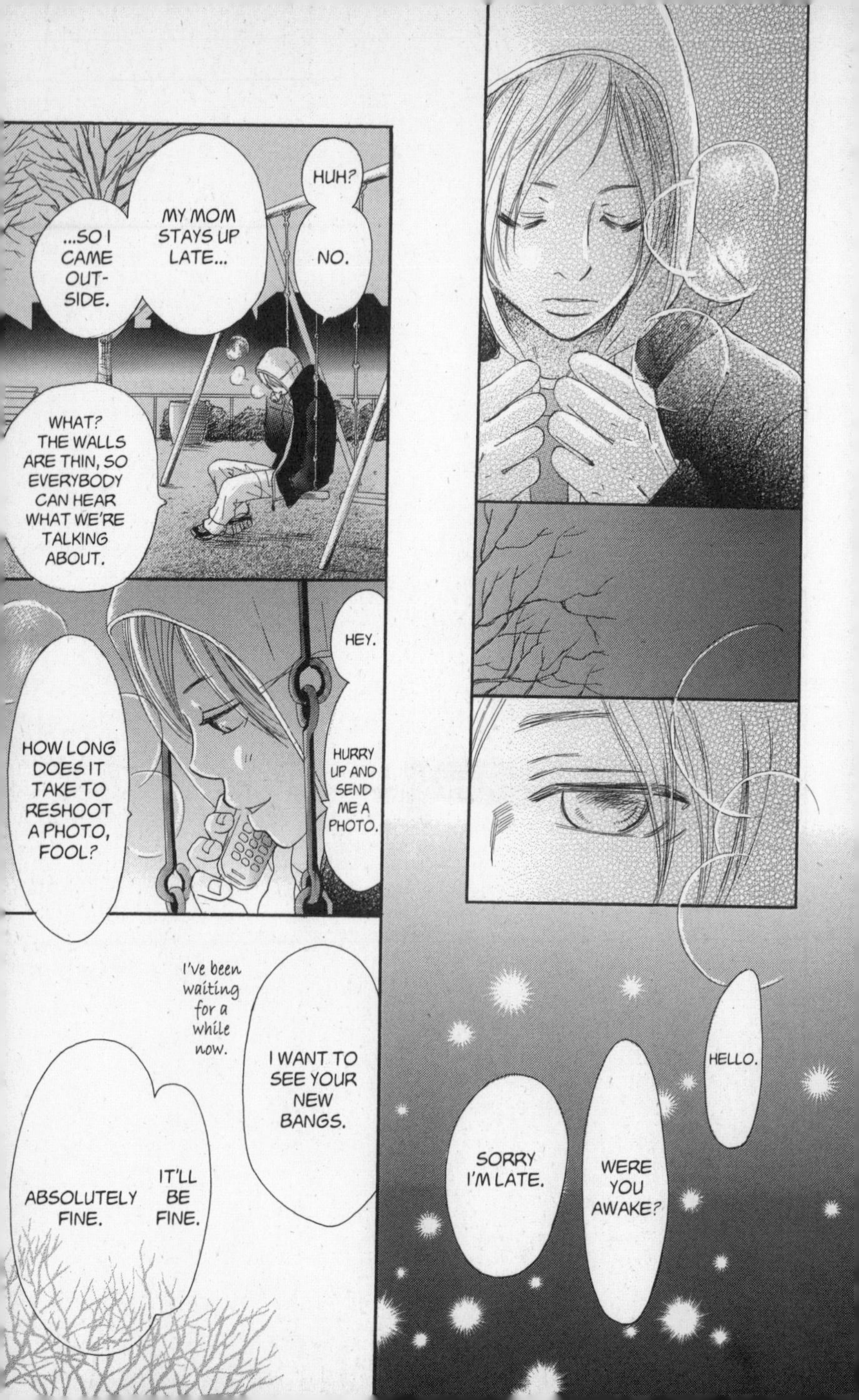
HELLO.
WERE YOU AWAKE?
SORRY I'M LATE.
HUH?
NO.
MY MOM STAYS UP LATE...
...SO I CAME OUT-SIDE.
WHAT? THE WALLS ARE THIN, SO EVERYBODY CAN HEAR WHAT WE'RE TALKING ABOUT.
HEY.
HURRY UP AND SEND ME A PHOTO.
HOW LONG DOES IT TAKE TO RESHOOT A PHOTO, FOOL?
I've been waiting for a while now.
I WANT TO SEE YOUR NEW BANGS.
IT'LL BE FINE.
ABSOLUTELY FINE.

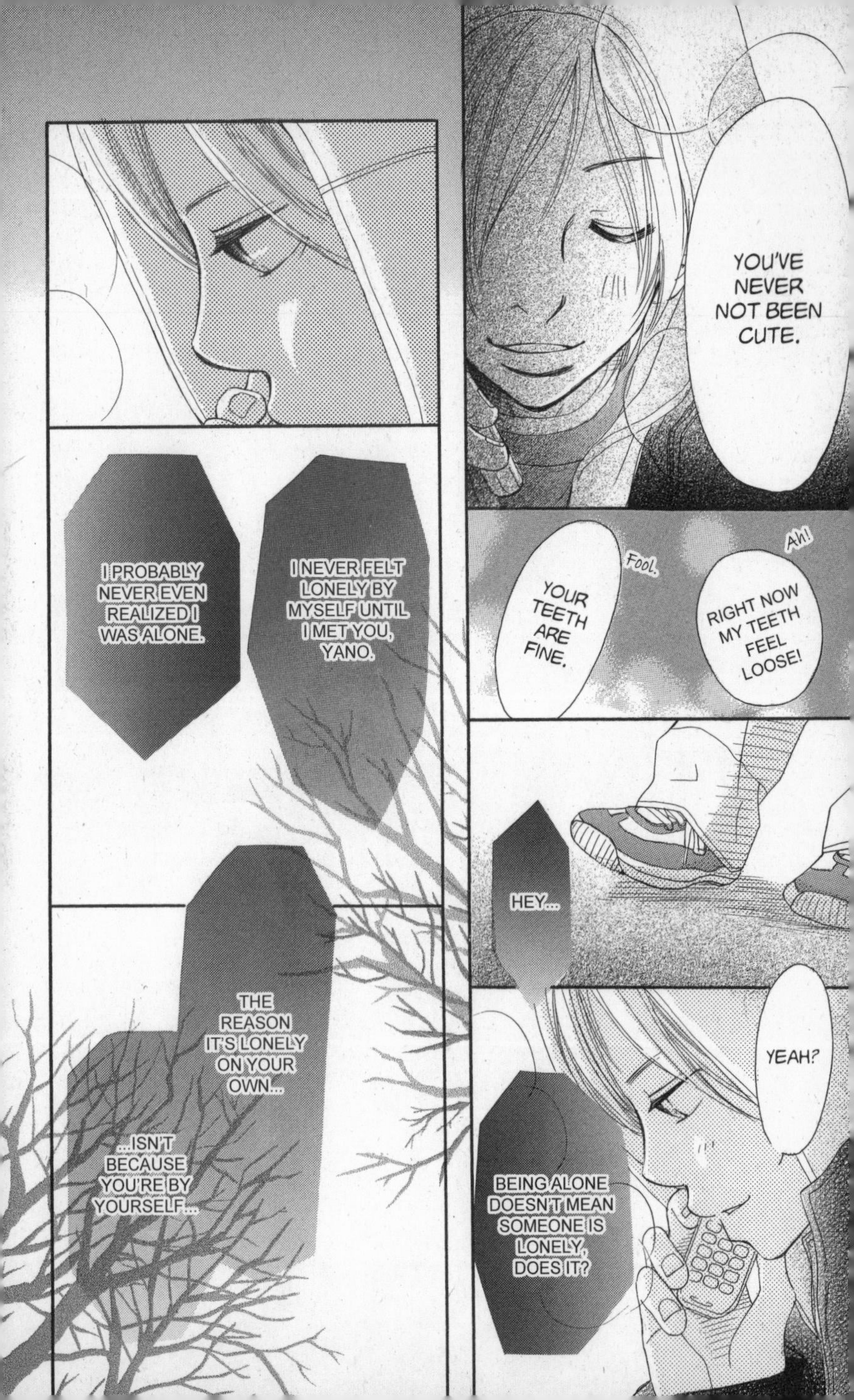
YOU'VE NEVER NOT BEEN CUTE.
Ah!
RIGHT NOW MY TEETH FEEL LOOSE!
Fool.
YOUR TEETH ARE FINE.
HEY...
YEAH?
BEING ALONE DOESN'T MEAN SOMEONE IS LONELY, DOES IT?
I NEVER FELT LONELY BY MYSELF UNTIL I MET YOU, YANO.
I PROBABLY NEVER EVEN REALIZED I WAS ALONE.
THE REASON IT'S LONELY ON YOUR OWN...
...ISN'T BECAUSE YOU'RE BY YOURSELF...

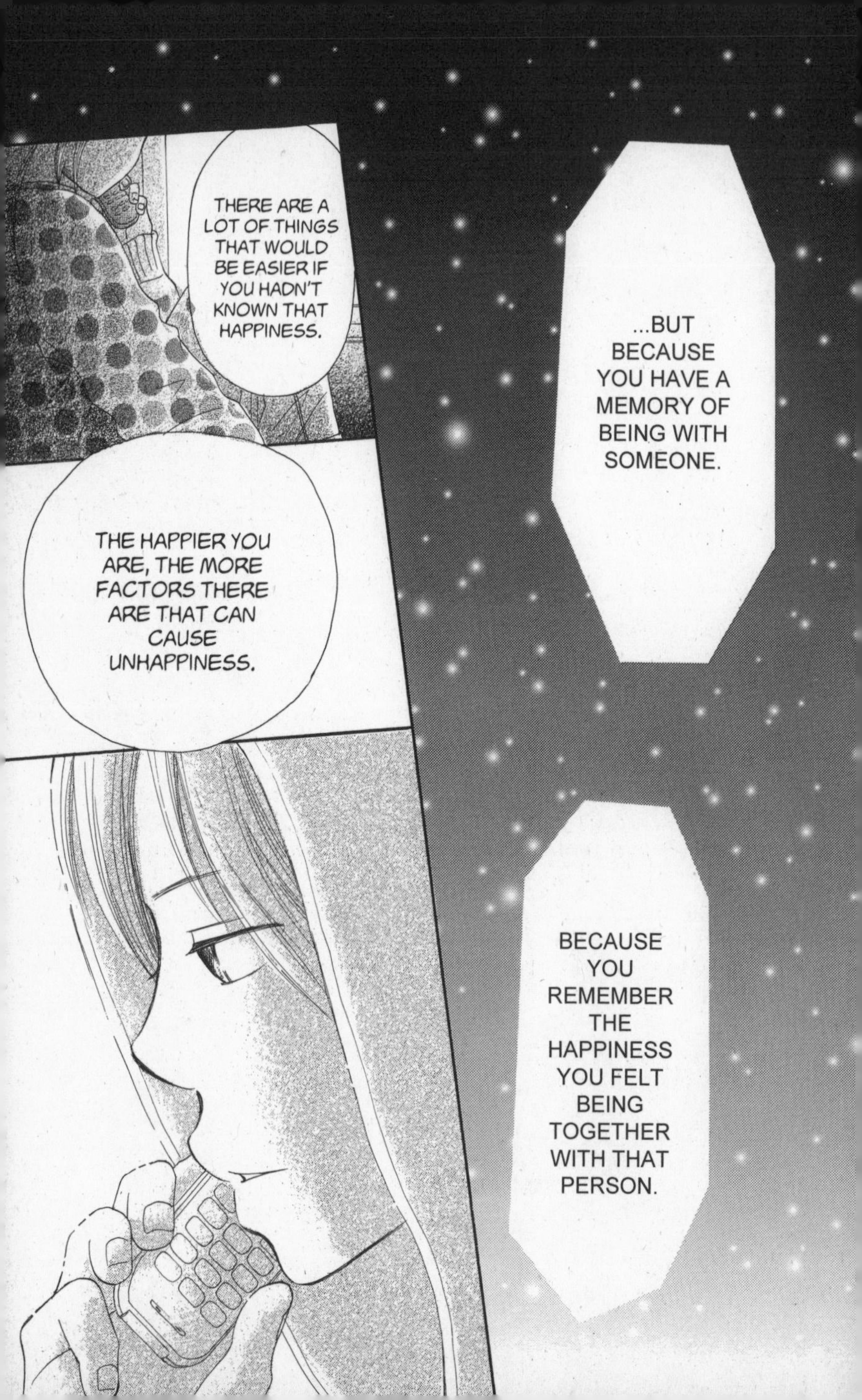
THERE ARE A LOT OF THINGS THAT WOULD BE EASIER IF YOU HADN'T KNOWN THAT HAPPINESS.
THE HAPPIER YOU ARE, THE MORE FACTORS THERE ARE THAT CAN CAUSE UNHAPPINESS.
...BUT BECAUSE YOU HAVE A MEMORY OF BEING WITH SOMEONE.
BECAUSE YOU REMEMBER THE HAPPINESS YOU FELT BEING TOGETHER WITH THAT PERSON.

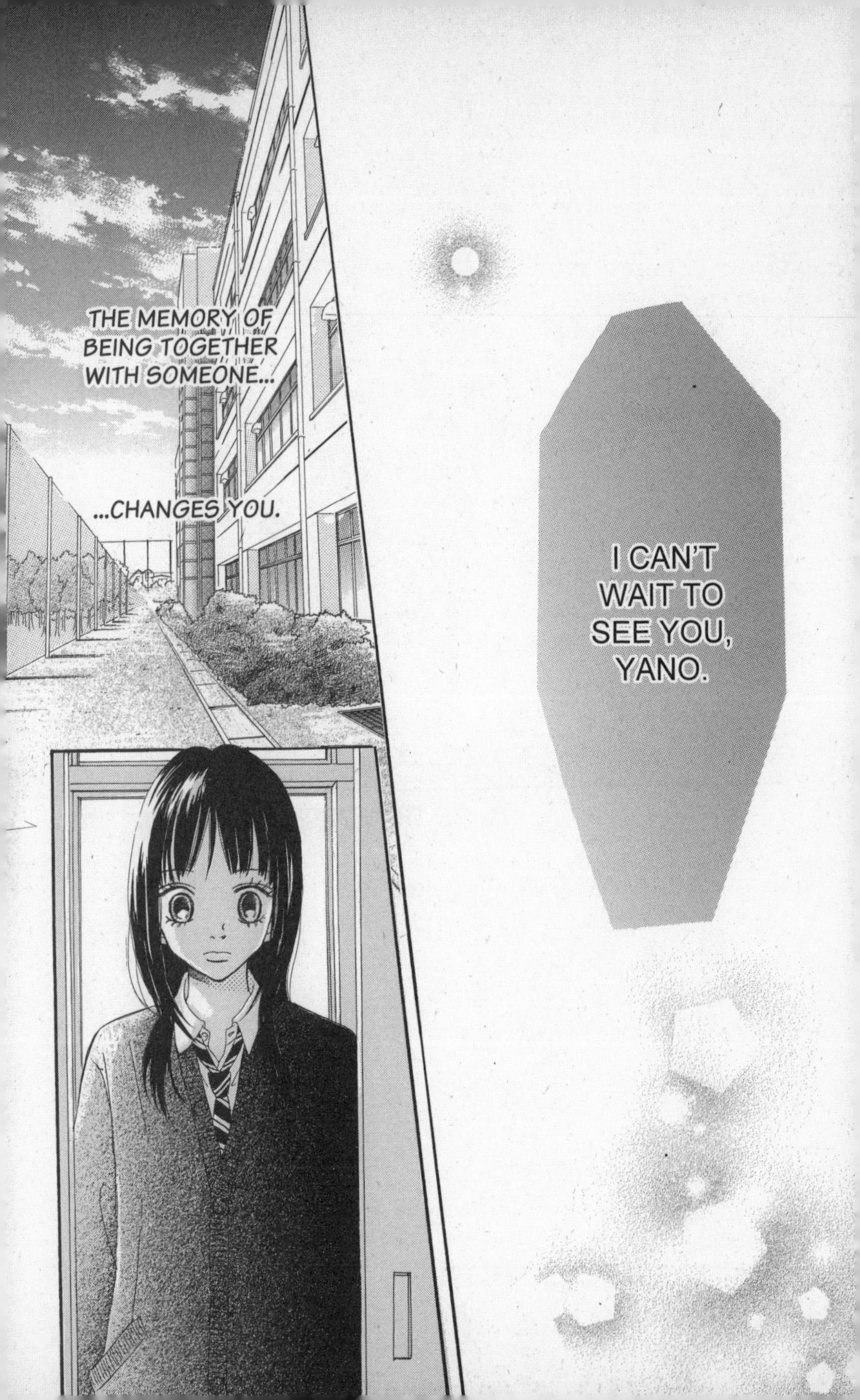
I CAN'T WAIT TO SEE YOU, YANO.
THE MEMORY OF BEING TOGETHER WITH SOMEONE...
...CHANGES YOU.

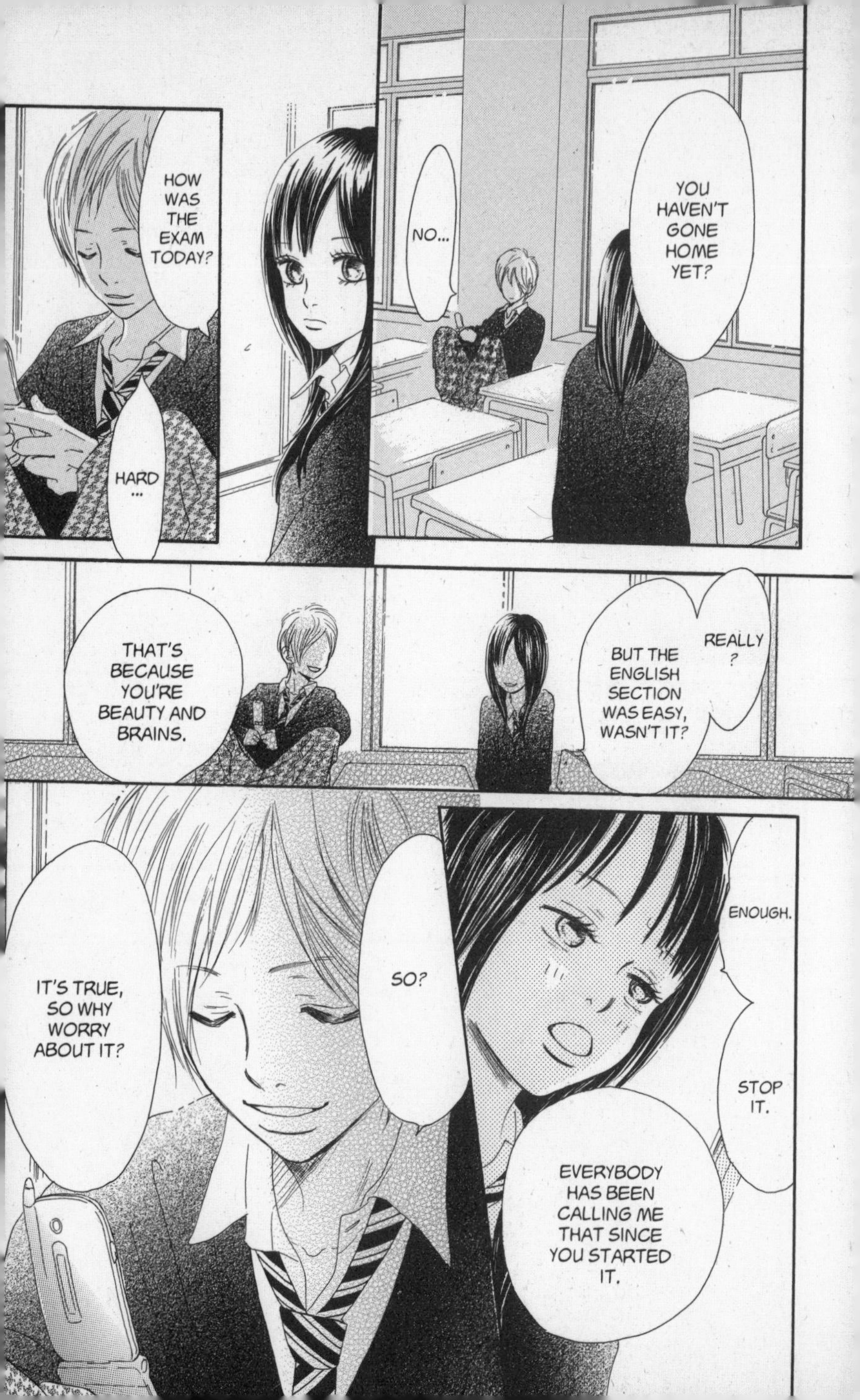
YOU HAVEN'T GONE HOME YET?
NO...
HOW WAS THE EXAM TODAY?
HARD...
REALLY?
BUT THE ENGLISH SECTION WAS EASY, WASN'T IT?
THAT'S BECAUSE YOU'RE BEAUTY AND BRAINS.
ENOUGH.
STOP IT.
EVERYBODY HAS BEEN CALLING ME THAT SINCE YOU STARTED IT.
SO?
IT'S TRUE, SO WHY WORRY ABOUT IT?

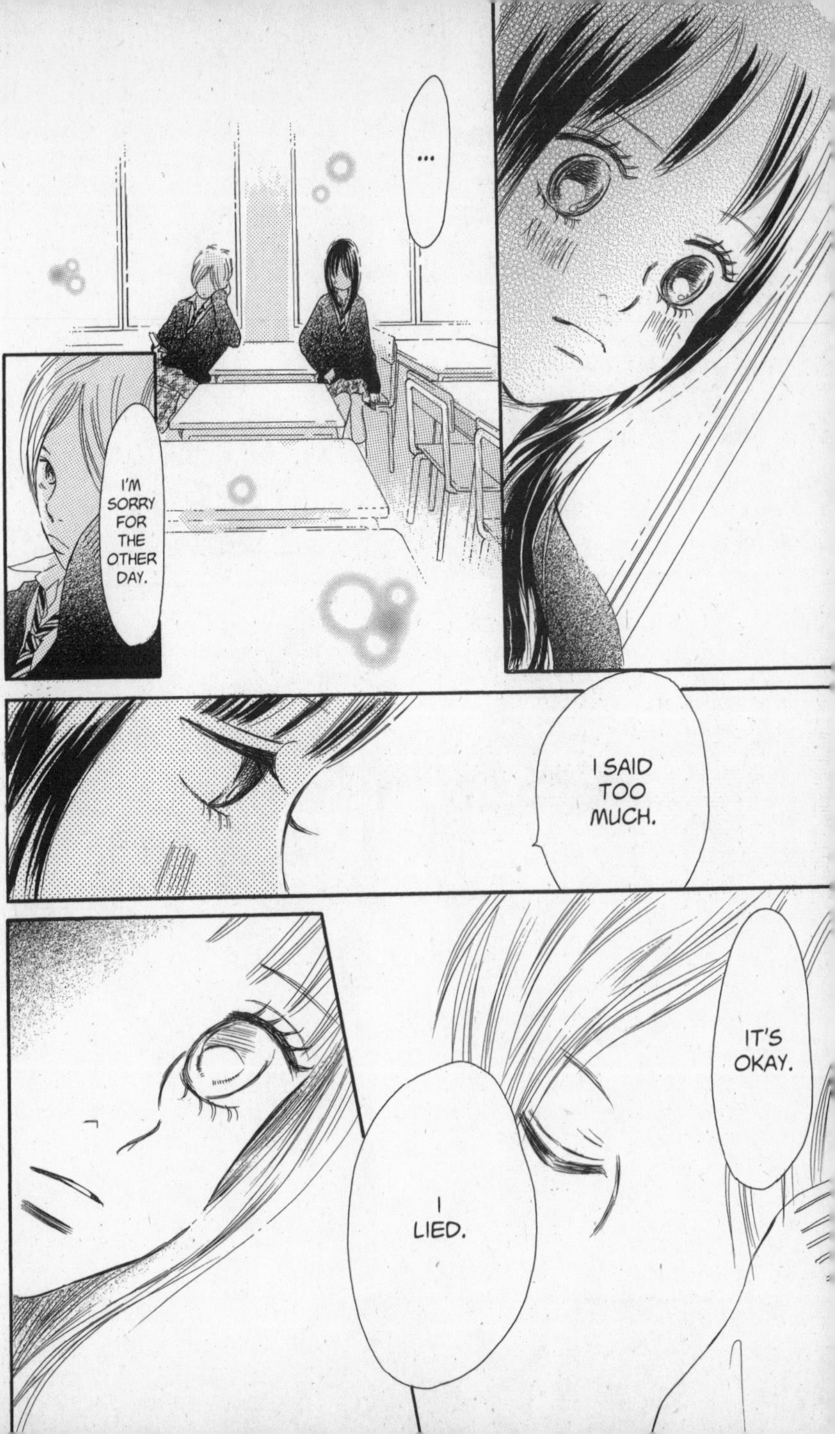
...
I'M SORRY FOR THE OTHER DAY.
I SAID TOO MUCH.
IT'S OKAY.
I LIED.

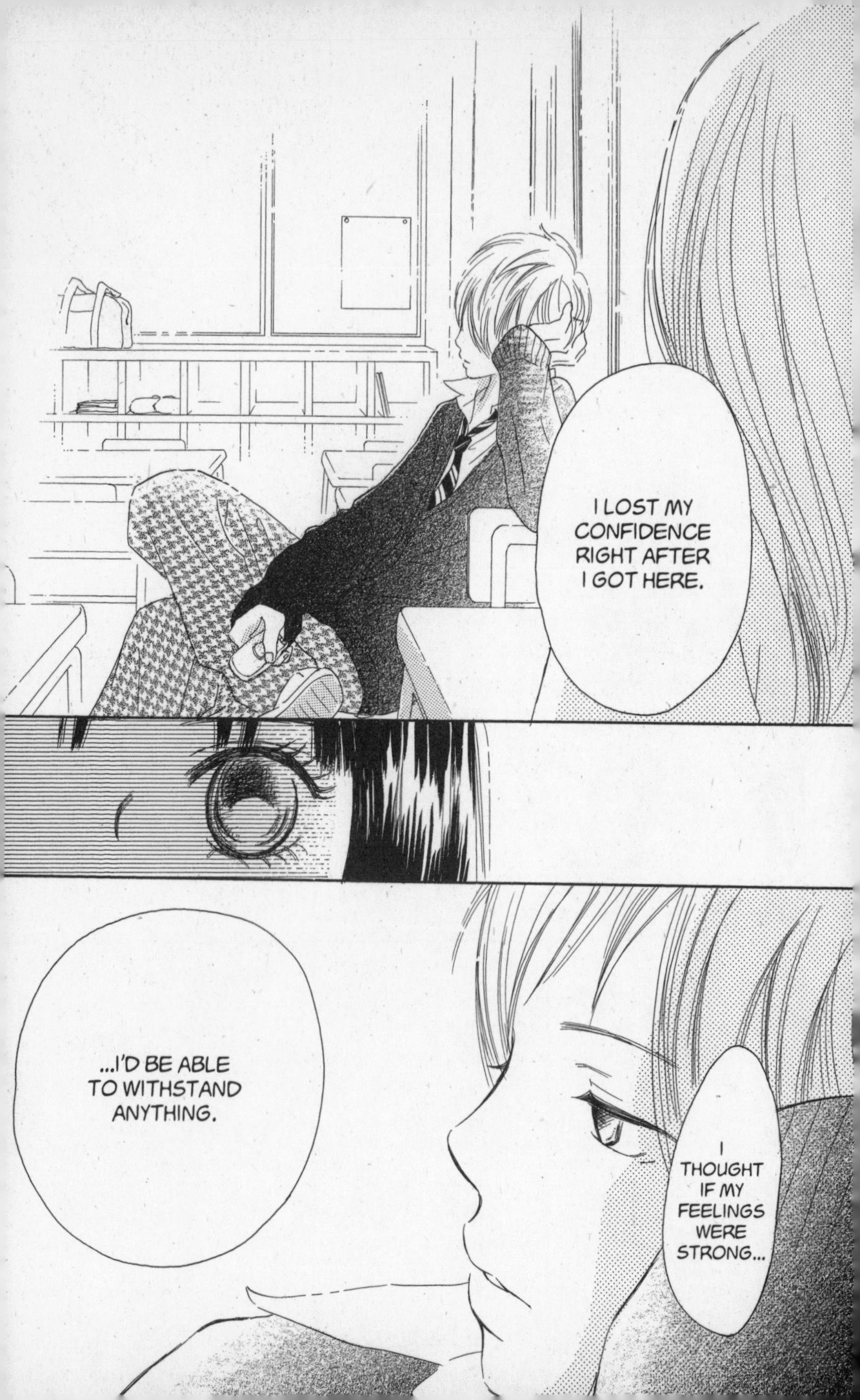
I LOST MY CONFIDENCE RIGHT AFTER I GOT HERE.
I THOUGHT IF MY FEELINGS WERE STRONG...
...I'D BE ABLE TO WITHSTAND ANYTHING.

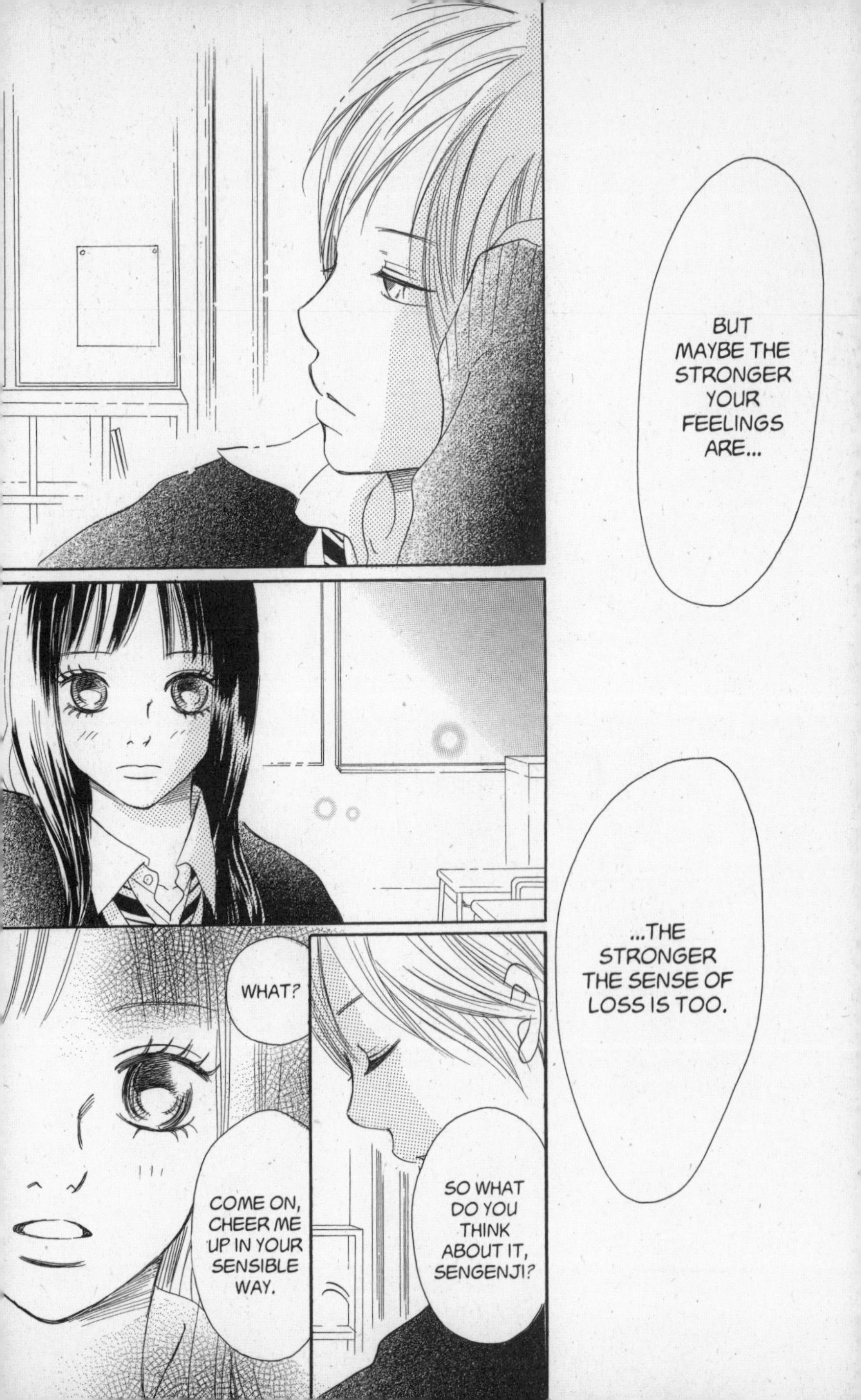
BUT MAYBE THE STRONGER YOUR FEELINGS ARE...
...THE STRONGER THE SENSE OF LOSS IS TOO.
SO WHAT DO YOU THINK ABOUT IT, SENGENJI?
WHAT?
COME ON, CHEER ME UP IN YOUR SENSIBLE WAY.

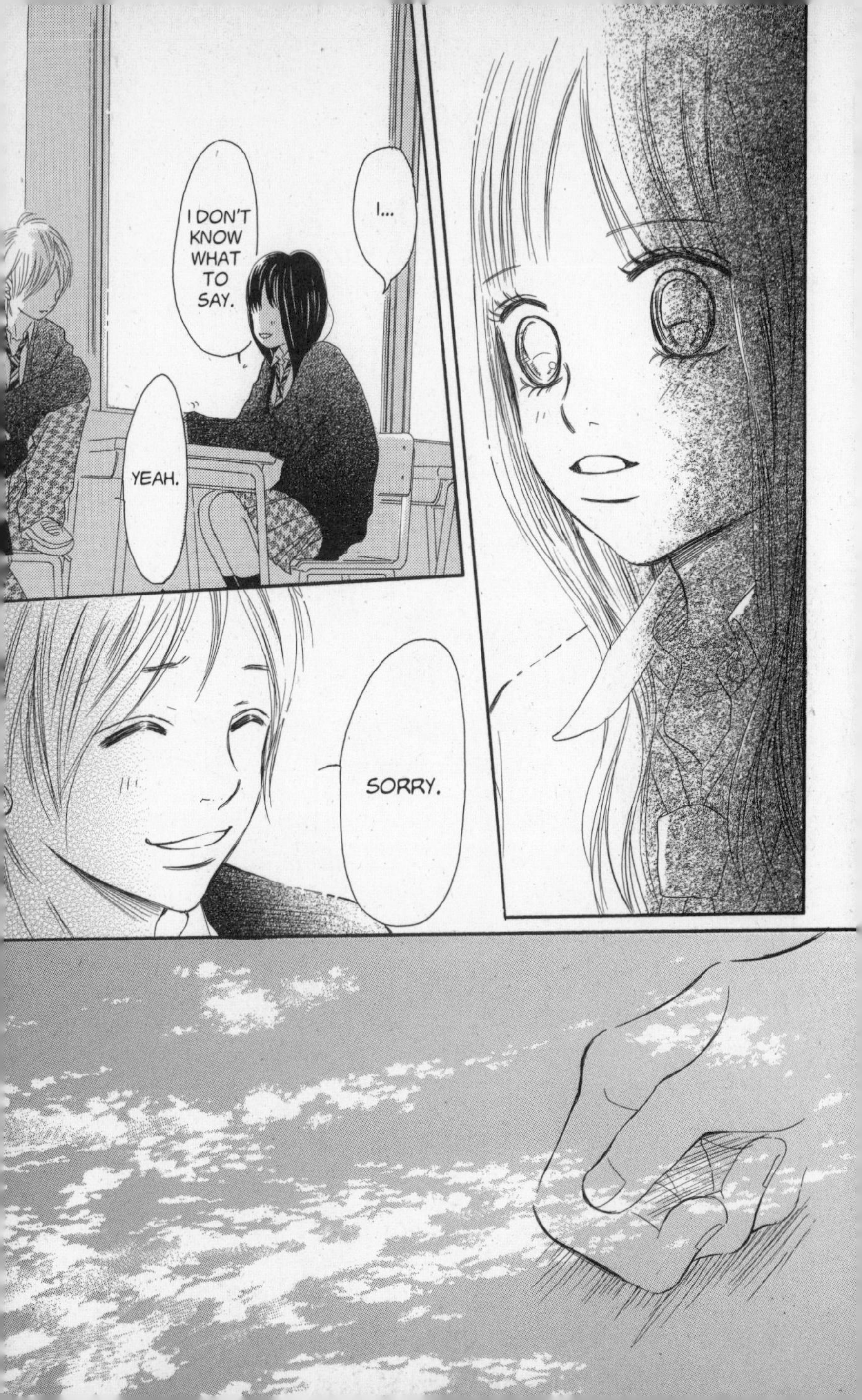
I...
I DON'T KNOW WHAT TO SAY.
YEAH.
SORRY.

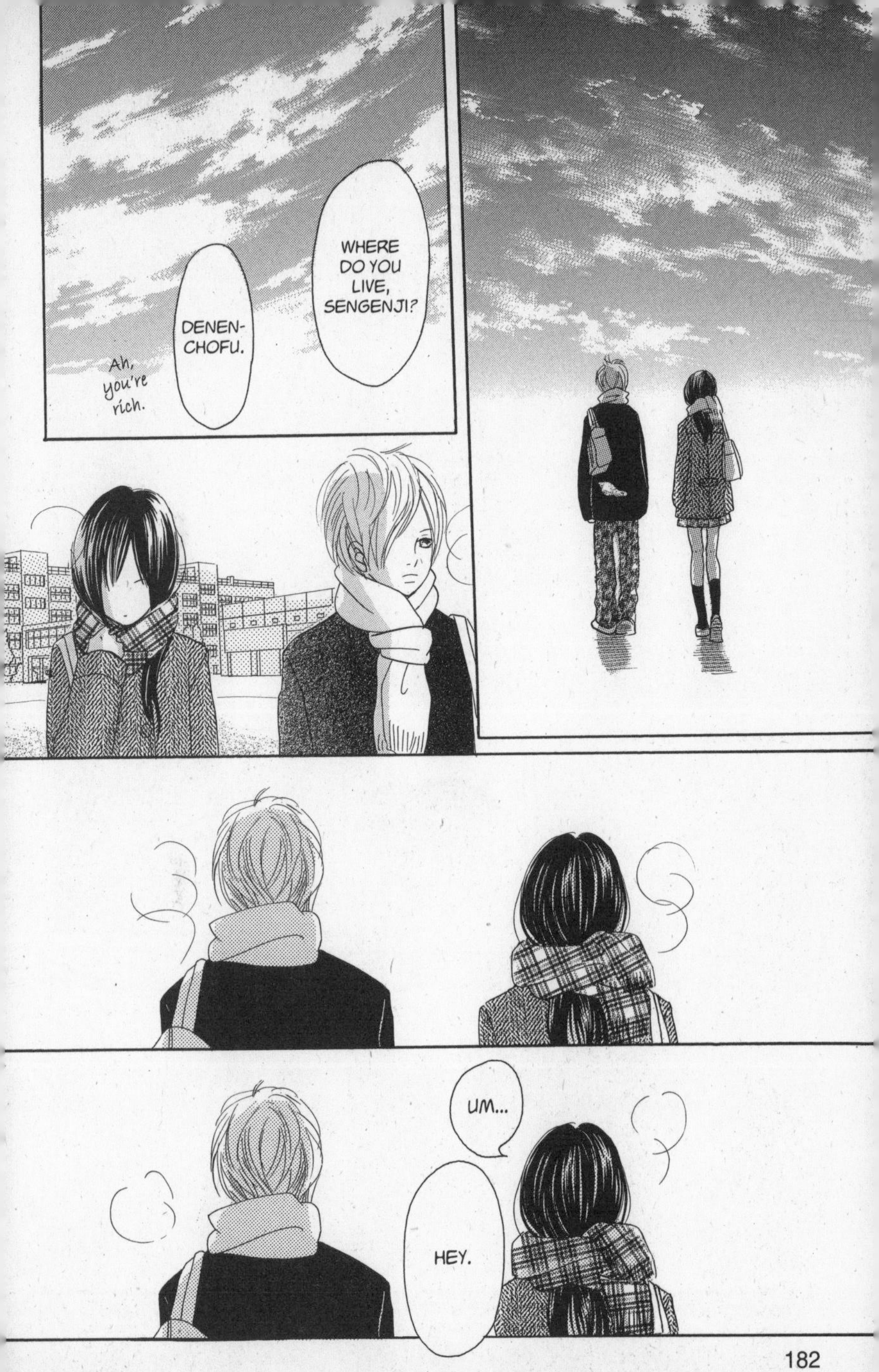
WHERE DO YOU LIVE, SENGENJI?
DENEN-CHOFU.
Ah, you're rich.
UM...
HEY.

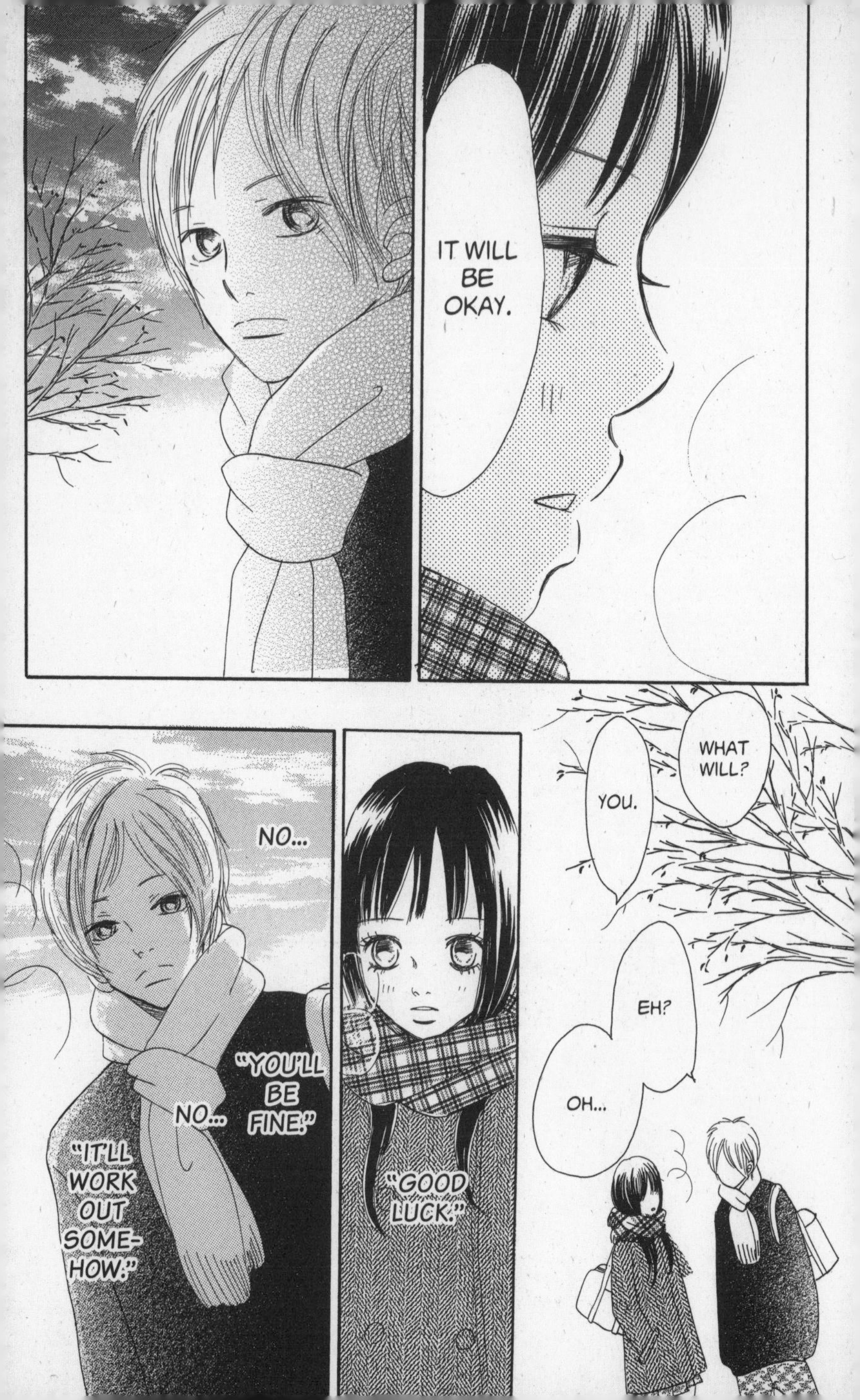
IT WILL BE OKAY.
WHAT WILL?
YOU.
EH?
OH...
"GOOD LUCK."
NO...
"YOU'LL BE FINE."
NO...
"IT'LL WORK OUT SOME-HOW."

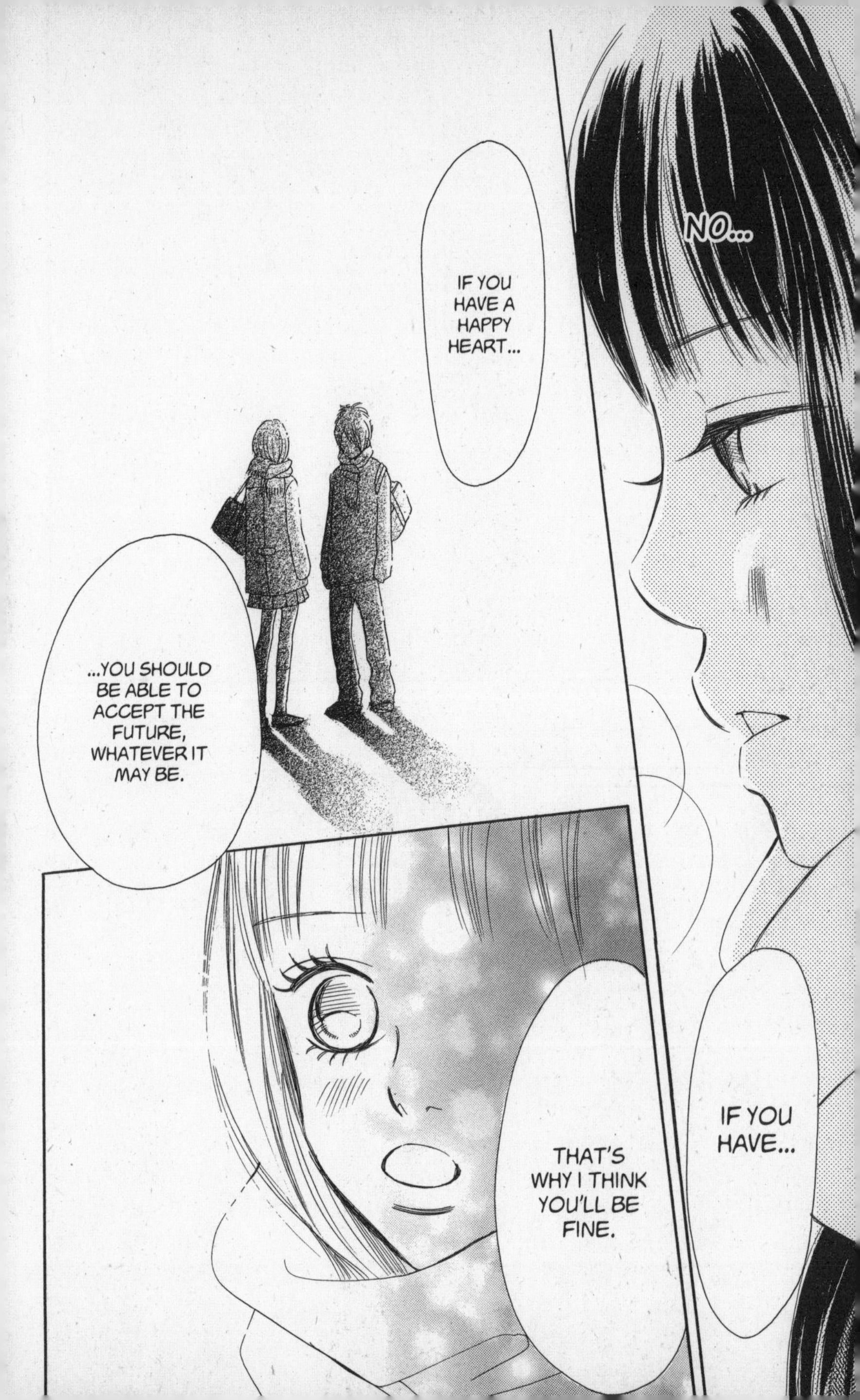
NO...
IF YOU HAVE...
IF YOU HAVE A HAPPY HEART...
...YOU SHOULD BE ABLE TO ACCEPT THE FUTURE, WHATEVER IT MAY BE.
THAT'S WHY I THINK YOU'LL BE FINE.

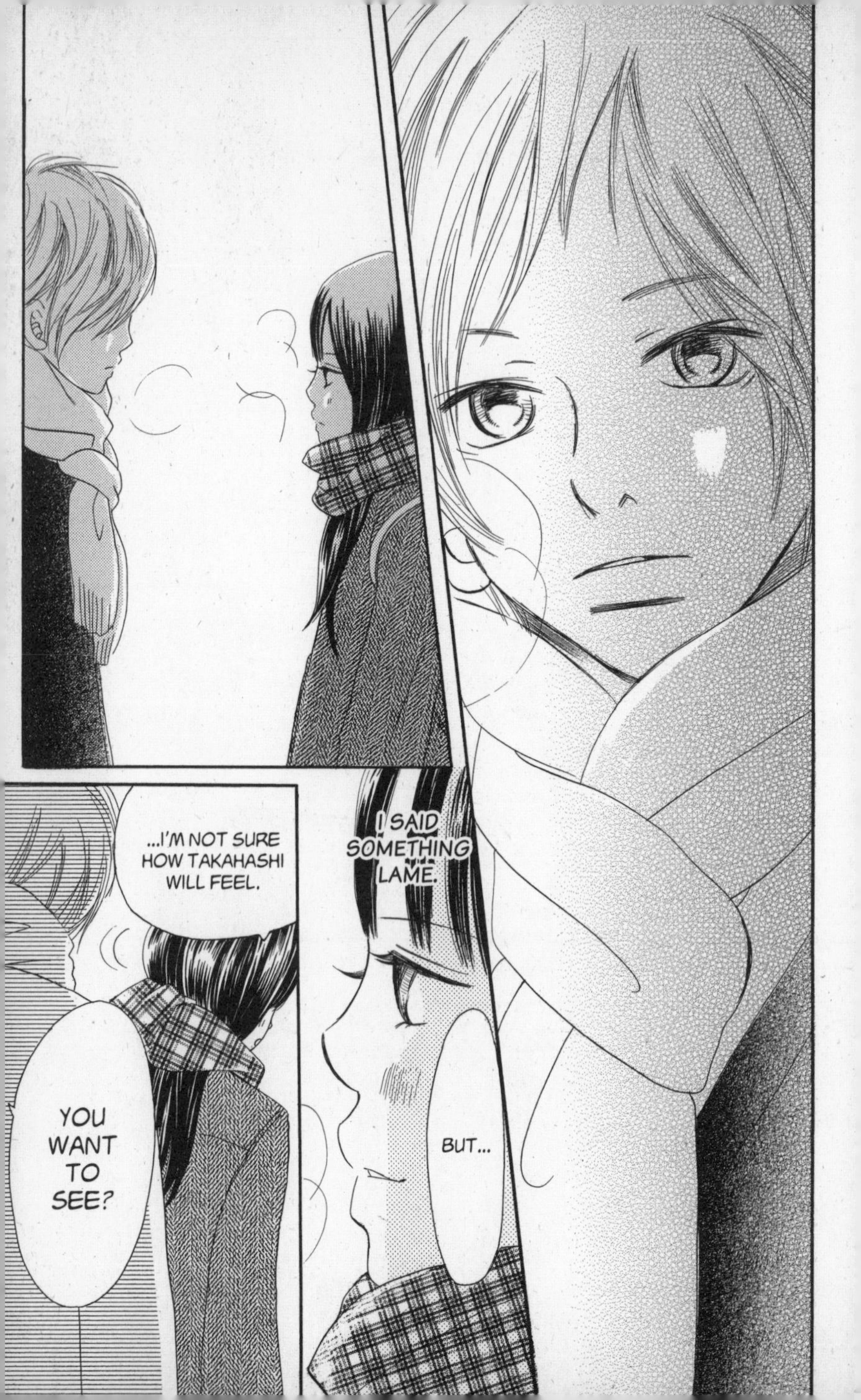
I SAID SOMETHING LAME.
BUT...
...I'M NOT SURE HOW TAKAHASHI WILL FEEL.
YOU WANT TO SEE?

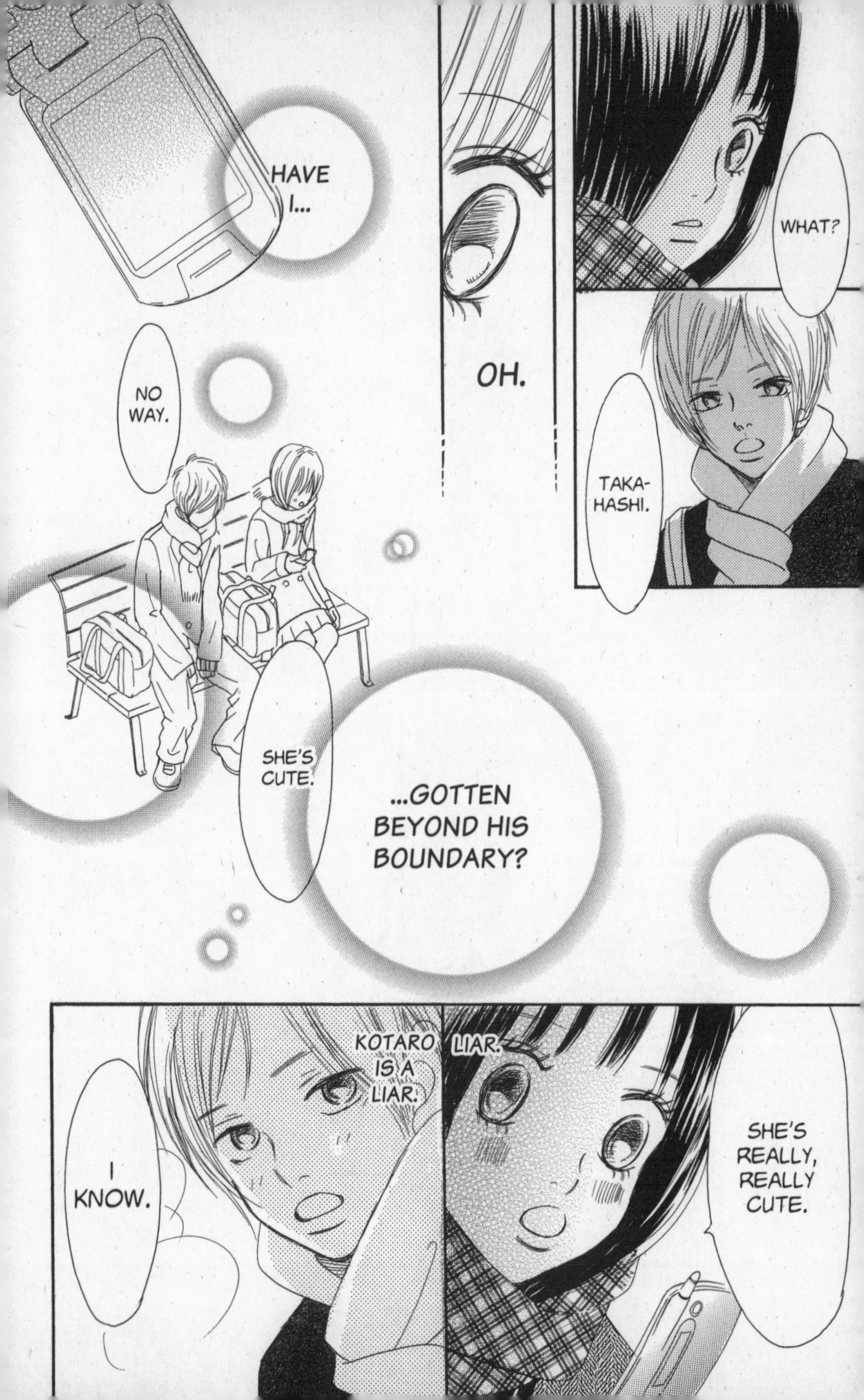
WHAT?
TAKA-HASHI.
OH.
HAVE I...
NO WAY.
SHE'S CUTE.
...GOTTEN BEYOND HIS BOUNDARY?
SHE'S REALLY, REALLY CUTE.
LIAR.
KOTARO IS A LIAR.
I KNOW.

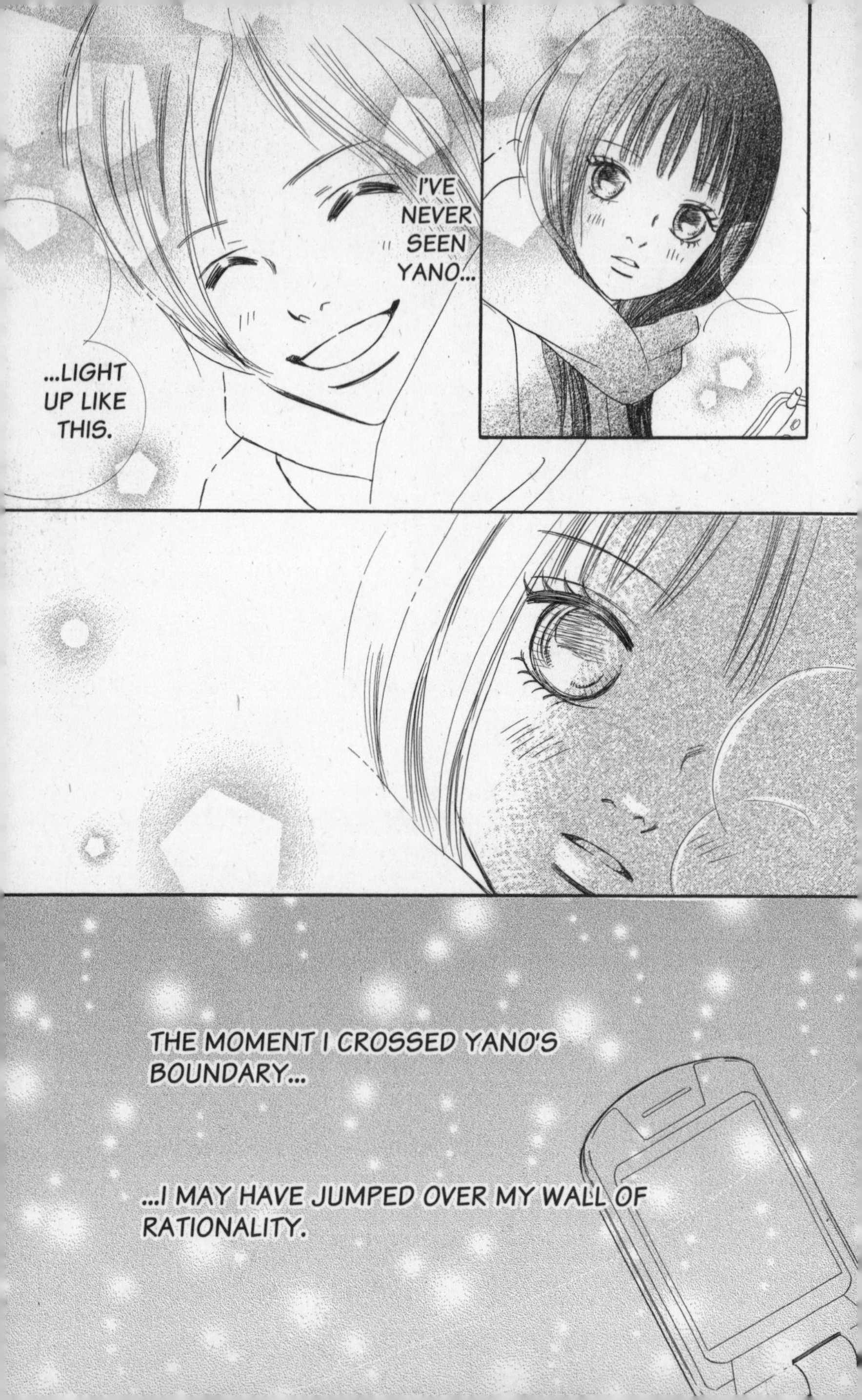
I'VE NEVER SEEN YANO...
...LIGHT UP LIKE THIS.
THE MOMENT I CROSSED YANO'S BOUNDARY...
...I MAY HAVE JUMPED OVER MY WALL OF RATIONALITY.

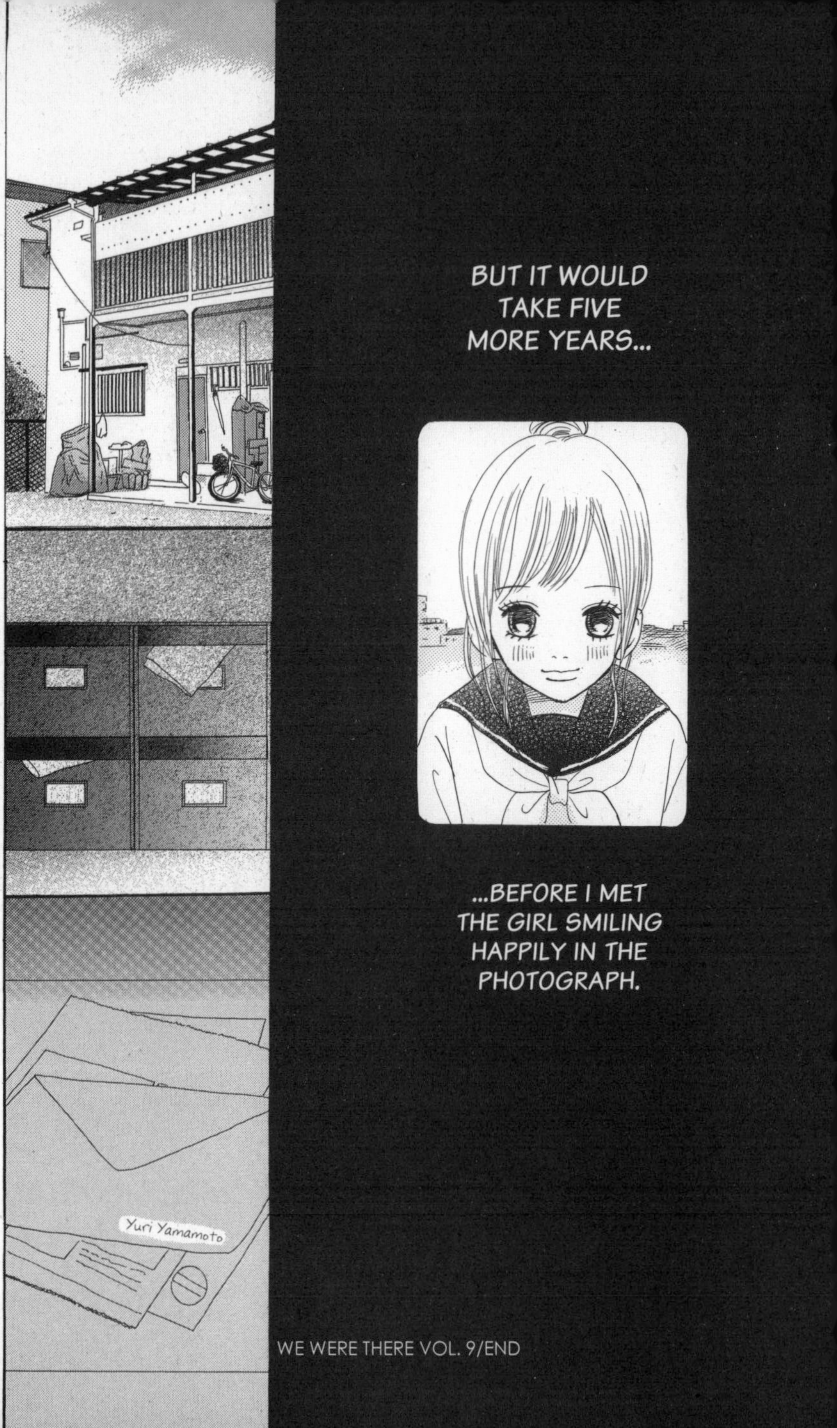
BUT IT WOULD TAKE FIVE MORE YEARS...
...BEFORE I MET THE GIRL SMILING HAPPILY IN THE PHOTOGRAPH.
Yuri Yamamoto
WE WERE THERE VOL. 9/END

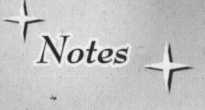

## Notes

### Honorifics

In Japan, people are usually addressed by their name followed by a suffix.
The suffix shows familiarity or respect, depending on the relationship.
Male (familiar): first or last name + kun
Female (familiar): first or last name + chan
Adult (polite): last name + san
Upperclassman (polite): last name + senpai
Teacher or professional: last name + sensei
Close friends or lovers: first name only, no suffix

### Nana-chan vs. Nana-san

Nanami's nickname is "Nana-chan." Yano's ex-girlfriend
was a year older, so she was known as "Nana-san."

### Terms

A *gokon* is a group date.
"*Kojo no Tsuki*" (The Moon over the Ancient Castle) is a famous
Japanese song.
*Obon* is a period during summer that honors the spirits of
deceased ancestors.
*Shiroi Koibito*, Butter Sandwich, and *Wakasaimo* are sweets from
Hokkaido. *Shiroi Koibito*, or "white lover," is a cookie with white
chocolate inside. A "Butter Sandwich" is white chocolate, butter and
raisins in a soft biscuit. *Wakasaimo* is made out of white bean paste
and kelp and shaped to look like a sweet potato. Hokkaido is also
known for crab.

All the movies out on DVD that I want to watch
are discontinued, so I'm having a hard time
deciding whether I want to buy the DVDs being
sold on the Internet at expensive prices or wait
until they are reissued. I'm in a quandary...
—Yuki Obata

Yuki Obata's birthday is January 9. Her debut manga, *Raindrops*, won
the Shogakukan Shinjin Comics Taisho Kasaku Award in 1998. Her
current series, *We Were There* (*Bokura ga Ita*), won the 50th Shogakukan
Manga Award and was adapted into an animated television series. She
likes sweets, coffee, drinking with friends, and scary stories. Her hobby
is browsing in bookshops.